The Essentials of
Technical Communication

SECOND EDITION

ELIZABETH TEBEAUX
TEXAS A&M UNIVERSITY

SAM DRAGGA
TEXAS TECH UNIVERSITY

New York   Oxford
Oxford University Press

Oxford University Press, Inc., publishes works that further Oxford University's
objective of excellence in research, scholarship, and education.

Oxford   New York
Auckland   Cape Town   Dar es Salaam   Hong Kong   Karachi
Kuala Lumpur   Madrid   Melbourne   Mexico City   Nairobi
New Delhi   Shanghai   Taipei   Toronto

With offices in
Argentina   Austria   Brazil   Chile   Czech Republic   France   Greece
Guatemala   Hungary   Italy   Japan   Poland   Portugal   Singapore
South Korea   Switzerland   Thailand   Turkey   Ukraine   Vietnam

For titles covered by Section 112 of the U.S. Higher Education
Opportunity Act, please visit www.oup.com/us/he for the latest
information about pricing and alternate formats.

Published by Oxford University Press, Inc.
198 Madison Avenue, New York, New York 10016
http://www.oup.com

Oxford is a registered trademark of Oxford University Press

Library of Congress Cataloging-in-Publication Data
Tebeaux, Elizabeth.
The essentials of technical communication / Elizabeth Tebeaux, Sam Dragga.
  p. cm.
ISBN 978-0-19-989078-1
1. Technical writing. 2. Communication of technical information.
I. Dragga, Sam. II. Title.
T11.T295 2011
808'.0666—dc23
                                                    2011044299

Printing number: 9 8 7 6 5

Printed in the United States of America
on acid-free paper

Dedicated to
David H. Stewart
1926–2009

Our first English department head, a scholar fully committed to the teaching of both writing and great literature.

Without his support at the beginning of our careers, neither of us would have enjoyed as productive a life in technical communication as we have had. *The Essentials of Technical Communication* emerges from that support.

Brief **Contents**

Detailed Contents

Part Two: **Applications**

Checklists

Preface

In the workplace, no one wants to read what you write—seriously. In addition, they will read as little of what you write as they possibly can. Your boss or co-workers may not have the necessary background, the time, or the inclination to wade through your e-mail, memo, or report. We have developed *The Essentials of Technical Communication* with this in mind, as a practical introduction to all aspects of effective professional communication—a handbook to help you get your message across on the job, where time equals money and poorly crafted documents can have a host of unwelcome consequences.

As teachers of technical writing with more than 50 years of experience between us, we know that following a few simple guidelines leads to more efficient and effective communications. In this book we want to provide the guidelines you need as you plan, draft, and revise documents. Understanding these guidelines will help you avoid blank-page terror and enable you to write effectively and quickly, both requirements of employees who write for their jobs.

Approach

Our rationale is simple: we believe that the effective writer in a work situation must learn and internalize basic concepts of rhetoric and then apply these in developing documents. We've filled this brief book with memorable, concise guidelines. Each chapter in Part One focuses on basic rhetorical principles, and Part Two applies those principles to the planning and writing of particular types of documents.

A brief book enables instructors to adapt the book to their own uses. Many teachers want to build on principles by adding their unique approaches. This book provides the flexibility to allow for that possibility. In addition, many employees who did not study technical or business writing in college will find this book useful in learning how to write in the workplace.

Organization

The book is organized into two parts. Part One (Chapters 1 through 6) lays out essential communication principles:

+ Chapter 1, Characteristics of Writing at Work, describes technical writing, or writing in the workplace, to show how it differs from academic writing.
+ Chapter 2, Writing for Your Readers, presents the essential elements of analyzing readers and then choosing content, format, and style as these meet the needs of the intended readers. We embed a discussion of the composing process in this chapter.

✦ Chapter 3, Writing Ethically, discusses the ethics of technical documents. While most professionals have standards of good practice, writers should also follow principles of communication ethics.

✦ Chapter 4, Achieving a Readable Style, explains how to write concise, pristine sentences and paragraphs.

✦ Chapter 5, Designing Documents, illustrates basic principles for creating accessible and inviting documents. In a world of too much information, readers often miss or ignore important messages not presented in an easy-to-read format.

✦ Chapter 6, Designing Illustrations, provides guidelines for developing effective visuals. Graphics software creates practically infinite possibilities for visuals, but effective use requires an understanding of fundamental graphic design principles.

Part Two (Chapters 7 through 12) then applies the principles from Part One to the types of documents most commonly prepared in the workplace:

✦ Chapter 7, E-mails, Texts, Memos, and Letters, presents the basics of correspondence and demonstrates how to ensure that these routine messages are clear, readable, and effective.

✦ Chapter 8, Technical Reports, presents the elements of report development along with examples, including an annotated abstract. We provide a formal report in Appendix C and on the book's companion website, **www.oup.com/us/tebeaux.** (We also include links to documentation resources on the website. With the emergence of bibliography and citation software we believe extensive instruction in documentation is no longer needed in the text, though we do include a brief guide to the most common documentation systems in Appendix B.)

✦ Chapter 9, Proposals and Progress Reports, provides guidelines for developing business proposals and status reports. In this chapter, we use several student examples, as these respond to real situations in a university setting.

✦ Chapter 10, Instructions, Procedures, and Policies, describes how to develop clear instructions for a variety of situations.

✦ Chapter 11, Oral Reports, provides a short guide to developing and then presenting a concise, effective PowerPoint presentation.

✦ Chapter 12, Résumés and Job Applications, describes how to prepare job application documents.

FEATURES

• **Sample Documents:** This text, although concise, includes a range of sample documents covering the essential types and styles you're likely to encounter in the workplace. Many of these documents are available for download on the book's companion website, **www.oup.com/us/tebeaux,** along with links to documentation resources.

- **Case Studies:** In Chapters 2, 7, 8, 9, and 10, case studies show how different types of documents function in different situations. These cases contextualize the documents to give you a sense of how and when the techniques we outline can and should be applied.
- **Checklists:** At chapter ends, we have included checklists—lists of questions you can use to ensure that your professional documents achieve your purpose. We hope you find that these are a handy reference tool. They are indexed in the front of the book.
- **Exercises:** Exercises at the end of each chapter guide practice in the techniques outlined in the text. Some of the exercises are designed to be done in class and could be done or discussed in small groups, and others are take-home assignments.
- **Appendices:** Three appendices contain a brief guide to grammar, punctuation, and usage (A); a synopsis of information literacy and three widely used documentation systems (B); and a sample report (C).
- **Companion Website:** The book's companion website at **www.oup.com/us/ tebeaux** offers additional resources for students, including chapter overviews, self-quizzes, downloadable versions of the checklists from the book, helpful links, annotated document pages, and downloadable sample documents, including those from the exercises at chapter ends. The site also includes an Instructor's Manual, featuring downloadable PowerPoint files for use as lecture aids, chapter objectives, teaching strategies, workshop activities, writing projects, worksheets, and discussion questions. The Companion Website also includes revision assignments, multimodal writing assignments, and multilingual writing assignments.
- **Instructor's Manual:** The Instructor's Manual is available in a CD version that includes a Test Bank.

NEW TO THIS EDITION

While improving upon our first edition, we did not change those aspects of the book that made it popular with professors and students of technical communication. This new edition maintains the concise and practical nature of the first.

But we have made several important changes based on the excellent suggestions from our expert panel of reviewers. We made each change to prepare students (1) to write in an increasingly dynamic, digital age and (2) to write for an increasingly diverse audience—both in the classroom and in the workplace.

Changes we've made for this second edition include the following:

- Chapter 1: We've included material on the need for information security as the most important difference between writing at school and writing at work.
- Chapter 2: We've added a new case document that incorporates both issues in e-mail design and audience perspective.

- Chapter 3: We've added a caution about distributing information without evaluating its validity or reliability. We believe ethical communicators must assume responsibility for the accuracy of their information. We've also included the IEEE Code of Ethics for comparison with STC's Ethical Guidelines.
- Chapter 4: We've added additional examples of common style problems: excessive "be" verbs and use of "there is, there are" constructions that reduce the directness of sentences and often increase sentence length. We have also added a short report that includes excessive use of "be" constructions and other sentence problems.
- Chapter 5: New here is greater emphasis on designing for mobile readers who are accessing documents from mobile devices.
- Chapter 6: We've included animation and film clips among the kinds of visual communication that could readily substitute for words on the page.
- Chapter 7: We discuss how text messages make the need for clear and concise wording all the more important.
- Chapter 8: We've separated discussion of informal and formal reports and added additional examples of informal reports. We've added a new example student formal report, included in Appendix C.
- Chapter 9: We've added the proposal and progress report for the student report example included in Appendix C.
- Chapter 10: We've added an example of work procedures prepared by a student, as this form of instructional writing occurs commonly in organizations.
- Chapter 11: We have changed all the examples of PowerPoint slides, included a full slide presentation that exhibits qualities of good PowerPoint presentations, and included new examples of ineffective slides that demonstrate common errors.
- Chapter 12: We've included new examples of résumés and discussed the necessity of managing your professional identity on social networking sites.

For all chapters, we have examined and in many cases modified and expanded exercises. These require students to think critically about the topics discussed in the chapter.

Finally, the Companion Website and Instructor's Resources have been updated with new examples, exercises, and materials. Of particular note is the revised Instructor's Manual, which now contains sections in each chapter on Multimodal and Multilingual Writing, as well as new links, writing projects, and teaching strategies. The test bank has been updated as well and now offers a revised and expanded selection of test questions.

ACKNOWLEDGMENTS

We are grateful to the dedicated book publishers of Oxford University Press for their conscientious efforts to make this book eloquent, elegant, concise, and cogent. We extend our thanks to the reviewers commissioned by Oxford for the first edition of this text: Susan Aylworth, California State University, Chico; Scott Downing, Kenai Peninsula College, University of Alaska Anchorage; Leslie Fife, Oklahoma State University; Maureen Fitzsimmons, Syracuse University; Elizabeth Holtzinger-Jennings, Pennsylvania State University; Danica Hubbard, College of DuPage; Kevin LaGrandeur, New York Institute of Technology; Lisa McClure, Southern Illinois University, Carbondale; Elizabeth Monske, Northern Michigan University; Brenda Moore, New Jersey Institute of Technology; Marguerite Newcomb, University of Texas at San Antonio; Roxanna Pisiak, Morrisville State College; Liza Potts, Old Dominion University; Denise Stodola, Kettering University; Aaron Toscano, University of North Carolina at Charlotte; and Linda Young, Oregon Institute of Technology. And we add on our thanks to those who reviewed for this new edition: Latonia Bailey, Crowder College; Elizabeth Childs, Auburn University; Cathy Corr, University of Montana-Missoula; Ed Cottrill, University of Massachusetts-Amherst; Richie Crider, University of Maryland; Melody DeMeritt, California Polytechnic State University; Kendall Kelly, Southwest Texas State University; Elizabeth Lopez, Georgia State University; Raynette Meyer, Aiken Technical College; Marguerite Newcomb, University of Texas-San Antonio; Mark Noe, University of Texas-Pan American; Ritu Raju, Houston Community College; Leslie St. Martin, College of the Canyons; Dawn Taylor, South Texas College; and Michelle Weisman, College of the Ozarks.

We also thank the innumerable colleagues and students who have challenged and inspired us in the teaching of technical communication. And, as always, special thanks to Jene and Linda for their love and support.

PART **ONE**

Principles

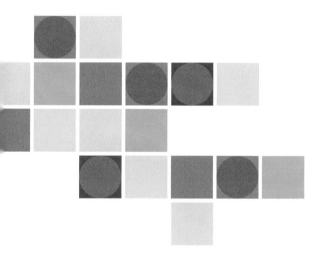

Characteristics of Writing at Work

Technical or business writing describes writing that occurs in a business or work setting. University offices, corporations, research centers, hospitals, businesses of all sizes, even nonprofit organizations produce large quantities of technical writing, which differs from academic writing in a number of important ways. These differences mean that you cannot write on the job the way you have written in school. Writing in school and writing at work differ because the purposes and the context of each differ. Thus, the products of each contrast sharply.

Technical writing is like any sport you want to pursue: you must first learn the foundational concepts, then understand how these concepts affect the sport before you apply the principles as a participant.

Quick Tips

On the job, keep in mind that **no one wants to read anything you write**. **Most of the time they will not read all of what you write**. They will read because they need to, not because they want to. They will read because you have information they need to take actions or make decisions. They don't get paid to read: they get paid to take actions and make decisions. The more time they need to read your document, the less productive time they have. Make sure everything you write is clear, correct, necessary, and polite. And don't assume that anything you write is confidential.

Modern organizations have to keep their technical and business writing secure, whether it exists in paper or virtual form. Organizations that lose information to cyber thieves often face severe consequences.

WRITING AT WORK VERSUS WRITING AT SCHOOL

Workplace writing requires that you continue to apply what you have learned about effective paragraph development, correct sentence structure, punctuation, and usage. As an educated adult, your writing should exemplify correctness. Beyond these fundamental principles, business or technical writing will differ from writing you have done as a student in four important ways.

Writing at work:

1. Requires acute awareness of security and legal liability
2. Requires awareness that documents may be read by unknown readers, inside and outside the organization, for an infinite time
3. Achieves job goals
4. Addresses a variety of readers who have different perspectives from those of the writer
5. Requires a variety of written documents

Requires acute awareness of security and legal liability. The most fundamental characteristic of technical writing rests in the legal liability associated with workplace information. This liability extends from federal privacy acts, such as FERPA (Family Educational Rights and Privacy Act), that protect you, as a student in college, and extends to protection of the research and intellectual property of the university from cyber thieves.

Chief information officers (CIOs) in educational, business, government, and research organizations work diligently to protect the privacy of information about their employees and the knowledge generated by these employees by following both federal and state privacy laws. Identity and information theft can occur at any time, despite the best efforts of any CIO's staff and security team. People throughout the world continue to attack computing systems to gain access to credit card numbers, personal and medical information, transcripts of academic work, creative work, and research data—essentially whatever hackers can access, either for their own use or to sell to crime cartels.

Electronic communication has become a blessing and a curse. Today's workplace requires extensive technology. Research organizations, hospitals, banks, financial organizations, law firms, physicians, even small, locally owned businesses have to pursue strict security on all information they have about customers, clients, and patients. Organizations, like architectural firms, computer companies, engineering companies, and manufacturers, must protect their intellectual property from theft. The knowledge they produce for clients becomes the value of the organization. When you begin a job, you need to learn the security rules and follow them. For example, you will likely not be allowed to use your company e-mail for any purpose other than for company business. Your company telephones will likely require the same restrictions. You should never access your personal blogs or social networking sites from your employer's computer.

To avoid potential security breaches,

- Remember that any text message you send will not be secure and may be legally accessed, whether the cell phone you use belongs to you or your employer. Company e-mail can be viewed by the company webmaster. Once you begin working for an organization, use caution in what you discuss via text messages and e-mail.
- Avoid blogs, unless your company uses secure blogs for creating collaborative reports, for example. Remember that others can see what you have written. Be sure that your comments are tasteful, helpful, and accurate.
- Avoid using browsers available on company computers to locate information on any topic not related to your work.
- Use social media carefully. Your company may have a page on one of the social media sites, but do not use it or respond to it. First, ask the purpose of the site and the rules for its use by employees. Note: Many students have been expelled from their universities for inappropriate use of social media. A business organization, because of concerns for information security, will watch how employees use social media. You can be terminated if your comments on blogs, wikis, and other forms of social media disparage the organization and perhaps divulge proprietary information.
- Many organizations, before they hire new employees, will check social media to see what potential employees have said about themselves. Again, criminals across the world also check. Divulging confidential information, personal or professional, can have major consequences for you and organizations for whom you work, have worked, or will work. Nothing you place in cyberspace ever goes away. Ask yourself: "If I decided to run for public office in 20 years, would I want people I don't even know to see what I said about myself today?"
- If you have a personal webpage, be sure that what you place on the page makes a positive statement about you and does not discredit your employer in any way.
- Remember that anything you write and send in cyberspace can and will likely be accessed by others. Tip: Always write as if someone you do not know might be reading over your shoulder. And follow all rules that your employer stipulates. Accepting and agreeing to follow rules of confidentiality of company information may be a condition of employment with that organization.

In school, your primary obligation is to avoid plagiarism. But what you write at work can be used against you in lawsuits. Once you sign your name to a report or letter, your signature makes you responsible for the content. Hostile readers can use what you say to support claims against you and the organization you represent. Because we live in an increasingly litigious society, designing documents that will prevent their misuse should be one of your primary goals.

Requires awareness that documents may be read by unknown readers.
Always anticipate unknown readers who may receive copies of your reports or
e-mail. Ask yourself this important question: "Does my report or e-mail contain
any information that could be misconstrued and affect me or the organization
adversely if unknown readers see my communication?" While academic writing
responds to assignments, applicable only for a specific semester, course, and professor, workplace communications have no specific lifespan. They can be read and
then used in ways you never intended or envisioned.

You cannot underestimate the problem that unknown readers present.
Nearly everything you write for an organization will remain in the organization's archive indefinitely. Copies of your reports and letters will be placed in
files accessible by readers who may not know anything about you or the situation you are writing about. These documents will often be used in assessing
your performance and in determining your promotion potential. What you say
suggests how well you have done your job. Unknown readers may also use your
reports to gain understanding of a work situation they have inherited with a new
job assignment. On the job, what you write becomes much more than a knowledge indicator for a grade.

Achieves job goals. In school, you write to show your professor that you know
the subject matter and to make a good grade. But in the workplace, writing is the
major way that people achieve their job goals and document their work. Writing
becomes documentation that you have done your work and how you have done it.
How well you write will suggest how well you have done your work. It will become
part of the organization's permanent archives.

Addresses a variety of readers who have different perspectives. In college, you write your assignments for a single reader, a professor, a specialist in a
subject area. But in a work setting, you can expect to write to readers who have
varied educational and technical backgrounds, readers who have different roles
inside and outside the organization, and readers who may know less about a topic
than you do. Your supervisor, for example, may have majored in a field of study
very different from yours, or your supervisor's responsibilities may have channeled
his or her technical knowledge into other areas. For example, you may report directly to a person whose educational background has been in physical chemistry or electrical engineering but whose responsibilities may now be in personnel
management, database administration, quality control, or financial analysis. Many
technical people earn MBAs to assist them in management roles.

In a work context, these readers will feel no commitment to read what you
write unless your messages help them as they do their own work. They will generally not read all documents completely. Each will be interested in how your
message affects his or her job goals. What is clear and important to you may not
be clear or important to others. Because e-mail has become a common way of
communicating within organizations, you really have no idea who will read what

you write, as any message and its attachments may be forwarded. Documents posted online on an organization's website are far from secure from prying eyes and hackers.

Creates excessive paperwork and e-mails. We live and work in an information age where the quantity of information grows rapidly, where people have more to read than they can ever hope to read. As they see your report or your e-mail subject line, they will immediately ask themselves questions such as "What is this?" "Why should I read it?" "How does it affect me?" "What am I going to have to do?" Without a carefully stated subject line, your readers may delete your message before opening it. If they do open your e-mail, they will want to find the main points and ideas quickly, and they will become impatient if they are unable to find them by glancing at the page. They will not usually read any document completely or bother to respond to it unless, at the beginning, the message indicates that reading your document serves their best interests. How they respond to the first few sentences of your writing will often determine how much more of it they read.

On the job, your readers are not a captive audience, as your teachers have been. They do not have to read what you write. If you want your writing read, make your message clear and easy to read; make your message as interesting, relevant, and concise as possible. Because your readers often read selectively, conciseness and clarity are basic ingredients of effective business communication. Mechanical correctness will still be a desirable quality, but correct writing that cannot be read easily and quickly will not be read.

Uses a variety of documents. Most academic writing includes essays, essay examinations, research papers, and laboratory reports. All are directed to your teachers. At work, however, employees can expect to write a variety of documents not relevant to academic writing assignments: letters, e-mails, information and procedure memos, proposals, progress reports, project reports, feasibility studies, economic justification reports, policy statements, travel reports, news releases, speeches, training procedures, budget forecasts, employee evaluations, user documentation, and perhaps articles for publication in trade journals. What you write will change with your responsibilities, the kind of job you have, and your position in the organization. How you write each document will depend on the topic being discussed, the situation leading to the document, your readers' needs and perspectives, and your purpose in writing.

THE FOUNDATIONS OF EFFECTIVE WRITING AT WORK

Developing effective documents requires a process involving at least six stages:

1. Planning the document
2. Determining content

3. Arranging ideas
4. Drafting
5. Revising
6. Editing

While each of these stages can be a separate activity, when you write you will more than likely be moving back and forth from one activity to the other, as you develop your document. Following this process will help ensure that content is appropriate as well as correctly and effectively presented.

THE QUALITIES OF GOOD TECHNICAL WRITING

Surveys show that organizations rank writing skills in this order of importance:

1. Accuracy
2. Clarity
3. Conciseness
4. Readability
5. Usability
6. Correctness

These qualities mean that a document

- makes a good impression when readers first interact with it: document is neat, readable, well organized, and inviting.
- can be read selectively—for instance, by some users, only the summary; by other users, only the introduction and conclusions; by still other users, the entire report.
- shows a plan that reveals the purpose and value of the document.
- makes sense: ideas appear in a logical sequence immediately evident from document design.
- uses visuals, if necessary, to help readers understand ideas or data.
- conveys an overall impression of authority, thoroughness, soundness, and honest work.
- makes sense to people who were not part of the initial readership.
- makes a positive statement about the writer and the organization.
- enables people who need to use your writing to perform a task to do so.

Beyond all these basic characteristics, good technical writing is free of typographical errors, grammatical slips, and misspelled words. Little flaws distract attention from the writer's main points and call into question the writer's literacy.

As you study, understand, and practice writing for a workplace setting, keep in mind these qualities as well as the differences between the writing you do as an employee and the writing you have done as a student.

Exercises

1. Professional associations will often publish articles in their newsletter or magazine or on their official website that describe a day in the life of a prominent individual in the field. Locate such a news article for a professional in your field. How much of this individual's typical day is occupied with speaking and writing? What kinds of letters and reports does this individual compose? How much e-mail does he or she send and receive? Summarize your findings in a one-page memo. Also explain in your memo how your findings compare and contrast with your experience and expectations for this profession.

2. Visit the website of a major employer in your field. What kinds of documents do you find at this site? What do you notice about the writing style or use of illustrations? Do you think you could create documents like these for this employer? Do you think you could help create better documents? Based on your examination of these documents, what is your impression of this employer?

3. Examine Figure 1-1. If you were the author of this document and were given 15 more minutes to make it better, what changes would you make?

CYBERSECURITY
CONSUMER TIPS FOR INTERNATIONAL TRAVELERS

Be Aware

1. When traveling internationally, in addition to taking your passport, *take responsibility for your cybersecurity.*

2. Your information and communications – and the devices that contain and transmit them – are as much a part of you as the valuables in your suitcase. The more you do to protect yourself, the more secure your information and devices likely will be.

3. While in a foreign country, you are subject to its laws. Laws and policies regarding online security and privacy may be different in other countries than in the United States. If you would like to become familiar with other laws, the State Department website contains safety information for every country in the world, including regarding communications.[1]

4. Protect yourself by leaving at home any electronic equipment you don't need during your travel.

Before You Go

5. If you take it, protect it:
    *   Back up your electronic files
    *   Remove sensitive data
    *   Install strong passwords
    *   Ensure antivirus software is up-to-date

While Traveling

6. Be vigilant about possession and use of your equipment and information. Don't assume it's safe. Culprits are visible and invisible.

---

[1] www.travel.state.gov/travel/cis_pa_tw/cis/cis_1765.html. For information regarding treaties, laws and policies, see: www.travel.state.gov/law/legal/legal_818.html. For general international travel tips, see: www.travel.state.gov/travel/tips/tips_1232.html.

FIGURE 1-1 Document for Exercise 3

Source: Federal Communications Commission. Cybersecurity Tips for International Travelers. http://
www.fcc.gov/cgb/consumerfacts/cybertipsinternational.pdf

- Keep *your* eyes on your electronics. Keep your devices with you in airports, hotels, and restaurants, etc.
- Be aware of your surroundings. *Other* eyes can take information from you by looking at your devices.
- Consider using a privacy screen on your laptop.

7. Your mobile phone and other electronic devices may be vulnerable to malware because they will connect with local networks abroad. They also may identify your personal location information to others.

8. Electronic communications, equipment and services (*e.g.*, phones, computers and fax machines) in public places such as Internet cafes, coffee shops, book stores, travel agencies, clinics, libraries, airports, and hotels may be vulnerable. You may choose not to use these services at all, or avoid using them for sensitive communications.

9. Don't use the same passwords or PIN numbers abroad that you use in the United States. For example, if the hotel safety deposit box requires a PIN number, use a unique one.

Upon Return Home

10. Electronics and devices used or obtained abroad can be compromised. Consider safety measures such as changing passwords for your laptop or smartphone.

Additional Cybersecurity Resources

- Department of Homeland Security, Computer Emergency Readiness Team Tips[2]
- FCC Privacy and Online Security Tips[3]

---

[2] www.us-cert.gov/cas/tips/

[3] reboot.fcc.gov/privacy-and-online-security

FIGURE 1-1 *Continued*

Writing for Your Readers

Before you begin to plan your document, think first about your readers and then your purpose. Every decision you make in developing your document should reflect your audience, their needs, and your purpose.

Avoid becoming absorbed in ideas and information you plan to include. Never forget that the person or group who will read the document may have a very different perspective of the content. Your readers cannot climb into your mind and know your thoughts. When you carefully analyze your readers, you can often design and write your report in a way that helps them understand what's in your mind.

Quick Tips

To develop any communication, you have three main goals that connect reader, purpose, and context:

1. You want your readers to understand your meaning exactly in the way you intend.
2. You want your writing to achieve its goal with the designated readers.
3. You want to keep the goodwill of those with whom you communicate.

UNDERSTAND YOUR READERS—THE HEART OF THE PLANNING PROCESS

To achieve the three goals just listed, you must pursue the following four tasks, both before you begin to write and while you are actually composing your document:

1. Determine as fully as possible who will read what you write.

2. Know the goals you want your writing to achieve and the business context in which you need to communicate.
3. Understand your role in the organization as a writer and how your role should be reflected in what you write.
4. Determine the content by considering your readers' frame of reference and your purpose in writing.

Keep in mind that business readers want answers now. Employees in most organizations, particularly large ones, have more to read than they can and will read. If you want your letter or report to be read, be sure that important information occurs on the first page of a report and in the first paragraph of an e-mail, memo, or letter and that you answer the following questions your readers will ask:

- What is this?
- Do I have to read it?
- How does it affect me?
- What will I have to do?
- What are the main ideas?

If you answer their questions at the beginning of your document, readers may be willing to read more of your report, e-mail, or letter.

In order to answer these questions in the minds of your readers, you will have to answer three questions yourself about the document you are writing:

- Who will read what I write?
- Who will act on what I write?
- Who else may read what I write?

In many cases, your primary reader will transmit your document to someone else for action. Perhaps this individual is one of your secondary readers or someone unknown to you.

Determine your readers and their perspectives. When you consider your readers, determine as much as you can about them.

- How much do your readers know about your topic?
- Do your readers have expertise in this area?

Readers with technical expertise in the area you discuss have different needs (and often different perspectives) from readers who lack technical expertise.

- How much do your readers know about your topic?
- What are your readers' educational levels?
- What are your readers' cultural backgrounds?

If you work in an organization that does business with readers from other cultures, plan to do background reading on these cultures.

- Will your readers be interested in what you write? If not, how could you present your message to make it appealing?

- What kind of relationship do you have with these readers? What is the readers' attitude toward you, the subject matter you need to communicate, the job you have, and your area within the organization? Do you have credibility with these readers?

A host of factors determine your reader(s)' perception: education, family, geographical and cultural background, job responsibilities, rank in the organization, age, life experiences, and gender—just to name a few demographics that define how people see the world. How much your readers know about your topic determines what you say and the technical level of your presentation.

- How well do you know your readers?

You may not know your readers personally. However, if you know an individual's level in the organization, the responsibilities associated with that level, and the kind of technical expertise your reader has, this information will help you decide what you need to say and how to present your information. Knowing your readers' responsibilities in the organization can help you anticipate their attitude—if your subject will interest them. Because people tend to read only what will help them, try to relate your message to your readers' job. Knowing the readers' attitude toward the topic addressed in your message will help you determine how to present your information.

- Who else is likely to read what you write?

Most reports and letters have distribution lists: the names of those who receive copies. A person on the distribution list may be the person who will ultimately act on what you write. Thus, the needs and perceptions of those who receive copies should be considered.

- Why is each person on the distribution list receiving a copy?
- How much does each person on this list know about your topic?

Sometimes your primary reader may know the situation you are discussing, and the purpose of the report may be to inform others within the organization by going through proper channels.

- What situation led to the need for this document?

Often, you can better understand your reader's perspective if you understand the situation that requires you to write this document. The need for written communications develops from interactions of people involved in a work environment. To be able to select content, level of language (technical or general), and amount of explanation needed in a business context, a writer must be careful to determine the needs of each reader. Closely examining a situation requiring a written response may even help you determine what you need to tell your readers and how to present your message.

Determine your purpose.

- Why are you writing?
- What do you want to achieve with your document?

Determining why you are writing—what you want to achieve—is as important as determining your readers. *Purpose always relates to readers.* And, you may have more than one purpose. For example, you may be writing to inform, to provide information, to recommend action. In addition, what you say may serve as documentation—proof of your efforts—to show that you have provided the information requested. Written messages that document employees' activities serve a major function in today's business organizations. Without documentation, you may have difficulty proving that you performed specific tasks.

Understand your role as a writer.

- What is your position in the organization?

As an employee, you will be hired to perform the duties that define a particular job. As the one responsible for performing specific tasks, you will be communicating with employees above you, below you, and on your own level. In writing to individuals in any group, you will communicate, not as you would with a friend or family member, but as the person responsible for the work associated with that position. When you write, you create a personality that should fit the position you hold.

To have credibility as a writer in an organization, the image that you project should be appropriate to your position. What you say and how you say it should reflect your level of responsibility in the organization—the power relationship that exists between you and the reader. The image you project will change, depending on your readers. You will project the image of a subordinate when you write to those higher than you, but you will transmit the image of the supervisor to those who work directly under you. When you communicate with others on your own job level, you will convey the image of a colleague. Good writers have the ability to fit their message to each reader.

Plan the content.

- What ideas should you use to achieve the goals of the message?
- What ideas should you omit?
- How should you arrange your ideas?

Once you have analyzed your readers and your purpose, you can begin to decide what you want and need to say, then how you will phrase and arrange your ideas.

- How do you want your message to sound?

Knowing how your message should sound will always be critical. Always try to convey a respectful tone commensurate with your position in the organization. How a message is conveyed may often be as important as the content.

Case 2-1 shows how a writer's assessment of audience and purpose change his content and presentation in the e-mails for each reader involved in the situation.

Case 2-1: Process Instructions

Bill Ramirez develops and manages training programs for his company. Reading an e-mail from one of the other supervisors, Mark Jaron, Bill finds that a number of employees have been allowed to enroll in a training course for which they do not have qualifications. Unable to talk with Joyce Smith, who enrolls employees for all training programs, Bill sends Joyce the following e-mail. Bill knows that Joyce has been on extended family leave because of one of her children and has just returned to work. Her temporary replacement, Sandra Herzberg, was pulled back to her human resources job two weeks before Joyce returned. Bill is polite and concerned but specific in stating his request (Case Document 2-1a).

CASE DOCUMENT 2-1A

Bill's E-mail to Joyce

To: joyce_smith@gyros.net
Sub: Checking Appropriate enrollments for MSW—3

Joyce: Please remove all managers lower than level 2 from the level three managerial skills workshops (MSW—3). We currently have 6-8 people enrolled who don't yet have the service records that qualify them for any of the MSWs. In addition, four people with more than enough time in grade must be enrolled by Friday.

I know you need help in checking lists, as Sandra had to return to HR sooner than we anticipated. But a number of people, not just the four from Mark's group, have been waiting for this class for months. If we fill existing vacancies from the wait list, we can enroll everybody who needs to be in this session.

Please stop by after lunch today so that we can go over the list of everyone enrolled in all the MSW workshops scheduled to begin in two weeks. Be sure to discuss anyone you are not sure about. I will help you sort this out. A number of department heads are unhappy, but they understand the situation.

Bill then sends an e-mail to Mark Jaron (Case Document 2-1b), who was extremely unhappy when he found out that his four employees couldn't enroll in the workshop, particularly when he discovered that a number of level 2 employees were enrolled.

CASE DOCUMENT 2-1B

Bill's E-mail to Mark

To: Mark_Jaron@gyros.net
Sub: Checking appropriate enrollments for MSW—3

Thanks for your voice mail. I appreciate your telling me about the problem, and I will have it resolved this afternoon.

Joyce, as you may know, has just returned from extended family leave. She's swamped, as Sandra was pulled back to HR two weeks early because of staff reductions. Joyce and I will be working on the MSW lists this afternoon and will send new enrollment lists to all departments by the end of the day. With our regular team now in place, training schedules/enrollments should be fine.

Bill also decides to send a short e-mail to his supervisor, Marshall Remick, to let him know what has happened (Case Document 2-1c). That way, Bill reasons, Marshall will be prepared if he hears about the problems the training division has had in enrolling people in the wrong classes. Bill wants to protect himself as well as Joyce by explaining the situation to his supervisor.

CASE DOCUMENT 2-1C

Bill's E-mail to Marshall

To: Marshall_Remick@gyros.net
Sub: Checking appropriate enrollments for MSW—3

Marshall: You may hear that we have enrolled the wrong people for some of the MSW workshops. That's true, but the problem will be rectified by the end of today.

Joyce Smith, as you probably recall, has been on extended family leave. Sandra Herzberg, who assumed much of Joyce's job, had to return to HR because of staffing cuts. For two weeks, enrollments were not monitored. Hence the errors.

Joyce and I will be evaluating everyone who has enrolled, and we will (1) notify those who should not have enrolled, and (2) enroll people on the official waiting list. Everyone involved will receive an e-mail. I've already notified Mark.

Anticipate the context in which your writing will be received.

• How will your writing be used?

Once your document has reached its primary destination, it may be placed in a stack for later reading; it may be skimmed and then routed to the person who will be responsible for acting on it; it may be read, copied, and distributed to readers unknown to you; it may be read and used as an agenda item for discussing a particular point; or it may be read carefully and later used as a reference. Knowing how readers to whom you write frequently use the documents they receive can often guide you in deciding not only what to say but also how to organize the information and arrange it on the page.

Case 2-2 shows how consideration of the context helped a writer know how to plan an e-mail.

The Basic Parts of the Composing Process

This composing process, integral to your analysis of audience, has six main stages:

1. **Analyzing** the situation
2. **Choosing/discovering** content
3. **Arranging** content
4. **Drafting**
5. **Revising**
6. **Editing** the finished draft

A writer who tries to do all stages at once usually creates a document that will fail. Research has shown that good writers usually follow a standard process—one that will make your writing tasks easier and the results more effective.

Analyzing the writing situation—purpose, readers, and context. The first step in composing is the most critical. In this step, you need to know *why* you need to write: what you want to achieve with your document, what situation or problem has led to the necessity of your writing this document. Then, you need to consider your readers—those who will or may read your document.

Every technical or workplace document responds to a specific situation. Each document has a targeted audience. Writing responds to both—the situation and the readers in that situation. Writing is not simply compiling information about a subject.

Choosing/discovering content. You select content for your document based on your purpose, *what* your reader needs, and *how* you think your reader perceives the subject.

As you search for information, remember your purpose, what you want your reader to know and do with what you write.

Then, begin to list ideas you can use to develop your topic. Based on these ideas, ask yourself what additional information you will need to locate. Don't like

Case 2-2

The director of online sales at Pine Avenue Books would like to perform a customer survey regarding the store's website in order to improve the efficiency of the online shopping experience. She drafts the following e-mail that she will send to all customers who made online or onsite purchases at the store in the last two years (Case Document 2-2a). The store manager, however, tells her that

---

CASE DOCUMENT 2-2A

SUBJECT: Please take a 5-minute, multiple-choice survey; details follow.

I am the director of online sales at Pine Avenue Books and am conducting a study of the online shopping sections of the store's website. If you have purchased books online in the last two years, please consider participating, and passing the attached invitation on to your friends for their potential participation.

The purpose of this study is to determine how customers view the store's website and, in particular, the sections related to online shopping. Your participation may provide useful information about online shopping, and help us to improve your online shopping experience in the future. I am looking for customers who have bought books online at Pine Avenue Books in the last two years.

If you participate, your obligations will be low. You will complete a short, anonymous survey via the Internet that will require approximately 5 minutes of your time, and will be returned to me via Survey Monkey, an online data collection service. If you complete a survey, your responses will be returned to me anonymously (I will not be able to identify your e-mail address, your IP address, or any other information that would inform me as to your identity or your location). If you agree to do so, you will also participate in a 15- to 20-minute follow-up session (this meeting will occur by telephone or e-mail as you choose). All data for surveys and follow-up interviews will be strictly confidential. Your identity will never be revealed in any results, discussions, or presentation of the research. In addition, all information will be destroyed after I have analyzed the data.

Completion of the survey and postsurvey interviews is voluntary; you may skip questions, and can quit any portion of the study at any time. If you are willing to participate in this study, please click on the following link http://www.surveymonkey.com/PineAvenueBooks and complete the survey. If you wish to participate in a follow-up interview, please include contact information at the end of the survey.

You may contact me via e-mail or telephone as follows:

her draft, if sent by e-mail, will likely not be read: (1) The subject line does not encourage busy readers to open the e-mail. (2) The purpose of the message does not appear until the second paragraph. (3) The e-mail as a whole is dense and difficult for readers to skim. The online sales director revises the original to respond to the three issues (Case Document 2-2b).

CASE DOCUMENT 2-2B

SUBJECT: Please take a 5-minute survey about online shopping at Pine Avenue Books.

SURVEY PURPOSE
The purpose of this study is to gauge your opinion of the online shopping sections of the Pine Avenue Books website (www.pineavenuebooks.com). Your participation will help us to improve your future online shopping experience.

If you have purchased books online in the last two years, please consider participating, and passing the attached invitation on to your friends for their potential participation.

SURVEY REQUIREMENTS
If you participate, your obligations will be minimal.

1. You will complete a short, anonymous survey via the Internet that will require approximately 5 minutes of your time and will be returned to me via Survey Monkey, an online data collection service.
2. If you complete a survey, your responses will be returned to me anonymously (I will not be able to identify your e-mail address, your IP address, or any other information that would inform me as to your identity, or your location).
3. If you agree to do so, you will also participate in a 15- to 20-minute follow-up session (this meeting will occur by telephone or e-mail as you choose).
4. All data for surveys and follow-up interviews will be strictly confidential. Your identity will never be revealed in any results, discussions, or presentation of the research. In addition, all information will be destroyed after I have analyzed the data.
5. Completion of the survey and follow-up interviews is voluntary; you may skip questions, and can quit any portion of the study at any time.
6. If you are willing to participate in this study, please click on the link http://www.surveymonkey.com/PineAvenueBooks and complete the survey. If you wish to participate in a follow-up interview, please include contact information at the end of the survey.

If you have questions, you may contact me via e-mail or telephone as follows:

what you wrote? Delete it. You may want to begin your document by writing your purpose at the beginning to help you stay on track.

Arranging content. As you collect and begin summarizing information and data, consider how to arrange the material. In what order should you present your content? Memos, for example, need to begin with the news or essential information to ensure that readers at least read what's most important before they start skimming the document or stop reading it altogether. Most reports begin with an introduction, followed by a summary of the report. Alternately, you can combine the introduction with a summary of the report. The discussion section, in which you present the supporting information, follows. Most reports follow some version of this plan. Many business organizations have templates for reports.

You can arrange content by placing material in "stacks," which can be used as a resource when you begin writing. If you know what arrangement you want/have to use, sort material so that you can easily find it when you begin drafting specific segments of your document. You can also sort material electronically: create folders for each segment of your report. Then arrange material within each folder before you begin drafting. This method allows you to track material you use and insert appropriate citations when you use material from a specific source.

If you use electronic articles from your library's database, insert these articles into files that can be accessed later when you begin to draft your document.

Drafting. Every individual drafts differently. Most writers work on a document in a start/stop fashion. When you begin your draft, open your file and save it with the name of your report. Then, begin typing ideas or sections. (You may wish to move/paste material you listed, arranged, and then developed in Step 2.) You may wish to type the names of your main segments, boldface those, and insert information beneath the appropriate segment. This method helps you keep track of the information that you are using to develop your draft. Note that some of the ideas in your list become headings. Some may be combined with other ideas. You can arrange, delete, and add ideas as you need to.

As you continue to draft, you will revise. But during the drafting stage you should revise only to improve the meaning. Try to avoid worrying about sentences that don't sound "quite right." If the sentence you write captures what you want to say, even clumsily, don't stop to revise. You can "clean up" these sentences later. Don't attempt to correct mechanical problems unless you feel you can do so without slowing your ability to transfer your ideas from your mind to the screen. Focus on presenting your material to your readers: then you can begin a formal revision process once you believe you have your basic ideas on the screen or page.

Revising. During the formal revision process you need to revise several times and focus on different issues:

- **Logic.** Does your presentation make sense? Try reading paragraphs aloud that seem to you to be "scrambled." Hearing what you have written often tells you if/where problems in logic occur. Does your material occur in the appropriate order for your purpose and for your readers?

- **Completeness.** Does you presentation seem complete, in terms of your purpose and your readers' needs and requirements? Is your information correct? Does your document contain all requested information?

- **Style.** Examine each paragraph and each sentence. Are your paragraphs really paragraphs? Do they have topic sentences? Do all the sentences in the paragraph pertain to the meaning you are building in the paragraph? Start each paragraph with a topic sentence. Eliminate or recast sentences that provide little support for the topic sentence. Today's readers usually dislike wordy, dense, complicated sentences. Make your sentences clear, concise, and precise to encourage your readers to follow your ideas. Also watch the length of your paragraphs. Long paragraphs discourage readers and tend to become incoherent.

- **Visuals.** Do you need visuals—photos, graphs, drawings, pictorial illustrations—to help your reader "see" and remember key ideas? Visuals combined with text often provide the best means of communicating with your readers.

- **Document design.** When you began drafting, if you used headings or names of report segments to help you organize your draft, you began at that point to design your document. Document design refers to the way information is arranged and displayed on the page. The importance of how information looks on the page cannot be stressed enough. If you want your writing to be read, design the page so that information is inviting and accessible.

Editing.   Get into the habit of performing several "edits" for any document: one for mechanics—spelling, usage, punctuation, and sentence structure.

A second edit focuses on the document as a whole. How does it look? How does it sound? Is the important information easy to locate? Is the document complete?

Another edit focuses on citing sources: check your documentation to be sure that you give credit or sources of all information you have used. Be sure that when you use illustrations and ideas from other sources you give credit to the source.

In short, don't try to check for every error at once, in one reading. Editing requires care, objective reading, and diligence.

For an example of how the composing process works when it is applied to a routine business document, read Case 2-3 and track the development of this memorandum. Note how the message looks after Bob's initial revision of his draft.

Case 2-3

Bob Johnson, an engineering project manager with a local civil engineering firm, has been named local arrangement chair of the forthcoming construction engineering conference. Two months before the conference, Bob needs to send a memo to everyone in his group to let them know what responsibilities they will have at the conference. While all employees know about the conference, Bob has informed his group via e-mail that each office group will have responsibilities throughout the conference. Bob wants the memo to inform his group specifically about what they will need to do.

Bob uses the planning stage of developing the memo to decide what topics he wants to present to his group. He will send this memo as an e-mail attachment. As he plans his memo, Bob types the following list of topics:

Location, date, time info of conference
Specific duties of the SE Group
General instructions
Conference schedule
Other information SE Group needs to know

As he develops the memo, he inserts information beneath each heading and highlights incomplete sections. His first draft looks like this (Case Document 2-3a):

CASE DOCUMENT 2-3A

Bob's first draft

Conference Location, Date, Time

CE conference—October 28-29—Lancaster Center. Our group's responsibility—serve as greeters, help prevent glitches. Over 150 engineers have already registered, and the cut-off date is still three weeks away. We need to be sure we are organized. Conference may be larger than last year. We want to do our part to ensure the success of the meeting. Help all attendees have a good conference. Be proactive in anticipating problems with people getting where they need to be:

Please be at the Lancaster Center at the following times:

Oct. 28: noon-end of the day
Oct. 29: 7:00-end of the conference. Last session begins at 3:30
Refreshments will be available during break periods. WATER IN ALL ROOMS.

Our Responsibilities
Helping visitors locate the section meetings, answer any questions, deal with any hotel reservation glitches, transportation problems, questions about restaurants. Remain available until after the dinner on Oct. 28. Oct. 29: On site throughout the day.

General Instructions Information
- Number expected to register and attend: 200+.
- Visitors will arrive at the hotel by mid-morning on the 28th. Some will come the evening before. [Contact Ralph to see if we need to be at the hotel on Oct. 27 after 5:00? Check information folder for sponsor letters.]
- Be available no later than noon on 28th. If possible, arrive at the Lancaster Center earlier than that. Dress is business casual.
- If those flying in arrive late, contract Jim or Joanna via their cell phones to ensure that registrations are not cancelled. Jim: 228-3459; Joanna: 322-1875.

Conference Schedule

Oct. 28
Light lunch: noon-1:15
Opening session: 1:30-3:00
Second session: 3:30-5:00 [check sponsors for all sessions. These have to be correct!!!! Check with central planning group.]
Dinner: 6:30—Holcomb Room, 2nd floor of the LC

Oct. 29
Breakfast: Room 104 of the LC, 7:00-8:00 [sponsor? Be sure we have a complete list with all names spelled correctly. Contact info for each.]
Third session: 8:30-10:00 [session sponsor?]
Closing Session: 10:30-noon [sponsor?]
Lunch: noon

Displays
Nine vendors will display software all day the 29th in room 106. Consultants will be on hand to discuss compatibility issues. Be available to help vendors set up.

Conference Materials
Will be available at the check-in desk at the front door
Each folder will contain brochures about new products and a schedule. Add a list of restaurants downtown?

Other
Breakout rooms will be available for the second part of the sessions.
Phone and faxes are available in Room 110 8:00-5:00.

Bob's revision follows (Case Document 2-3b). How could he have improved it with the following goals in mind? He wants his employees to

- report on time,
- know what they should do when they arrive,
- have cell phone numbers for quick contact purposes, and
- know whom to contact throughout the conference.

Does the memo enable Bob's employees to achieve those goals?

CASE DOCUMENT 2-3B

Bob's revision

TO: SE Group   **DATE:**   October 1, 2011
FROM: Bob Johnson
SUBJECT: Preparations for the Construction Engineering Conference

Conference Location, Date, Time
The construction engineering conference is scheduled October 28-29 at the Lancaster Center. Our group will serve as greeters. Over 150 engineers have already registered, and the cut-off date is still three weeks away. We need to be sure we are organized to help visitors as they arrive.

Please be at the Lancaster Center at the following times:

Oct. 28:   noon-end of the day
Oct. 29:   7:00-end of the conference. Last session begins at 3:30

SE Group—Specific Duties
We will be responsible for helping visitors locate the section meetings, answer any questions, deal with any hotel reservation and transportation glitches, and remain available until after the dinner on Oct. 28. Oct. 29—We need to be on site throughout the day and help guests who need to leave promptly at the close of the morning session.

General Information
- Number expected to register and attend: 200+
- Visitors will arrive at the hotel by mid-morning on the 28th. Some will come the evening before.
- Be available no later than noon. If possible, arrive at the Lancaster Center earlier than that.
- If those flying in arrive late, contract Jim or Joanna via their cell phones to ensure that registrations are not cancelled. Jim: 228-3459; Joanna: 322-1875.

Conference Schedule

Oct. 28

Noon-1:15	Lite lunch—Mellon Room (Sponsor: KLM Ltd.)
1:30-3:30	Room 105, Opening session
3:30-5:00	Room 105, Second session (Sponsor: Bickle and Lauren)
6:30	Buffet in Holcomb Room, 2nd floor of the LC

Oct. 29

7:00-8:00	Breakfast: Room 104 of the LC
8:30-10:00	Room 105, Third session (Sponsor: MERK Inc.)
10:30-noon	Room 105 Closing Session (Sponsor: Malcolm, Fisher, & Peabody)
Lunch: noon	Mellon Room

Software Displays

Nine vendors will display software all day the 29th in room 106. Consultants will be on hand to discuss compatibility issues. Be available to help vendors with set-up.

Conference Materials
- Available at the check-in desk at the front door
- Registration folder with name tags: will contain brochures about new products and a schedule of activities. List of restaurants in town for those who are staying for the weekend.

Other Information
- Phone and faxes are available in room 110 8:00-5:00.
- Refreshments will be available during break periods. Bottled water in all rooms.

Call me on my cell phone if anything comes up that isn't covered here.

PLANNING AND REVISION CHECKLIST

Analyzing the Situation

- ☐ What is your subject or topic?
- ☐ What is the purpose of the document?
- ☐ Who are your readers, known and potential?
- ☐ Why are you writing? Why is this document required? What is the situation that led to the need for this document? Who cares?

Selecting Content

- ☐ What topics do you need to cover? What do your readers need to know? What do you want your readers to do?
- ☐ What structure do you plan to use? If you have required report sections, what are they?
- ☐ What information resources do you have available? What resources do you need to locate?
- ☐ What types of visuals—e.g., graphs, photos, diagrams—are you considering using? Will they help convey the message?

Arranging Content

- ☐ In what order should the information be placed? What does your reader need to know first?
- ☐ Have you sorted your material into specific groups?
- ☐ Can you see a plan for headings that announce the content to your reader?
- ☐ Is all the material relevant to your purpose?

Drafting

- ☐ Have you inserted information under each of your headings?
- ☐ Have you recorded the sources of all information you will use so that you can develop correct citations after you have completed your draft?
- ☐ Have you noted where you will use graphics? Have you noted the source of each graphic you use from another source?

Revising

- ☐ Have you stated clearly the purpose of your report?
- ☐ Does your content support your purpose?
- ☐ Is your tone appropriate?
- ☐ Will your readers be able to follow your logic?
- ☐ Have you included all required items—report sections and required information?

continued

PLANNING AND REVISION CHECKLIST ✔ *continued*

☐ Have you checked all facts and numbers?
☐ Could any material be deleted?
☐ Is your document easy to read? Are your paragraphs well organized and of a reasonable length?
☐ Have you had someone read your draft and suggest improvements?

Editing

☐ Have you checked for misspellings and for other mechanical errors, such as misplaced commas, semicolons, colons, and quotation marks?
☐ Have you checked all points of the completed draft at which your word processing program suggests that you have errors in either sentence structure, mechanics, or spelling?
☐ Have you included all the formal elements that your report needs/is required to include?
☐ Is your system of documentation complete and accurate (if you are following a style sheet)?
☐ Are your pages numbered?
☐ Are all graphics placed in the appropriate locations within the text?
☐ Is the format consistent—font selected, size, placement of headings?

EXERCISES

1. Interview a professional in your field about his or her writing practices. Who are the different audiences that this individual must write for? Does he or she typically write for colleagues, superiors, or subordinates? For international or local readers? For readers inside or outside the organization? For readers in the same field or in different fields? How does he or she adjust the message for each audience? What stories of noteworthy success or failure in addressing a specific audience is this individual willing to share with you? Summarize your findings in a brief slide presentation, explaining the insights you've gained from this interview about analyzing your audience.

2. Your employer has always provided free child care to all employees with children ages 3 months to 5 years. For its 50 years of operation, the company has taken great pride in being a family-friendly employer. Tough economic times for the industry and rising costs of operation for the child care center, however, now require that the company begin charging parents $100 per month per child for the services of the child care center. According to the president of the company,

it was either that or freeze wages for all employees or lower the already slim dividend paid to the company's stockholders and risk a loss of investors. The president of the company directs you to write three letters regarding this important change: one to parents using the child care center, one to all employees, and one to the stockholders. Note that parents will also receive the letter addressed to employees. Note also that some employees are also stockholders. The president recognizes the sensitivity of this policy change and thus will also expect from you a memo justifying the variations you made in the three letters.

3. Find a blog posting aimed at specialists in your field. Revise the posting for a specific group of readers outside your field who might need to know this information (e.g., business managers, city officials, school administrators). Attach the original to your revision and submit both to your instructor.

4. Examine Figure 2-1. If you were the author of this document and were given 15 more minutes to make it more suitable for its audience, what changes would you make?

One Child's Death is One Too Many

Preventing Backovers in America's Driveways

Vehicle backover injuries and deaths occur when someone, without a driver's knowledge or awareness, is positioned behind a vehicle as the driver is backing out of a driveway or other parking spot. Most victims of backovers are the elderly and children.

To add to the tragedy of backover injuries and deaths, the driver is often a neighbor or relative. When a child is the victim, the driver may even be the child's mother or father.

Since most of these heartbreaking incidents occur in private driveways rather than on the road, they are not typically included in traffic-crash fatality data. Therefore, experts often don't agree on the exact number of children injured or killed in backover incidents each year.

But even one child who dies from a backover incident is one too many. Awareness and understanding of the problem are the first steps toward reducing the risk of backover deaths.

All Vehicles Have Blind Spots

In the case of a backover incident, the blind spot is the place behind your vehicle that you cannot see in the rear or side view mirrors — or even by craning your neck out the driver's side window. Generally speaking, the larger the vehicle, the larger the blind spot.

Blind spots for shorter drivers tend to be significantly larger as well. In addition, the elevation of the driver's seat, the shape of a vehicle's windows and mirrors, and the slope of a driveway can affect the size of the blind spot behind a vehicle.

In addition, the smaller stature of children can make them particularly difficult for a driver to see when backing up. So how do you protect a child from becoming a victim of backover?

FIGURE 2-1 Document for Exercise 4

Source: National Highway Traffic Safety Administration. One Child's Death Is One Too Many: Preventing Backovers in America's Driveways. http://www.nhtsa.gov/people/injury/pedbimot/ped/BackoversTry2/PreventingBackovers.pdf

Safety Tips for Parents

Keeping your children out of harm's way requires ongoing education, supervision, and vigilance: there simply is no single fail-safe solution. However, safety experts advise employing the following strategies to help reduce the risk of a backover tragedy occurring:

- Ensure your children are properly supervised at all times, especially wherever motor vehicles might be present.

- Teach children not to play in, under, or around vehicles — ever.

- Always assume children could be present and carefully check the street, driveway, and area around your vehicle before backing out.

- Avoid making your driveway a "playground." If you do allow children in this area, make sure that it's only when there are no vehicles present. To further protect children who may be outside playing, separate the driveway from the roadway with a physical barrier to prevent any cars from entering.

- To prevent curious children from ever putting a vehicle in gear, never leave vehicles running, and keep all vehicles, even those in driveways and garages, locked up tight.

- When backing up, always know where all children are and have them stay in your full view and well away from your vehicle.

- Look behind you as you back out S-L-O-W-L-Y with your windows rolled down to listen for children who may have dashed behind your vehicle suddenly — and be prepared to stop!

- If you're driving an SUV or truck, remember that the blind spot behind your vehicle can be especially large: use extreme care whenever you back up.

Finally, talk with neighborhood parents about backover incidents and ask them to teach their children not to play in or around any vehicle or driveway. By working together to promote awareness and protective home and neighborhood environments, we can help to keep all our children safe.

FIGURE 2-1 *Continued*

3

Writing Ethically

Quick Tips

On the job, you typically won't have time to analyze all the issues or answer all the questions relating to a given ethical dilemma. You might have to make a decision quickly—in minutes or seconds.

In cases like this, think of a person in your company or in your profession you admire for his or her integrity and good judgment (e.g., a colleague, a supervisor, a mentor). Ask yourself, "How would he or she manage this dilemma?" Allow your answer to this question to guide your actions.

YOUR PROFESSIONAL OBLIGATIONS

None of us are isolated individuals, operating entirely separate from the traffic of human society. Your ethical obligations are several, often intersecting, and from time to time competing. Consider, for example, your duties to the following:

- **To yourself:** You will have to make decisions and take actions that allow you to support yourself financially while establishing (and maintaining) your reputation in your field. You can't quit (or lose) your job every time you object to a policy of your boss.
- **To your discipline and profession:** As a member of your profession, you have a responsibility to advance the knowledge and reputation of your field. You must share information with your colleagues that will improve the practices of your profession, clarify understanding, offer new insights, and promote better training of new students of your discipline. You must communicate in a manner that brings credit to your profession and inspires the next generation to want to study and join your profession.

- **To your academic institution:** You have a moral obligation to the institution that trained you for your profession. Your successes or failures will be indicative of the merits of that institution and its faculty. If you disgrace yourself by illegal or unethical actions, for example, investigating officials and the public might ask why you weren't taught better behavior.
- **To your employer:** Your responsibility as an employee is to serve the interests of your organization, to help it make money, to promote its products and services, and to shield confidential information and intellectual property, especially if doing so offers a competitive advantage.
- **To your colleagues:** You have a duty to your colleagues on the job to do your fair share of the work assigned and to do it with integrity, accuracy, and efficiency. You also have responsibility to use no more than your fair share of the resources allotted and to take no more than your fair share of the credit (or blame) given.
- **To the public:** Your obligation to society is to promote the public good through greater safety, fuller liberty, and a better quality of life. Your decisions and actions on the job could allow communities to thrive in resilient and sustainable environments or to be poisoned by private greed and callous disregard for civic aspirations.

In communicating on the job, you will have to juggle your various obligations and determine which has priority. You can't simply do whatever the boss tells you to because you also have important responsibilities to yourself, your profession, your schools and teachers, your colleagues, and the public itself. You will need to make every effort to avoid being either submissive or self-righteous.

CODES OF CONDUCT

Both your professional association and your employing organization are likely to have codes of conduct or ethical guidelines that specify their expectations regarding appropriate behavior on the job. For example, the Society for Technical Communication, a leading international association for technical writers and graphic artists, has composed its guidelines as a list of six principles (Figure 3-1), while the Institute of Electrical and Electronic Engineers offers 10 ideals (Figure 3-2).

Familiarize yourself with the codes of conduct that regulate ethical communication for your company and your profession because from time to time you might have to cite their guidelines to justify your decisions regarding ethical dilemmas on the job. Ordinarily, a code of conduct asserts only guiding principles that you must interpret and apply to specific situations, but it might also be the entry point to a wider array of available ethics resources, including frequently asked questions (FAQs) and help lines for reporting violations and soliciting advice.

Society for Technical Communication: Ethical Principles for Technical Communicators

As technical communicators, we observe the following ethical principles in our professional activities.

Legality
We observe the laws and regulations governing our profession. We meet the terms of contracts we undertake. We ensure that all terms are consistent with laws and regulations locally and globally, as applicable, and with STC ethical principles.

Honesty
We seek to promote the public good in our activities. To the best of our ability, we provide truthful and accurate communications. We also dedicate ourselves to conciseness, clarity, coherence, and creativity, striving to meet the needs of those who use our products and services. We alert our clients and employers when we believe that material is ambiguous. Before using another person's work, we obtain permission. We attribute authorship of material and ideas only to those who make an original and substantive contribution. We do not perform work outside our job scope during hours compensated by clients or employers, except with their permission; nor do we use their facilities, equipment, or supplies without their approval. When we advertise our services, we do so truthfully.

Confidentiality
We respect the confidentiality of our clients, employers, and professional organizations. We disclose business-sensitive information only with their consent or when legally required to do so. We obtain releases from clients and employers before including any business sensitive materials in our portfolios or commercial demonstrations or before using such materials for another client or employer.

Quality
We endeavor to produce excellence in our communication products. We negotiate realistic agreements with clients and employers on schedules, budgets, and deliverables during project planning. Then we strive to fulfill our obligations in a timely, responsible manner.

Fairness
We respect cultural variety and other aspects of diversity in our clients, employers, development teams, and audiences. We serve the business interests of our clients and employers as long as they are consistent with the public good. Whenever possible, we avoid conflicts of interest in fulfilling our professional responsibilities and activities. If we discern a conflict of interest, we disclose it to those concerned and obtain their approval before proceeding.

Professionalism
We evaluate communication products and services constructively and tactfully, and seek definitive assessments of our own professional performance. We advance technical communication through our integrity and excellence in performing each task we undertake. Additionally, we assist other persons in our profession through mentoring, networking, and instruction. We also pursue professional self-improvement, especially through courses and conferences.

http://www.stc.org/about-stc/the-profession-all-about-technical-communication/ethical-principles

FIGURE 3-1 STC Ethical Principles for Technical Communicators

Source: Society for Technical Communication, http://www.stc.org/about-stc/
the-profession-all-about-technical-communication/ethical-principles

IEEE CODE OF ETHICS

WE, THE MEMBERS OF THE IEEE, in recognition of the importance of our technologies in affecting the quality of life throughout the world and in accepting a personal obligation to our profession, its members and the communities we serve, do hereby commit ourselves to the highest ethical and professional conduct and agree:

1. to accept responsibility in making decisions consistent with the safety, health and welfare of the public, and to disclose promptly factors that might endanger the public or the environment;

2. to avoid real or perceived conflicts of interest whenever possible, and to disclose them to affected parties when they do exist;

3. to be honest and realistic in stating claims or estimates based on available data;

4. to reject bribery in all its forms;

5. to improve the understanding of technology, its appropriate application, and potential consequences;

6. to maintain and improve our technical competence and to undertake technological tasks for others only if qualified by training or experience, or after full disclosure of pertinent limitations;

7. to seek, accept, and offer honest criticism of technical work, to acknowledge and correct errors, and to credit properly the contributions of others;

8. to treat fairly all persons regardless of such factors as race, religion, gender, disability, age, or national origin;

9. to avoid injuring others, their property, reputation, or employment by false or malicious action;

10. to assist colleagues and co-workers in their professional development and to support them in following this code of ethics.

Approved by the IEEE Board of Directors | February 2006

FIGURE 3-2 IEEE Code of Ethics

Source: http://www.ieee.org/portal/cms_docs/about/CoE_poster.pdf

Recognizing Unethical Communication

Also essential to communicating ethically is to recognize the ways in which individuals on the job might be unethical in their communications. Chief among the possibilities are plagiarizing, deliberately using imprecise or ambiguous language, manipulating statistics, using misleading visuals, promoting prejudice, and distributing misinformation.

Plagiarism and theft of intellectual property. On the job, you may be responsible for the security of five kinds of intellectual property:

1. Copyrightable Material: A composition of original material fixed in a tangible medium, such as books, journals, software applications, computer programs, video or audio recordings, illustrations, etc. This includes materials available in digital files, e-mail messages, and World Wide Web pages.
2. Trademark: A display of words or symbols communicated in text, illustrations, or sounds that identify and distinguish the goods and services of a manufacturer or supplier, such as the name or logo of a company.
3. Trade Secret: A design, formula, list, method, pattern, or process that offers a competitive advantage over parties who don't have the same information, such as a special recipe.
4. Invention: A new and unique design, device, method, or process that is subject to patent protection.
5. Tangible Research Property: Tangible items created during research related to copyrightable materials, trademarks, trade secrets, and inventions, such as databases, diagrams, drawings, notes, prototypes, samples, and associated equipment and supplies.

Copyrightable material is unique in that for certain purposes (e.g., criticism, news reporting, research, teaching) you have the right to borrow limited portions for presentation or publication without the explicit permission of the owner. If the borrowing is extensive, however, permission is necessary.

On the job, writers will often recycle the words and images from various documents of their company without identifying the original source. They will readily lift paragraphs from the corporate website, for example, to use in a business letter to a potential client, or they will borrow a table from the annual report to use again in a proposal to a potential funding agency. Such recycling of material is efficient, and it is entirely legal and ethical as long as the participating writers recognize and allow this sharing of effort. In such cases, the company has ownership of the words and images that are being recycled. (If you have doubts about the propriety of such recycling within your company, ask the writer directly for his or her permission.)

If it isn't your company's materials that are being used, however, you must acknowledge the sources of borrowed words, images, and ideas. In the majority of documents you write (such as letters, e-mail messages, blog postings, and memos), the acknowledgment may be a brief and simple introduction to the borrowed material: for example, "As Dr. Shirley Olson discovered, it's possible to vaccinate mosquitoes to prevent their developing and passing the disease on to human beings."

In formal reports, however, some official system of documentation would be necessary to identify the source of the information and to give full credit to Dr. Olson. Your organization might develop a special style for such source citations or adopt a standard style guide such as *The Chicago Manual of Style* of the University of Chicago Press, the *Publication Manual of the American Psychological Association*, or the *MLA Style Manual* of the Modern Language Association.

To use the words, images, or ideas of others without attribution is plagiarism. It constitutes a theft of intellectual property and is highly unethical and potentially illegal. Your intentions are immaterial: that is, it would be plagiarism if it were deliberate or if it were entirely inadvertent. You must, therefore, be especially cautious to avoid plagiarism: your organization could find itself the subject of a criminal case or a civil suit, and you could lose your job and your reputation.

Note also that material is automatically copyrighted as soon as it is created: it need not carry a copyright notice, and the copyright need not be registered with the United States Copyright Office (copyright.gov), though both actions will help to deter infringement.

If you quote a source (including material from e-mail messages, blog postings, or video clips), put the borrowed material inside quotation marks (or display it in a separate indented paragraph) and specify the source. If you paraphrase or summarize, you don't need quotation marks but you still must specify the source. Make sure that even your acknowledged paraphrases and summaries differ from the wording and phrasing of the original passage so that you can't be accused of plagiarism.

Here, for example, is the original passage from a source:

> Ethylene oxide has a boiling point of 51°F. It is processed as a liquid through the application of pressure. As the temperature of the ethylene oxide increases, the pressure in the feed line will correspondingly increase. At the time of the explosion, the ambient temperature was around 93°F. The feed line was not insulated or cooled. (from United States Environmental Protection Agency, Office of Solid Waste and Emergency Response. 2000. EPA chemical accident investigation report, Accra Pac Group, Inc. North Plant, Elkhart, Indiana. EPA 550-R-00-001. Washington, DC.)

Here is a summary that would constitute plagiarism even if the source were cited. Note how this passage changes words here and there but essentially duplicates the original passage:

> The boiling point of ethylene oxide is 51°F. Pressure is applied to process it as a liquid. As the temperature of the ethylene oxide rises, so does the pressure in the feed line. The temperature in the vicinity was roughly 93°F at the time of the explosion, and the feed line was neither insulated nor cooled.

Here is a summary that would be considered ethically appropriate. Note how the order of the sentences as well as the words have been substantially changed. Nevertheless, the source of the information must still be identified:

> Ethylene oxide was pressurized as a liquid in a feed line that was neither insulated from external temperatures nor subjected to any kind of special cooling. Ethylene oxide boils at 51°, but the ambient temperature rose to approximately 93°F. Increased pressure from the boiling chemical inside the feed line caused the line to rupture, resulting in the explosion.

If the borrowing is a substantial portion of the original source (e.g., several paragraphs or a single image), you will have two ethical and legal duties:

1. Acknowledge the source.
2. Request permission from the owner of the intellectual property.

The extensive borrowing of copyrighted material will ordinarily be permitted, but often with restrictions and often for a cost. You may contact the copyright owner directly or make your request through a service such as the Copyright Clearance Center (copyright.com). In this case, the borrowed material carries a note indicating both the source and the receipt of permission:

> From *Understanding Intercultural Communication*, by Stella Ting-Toomey and Leeva C. Chung. Copyright 2007 by Oxford University Press. Reprinted by permission.

If you change the original material (e.g., summarizing passages, revising illustrations, pulling still slides from digital video), you would specify the adaptation of the borrowing:

> From Lisk, John. (2011, March 10). Ways to Relieve Stress [Video]. CNN.com. http://www.cnn.com/video/#/video/health/2011/03/10/hm.stress.buster.cnn. Adapted by permission.

Permission is not needed for material in the public domain (i.e., intellectual property for which copyright protection has already expired or material created by agencies of the government of the United States), but such sources must always be acknowledged.

Deliberately imprecise or ambiguous language. Ordinarily, unclear and ambiguous language is a result of the writer's negligence, but it could also be a sign of a deliberate effort to mislead or manipulate the reader by hiding or disguising information.

Writers can imply that things are better or worse than they really are through the choice of words. For example, a writer answering inquiries about the company's electric vehicle could reply, "This automobile was designed to travel 1,000 miles on a single electric charge." It could be that the vehicle was designed with this objective in mind, but if it doesn't genuinely operate with this level of efficiency, the writer has made a false implication without telling a straight lie. And if this promised 1,000 miles doesn't include the weight of the average driver, the deception is all the greater.

Negative assertions are often deceptive. For example, consider a marketing claim such as "No anti-virus software does more or costs less than Infolator." With the words "does more" and "cost less" in the claim, you might be inclined to think that Infolator is truly better and lower in price. Notice, however, that Infolator doesn't really have to be better or lower in price to make its claim: it could have the same functions and be the same price as other antivirus software. The real claim here isn't that it's a better and cheaper product but that it's just as good and just as cheap.

Manipulation of numerical information. A leading way for individuals to be deceived is through the manipulation of statistics. For example, imagine the writer of a recommendation report who would like to give the impression that a controversial change in security practices really has wide support. She surveys only the managers in the company and finds that 51 percent of the 19 percent who returned the survey favor the change. In the report she writes, "A majority of those who completed the survey favored the change." By not revealing that this "majority" is only 51 percent and that it represents only about 10 percent of the company's managers, she magnifies the thin support for the controversial change. She has not exactly lied, but she has likely deceived most readers of the report.

Use of misleading illustrations. Like words, illustrations have the capacity to misrepresent and mislead. For example, a company of one hundred employees has only two who are African Americans. In the recruiting materials it carries to college campuses, the company shows a dozen of its employees doing different jobs, including both of its African Americans. This is unethical communication because it implies that African Americans constitute almost 17 percent of the employees—a gross distortion of the real situation. Prospective job candidates would be substantially deceived about the diversity of colleagues and the working environment this company offers.

Or consider a line graph such as Figure 3-3 that might be given to prospective clients of ABC Manufacturing. Here we see a picture of volatile change year to year.

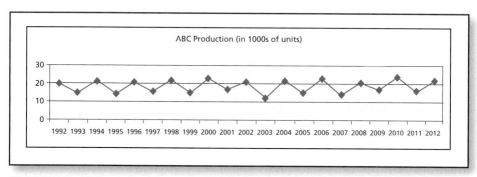

FIGURE 3-3 ABC production reported in one-year intervals

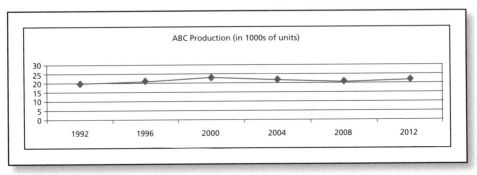

FIGURE 3-4 ABC production reported in four-year intervals

If the increments on the line graph are changed from every year to every four years, however, ABC's disturbing record of erratic production almost vanishes entirely (see Figure 3-4). Viewers of this line graph would be given only the impression of relative stability. Prospective clients would be thoroughly deceived and would be quite surprised if ABC failed to meet its production goals in subsequent years.

Promotion of prejudice. Writers also communicate unethically by voicing prejudice through their choice of words and illustrations. For example, consider the following passage from a company memo:

> One of the constraints that the company operates under is the need to recruit women candidates for managerial positions. Harriet Smith was clearly ineffective as operations manager.

The unmistakable implication here is that women candidates constitute a negative impact on the business (i.e., "a constraint") and that Harriet Smith is representative of all women. It is unlikely that a man who proved to be ineffective as a manager would be considered representative of all men.

If titles are always used for men in the company but never used for women (e.g., Mr. William Jones, advertising manager, and Harriet Smith, operations manager), women don't seem as credible and authoritative. If photographs in the company's annual report always show the women sitting at desks staring at computer screens but the men sitting at big conference tables hearing reports and making decisions, the clear message is that men are (or ought to be) important executives while women are suited exclusively for clerical positions.

Your job as a communicator is to make sure that you don't reinforce or inspire prejudice and bigotry. Your ethical obligation is to offer only valid and reliable findings, fair and unbiased analyses, and logically justified conclusions.

Uncritical use of information. On the Internet especially, it is possible to find all kinds of erroneous information, manipulated images, distorted depictions, and dubious claims. If you are using the information you find without judging its accuracy, assessing the credibility of your sources, or verifying information across multiple sources, you could easily be distributing dangerous and damaging misinformation. Your negligence here is as unethical as it is inept. To build a reputation for integrity, you must accept responsibility for the accuracy of the information you communicate.

MANAGING UNETHICAL SITUATIONS

If you find yourself asked by a boss, colleague, or client to do something that you don't consider right, don't hesitate to ask polite questions. Don't accuse or immediately declare the request unethical. Explain your dilemma. Ask the individual to clarify. He or she might be unaware of the difficult moral position you're being put in by such a request or might immediately modify the request.

Keep in mind also that people of different cultures might have different ethical perspectives. For example, the dominant ethical perspective in the United States assumes that to be fair you must consider all people as equal and give privilege to none, but in China this idea could be considered unfair because family, friends, and neighbors are ordinarily thought to be special. In this situation, you would be wise to acknowledge each side's intention to be ethical as you try to find a solution satisfactory to both.

If explanations and negotiations don't satisfy you and if time allows, visit with a supervisor or mentor for guidance. Review the code of conduct of your profession or company for passages that might support or challenge your position.

If all of your investigation and deliberation fail to quiet your moral doubts, explain (in writing, if possible) that you don't feel comfortable doing X, but you could do Y. That is, identify both the thing you can't do (the unethical action requested), but also the thing that you could do (the ethical option).

If asked to justify your decision, cite the appropriate passages of your profession's or company's code of conduct. That is, make it clear that it isn't only you who is rejecting the request, but that it is your profession or your company that proscribes this behavior. Again, don't be impolite and don't accuse.

If you see something occurring on the job that you don't think is right, discuss the situation with your supervisor or mentor (in writing, if possible). If your investigation fails to satisfy you that the activity is justified, consider your several ethical obligations, including to your profession and to the public. Always make the decision that you could live with if your decision were made public.

A final piece of advice. Keep in mind that you bring two important credentials to a job: a knowledge of your field and a reputation for integrity. If you don't have a reputation for integrity, your knowledge of your field can't be trusted.

ETHICS DECISION CHECKLIST ✔

☐ What is the nature of the ethical dilemma?
☐ What are the specific aspects of this dilemma that make you uncomfortable?
☐ What are your competing obligations in this dilemma?
☐ What advice does a trusted supervisor or mentor offer?
☐ Does your company's code of conduct address this issue?
☐ Does your professional association's code of conduct address this issue?
☐ What are you unwilling to do? What are you willing to do?
☐ How will you explain or justify your decision?

EXERCISES

1. Visit the website of two major employers in your field. Locate the code of conduct for each. What are the similarities and differences in the two codes of conduct? What are the values that each employer espouses? What does each employer expect from its employees? From its executives? What additional ethics resources does each employer make available to employees? What can you tell about each employer from the code of conduct? Based on your review of the two codes of conduct, which employer would you prefer to work for? Why? Summarize your findings in a memo and share this memo with your colleagues.

2. The Ethisphere Institute (www.ethisphere.org) every year publishes a list of the world's most ethical companies. Check this year's list and choose one of the companies to investigate. What makes it one of the world's most ethical companies? Do you agree or disagree with this assessment? Report your findings in a slide presentation addressed to majors in your field.

3. You are a claims manager at the local office of a national insurance company. A claim for insurance coverage has come in from a pet store that is going out of business. A clerk at the store claims to have been severely traumatized after she assisted in euthanizing 13 young and healthy dogs that the store could neither sell nor donate and could no longer afford to feed and house. Reading the details in the claim makes you ill. Your administrative assistant, George, has always been scrupulous about keeping claims information confidential, but this time he decides to leak the case to a newspaper reporter. Public outrage about the dog killing is almost immediate, and the police are investigating. While you admire George for making a heroic decision, he has violated the client's privacy,

and your district supervisor is insisting that George be terminated. Write a letter to George explaining why he is losing his job. Or write a memo to your district supervisor explaining why George deserves to keep his job.

4. Examine Figure 3-5. If you were the author of this document and were given 15 more minutes to revise it, what changes would you make so that it better satisfies each of your competing ethical obligations?

PUBLIC NOTICE

Federal Communications Commission
445 12th St., S.W.
Washington, D.C. 20554

News Media Information 202 / 418-0500
Internet: http://www.fcc.gov
TTY: 1-888-835-5322

DA 11-250
February 9, 2011
Enforcement Advisory No. 2011-04

FCC ENFORCEMENT ADVISORY

CELL JAMMERS, GPS JAMMERS, and OTHER JAMMING DEVICES

CONSUMERS BEWARE: It is Unlawful to Use "Cell Jammers" and Other Equipment
that Blocks, Jams, or Interferes with Authorized Radio Communications in the U.S.

In recent years, the number of websites offering "cell jammers" or similar devices designed to block communications and create a "quiet zone" in vehicles, schools, theaters, restaurants, and other places has increased substantially. While these devices are marketed under different names – such as signal blockers, GPS jammers, or text stoppers – they have the same purpose. We remind consumers that it is a violation of federal law to use devices that intentionally block, jam, or interfere with authorized radio communications such as cell phones, police radar, GPS, and Wi-Fi.[1] Despite some marketers' claims, consumers cannot legally use cell and GPS jammers within the United States, nor can retailers lawfully sell them.

Why are jammers prohibited? Use of jamming devices can place you or other people in danger. For instance, jammers can prevent 9-1-1 and other emergency phone calls from getting through or interfere with law enforcement communications (ambulance, fire, police, etc). In order to protect the public and ensure access to emergency and other communications services, without interference, the FCC strictly prohibits the use, marketing, manufacture, and sale of jammers.

What happens if you use a jammer? Operation of a jammer in the United States is illegal and may subject you to substantial monetary penalties, seizure of the unlawful equipment, and criminal sanctions including imprisonment.[2] Therefore, this advisory emphasizes the importance of strict compliance with the legal prohibition against jammers.

Need more information? To file a complaint, visit www.fcc.gov/complaints or call 1-888-CALL-FCC. For additional information regarding enforcement of the jamming prohibition, visit www.fcc.gov/eb/jammerenforcement or contact Kevin Pittman or Neal McNeil of the Enforcement Bureau at (202) 418-1160 or jammerinfo@fcc.gov. Media inquiries should be directed to David Fiske at (202) 418-0513 or David.Fiske@fcc.gov.

To request materials in accessible formats for people with disabilities (Braille, large print, electronic files, audio format), send an e-mail to fcc504@fcc.gov or call the Consumer & Governmental Affairs Bureau at (202) 418-0530 (voice), (202) 418-0432 (TTY). You may also contact the Enforcement Bureau on its TTY line at (202) 418-1148 for further information about this Enforcement Advisory, or the FCC on its TTY line at 1-888-TELL-FCC (1-888-835-5322) for further information about the jamming prohibitions.

Issued by: Chief, Enforcement Bureau

---

[1] See 47 U.S.C. § 333 (prohibiting willful or malicious interference with the radio communications of any station licensed or authorized under the Communications Act or operated by the United States Government); 47 U.S.C. § 301 (requiring persons operating or using radio transmitters to be licensed or authorized under the Communications Act and the Commission's rules).

[2] See 47 U.S.C. §§ 401, 501, 503, 510.

Page 1 of 1

FIGURE 3-5 Document for Exercise 4

Achieving a Readable Style

Style refers to the overall way you express your ideas in a document, from the paragraph level to sentence structure and the words and phrases you choose.

Quick Tips

If you want your report to be read, use a style that your readers can follow easily. If your readers can't understand your report as they read it and have to constantly reread sentences and paragraphs, they may just disregard it or toss it out. Unreadable documents usually result from ineffective style.

THE PARAGRAPH

A reminder: the paragraph is a group of sentences that work together to produce a coherent idea. Paragraphs should be a moderate length—long paragraphs discourage readers—and begin with a topic sentence (a central statement) of their content. The supporting sentences build on the idea stated in the topic sentence and should occur in a logical order. In short:

- Begin each paragraph with a topic sentence that summarizes content to come.
- Include only information relevant to the topic sentence.
- Place sentences in a logical order.
- Avoid long paragraphs.

Examples for study. Effective report segments result from effective paragraphs. Examine the following introduction to a technical report (Figure 4-1). Because each paragraph begins with a topic sentence (highlighted in each example), you

45

Introduction

In 1996, the U.S. Department of Energy (DOE), Office of Fossil Energy, asked Argonne National Laboratory (ANL) to conduct a preliminary technical and legal evaluation of disposing of nonhazardous oil field wastes (NOW) into salt caverns. The conclusions of that study, based on preliminary research, were that disposal of oil field wastes into salt caverns is feasible and legal. If caverns are sited and designed well, operated carefully, closed properly, and monitored routinely, they can be a suitable means for disposing of oil field waste (Veil et al. 1996). Considering these findings and the increased U.S. interest in using salt caverns for nonhazardous oil field waste disposal, the Office of Fossil Energy asked ANL to conduct a preliminary identification and investigation of the risks associated with such disposal.

As Chapter 8 discusses, report introductions must have purpose statements to tell readers what the report will do. Having the purpose statement at the beginning of a paragraph helps readers find the purpose statement.

Report Purpose

The purpose of this report is to evaluate the possibility that adverse human health effects (carcinogenic and noncarcinogenic) could result from exposure to contaminants released from the caverns in domal salt formations used for nonhazardous oil field waste disposal. The evaluation assumes normal operations but considers the possibility of leaks in cavern seals and cavern walls during the post-closure phase of operation. It does not consider the risks associated with emissions from surface equipment operating at the site, nor does it consider the risks associated with surface oil leaks or other equipment-related spills or accidents.

The study focuses on possible long-term risks to human health. It does not address potential ecological effects, although such effects could result. Also, risks associated with naturally occurring radioactive materials (NORM) are not addressed. This preliminary assessment estimates risks associated with disposal in a single generic cavern only. No attempt has been made to address the possibly or likelihood that several caverns may be located in relatively close proximity and that more than one cavern could be a source of contamination to a given receptor. Also, no attempt has been made to evaluate the possible impacts of synergistic effects of multiple contaminants on a single receptor.

Because the history of salt cavern use for solid waste disposal is very limited, no readily available data could be accessed for this study. As a result, data from similar operations and professional judgment were used to develop the possible release mechanisms assumed in this hypothetical, generic analysis. The validity of the results would be enhanced if real data could be used. As data are generated on the use and post-closure operations of salt caverns used for solid waste disposal, they should be incorporated to update this study.

Report Development Process

Moves from broad to specific in supporting information

In this assessment, several steps were followed to identify possible human health risks. At the broadest level, these steps include identifying a reasonable set of contaminants of possible concern, identifying how humans could be exposed to these contaminants, assessing the toxicities of these contaminants, estimating their intakes, and characterizing their associated human health risks. The risk assessment methodology and

FIGURE 4-1 Effective Introduction to a Technical Report

techniques used in this report are based in large part on two documents. The first document is a training manual that was developed for a risk assessment workshop sponsored by DOE (DOE 1996). The second is the Risk Assessment Guidance for Superfund (U.S. Environmental Protection Agency [EPA] 1989).

Report Plan

The remainder of this report consists of nine sections. Section 2 provides background on the development, use, and closure of salt caverns that may be used for disposal of nonhazardous oil field wastes and possible cavern release scenarios. Section 3 identifies contaminants of potential concern that could cause harm to human health. Sections 4, 5, and 6 provide information for assessing potential exposure pathways that the contaminants of concern could take to reach human populations. Specifically, Section 4 describes fate and transport mechanisms of the contaminants of concern; Section 5 describes specific hydrogeologic conditions of locations where salt caverns are most likely to be used for oil field disposal (Gulf Coast, Texas, and New Mexico); and Section 6 describes potential release modes that could cause contaminants to leak from the cavern and be transported to areas where human populations may be exposed. Section 6 also estimates possible concentrations of the contaminants to which humans could be exposed under various release scenarios. Section 7 describes the toxicity of those contaminants that could come in contact with humans, given the fate and transport mechanisms identified in Section 5 combined with the potential exposure pathways described in Section 6. Section 8 estimates the potential intakes of those contaminants by humans and characterizes the risks to which those humans may be subjected on the basis of the intake of the contaminants (the potential for harm), their toxicities, and the release assumptions. Section 9 addresses the sensitivity of the estimated risks to operating procedures and potential regulatory structures, and Section 10 summarizes the results of the analyses.

> Topic sentence helps readers anticipate presentation of the nine sections. Naming each section allows the writer to show relationships among the sections.

FIGURE 4-1 *continued*

can read just the topic sentences and have a clear sense of the content of the introduction. While the final paragraph is the longest of this introduction, its structure allows you to follow easily the development of the paragraph.

This next example paragraph (Figure 4-2) uses a list to draw the reader's eyes to the central idea presented in the paragraph, the criteria for approval. The topic sentence introduces the paragraph and the list.

The listing strategy emphasizes the six items that take front and center in the Lake Ashton project. In this situation, listing highlights the rhetorical immediacy of the problem. A traditional paragraph with linear text would obscure the concerns (Figure 4-3).

Avoid excessive use of any writing technique—too many short paragraphs, too much enumeration (first, second, third, etc.), as well as too many lists. Concise paragraphs that begin with topic sentences and well-structured sentences of

The City of Ashtonville Economic Development Council presented six main concerns to the City Parks and Recreation Department about the proposed Ashton Lake development proposal:

1. Financial feasibility of the project
2. Ability to raise the necessary funds
3. Project maintenance, including long-term
4. Protection/Enhancement of the shoreline
5. Effect of project on changing lake water levels
6. Erosion of project's materials caused by water/sand

The EDC expressed a major concern that the project may not be as family-friendly as needed because it would require extensive funding to develop the recommended recreation facilities. In addition, the concerns stated suggest that the project, if approved, will have to be funded strictly by private donations rather than city or county parks money.

FIGURE 4-2 Effective Use of a List within a Paragraph

moderate length create clear, readable documents. Why is Figure 4-5 easier to read than Figure 4-4?

Note that each paragraph of Figure 4-5 begins with a topic sentence and a clearly stated subheading introduces each segment of the introduction. (Chapter 5 will explain how to design documents, but this revision also exemplifies excellent document design.)

BASIC PRINCIPLES OF EFFECTIVE STYLE

Effective writers adjust their style to the needs of their readers: (1) readers' knowledge of the subject, (2) readers' expectations about style based on the specific kind of writing, (3) readers' probable reading level based on the context in which the document will be read, and (4) the writer's relationship to readers—the professional roles of both writer and readers.

Determine your readers' knowledge of the subject. The reader's familiarity with the subject will determine how many specialized terms you can use. If the

The City of Ashtonville Economic Development Council presented six main concerns to the City Parks and Recreation Department about the proposed Ashton Lake development proposal: financial feasibility of the project; ability to raise the necessary funds; project maintenance, including long-term; protection/enhancement of the shoreline; effect of project on changing lake water levels; and erosion of project's materials caused by water/sand. The EDC expressed a major concern that the project may not be as family-friendly as needed because it would require extensive funding to develop the recommended recreation facilities. In addition, the concerns stated suggest that the project, if approved, will have to be funded strictly by private donations rather than city or county parks money.

FIGURE 4-3 Ineffective Run-in List

How an MRI Works

Brain perfusion refers to the blood circulation around the brain while exchanging oxygen and nutrients between the blood and the brain tissue. The effectiveness of brain perfusion depends on "blood pressure, blood velocity[...], and diffusion rates of oxygen and nutrients" [1]. An MRI scanner can monitor the perfusion of the brain to determine if a neurological disease is present.

An MRI scan uses a magnetic field to generate enhanced images that show certain parts of the body. The hydrogen atom provides a crucial component in the generation of an MRI scan. The hydrogen atom contains a single proton that interacts with the magnetic field generated by the MRI. The hydrogen atoms in a specific area of the human body will behave differently due to the presence of a magnetic field. The MRI scanner will detect the behavior of these hydrogen atoms to generate an enhanced image of that area.

In many MRI procedures, a contrast agent is used to further enhance the image of the body by increasing the brightness of the tissue being examined. The injection of contrast agents into the body will help the MRI scan retrieve information such as "blood flow [...] and related physiological parameters" [2]. These contrast agents work by altering the local magnetic field in the tissue being examined to generate an illuminated image of that tissue on the MRI scan.

Unfortunately, contrast agents have limited functions when physicians attempt to study the human brain. The brain contains a "membrane structure" known as the blood brain barrier. which protects the brain from foreign chemicals in the blood, while still allowing essential metabolic function [3]. The blood brain barrier filters out any unwanted chemicals that may travel through the brain. Since the blood brain barrier is very effective in its function, the chemicals in the contrast agents will be filtered out by this *membrane structure*. If a neurological disease is present in the brain, it can weaken the blood brain barrier and allow these unwanted chemicals to pass through [3]. The contrast agent would be useful for studying the disease in this situation.

Many methods have been created to penetrate the blood brain barrier. My proposed method will strengthen the interaction between hydrogen atoms with the magnetic field via electrical signals. During an MRI scan, an electrical signal will be emitted around the neck area. This signal will mark the hydrogen atoms that are in the vicinity of the emitted signal. Because no external chemicals are introduced, the blood brain barrier will not detect any foreign chemicals and will let the marked hydrogen atoms into the brain. The hydrogen atoms will travel through the bloodstream around the brain acting as beacons. They will then interact with the magnetic field of the MRI, allowing MRI to enhance the image of the brain, much like contrast agents [4].

FIGURE 4-4 Original Introduction to a Student Research Proposal

reader has a thorough knowledge of the subject, you can use acronyms, specialized nomenclature, and jargon that readers in a specific discipline regularly read and use. If the reader has little knowledge of the subject, limit the use of specialized vocabulary or perhaps define the terms. Another possibility—substitute phrases or words that clearly express your meaning.

In a work context, the better you know people who will read your writing, the better you can design your reports, memos, and e-mails. You can also ask people who know your readers to aid you in finding out preferences in organization, style, and length. When you begin a job assignment, ask your supervisor for his or her preferences in these three areas.

Note: Conciseness does not equal brevity. When you write concisely, you include all that you need to say without extra words and phrases that contribute little to the main idea. Brevity means that you aim only for economy, rather than completeness of thought.

Introduction

Importance of Brain Perfusion

Brain perfusion refers to the blood circulation around the brain while the circulatory system exchanges oxygen and nutrients between the blood and the brain tissue. Brain perfusion depends on "blood pressure, blood velocity [...], and diffusion (dispersal) rates of oxygen and nutrients" [1]. An MRI scanner can monitor the perfusion of the brain to determine if a neurological disease is present.

How an MRI Works

A magnetic resonance imaging (MRI) scan uses a magnetic field (an attractive force) to show enhanced images of certain parts of the body. A dynamic MRI scan displays a fuller and more detailed result, unlike a conventional MRI. The hydrogen atoms in the human body are very important in an MRI procedure. One hydrogen atom contains a single proton that behaves differently when the MRI emits a magnetic field around that area. The MRI scanner will detect the behavior of these hydrogen atoms to generate an enhanced image of that area.

In many MRI procedures, a contrast agent (a compound fluid) is used to further enhance the image of the body by increasing the brightness of the tissue being examined. The injection of contrast agents into the body will help the MRI scan retrieve information such as blood flow and other related physical characteristics [2].

Limits of the MRI

Unfortunately, contrast agents have limited functions when physicians attempt to study the human brain. The brain contains a "membrane structure" known as the blood brain barrier, which protects the brain from foreign chemicals in the blood, while still allowing essential metabolic function [3]. The blood brain barrier filters out any unwanted chemicals that may travel through the brain. Since the blood brain barrier is very effective in its function, the chemicals in the contrast agents will be filtered out by this *membrane structure*. If a neurological disease is present in the brain, it can weaken the blood brain barrier and allow these unwanted chemicals to pass through [3]. The contrast agent would be useful for studying the disease in this situation.

Value of My Method in Improving the MRI

Many methods have been created to penetrate the blood brain barrier. My proposed method will strengthen the interaction between hydrogen atoms with the magnetic field via electrical signals. During a dynamic MRI scan, an electrical signal will be emitted around the neck area. This signal will mark the hydrogen atoms that are in the vicinity of the emitted signal. Because no external chemicals are introduced, the blood brain barrier will not detect any foreign chemicals and will let the marked hydrogen atoms into the brain. The hydrogen atoms will travel through the bloodstream around the brain acting as beacons. They will then interact with the magnetic field of the MRI, allowing MRI to enhance the image of the brain, much like contrast agents [4].

Subject and Purpose

This research will focus on developing a new method of performing a dynamic MRI scan on the human brain. This new method involves emitting an electrical signal into the body to interact with the hydrogen atoms and performing a dynamic MRI scan. To determine the effectiveness of this new method, I will analyze the MRI scan to determine the rate of perfusion in the brain.

FIGURE 4-5 Revised Introduction to the Student Research Proposal

Determine whether a particular style will be expected. Use the company style sheet and templates. But remember that you still have to adapt what you say to your intended readers.

Adjust the style to the readers, the purpose, and the context. Most business and technical writing should strive for as much conciseness as possible because of the large quantity of information that most readers confront. E-mail messages should have concise paragraphs and concise sentences. Even in complex, highly technical reports, readers value conciseness: the longer the report, the less likely that anyone will read all of it.

Keys to Building Effective Sentences

English sentences work more effectively—they become easier to read, understand, and remember—if they follow basic rules of sentence structure.

Watch sentence length. Documents composed of consistently long sentences can become difficult to read. Sentence length should vary, but consider revising sentences over 15 to 20 words. Even legal documents can benefit from shorter sentences and have improved as a result of plain English laws that now govern insurance policies and many other legal documents in various states. Many government entities want their public documents written in concise, easily understood sentences:

Before:
This Appendix contains a brief discussion of certain economic and demographic characteristics of the Area in which the County is located and does not constitute a part of this Official Statement. Information in this Appendix has been obtained from the sources noted, which are believed to be reliable, although no investigation has been made to verify the accuracy of such information.

Characteristics of Bad and Good Writing

Bad Writing	Good Writing
few verbs/number of words per sentence	many verbs/number of words per sentence
excessive *is/are* verb forms	concrete verbs
abstract nouns	concrete nouns
many prepositional phrases	few prepositional phrases
few clauses	linked clauses
passive voice	active voice
separation of key words: subject-verb, actor-action	clear actor-action relationship
long, rambling sentences	specific, precise sentences
main idea of sentences is difficult to process	meaning of sentences is easy to find
sentences must be read several times	meaning is clear after one reading

After:
This Appendix contains a brief discussion of certain economic and demographic characteristics of the Area in which the County is located. The Appendix does not constitute part of this Official Statement. Information in the Appendix has been obtained from the sources noted. They are believed to be reliable. However, the accuracy of the information has not been verified.

Keep subjects and verbs close together. A recipe for sentence clarity: keep the subject of the sentence and the verb close together, and emphasize verbs. The more verbs in a sentence, the sharper and more direct the sentence. We call this characteristic verb/word ratio. For example,

     S   V   S   V

John <u>loves</u> Mary because she <u>inherited</u> money. (verb/word ratio = 2/7)

versus

                         S   V

Mary's inheritance of money <u>was</u> one of the reasons for John's interest in Mary.

(verb/word ratio = 1/12)

In this simple example, you can see the point: the more verbs, the sharper the sentence.

Let's take this method a step further: lengthy sentences become less distracting to the reader if the writer structures them to enhance clarity and readability. To achieve clarity, build sentences with clauses and as many verbs and verbals as possible. For example, the sentence,

When they plan investment portfolios, financial planners recommend a variety of investments because they resist rapid economic changes. (18 words)

develops about three clauses:

When they <u>plan</u> investment portfolios
financial planners <u>recommend</u> a variety of investments
because they <u>resist</u> economic change.

Note that the sentence follows the three guidelines:

Interlocking clauses (three in this sentence)
Specific action verbs: plan, recommend, and resist
Subject next to the verb in each clause

they plan
planners recommend
they resist

The sentence has a verb/word ratio of 3/17.

Assume that the writer did not follow the guidelines and avoided verbs:

> In plans for investment portfolios, a variety of investments is recommended by financial planners because of their resistance to economic changes.

The verb/word ratio is 1/21. The sentence lacks directness and conciseness. Compare the two versions. Can you see the difference? In English sentences, the more verbs and verbals a writer uses, the easier the sentence becomes to read and understand. In addition, when you have the actors as the subject, followed by a concrete verb—what the actor does—the sentence becomes direct and concise.

For most writing, use specific concrete subjects and verbs. Write to express, not to impress.

Instead of:
There is now no effective existing mechanism for introducing into the beginning initiation and development stages requirements on how to guide employees on how to minimize errors in product development efforts.

(verb/word ratio = 3/31; one "is" verb and two verbals)

Use:
The company has no way to guide employees on how to minimize product development errors during the early development stages.

(verb/word ratio = 3/20) Note that the sentence begins with the actor in the subject position and two verbals.

Note: When a sentence lacks a clear subject/agent doing the action (verb), writers can often drift into the phrases "there is, there are, there was, there were," which have no meaning and deter conciseness and directness.

Instead of:
Our lack of pertinent data prevented determination of committee action effectiveness in funding target areas that needed assistance the most.

(Note that the sentence incorporates two clauses and two verbs. Verb/word ratio = 2/21)

Or, even worse:

There was a lack of pertinent data determination of committee action effectiveness in funding target areas that needed assistance the most.

Use, assuming we know who did what action:
Because we lacked pertinent data, our committee could not determine whether we had targeted funds to areas that needed assistance the most.

(Note the revision of the sentence with four interlocking clauses and four verbs. Verb/word ratio = 4/22) In addition, clear subjects placed close to their verbs makes clear who does what action.

Or use:

We <u>didn't have</u> enough data: We <u>could not decide</u> if the committee <u>had sent</u> funds to areas that <u>needed</u> them most.

When we break the sentence into two sentences, we still have four verbs. In addition, the short sentence followed by the longer, explanatory sentence also clarifies the meaning.

Note that in this revision we place the actor as the subject of the sentence/clause and then follow the subject with the verb, a concrete, descriptive verb that explains what the actor/subject will do.

But always be aware of how direct/indirect words affect tone:

(A) We encourage you to anticipate the amount of correspondence you accumulate and suggest you endeavor to answer it promptly.

(B) Please expect large amounts of e-mail and try to answer it quickly.

Note that (B) is easier and quicker to read than (A). The tone of (A) sounds pompous.

Write squeaky-clean prose. The following excerpt from *DNA: The Secret of Life* addresses readers interested in science and possessing a basic understanding of genetics. Note the structure of each sentence, the use of topic sentences, and the development of each paragraph:

> The great size of DNA molecules posed a big problem in the early days of molecular biology. To come to grips with a particular gene—a particular stretch of DNA—we would have to devise some way of isolating it from all the rest of the DNA that sprawled around it in either direction. But it was not only a matter of isolating the gene; we also needed some way of "amplifying" it: obtaining a large enough sample of it to work with. In essence we needed a molecular editing system: a pair of molecular scissors that could cut the DNA text into manageable sections; a kind of molecular glue pot that would allow us to manipulate those pieces; and finally a molecular duplicating machine to amplify the pieces that we had cut out and isolated. We wanted to do the equivalent of what a word processor can now achieve: to cut, paste, and copy DNA.
>
> Developing the basic tools to perform these procedures seemed a tall order even after we cracked the genetic code. A number of discoveries made in the late sixties and early seventies, however, serendipitously came together in 1973 to give us so-called "recombinant DNA" technology—the capacity to edit DNA. This was no ordinary advance in lab techniques. Scientists were suddenly able to tailor DNA molecules, creating ones that had never before been seen in nature. We could "play God" with the molecular underpinning of all of life. This was an unsettling idea to many people. Jeremy Rifkin, an alarmist for whom every new genetic technology has about it the whiff of Dr. Frankenstein's monster, had it right when he remarked that recombinant DNA "rivaled the importance of the discovery of fire itself."

Source: Watson, James. *DNA: The Secret of Life*, pp. 87–88. Knopf, 2003. Used by permission.

This excerpt uses a variety of sentences of moderate length, close subject-verb patterns, familiar words, and a description of recombinant DNA in words easily understood by the nonscientific reader: the passage concisely and picturesquely expresses the meaning of recombinant DNA.

Avoid pompous language; write to express, not impress. The concept of simplicity relates to the concept of naturalness. Writers often believe they must sound learned, aloof, and sophisticated to impress readers. The idea that direct writing lacks sophistication frequently derives from writing done in secondary school. Teachers encourage high school students to expand their vocabularies. Academic writing in college reinforces the importance of using jargon-laden language to convince the professor that the student knows the subject and the nomenclature of the discipline. Instructors may reward students for writing ponderous verbiage in research papers. On the job, however, verbose writing may be ignored or misread by readers who are interested in gleaning information relevant to their job needs.

Remember that writing exists for human beings, and few of us enjoy writing that is harder to read than it needs to be. What constitutes "difficult" writing depends on the reader, the topic, and the purpose of the document. But direct, concise writing that uses a conversational style will usually be appreciated by your readers. Using shorter rather than longer sentences also helps readers follow your thoughts:

> Please give immediate attention to insure that the pages of all documents prepared for distribution are numbered sequentially and in a place of optimum visibility. This is needed to facilitate our ability to refer to items during meetings.

Versus

> Please correctly number the pages of all documents. Place numbers in the upper right-hand corner. Sequential numbering helps us locate material during meetings.

Or,

> Please number all pages sequentially.

Three additional examples:

> 1. It has recently been brought to my attention that only a small percentage of the employees in our division are contributors to the citizens' health research fund supported by this firm. This fund is a major source of money for the encouragement of significant discoveries and innovations made in behalf of research relevant to community health.

Versus

> I have discovered that only a small percentage of employees in our division contribute to the citizens' health research fund. Our firm supports this research because the products of this research improve community health.

> 2. As a result of their expertise, the consulting team is provided with the opportunity to make a reasonable determination of the appropriate direction to proceed regarding their selection of information systems.

Versus

> The consulting team has the expertise to select the best information systems.
>
> 3. It is our contention that the necessary modifications should be made to make the system operational because its complete replacement is economically prohibitive.

Versus

> We believe that the system should be modified to make it operational. Complete replacement costs too much.

Avoid excessive use of is/are verb forms. Choosing specific, concrete verbs for clarity means avoiding forms of the be verb, if possible. As the following sentences illustrate, excessive use of be verbs often obscures action verbs. Many times, a be verb is the best choice (as this sentence exemplifies). However, you can lessen the tendency to use be verbs by doing the following:

- Avoid beginning sentences with *there is* or *there are, there was* or *there were.*
- Avoid beginning sentences with phrases such as *it is clear that, it is evident that*, and *it should be noted that.*
- Choose a specific verb rather than *is, are, was*, and *were* verb forms.

Be verbs often create a longer, less direct sentence:

> Delegation <u>is</u> a means of lessening the manager's work load.

Versus

> Managers who delegate <u>reduce</u> their work load.
>
> Examine the following three examples:
>
> 1. Our appraisal system is broken: it is inefficient, it is unfair, and it is costly.

Versus

> Our appraisal system lacks efficiency, fairness, and cost.
>
> 2. My decision <u>is based on the assumption</u> that his statement <u>is erroneous</u>.

Versus

> My decision <u>assumed</u> that his statement <u>is erroneous</u>.
>
> 3. Our office <u>has been provided with the authority to make a determination about the selection</u> of a computing system.

Versus

> Our office was authorized to select a computing system.

As these examples, and the ones that follow, show, the clearest sentences focus on the agent and the action (the verb):

1. There are two systems presently available for testing job candidates.

Versus

Two available systems can test job candidates.

2. There are several national and global organizations dedicated to promoting environmental sustainability for health care facilities.

Versus

Several national and global organizations promote environmental sustainability for health care facilities.

Use active voice for clarity. The structure of a sentence—the arrangement of words—affects the clarity of the sentence. In active voice, the agent that does the action occurs next to the verb, the agent and the action both appear in the sentence, and the agent appears as the subject of the sentence.

> *agent   verb*
> The department teaches the course every spring term.

> *agent   verb*
> Our office submits all travel vouchers within 24 hours of their completion.

The result? Clear, concise, direct sentences.

> *Before:*
> (A) Attempts were made by the division staff to assess the project.

> *After:*
> > *agent   verb*
> (B) The division staff attempted to assess the project.

Sentence (A) uses passive voice. Sentence (B) uses active voice: the agent (staff) occurs as the subject and appears next to the verb (attempted).

Research to determine the most readable sentence structures indicates that active voice sentences may be more readable than passive sentences. Readers often need the agent (the actor) placed near the action (the verb) to determine the sentence meaning. The subject and verb contain the essence of the sentence. The following examples illustrate this concept.

The door is to be locked at 6:00 P.M.

This sentence, which does not specify the agent, could mean either of the following:

The guard (or some designated person) will lock the door at 6:00 P.M.

The last person leaving the building at 6:00 P.M. must lock the door.

As both revisions illustrate, to understand a sentence, readers must know the agent and the action carried out by the agent. When you write, be sure your sentences indicate who or what performs the action.

Passive voice sentences often intentionally do not include the actor or agent doing the action to hide responsibility. The result may produce a sentence more verbose and less accurate than an active voice version. Passive voice sentences often use "there is" and "there are" constructions. Even in engineering writing, such as articles for academic journals, many editors want active voice sentences because of the increased clarity of the sentences. As in the examples below, the use of active subjects will usually make an explanation easier to read and easier to understand:

Before:

With the growing request of high quality multimedia service, especially in portable systems, efficient algorithms for audio and/or video data processing have been developed. These algorithms have the characteristics of high complexity data-intensive computation. For these applications, there exist two extreme implementations. One is software implementation running on a general purpose processor and the other is hardware implementation in the form of application-specific integrated circuit (ASIC). In the first case, it is flexible enough to support various applications but may not yield sufficient performance to cope with the complexity of application. In the second case, optimization is better in respect of both power and performance but only for a specific application. A coarse-grained reconfigurable architecture fills the gap between the two approaches, providing higher performance than software implementation and wider applicability than hardware implementation.

After:

(Note: We separate sentences in the original passage here so that you can follow the changes in sentence structure.)

To respond to growing requests for high quality multimedia services, especially in portable systems, engineers have developed efficient algorithms for audio and/or video data processing.

These algorithms exemplify high complexity data-intensive computation.

In addition, these applications use two extreme implementations: (1) a *software implementation* running on a general purpose processor and (2) a *hardware implementation*, an application-specific integrated circuit (ASIC). The first has flexibility needed to support various applications, but it may not yield sufficient performance to cope with complex applications. In the second, we can optimize by power and performance but only for a specific application. A coarse-grained reconfigurable architecture fills the gap between the two approaches. This architecture provides higher performance than software implementation and wider applicability than hardware implementation.

Breaking long sentences into shorter ones and creating short paragraphs can also produce clarity:

Before:

To ensure dimensional quality of manufactured products, a crucial step is to take coordinate measurements of the geometric features to reconstruct product surface and then to check their compliance with tolerance specifications: my research develops a method to integrate the coordinate measurements from measuring devices of different resolutions for a better reconstruction of the product surface.

After:

To ensure dimensional quality of manufactured products, researchers must take coordinate[d] measurements of the geometric features. The goal: to reconstruct product surface and then check surface compliance with tolerance specifications.

My research develops a method to integrate the coordinate[d] measurements from measuring devices of different resolutions to better reconstruct the product surface.

WORD CHOICE

To write concise sentences, use clear, concise words and phrases. Avoid using longer words when shorter ones will do just as well. (Write to express, not to impress.)

instead of	write	instead of	write
accordingly	so	hence	so
accumulate	gather	implement	carry out
acquire	get	initiate	begin
acquaint	tell	maximum	most
activate	begin	modification	change
aggregate	total	nevertheless	but, however,
assist	help	objective	aim
communicate	write, talk, tell	optimum	best
compensation	pay	personnel	people, staff
consequently	so	procure	get
continue	keep up	purchase	buy
demonstrate	show	terminate	end
discontinue	stop	transmit	send
endeavor	try	utilize	use
facilitate	ease, simplify		

Eliminate dead phrases—words that add nothing to the meaning of the sentence.

to the extent that	in view of
with your permission	inasmuch as
hence	as a matter of fact
with reference to	for the purpose of
in connection with	in order
with respect to	
as already stated	

Avoid words that sound knowledgeable without being specific. Many are technical words that have been overused and poorly adapted to nontechnical situations.

parameters	warrants further investigation
logistical interface	broad-based
contact	dynamics
impact	infrastructure
input/output	longitudinal study
conceptualize	matrix
formalize	meaningful
multifaceted	monolithic
systematized	paradigm
prioritize	participatory involvement
time frame	resource utilization
hard date	viability
in-depth study	

Avoid redundant phrases.

absolutely complete	human volunteer
absolutely essential	insist and demand
agreeable and satisfactory	my personal opinion
anxious and eager	necessary essentially
basic fundamentals	past memories
complete absence	point in time
consensus of opinion	right and proper
each and every	sincere and earnest
exactly identical	small in size
example to illustrate	summarize briefly
few in number	thought and consideration

first and foremost   true facts
general consensus   very unique
green in color

Avoid business jargon

---

instead of	**write**
consideration was given	I considered
prior to the	before
at the present writing	now
effect an improvement	improve
in the neighborhood of	about
beg to advise	tell
cognizant of	know
thanking you in advance	I would appreciate
endeavor	try
viable alternative	possibility
in regard/reference to	about
send under separate cover	send separately
return same to the above	return to us
needless to say	[omit]
it goes without saying	[omit]
in the normal course of procedure	normally
in this day and age	today
in my opinion	I believe
it is our opinion	we think
on a daily basis	daily
on the grounds that	because
pursuant to our agreement	as we agreed
we are not in a position to	we cannot
without further delay	now
please be advised that	[omit]

STYLE CHECKLIST ✔

Planning

☐ How will you adjust your writing style to accommodate your readers' knowledge of the subject?

☐ How will you meet your readers' expectations about style for the specific kind of document you are writing?

☐ What is the appropriate reading level for the context in which the document will be read?

☐ How will you adjust your style so that it is appropriate for the professional relationship you have to your readers?

Revision

☐ Do paragraphs start with a topic sentence? Do the following sentences in the paragraph build on the idea in the topic sentence?

☐ Are most sentences 20 words or shorter? Could longer sentences be made shorter?

☐ Are subjects and verbs close together in your sentences?

☐ Have you used specific nouns and concrete verbs?

☐ Have you avoided ponderous and impersonal language?

☐ Have you avoided is/are verb forms whenever possible?

☐ Are most of your sentences written in active voice? Could any sentences with passive voice be changed to active voice?

☐ Have you defined everything that might require defining?

☐ Could any of your sentences be written with equal clarity but fewer words?

EXERCISES

1. Visit the website of two major employers in your field. What kinds of documents do you find at each site? Do the organizations have a style guide for their documents? From looking at a number of the documents at each site (e.g., letter from the president, mission statement, code of conduct), how would you characterize each organization's style? Which organization has the more readable style? How would you make each organization's style more readable?

2. Figure 4-6 is a memo composed by the manager of The Plaza, a relatively new apartment building in Lubbock, Texas. The manager would like to distribute the memo to all residents as soon as possible. As the regional manager of Rite Properties, which operates The Plaza, you must review the official communications

coming from managers to residents. What changes would you advise the manager to make to this memo?

3. Examine Figure 4-7. If you were the author of this document and were given 15 more minutes to make it more readable, what changes would you make?

4. Examine Figure 4-8. Note the number of stylistic weaknesses highlighted. Revise the report to remove these weaknesses and others you find.

Rite Properties

7001 South Loop 289
Lubbock, Texas 79425
806-555-1327
manager@theplaza.com

May 15, 2012

TO: ALL PLAZA RESIDENTS
FROM: The Management
SUBJECT: problems

Over recent weeks and months we have had an issue with dogs urinating and defecating in staircases, sidewalks, the courtyard, and in the parking lot. This has required daily cleaning of these areas and is consuming additional janitor hours, which costs money and could soon lead to rent increases. Please be respectful of the buildings and your neighbors and curb your dog from using these public areas as a rest-room. If your pet has an accident, it is your responsibility to clean up after it. Okay? If you ever witness this activity, please report it to Management. Monetary penalties will be imposed on the responsible party.

Also effective today, May 15, 2012, Bailey's will tow any Plaza resident vehicles or Plaza visitor vehicles that park in their parking lot. One visitor vehicle from Plaza was parked directly in front of their back door, blocking the way for a big delivery truck coming in this morning, consequently, no one may park over there any more. Residents, we have been over the parking situation over and over, if you or your guests get towed, don't call me. I've put out several newsletters or spoke with individuals about the parking. It is your responsibility to tell your guests where to park. We have had a good relationship with Bailey's for along time, but when we get in the way, everyone must pay the price. Stop and think where you park! Is it going to be in someone's way in the morning? The next time I am called to clear out the cars to avoid being towed because it is blocking a door or driveway at Bailey's, I promise, I will call the tow truck myself.

We have also been changing the filters and checking the smoke alarm batteries this week and there are those of you that are tampering with your smoke alarms! Repeatedly we have told you not to take the battery out of your smoke alarm. IT IS AGAINST THE LAW. Do you have enough insurance to cover all your home's contents in addition to all the contents of several other homes if a fire breaks out in your apartment and because you have no battery in your smoke alarm, no one was warned before it was too late. When your alarm beeps, it means you need a new battery. We have the batteries in the office, come and get a new battery. There is absolutely no excuse that can be justified for removing or tampering with any part of the smoke alarm that I will accept. If we didn't have an alarm in your apartment and you had a fire, you would immediately blame us, do we get to blame you when you have removed the battery or tampered with the alarm? Each of you that had removed your alarm battery will be fined $25.00 which is clearly stated in your lease and had been explained in several newsletters.

Again, it is your responsibility for telling your guests where to park. You know how it feels when there are no parking spaces because they are filled with guests. I constantly see the same guests parking on the lot, the lot is posted for resident parking with all others towed, I have threatened to tow in the past, but once again, it has gotten out of hand and we are almost full and it takes every space on the lot just so our residents are allowed to park on the lot. Effective today, all non stickered vehicles will be towed with no advance warning. When this happens, perhaps you will want to pay the towing charge to your guest since you did not tell them where to park. When your guests vehicles get towed, please do not contact me. There will be a sticker telling them exactly where to get in touch with the wrecker service to retrieve their vehicle.

continued

FIGURE 4-6 Document for Exercise 2

Once again there is trash being left outside apartments overnight and during the day. Please, we take prospective residents through the courtyard nearly every day and it is very embarrassing to have to pass other people's trash. If you can't carry it out to the dumpster, leave it in your house until you can. It will be greatly appreciated.

Finally, as the weather heats up and you open your windows to cool off, remember that this allows sound to travel. If your windows are open after 10 PM, keep the noise in your apartment down. No loud televisions, parties, or music, please. Your neighbors will thank you. Have a wonderful day!

FIGURE 4-6 *continued*

HEADS×UP
CONCUSSION IN HIGH SCHOOL SPORTS

A FACT SHEET FOR **PARENTS**

What is a concussion?
A concussion is a brain injury. Concussions are caused by a bump, blow, or jolt to the head or body. Even a "ding," "getting your bell rung," or what seems to be a mild bump or blow to the head can be serious.

What are the signs and symptoms?
You can't see a concussion. Signs and symptoms of concussion can show up right after the injury or may not appear or be noticed until days after the injury. If your teen reports **one or more** symptoms of concussion listed below, or if you notice the symptoms yourself, keep your teen out of play and seek medical attention right away.

Signs Observed by Parents or Guardians	Symptoms Reported by Athlete
• Appears dazed or stunned • Is confused about assignment or position • Forgets an instruction • Is unsure of game, score, or opponent • Moves clumsily • Answers questions slowly • Loses consciousness *(even briefly)* • Shows mood, behavior, or personality changes • Can't recall events *prior* to hit or fall • Can't recall events *after* hit or fall	• Headache or "pressure" in head • Nausea or vomiting • Balance problems or dizziness • Double or blurry vision • Sensitivity to light or noise • Feeling sluggish, hazy, foggy, or groggy • Concentration or memory problems • Confusion • Just not "feeling right" or is "feeling down"

How can you help your teen prevent a concussion?
Every sport is different, but there are steps your teens can take to protect themselves from concussion and other injuries.
• Make sure they wear the right protective equipment for their activity. It should fit properly, be well maintained, and be worn consistently and correctly.
• Ensure that they follow their coaches' rules for safety and the rules of the sport.
• Encourage them to practice good sportsmanship at all times.

What should you do if you think your teen has a concussion?

1. **Keep your teen out of play.** If your teen has a concussion, her/his brain needs time to heal. Don't let your teen return to play the day of the injury and until a health care professional, experienced in evaluating for concussion, says your teen is symptom-free and it's OK to return to play. A repeat concussion that occurs before the brain recovers from the first—usually within a short period of time (hours, days, or weeks)—can slow recovery or increase the likelihood of having long-term problems. In rare cases, repeat concussions can result in edema (brain swelling), permanent brain damage, and even death.

2. **Seek medical attention right away.** A health care professional experienced in evaluating for concussion will be able to decide how serious the concussion is and when it is safe for your teen to return to sports.

3. **Teach your teen that it's not smart to play with a concussion.** Rest is key after a concussion. Sometimes athletes wrongly believe that it shows strength and courage to play injured. Discourage others from pressuring injured athletes to play. Don't let your teen convince you that s/he's "just fine."

4. **Tell all of your teen's coaches and the student's school nurse about ANY concussion.** Coaches, school nurses, and other school staff should know if your teen has ever had a concussion. Your teen may need to limit activities while s/he is recovering from a concussion. Things such as studying, driving, working on a computer, playing video games, or exercising may cause concussion symptoms to reappear or get worse. Talk to your health care professional, as well as your teen's coaches, school nurse, and teachers. If needed, they can help adjust your teen's school activities during her/his recovery.

> **If you think your teen has a concussion:**
> Don't assess it yourself. Take him/her out of play.
> Seek the advice of a health care professional.

It's better to miss one game than the whole season.

For more information and to order additional materials *free-of-charge*, visit: **www.cdc.gov/Concussion**.

U.S. DEPARTMENT OF HEALTH AND HUMAN SERVICES
CENTERS FOR DISEASE CONTROL AND PREVENTION

June 2010

FIGURE 4-7 Document for Exercise 3

Memorandum

TO: Jerry Bradshaw   DATE: March 29, 2011
FROM: Bill Jones
SUBJECT: **The Best Approaches in Alternative Fuel Research**

Purpose

Alternative fuels are becoming an important area of research. There are two main reasons researchers are looking for a new and reliable fuel source. The first is to combat the reliance of the U.S on foreign oil. The second is to reduce the amount of harmful emissions into the atmosphere. The heavy reliance on gasoline is harmful to both our economy and the environment. In this report I will discuss the best approaches in alternative fuel research. The three main approaches that will be covered are ethanol, the hydrogen fuel cell, and biodiesel. For each approach I will explain the process of producing the fuel, the benefits, costs, and the negative aspects. The information provided will show what the best alternative fuel will be.

Research Methods

The data and information collected was obtained from several websites and online databases. I found which alternative fuels were currently in use from the U.S. Department of Energy website. It had useful information about new alternatives being researched and also information about fuels currently in use. After determining which three fuels had the most potential I went into more in depth research and looked for articles on the online databases.

Findings

Approach 1-Ethanol

Ethanol is an alcohol produced by the fermentation of the grains or seeds of a plant. The most common ingredient used in ethanol production is corn. The production process of ethanol begins with the harvesting of the corn. The kernels of corn are shipped to a plant where they are first ground and then cooked in a large cooker. After the ground corn is cooked, the fermentation process can begin. For fermentation to take place a single celled fungus called yeast is added to the processed corn. The yeast feeds on the starches in the grain and produces alcohol as a by-product. Ethanol is retrieved from the fermentation chamber by distilling the fluid inside the chamber. Then trucks are used to

FIGURE 4-8 Memo Report Needing Stylistic Conciseness

transport the ethanol to consumers. Pipes are not used because ethanol is corrosive and would damage the pipes after a certain amount of time.

The main benefit of producing ethanol is that it is renewable. However, most cars cannot use straight ethanol because it is more corrosive than gasoline. Many times ethanol is mixed with gasoline in different ratios so that regular cars are able to function properly without any corrosive damage. The ethanol/gasoline mixture still emits carbon dioxide, but it is cleaner burning than pure gasoline. Plants absorb carbon dioxide, so the carbon dioxide released by the ethanol is recycled by the plants that are used to produce the ethanol.

Some researchers argue that because of all the farm equipment used to produce the corn and the energy needed by the factory, we use more energy producing ethanol than we get out of it. Mass production of corn also takes a heavy toll on the environment. The fertilizers used on the corn release N2O, which is a very strong green house gas. Farming only corn also takes essential minerals from the soil and can cause erosion. There are efforts being made to negate these problems by finding new processes that will use the whole plant to produce cellulose ethanol instead of just the corn kernels. Using the whole plant would allow ethanol production to become more efficient. It would also allow us to use different grass species. The use of native grass species would require less fertilization and not damage the soil.

Approach 2-Hydrogen Fuel Cells

Fuel cells are able to convert chemical processes into electricity. The type of fuel cell that is best suited to power a vehicle is called a polymer exchange membrane fuel cell (PEMFC). The main reaction that these cells use is converting Hydrogen and Oxygen into water. There are four main components of the PEMFC and each component has a specific job. First is the anode. The anode captures the electrons that are freed during the reaction. These electrons are used in an external circuit that is able to produce work. It also disperses the Hydrogen evenly over the surface of the catalyst. The catalyst is what helps the reaction take place. For this process the catalyst is usually made of platinum nanoparticles that are thinly spread on a thin carbon sheet. The nanoparticles allow for the highest surface as possible, which increases the reaction rate. Third is the electrolyte or proton exchange membrane. This membrane only conducts positively charged ions, while blocking electrons. A downside is that the membrane must remain hydrated in order to function properly. Last is the cathode, it distributes the Oxygen across the catalyst and conducts the electrons from the outer circuit to complete the reaction of Oxygen and Hydrogen to make water. The overall process has four main steps. First the H2 splits when it contacts the catalyst and releases 2 electrons. These electrons travel to the anode and through the outer circuit to the cathode. Second the

FIGURE 4-8 *continued*

O2 also splits forming two highly negative ions. Third, the O- ions attract the H+ ions and draw them through the membrane. Last the Hydrogen and Oxygen pair up with the electrons from the circuit and form water.

This is complicated, but has some excellent benefits. First is the amount of pollution reduction. The only by-product is water. Second is that the process is said to be 64% efficient compared to 20% efficiency of gas combustion engines. However, since the process is complicated the components are expensive, especially the platinum catalysts. The membranes are also not very durable. They tend to degrade under the conditions of turning on and off your car. Very high or low temperatures are also a problem for the membranes. The membranes must stay hydrated to function and in high temperatures they dry out, while in cold temperatures there is the possibility of freezing. There is also a problem with the fuel. To be able to travel a considerable distance, a lot of hydrogen is needed, and we don't have the technology to compress the hydrogen into a small enough tank. We also have no infrastructure to distribute the hydrogen. Therefore this process may need to wait until we have better technology to utilize the fuel cell's capabilities.

Approach 3-Biodiesel

Biodiesel is a form of diesel that is produced from organic renewable oils like vegetable oils and animal fat. Production from these oils is a benefit because they are non-toxic, biodegradable, and renewable. The process of making biodiesel is a simple process. First the recycled oils or fats are filtered and preprocessed to remove any water or contaminants. The oils and fats are then mixed with an alcohol, usually methanol, and a catalyst like sodium hydroxide or potassium hydroxide. The oil molecules are broken apart and reformed into methyl esters and glycerin. Glycerin is a by-product that can be separated out and used in other industries. The methyl esters become the biodiesel.

Using biodiesel has many advantages. Unlike ethanol which is produced from corn, biodiesel can be created from non-food crops or recycled greases. Soybeans are of the major crops that are used in biodiesel production. The oils are extracted from the soybeans and used to make fuel while the rest of the soybean can still be used for livestock feed or other applications, so nothing is wasted. Algae are another source for biodiesel production. Oils can be extracted from the algae and processed. Algae allow for a renewable resource that grows rapidly and is easy to maintain, so it is an excellent option. Some researchers have found that the biodiesel produced contains 3.2 times the amount of energy it takes to produce. This shows that biodiesel production is an efficient process. Most diesel engines are already compatible with using biodiesel,

FIGURE 4-8 *continued*

so fewer changes need to be made. However, biodiesel still needs to be mixed with petrodiesel in order to get the right viscosity, so cars can't run entirely on biodiesel.

Conclusion

There are many reasons why we must take steps to reduce our dependence on fossil fuels. One of the main reasons is to regain energy independence. If we find an alternative fuel that is efficient and easy to produce, we will lessen our dependence on foreign oil and form a more stable economy and country. The three approaches that I researched are some of the best possibilities. Each one has their pros and cons. Although ethanol is renewable it relies too much on food crops and is not efficient enough yet. More research is needed to produce a more efficient procedure. Fuel cells are also a great idea that have no harmful emissions and are very efficient, but we still don't have the technology to make them practical yet. Therefore the most reliable fuel source is biodiesel. The production of biodiesel is simple and efficient. The renewable resources used are abundant, easy to obtain and aren't specifically food crops. Algae are an especially good resource. They would be cheap and easy to mass produce, yet they would provide enough oil for a processing plant. Biodiesel could have an impact on our fossil fuel consumption in the future.

Citations

Kelly, Tom. "Biodiesel Basics." *Beverage World* 129.10 (2010): S20-S21. Web. 29 Mar 2011.

Jozefowics, Chris. "Fuel for Thought." *Current Science* 92.11 (2007): P6-7. Web. 29 Mar 2011.

Lin, Lin. "Opportunities and Challenges for Biodiesel Fuel." *Applied Energy* 88.4 (2011): p1020-1031. Web. 29 Mar 2011.

Nice, Karim, and Jonathan Strickland. "How Fuel Cells Work." *How Stuff Works.* Discovery Company, n.d. Web. 29 Mar 2011. <http://auto.howstuffworks.com/fuel-efficiency/alternative-fuels/fuel-ce112.htm>.

"Alternative Fuels and Advanced Vehicles Data Center." *U.S Department of Energy.* N.p., n.d. Web. 29 Mar 2011. <http://www.afdc.energy.gov/afdc/fuels/biodiesel_production.html>.

FIGURE 4-8 *continued*

5

Designing Documents

Effective writing is more than just putting words on the page or computer screen. And it's more than correct sentences organized in logical paragraphs. To be effective, your document must also be visually intelligible.

You have many choices about how your document will appear to your readers. It is easy, for example, to integrate illustrations, to include audio and video, and to link to other documents. It is also easy to overwhelm and confuse your readers with these elements. This chapter will help you make the careful choices that allow for easy reading and navigation of your documents.

Quick Tips

On the job, you will probably write and receive more e-mail messages than any other kind of document. And more and more often you will be writing your messages and your readers will be receiving your messages on mobile devices. If you design your e-mail messages for quick and easy reading, your recipients will be able to decipher your intended meaning efficiently and respond readily and appropriately to your instructions, questions, and requests regardless of their location. Here are five simple guidelines to follow:

1. **Keep your messages brief.** E-mail is especially effective for brief messages that the recipient will read and reply to quickly. Long, scrolling messages with extensive detail are often better relegated to attachments that could be accessed and studied later.
2. **Use short paragraphs.** Short paragraphs separated by white space encourage quick reading and make it easy for your recipient to perceive and retrieve the chief points of your message.
3. **Use the subject line to specify your message.** A clear and specific subject line will preview your message for your recipients, making their reading easier and aiding their understanding. You will also be helping

recipients to sort and find your messages later, especially if you write a separate message for each topic you address.

4. **Use headings to identify the sections of your message.** Headings make it easier for your recipient to skim your message for its chief points and assist in later retrieval of specific information in your message.

5. **Ask simple yes/no questions.** Make it easy for your recipient to reply to your message with the briefest possible answer. For example, ask, "Should I . . . ?" instead of "How would you like me to handle this situation?" If a series of yes/no questions are necessary, number the questions.

UNDERSTANDING THE BASICS OF DOCUMENT DESIGN

Readers judge a document by how it looks as much as by what it contains. In fact, their earliest impression comes from the appearance of the document, not its content. A dense page of long paragraphs will often discourage or annoy readers even before they begin reading. A page designed to help readers locate important information, however, may add to the persuasiveness of your position or convince your readers to put a little more effort into finding what they need and understanding what they find.

These five principles will help you plan your document's visual design:

- Know what decisions are yours to make.
- Choose a design that fits your situation.
- Plan your design from the beginning.
- Reveal your design to your readers.
- Keep your design consistent.

Know what decisions are yours to make.   Many companies have a standard format or template for reports, letters, proposals, e-mail messages, and websites. Before you develop your document, determine the pertinent design requirements. Don't change the format arbitrarily just to be different. If you think the template you are supposed to use isn't appropriate for your audience and your message, find out who makes decisions on such design issues and make a case for the changes that you would like to see.

Keep in mind also that you don't have to use exotic or sophisticated software applications to apply basic principles of document design. The typical word processing program has all the functions you will likely need to create a visually effective document like the one shown in Figure 5-1.

Choose a design that fits your situation.   Don't make your document any more complex than the situation requires. You typically don't need a table of contents or a glossary for reports that are under five pages. Add appendix material only if it is necessary and will be useful for your readers.

Vacation Time Allowed Management Employees

The following schedule describes the new vacation schedule approved by the company. This schedule is effective immediately and will remain in effect until a further update is issued.

Vacation Eligibility
Vacation with pay shall be granted during the calendar year to each management employee who has completed 6 months of service since the date of employment. Employees who have been dismissed for misconduct will not receive vacation with pay.

Net Credited Service and Eligible Weeks
Net Credited Service is determined by the Employee Benefits Committee.

Net Credited Service	Eligible Weeks
▪ 6–12 months	1
▪ 12 months–7 years	2
▪ 7–15 years (or District level with 6 months service)	3
▪ 15–25 years (or Division level with 6 months service)	4
▪ 25+ years (or Department head or higher with 6 months service)	5

Guidelines
- If eligibility occurs on or after December 1, vacation may be taken in the next following year if it is taken before April 1.
- If an authorized holiday falls in a vacation week, an additional day of vacation may be taken before April 1 of the following year.

FIGURE 5-1 An Example of Effective Formatting

You'll impress readers most by providing just the information they need in a way that makes it easy for them to find it and understand it. Most people read technical and business documents selectively. They scan the document, looking for sections that are relevant to their needs. They try to grasp the main points quickly because they are busy and have far too much to read. Remember that your readers don't get paid to read documents: they get paid to make decisions and take actions. The more time needed to read your document, the less productive is their paid time on the job. And always keep in mind that they could be reading your document on their phones, tablets, or laptops while traveling to and from the job site, while sitting in meetings, and while multitasking in their offices.

For example, users working with a software application are unlikely to read the entire user's manual. They resort to the manual or to online help when they have a specific problem or need instructions for a specific task and can't figure it out by trial and error. They want to get to the right page or screen immediately. They want the instructions to stand out on the page or screen. Look at Figures 5-2 and 5-3. Notice how the numbered steps make for quick reading and easy understanding relative to the long and confusing paragraph of instructions.

Plan your design from the beginning. Before you start writing, carefully consider how you will organize and display your information. Ask questions like the following:

- How will your readers use the document? Will most people read it from beginning to end? Will they want to skim it and grab the main points without reading more? Will they want to jump to a specific topic? Even if they read the

All managers must report on the achievement of sales targets by their full-time and part-time salespeople, specifically the number of salespeople meeting weekly, monthly, and quarterly sales targets. These figures are based on the official sales targets issued by the Vice President of Merchandising and the number of full-time and part-time salespeople identified by Human Resources as assigned to each department at the beginning of the reporting period. To submit reports, start by logging in to your digital profile in Corporate Measures (http://www.corporatesmeasures .com/login/managers). Then, in the Manager section, select Weekly, Monthly, or Quarterly Sales Report, as appropriate. Next, in the Department section, locate each department managed during the reporting period and choose the pencil icon to edit the information for that department. Then, in the list of information for each department, scroll to Sales Targets. Then enter the appropriate figures for both full-time and part-time salespeople. Finally, in the adjacent text box, explain anything new or different during this reporting period that might be related to the achievement of sales targets (e.g., special promotions, changes in aisle displays, suggestive selling techniques).

FIGURE 5-2 Instructions in Paragraph Style
This format is difficult to follow, both on screen and on paper.

document through once, will they want to come back later and find a specific point quickly?
- How familiar are your readers with the subject of the document? How much support will they need in understanding and navigating the information you offer?
- How familiar are your readers with the kind of document you are writing? Do they come to the document with certain expectations about how the information will be organized and exhibited?
- Will most of your readers see this document on paper or on a screen?
- Will most of your readers be stationary or mobile? Will their attention to your document be focused or distracted?

If people will skim a document, for example, a table of contents and headings on every page will help them find information quickly. (The rest of this chapter includes techniques for developing effective designs to help people find what they need.)

If readers don't know much about the subject of the document, a glossary of keywords and abbreviations might be necessary. Illustrations might also be important because such readers won't have a store of pictures in their minds on which to call for support.

If readers are unfamiliar with the kind of document, they might benefit from a simple and explicit design that avoids potentially confusing variations. Experienced readers, however, might have rigid design expectations: website users, for example, ordinarily assume that underlined words and phrases are active links and will be annoyed if that isn't the case.

All managers must report on the achievement of sales targets by their full-time and part-time salespeople, specifically the number of salespeople meeting weekly, monthly, and quarterly sales targets.

These figures are based on

 a) official sales targets issued by the Vice President of Merchandising.
 b) the number of full-time and part-time salespeople identified by Human Resources as assigned to each department at the beginning of the reporting period.

To submit reports,

 1. Log in to your digital profile in CorporateMeasures (http://www.corporatemeasures.com/login/managers).

 2. In the Manager section, select Weekly, Monthly, or Quarterly Sales Report as appropriate.

 3. In the Department section, locate each department you managed during the reporting period and choose the pencil icon to edit the information for that department.

 4. In the list of information for each department, scroll to Sales Targets.

 5. Enter the appropriate figures for both full-time and part-time salespeople.

 6. In the adjacent text box, explain anything new or different during this reporting period that might be related to the achievement of sales targets (e.g., special promotions, changes in aisle displays, suggestive selling techniques).

FIGURE 5-3 Instructions in List Form

If the document is going to be read on a screen, you may have both more constraints and more choices than if the document were printed on paper. Limiting the amount of information and leaving blank space between paragraphs or list items is crucial in an online document. Illustrations and color will also be easier and less expensive to include in an online document than in a paper document.

If readers are mobile, your document could be competing for their attention with all the distractions in their changing environment. In this case, headings, lists, illustrations, and white space will be important focal points in helping readers to keep track of their location in your document and to recognize key items of information.

Reveal your design to your readers. Research on how people read and process information shows that readers must see how information is organized in order to make sense of it. That is, as you read, you try to do things at the same time: you try to make sense of the passage you're reading and you try to make sense of how this passage fits with previous passages and what it contributes to the entire document. The more difficult it is to do one or the other, the more difficult the document is to read.

Tables of contents and headings reveal the organization, scope, and direction of your document and give readers a clear overview or map with which to proceed. Using headings (at least one on every page or screen) in a memo will show the structure and logic of the discussion and help readers recognize, remember, and retrieve your major points. Longer reports definitely need headings and a table of contents that lists the headings. In online documents, a table of contents typically links to the pages listed.

Keep your design consistent. Consistency in design is essential to easy reading. When you have considered your audiences, the content you have to deliver, and the ways that people will read and use your document, you can develop a page or screen design that will work well for your situation. Once you have decided on the appropriate design, don't change it for arbitrary reasons. You want your readers to know immediately when they are beginning a new section, and when they are in another part of the same section, because they recognize the differences in the design of the headings at each level.

A good way to achieve this consistency is by identifying the different types of information in your document and using the styles function of your word processing program to duplicate the design.

First, think about all the types of information you will need to display, such as paragraphs, quotations, lists, examples, equations, formulas, and various levels of headings. Second, plan a design that always shows the same type of information in the same way throughout your document. The design could include the type size; the typeface, or font; placement of an element on the page or screen; whether the text has a border (also called a line or a rule) over or under it; whether the text or headings are bold or italic; the amount of space that comes before and after a heading; the style of the text that follows each kind of heading; and so forth. Third, use the style function of your word processing program to label and fix the design of each type of information.

Figure 5-4 shows a letter using document design to reveal the content and the relationships among the sections. This example shows how any document, including routine letters and memos, will benefit from the use of a consistent design.

DESIGNING EFFECTIVE PAGES AND SCREENS

Visually effective pages and screens are designed on a grid, so readers know where to look for information. They have space inside the text, around the graphics, and in the margins, so they look uncluttered and information is easy to locate. The line

DEPARTMENT OF HEALTH & HUMAN SERVICES   Public Health Service

_____

                                                              Centers for Disease Control
                                                              and Prevention

                                                              March 18, 2011

Dear Colleague,

April is STD Awareness Month, an annual observance to raise public awareness about
the impact of sexually transmitted diseases (STDs) on the lives of Americans and the
importance of discussing sexual health with healthcare providers and sex partners. This
letter summarizes CDC activities and resources that we hope will complement and
support your local activities.

CDC's Public Health Grand Rounds on Chlamydia
The Division of STD Prevention (DSTDP) participated in a series of presentations for the
CDC Public Health Grand Rounds on Chlamydia last May. A forthcoming article in the
Morbidity and Mortality Weekly Report (MMWR) will reprise these presentations.

The *GYT: Get Yourself Tested* Campaign
CDC is again partnering with MTV, the Kaiser Family Foundation, Planned Parenthood
Federation of America, and others to bring attention to the epidemic of STDs in the
United States. This year the GYT website is offering resources for providers to help them
better serve teen and young adult patients. The GYT provider site addresses young
people's common STD-related misconceptions and offers simple answers to patients'
questions. The website features CDC's 2010 STD Treatment Guidelines, reference guides
and charts (e.g. STD basics, who should be tested for what, where, and when); resources
for talking to patients about sexual history and STD testing; training resources; and GYT
materials for your office or clinic. You are invited to a March 24th webinar to learn about
this year's updates to the GYT campaign (prior registration is required).

National HIV and STD Testing Resources
CDC continues to update its interactive STD and HIV testing locator on the National HIV
and STD Testing Resource website www.findSTDtest.org. If you have not already done
so, please check to be sure your clinic(s) are included in the database and that the
information about them is current. Since the findSTDtest.org website will be promoted
throughout April as a source for STD testing locations, we want to ensure that the
information is accurate. Please contact Rachel Kachur (rlk4@cdc.gov) if you need
assistance updating your information.

STD Awareness Resource Site
CDC's STD Awareness Resource Site (formerly the STD Awareness Month website) has
been updated for 2011 and provides our STD prevention partners with information and
tools to support your local STD Awareness Month activities all year round. Included on
this site are resources for developing STD-related heath communication and social
marketing campaigns. Additionally, there is a media kit that includes sample press
releases, public service announcement scripts, and tips for media outreach. Widgets to

FIGURE 5-4 Letter That Uses Document Design Principles

length and margins help people read easily. The following suggestions will help
you develop visually effective pages and screens:

- Use blank space to frame and group information.
- Set the spacing for easy reading.
- Use a medium line length.
- Use a ragged right margin.

provide zip-code-based locator information for STD testing sites are available for download.

STD Prevention Materials
CDC is providing approximately 5,000 GYT clinic kits to state and local health departments. These kits will arrive by the end of March to the addresses provided by those who ordered them. If you have not ordered kits or need additional kits, you can download the kit materials and additional electronic resources now at the GYT Toolkit tab on the GYT website.

CDC STD Fact Sheets are available for download and local printing and are designed to print in either black and white or in color.

The following printed materials are available for shipment to you without charge through our online ordering page:

- STD "The Facts" brochure series. This award-winning series of brochures is available in English or Spanish, and is written in plain language. The brochures are available to health departments and other partners and may be ordered in quantities up to 500 per brochure. Electronic copies in PDF format can also be found on the STD Awareness Resource Site.
- *A Guide To Taking A Sexual Health History*. This practical guide is a good resource to share with healthcare providers in your community, especially if you are making them aware of STD Awareness Month activities. Five copies of this guide are included in each GYT clinic kit.
- The *2010 STD Treatment Guidelines* will be available soon for ordering in hard copy, wall chart, and pocket guide formats.

The Division of STD Prevention's Twitter account
The Twitter account @CDCSTD now has over 2,700 followers, is following more than 200 individuals and organizations, and is included in nearly 200 lists. It is now verified and listed as an official HHS Twitter account.

I look forward to hearing from you about your successes with your STD Awareness activities, not only in April, but throughout the year. Many thanks for your hard work and persistent efforts toward reducing the burden of sexually transmitted diseases on the American people.

Sincerely,

/Gail Bolan/

Gail Bolan, MD
Director, Division of STD Prevention
National Center for HIV/AIDS, Viral Hepatitis, STD and TB Prevention

FIGURE 5-4 *continued*

TO: All Department Heads

SUBJECT: New Media Request Procedures

A recent study of our media center request procedures indicates that we are not fulfilling media requests as efficiently as possible. A number of problems surfaced in the study. First, many requests, and particularly special requests (e.g., poster printing, laminating, close captioning of audio/videocasts, audio/video editing) are submitted in the evening after the media center has closed for the day or in the early morning before it has opened. As a result, the media center has an enormous backlog of orders to fill before it can begin servicing the orders submitted after 8:30 A.M., when it officially opens. This backlog may throw the center two or three hours behind schedule. Media requests submitted throughout the day cannot be completed promptly. By 2:00 P.M., requests submitted may not be filled that same day. If special orders arrive unexpectedly, even a routine copy request may take two business days to complete.

To remedy the situation, we will change to the following media request procedure beginning Monday, February 6. The media center will close at 3:00 every afternoon. Two employees will work at the center from 3:00 until 5:00 to complete all routine orders by 5:00. If you submit requests by 3:00, the center will have them ready by 5:00. In short, all requests will be filled the day they are submitted. However, do not leave requests after 3:00, as these will not be processed until the following day. However, we guarantee that if you submit your request between 8:00 and 3:00, you will have it fulfilled that day.

Special requests—including over 100 copies of one item, single/multiple copies of any document over 50 pages, front/back copying of one item up to 50 copies, poster (large-scale) printing, laminating, jobs involving trimming or folding, close captioning of audio/videocasts, and audio/video editing—will require that notice be given to the media center at least one day in advance (more time for unusual projects such as audio/videocasts in excess of five minutes or close captioning in multiple languages). That way, the center can prepare for your request and be sure to have it ready for you.

A copy of the special request form is attached to this message. Please complete this form and e-mail it to Lydia Rodriguez at the media center (at mediarequest@crsu.edu) so that she can schedule all special jobs. If you submit a special request without having completed the form, your project will be completed after all other special requests are completed.

Allow plenty of time for routine jobs—at least two hours, and three if possible. Beginning February 6, give all media requests to the receptionist in the media center. Be sure you attach complete instructions. Give your name, employee number, e-mail address, and department. Describe the project in detail, such as the number of copies required, paper color, collating and binding for multipage copies, color or black and white printing.

Pick-up procedures also change February 6. All jobs, after they are complete, will be placed in each department's mail box. No jobs will be left outside the media center after closing time. No jobs will be left with the receptionist. Large orders that will not fit mail boxes will be delivered to your office. Electronic projects will be delivered to the e-mail address listed on the request form.

If you have questions about this new procedure, please contact Lydia Rodriguez (by voice or text) at 742-2857.

FIGURE 5-5 Memo That Violates Format Guidelines

TO: All Department Heads
DATE: January 23, 2012
FROM: Lydia Rodriguez
SUBJECT: New Procedures for Ordering Jobs from the Media Center

EFFECTIVE DATE: MONDAY, FEBRUARY 6, 2012

To handle orders more quickly and efficiently, the Media Center is changing its procedures. Please inform everyone in your department and ask them to follow these new procedures.

Special Orders versus Routine Requests

Decide if you have a special order or a routine request. A special order is
- over 100 copies of one item
- single/multiple copies of any document over 50 pages
- front/back copying of one item up to 50 copies
- poster (large-scale) printing
- laminating
- jobs involving trimming or folding
- close captioning of audio/videocasts
- audio/video editing

Procedure for a Routine Request

1. Attach complete instructions to your request. Include
   - your name, employee number, e-mail address, and department
   - project details such as number of copies
   - special instructions such as collating and binding for multipage copies

2. Give all routine requests to the receptionist in the Media Center.

3. Allow two hours for your order to be filled.

NOTE: Routine requests submitted between 8:00 A.M. and 3:00 P.M. will be processed by 5:00 P.M. on the same day.

Procedure for a Special Order

1. Fill out the attached Special Order form.
2. E-mail the completed form to mediarequest@crsu.edu at least one day in advance of the day you need the job completed (two days in advance for unusual projects such as audio/videocasts in excess of five minutes or close captioning in multiple languages).

NOTE: This will allow us to schedule your job with the appropriate staff and equipment and complete your job promptly.

The Copy Center will close at 3:00 P.M. Orders submitted after that time will be processed the next business day.

Copy Pick-Up Procedures

Jobs will be delivered to your department's mailbox. If the order is too large for the mailbox, it will be delivered to your office. Electronic jobs will be delivered to your e-mail address.

If you have questions, text or call Lydia Rodriguez at 742-2857.

FIGURE 5-6 A Revision of Figure 5-5

Use blank space to frame and group information. Don't think of blank space as wasted or empty space. Space is a critical element in design for both paper and screens because it makes information easier to find and read. Look at Figures 5-5 and 5-6. Which do you think is easier to read?

You can incorporate blank space into documents in several ways. A critical location for blank space is at the margins. Here, blank space serves to enclose and contain the information and keep the page or screen from looking crowded and chaotic. Clear and generous margins make your information look organized and coherent.

If your document will be read on paper, also think about how it will be bound. If you are putting your work in a binder, be sure to leave room for the binding so that holes don't punch through the text. Similarly, think about whether a reader will want to punch holes in a copy later or put the work in a binder. These guidelines appear proportionately for margins on a standard 8½-by-11-inch page:

top margin	1 inch
bottom margin	1 inch
left margin	1 inch, if material is not being bound
	1½ inches, if material is being bound
right margin	1 inch

If you are going to photocopy on both the front and back of the page, leave space for the binding in the left margin of odd-numbered pages and in the right margin of even-numbered pages. Word processing programs allow you to choose mirror margins so that they alternate for right-hand (odd-numbered) pages and left-hand (even-numbered) pages. If you cannot set alternating margins, set both the right and the left margin at about 1½ inches to allow for binding two-sided copies.

The space in the margins is important, but it's not enough. Graphic designers call margins *passive space* because margins only define the block of the page or screen that readers should look at. Graphic designers know that *active space*—the space inside the text—makes the real difference in designing effective pages or screens. Blank space helps users to find information quickly, keep track of the location of information, process the information in identifiable chunks, and retrieve the information later.

Here are three techniques to bring active space to your pages and screens:

- Use headings frequently (and at least once per page or screen). Put them above the text or to the left of the text and put space before them.
- Use bulleted lists for three or more parallel points. Use numbered lists for steps in instructions. Lists are often indented inside the text, and each item may be separated from the others by a blank space.
- Separate paragraphs with an extra blank line, or indent the first line of each paragraph. In online documents, make your paragraphs even shorter than you would in paper documents so that there is notable space even on the small screens of mobile phones. Online, one instruction or one short sentence may make an appropriate paragraph.

Space the lines of text for easy reading. It's customary in paper documents to use single spacing. (For a brief letter or memo of a single paragraph, double spacing is appropriate.) When you use single spacing, insert an extra line between paragraphs.

Drafts of documents submitted for review and editing are often double-spaced to give writers and editors more room in which to write corrections and notes. When you use double spacing in drafts, you need to have some way to show where new paragraphs begin. Either indent the first line of each paragraph or add an extra line between paragraphs.

For documents that will be read on screens, use single spacing, with an extra line inserted between paragraphs. Double spacing is rarely used for continuous text on the screen because it increases the need for scrolling through the document: a typical screen displays only a portion of what a paper page does, especially the screens on mobile devices.

Adjust the line length to the size of the page or screen. The number of words that fit on a line depends in part on the size and style of type that you are using. Long lines of text fatigue readers and make them lose their place in moving from the right margin back to the left margin of the next line. Short lines are also difficult to read because readers are almost continuously shifting their eyes from the right margin to the left margin of the next line with little time for moving across each line. Figure 5-7 illustrates the problems with both long and short lines of text.

Use a ragged right margin. Although text is almost always lined up on the left margin, it is sometimes also aligned on the right margin, creating a tidy rectangle of text. The text of this book, for example, is aligned on both the left and the right margins. Most of the examples in the figures in this chapter, however, are aligned on the left but not on the right. The technique of making all the text align

---

Long lines of type are difficult for many people to read. Readers may find it difficult to get back to the correct place at the left margin. This difficulty is increased if the text is justified. The smaller the type, the harder it is for most people to read long lines of type.

Very short lines
look choppy
on a page
and make
comprehension
difficult

FIGURE 5-7 Line Length
Very long lines and very short lines are hard to read.

exactly on both the left and the right margin is called *justifying the text*. If the text is aligned on the left but not on the right, it has a *ragged right margin*.

Justified type gives a document a formal tone. Unjustified (ragged right) type gives a document a more friendly, informal feeling. Justified text is often more difficult for readers because every line is the same length, thus eliminating a visual signal that helps readers both to keep track of each line and to locate the next line of text. Online documents ordinarily have ragged right margins in order to make reading on screens of various sizes as easy as possible.

HELPING READERS LOCATE INFORMATION

To help your readers find what they need and make sense of what they find, you have to plan a useful structure for your document, and you have to make that structure evident to your readers. In the previous sections of this chapter, we showed you how to use page layout and fonts to make your document clear and easy to use. In this section, we explain how to give your readers signs of your document's overall structure.

On the job, people usually read technical and business documents selectively. Readers may glance over the table of contents to see what the document is about and then pick and choose the sections to read by looking for headings that match their needs and interests. They may go straight to the index of paper documents (or the search function for online documents) to find the location of a specific topic. They may skim through the pages, stopping when a heading or example or illustration strikes them as important. They may go back to the document later to retrieve or verify specific facts.

Following are four ways to help your readers find information easily:

- Use frequent headings.
- Write descriptive headings.
- Design distinctive headings.
- Use page numbers and headers or footers.

Use frequent headings. Frequent headings help readers know where they are in a document at all times. In a report, you probably want a heading for every subsection, which might cover two or three paragraphs. In general, in print you want to have clues to the text's arrangement on every page; online you should have a heading on every screen. On a website page you want to keep each topic short and give each topic a heading.

Write descriptive headings. Headings are the short titles that you use to label each section and subsection of your document. Even brief documents, such as letters and e-mail messages, can benefit from headings. Compare Figures 5-8 and 5-9 to see how useful headings are in a brief message.

Headings are the roadmap to your document, identifying the key topics and revealing the direction of thought.

UNITED STATES OF AMERICA
FEDERAL TRADE COMMISSION
WASHINGTON, D.C. 20580

Division of Advertising Practices

April 21, 2011

Nancy L. Stagg
Fish & Richardson P.C.
12390 El Camino Real
San Diego, CA 92130

     Re: Provide Commerce, Inc., FTC File No. 112-3111

Dear Ms. Stagg:

     As you know, the staff of the Federal Trade Commission's Division of Advertising Practices has conducted an investigation into advertising by your client, Provide Commerce, Inc., for possible violations of Section 5 of the Federal Trade Commission Act, 15 U.S.C. § 45. The staff's investigation followed a referral from the National Advertising Division of the Council of Better Business Bureaus ("NAD") regarding Provide Commerce's failure to comply with the NAD's decision regarding the use of a bar graph in making certain advertising claims for its ProFlowers brand of online flowers. For the reasons stated below, the staff has decided to close the investigation.

     The staff's investigation focused on whether certain ProFlowers advertising, which used a bar graph to depict the results of a consumer survey of three competing brand of online flowers, was misleading. FTC staff was concerned that the company's data, including the results of the consumer survey, did not support the bar graph depiction. In a recent letter, you stated that Provide Commerce had agreed to discontinue use of the bar graph to depict the claims at issue in the FTC's investigation.

     Upon review of this matter, including non-public information submitted to the staff, the staff has decided not to recommend enforcement action at this time. Among the factors considered is the company's decision to discontinue use of the bar graph in its advertising. This action is not to be construed as a determination that a violation may not have occurred, just as the pendency of an investigation should not be construed as a determination that a violation has occurred. The Commission reserves the right to take such further action as the public interest may require.

     Very truly yours,

     Mary K. Engle
     Associate Director

cc: Andrea Levine, NAD

FIGURE 5-8 Letter That Lacks Headings

These five suggestions will help you write useful headings:

- Use concrete language.
- Use questions, verb phrases, and sentences instead of nouns alone.
- Use standard keywords if readers expect them.
- Make the headings at a given level parallel.
- Make sure the headings match any list or table of contents in the document.

April 21, 2011

Re: Provide Commerce, Inc., FTC File No. 112-3111, Closing of Investigation

Dear Ms. Stagg:

As you know, the staff of the Federal Trade Commission's Division of Advertising Practices has conducted an investigation into advertising by your client, Provide Commerce, Inc., for possible violations of Section 5 of the Federal Trade Commission Act, 15 U.S.C. § 45. The staff's investigation followed a referral from the National Advertising Division of the Council of Better Business Bureaus ("NAD") regarding Provide Commerce's failure to comply with the NAD's decision regarding the use of a bar graph in making certain advertising claims for its ProFlowers brand of online flowers. For the reasons stated below, the staff has decided to close the investigation.

Provide Commerce will discontinue use of disputed bar graph
The staff's investigation focused on whether certain ProFlowers advertising, which used a bar graph to depict the results of a consumer survey of three competing brand of online flowers, was misleading. FTC staff was concerned that the company's data, including the results of the consumer survey, did not support the bar graph depiction. In a recent letter, you stated that Provide Commerce had agreed to discontinue use of the bar graph to depict the claims at issue in the FTC's investigation.

FTC will take no action now
Upon review of this matter, including non-public information submitted to the staff, the staff has decided not to recommend enforcement action at this time. Among the factors considered is the company's decision to discontinue use of the bar graph in its advertising.

FTC could take action later
This action is not to be construed as a determination that a violation may not have occurred, just as the pendency of an investigation should not be construed as a determination that a violation has occurred. The Commission reserves the right to take such further action as the public interest may require.

Very Truly yours,

Mary K. Engle
Associate Director

cc: Andrea Levine, NAD

FIGURE 5-9 Revision of Figure 5-8

Use concrete language. Generic headings such as *Introduction* or *Conclusion* give no indication of the topic you are discussing. Make your headings specific to your document. Make your headings reveal the subject and claims of your document. Readers should be able to read only your headings, without any of the accompanying text, to get a clear sense of your overall message.

Use questions, verb phrases, and sentences instead of nouns alone. The best way to write headings is to put yourself in your readers' place. Will readers come to your document with questions? Then questions will make good headings. Will they come wanting instructions for doing tasks? Then verb phrases that match the actions they need to take will make good headings. Will they come seeking knowledge about a situation? Then statements of fact about that situation will make good headings.

In addition, avoid headings that are individual nouns or strings of nouns: such headings are often perceived as ambiguous. For example, a heading such as "Evaluation Questionnaire Completion" makes it impossible to predict the kind of information that this section will offer. Much clearer would be a heading such as "How Do I Complete the Evaluation Questionnaire?" or "What Is the Deadline for Completing the Evaluation Questionnaires?" or "Who Must Complete the Evaluation Questionnaire?" Figure 5-10 shows how effective it can be to use questions, verb phrases, and statements as headings.

Use standard keywords if readers expect them. You may be working on a document for which readers expect to see a certain set of headings in a certain order, as in a standard proposal format. In that case, organize your material in the order and with the headings that your readers expect. Figure 5-11 shows the headings you might use in a standard proposal format.

Questions are useful as headings in a brochure.
What does the gypsy moth look like?
How can we protect trees from gypsy moths?
How often should we spray?

Verb phrases are useful in instruction manuals.
Verb phrases can be gerunds, like these:
- Adding a graphic
  Selecting the data
  Choosing type of graph to use
  Adding a title
Verb phrases can be imperatives, like these:
Make your attendance policy clear.
Explain your grading policy.
Announce your office hours.
Supply names of texts to be purchased.
Go over assignments and their due dates.

Short sentences are useful in memos and reports.
Our workload has doubled in the past year.
We are also being asked to do new tasks.
We have logged 560 hours of overtime this year.
We need three more staff positions.

FIGURE 5-10 Different Structures You Can Use for Effective Headings

Project Summary	Facilities and Equipment
Project Description	Personnel
Rationale and Significance	Budget
Plan of Work	

FIGURE 5-11 Keywords as Headings in a Proposal

Make the headings at a given level parallel. Like the items in a list, headings at any given level in a document should be parallel. Parallelism is a very powerful tool in writing because it helps readers to recognize the similarity among the listed items. See for yourself the difference parallelism makes by comparing the two sets of headings in Figure 5-12.

Make sure the headings match any list or table of contents in the document. To check how well your headings tell your story and to check how well you've maintained parallel structure in headings, use your word processing program to create an outline view or a table of contents for your draft document. Both in print and online, the headings will compose the table of contents. In a print document, readers can use the table of contents to locate a particular section. They know they're in the right place if the heading for that section matches the wording in the table of contents. The same is important online, where readers almost always navigate the document by jumping directly from a heading in the contents to a screen of information. If the heading on the screen they come to doesn't match the heading that they clicked on in the table of contents, they may be unsure of their location. Their confusion will quickly lead to annoyance.

Design distinctive headings. Headings do more than outline your document. They also help readers find specific parts quickly, and they show the relationship among the parts. To help readers, headings have to be easily distinguished from the text and each level of heading has to be easily distinguished from all the other levels. Figure 5-13 is a good example of a print document with four levels of headings. You can see how the writer uses boldface to distinguish all headings from the

Nonparallel Headings	**Parallel Headings**
Graph Modifications	Modifying a graph
Data selection updating	Changing the data
To add or delete columns	Adding or deleting columns
How to change color or patterns	Changing the color or patterns
Titles and legends can be included	Adding titles and legends

FIGURE 5-12 Nonparallel and Parallel Headings
Headings that use the same sentence structure—parallel headings—are easier for users to follow.

text and then uses type size, capitalization, and position on the page to distinguish each level of heading from the other levels.

These seven suggestions will help you design distinctive headings:

- Limit the number of heading levels.
- Create a pattern for the headings and stick to it.
- Match size to importance.
- Put more space before a heading than after it.
- Keep each heading with the section it covers.
- Use headings frequently.
- Consider using numbers with your headings.

Limit the number of heading levels. Don't make the hierarchy of levels more complicated than it needs to be. Headings are supposed to be an aid to reading, not an obstacle. The more levels of headings you use, the more that readers must do to keep the hierarchy straight in their minds. Paper documents don't need more than four levels of headings. If you have more than four levels, consider dividing the material into two major sections or two separate documents. Online documents don't need more than two levels of headings: readers scrolling through documents displayed on various sizes of screens will easily lose track of different levels of headings.

Create a pattern for the headings and stick to it. Although your choices depend in part on the technology you are using, you almost certainly have several options for showing levels of headings. Figure 5-13 demonstrates a variety of ways to show different levels of headings. You can combine these to create the pattern for your headings. For example, you can change size, position, and capitalization to show the different levels of headings.

Match size to importance. Changing the type size is one way to indicate levels of headings. If you use different type sizes, make sure that you match the

---

Controlling Soil-Borne Pathogens in Tree Nurseries

Types of Soil-Borne Pathogens and Their Effects on Trees
Simply stated, the effects of soil-borne pathogens . . .

Soil-borne fungi
At one time, it was thought that soil-borne fungi . . .

    Basiodiomycetes. The Basiodiomycetes are a class of fungi whose species . . .

    Phycomycetes. The class of Phycomycetes is a highly diversified type of fungus. It is the . . .

Plant parasitic nematodes
Nematodes are small, unsegmented . . .

Treatments and Controls for Soil-Borne Pathogens

FIGURE 5-13 Four Levels of Headings in a Report

size to the level of importance. If the headings are different sizes, readers expect first-level headings to be larger than second-level headings, second-level headings to be larger than third-level headings, and so on, as shown in Figure 5-13. The lower-level headings can be the same size as the text, but no level of heading should be smaller than the text. That would violate readers' expectations. If you use different type sizes for different heading levels, don't make the differences in type sizes excessive.

Put more space before a heading than after it. Headings announce the topic that is coming next in your document. Therefore, you want the heading to lead the reader's eye down the page or screen into the text that follows. One way to do that is to have more space, on the page or screen, before the heading rather than after it. In this way, the heading and its accompanying text constitute a visible chunk of information.

If you are going to use a rule with the heading, consider putting it *above* the heading rather than below it. A rule above the heading creates a "chunk" that includes both the heading and the text that it covers. A rule above the heading also draws the reader's eye down into the text that follows instead of up and away from that text.

Keep each heading with the section it covers. Don't leave a heading at the bottom of a page when the text appears on the next page. Make sure you have at least two lines of the first paragraph on the page with the heading. In some cases, you may want each topic to be on a separate page so that the heading and all the text of a topic appear together. Most word processing programs have functions that help you keep headings from being stranded at the bottom of a page and that allow you to set up your document so that all headings of a certain level start on a new page.

Consider using numbers with your headings. In many companies and agencies, the standard for organizing reports and manuals is to use a numbering system with headings. Figure 5-14 shows two such numbering systems: the alphanumeric system and the decimal system.

A numbering system allows you to refer precisely and concisely to a section of the report by the number of its heading (e.g., Section II.A.3.b or Section 4.3.7). If you add or delete a section later, however, you must be sure to revise the numbering of the report. In addition, a lot of readers find numbering systems confusing and, for example, would fail to recognize immediately that a section numbered 6.8.23 would come after a section numbered 6.8.2.3. If you use a numbering system with your headings, include the numbers before the entries in your table of contents.

Use page numbers and headers or footers. In addition to clearly worded and visually accessible headings, page numbers and running headers and footers are important aids to efficient reading.

Number the pages. Page numbers help readers keep track of where they are and provide easy reference points for talking about a document. Always number the pages of drafts and final documents that people are going to read on paper.

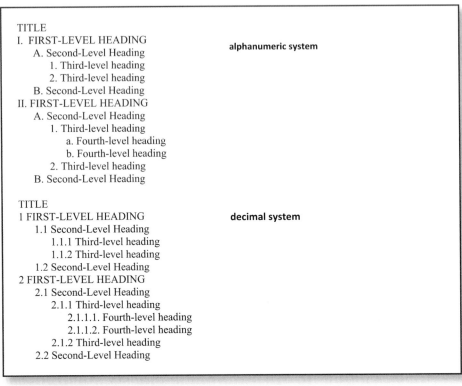

FIGURE 5-14 Two Types of Numbering Systems

If the document is going to be used online, inserting page numbers could be unnecessary. In websites, for example, readers jump from topic to topic and page to page instead of proceeding in a specified order from start to finish. In addition, word processing programs keep track automatically of the number of pages and typically display this information in the bottom margin of the document window as a reference point for writers and readers. If readers are likely to print your online document, however, they will certainly appreciate your inclusion of page numbers. In slides prepared for oral presentations, you will help your audience to track your progress and to stay attentive if you identify the slides with a numbering notation like this:

Slide 1 of 10

Short manuscripts and reports that have little prefatory material almost always use Arabic numerals (1, 2, 3). The common convention is to center the page number below the text at the bottom of the page or to put it in the upper outside corner (upper left corner for left-hand pages, upper right corner for right-hand pages). Always leave at least two lines of space between the text and the page number. Put the page number in the same place on each page. Page numbers at the bottom of the page often have a hyphen on each side, like this:

-17-

As reports grow longer and more complicated, the page-numbering system also may need to be more complex. If you have a preface or other material that comes before the main part of the report, it is customary to use lowercase Roman numerals (i, ii, iii) for that material and then to change to Arabic numerals for the body of the report.

In a report, the introduction may be part of the prefatory material or the main body. The title page doesn't show the number but is counted as the first page. The page following the title page is number 2 or ii.

You also have to know whether the document will be printed on one side of the paper or two. If both sides will carry printing, you may have to number several otherwise blank pages in word processing files. New chapters or major sections usually start on a right-hand page. The right-hand page always has an odd number. If the last page of your first chapter is page 9, for example, and your document will be printed double-sided, you have to include one otherwise blank page 10 so that the first page of your second chapter will be a right-hand page 11 when the document is printed, copied, and bound.

The body of a report is usually paginated continuously, from page 1 to the last page. For the appendices, you may continue the same series of numbers, or you may change to a letter-plus-number system. In that system, the pages in Appendix A are numbered A-1, A-2, and so on. The pages in Appendix B are numbered B-1, B-2, and so forth. If your report is part of a series, or if your company has a standard report format, you will need to make your page numbering match that of the series or standard format.

Numbering appendices with the letter-plus-number system has several advantages:

- It separates the appendices from the body. Readers can tell how long the body of the report is and how long each appendix is.
- It clearly shows that a page is part of an appendix and which appendix it belongs to. It makes pages in the appendices easier to locate.
- It allows the appendices to be printed separately from the body of the report. Sometimes the appendices are ready before the body of the report has been completed, and being able to print the appendices first may save time and help you meet a deadline.
- It allows the pagination of either an appendix or the body to be changed without requiring changes in the other parts.

Include headers or footers. In long documents, it helps readers if you give identifying information at the top or bottom of each page. Information at the top of the page is a header; information at the bottom of the page is a footer. Organizations often have standard practices regarding the information to be displayed in headers and footers. A typical header for a report might show the author's name, the title of the report, and the date. It might look like this:

Jane Fernstein   Feasibility Study   February 2012

In this case, the page numbers would likely appear in the footer.

A typical header for a letter might show the name of the person receiving the letter, the page number, and the date. It might look like this:

Dr. Jieru Chen   -2-   February 16, 2012

Or

Dr. Jieru Chen
Page 2
February 16, 2012

Note that headers and footers rarely appear on the first pages of documents because first pages already carry identifying information like the title, author, recipient, and date. Word processing programs allow you to start headers and footers on the second page.

DOCUMENT DESIGN CHECKLIST

☐ Is your document clean, organized, and attractive?

☐ Is your text easy to read?

☐ If your document is supposed to conform to a standard template, does it?

☐ Have you left adequate margins? (If necessary, have you left extra room for binding?)

☐ Is the spacing between the lines and paragraphs consistent and appropriate?

☐ Can the reader tell easily where sections and paragraphs begin?

☐ Have you checked the headings? Are the headings informative? Unambiguous? Consistent? Parallel?

☐ Will readers get an overall picture of the document by reading the headings?

☐ Is the hierarchy of the headings obvious?

☐ Can readers tell at a glance what is heading and what is text?

☐ If readers want to find a particular section quickly, will the size and placement of the heading help them?

☐ Have you checked the page breaks to be sure that you do not have a heading by itself at the bottom of a page?

☐ Are the pages of a paper document numbered?

☐ Are there appropriate headers or footers?

☐ If you are using a numbering system, is it consistent and correct?

☐ Did you test representative readers for their ability to locate information easily?

EXERCISES

1. Visit the website of two major employers in your field. What kinds of documents do you find at each site? Do the organizations seem to have a standard template for the design of their documents? From looking at a number of the documents at each site, how would you describe their design? Which organization does a better job of designing documents for its audience and purpose? How would you make the design of each organization's documents more effective?

2. Revise the headings used in Figure 5-4, substituting questions for the original phrases. Revise again, using short sentences for the headings. Which revision do you consider more appropriate for the audience and purpose of this letter?

3. Figure 5-15 is a first draft of the instructions for the GrillWizard.

    You are a friend and neighbor of the owner and founder of Fierce Products, a new company in Lubbock that manufactures the GrillWizard. Fierce Products is a family-owned company with 45 employees. The owner (and spouse of the author) has hired you to revise the design of the instructions in order to ensure safe and efficient operation of the product as well as to convey a positive impression of the quality of Fierce Products.

    After you design this document, you will return it to the company owner for final approval. Fierce Products is ready to release the GrillWizard to market. As soon as the instructions are ready, the product will be boxed and shipped. The sooner you submit your design, the sooner Fierce Products will start making money.

4. Examine Figure 5-16. If you were the author of this document and were given 15 more minutes to make it more effectively designed, what changes would you make?

GrillWizard

Fast and efficient frying and cooking with propane gas. Light the burner and instantly you have a hot 100,000 BTU continuous flame.

The **GrillWizard** will help you eliminate fish and other lingering cooking odors from your home.

The **GrillWizard** is used for fast frying of fish potatoes, onion rings, chicken, vegetables, and donuts. Substitute water for oil and it's also great for shrimp, crab, and lobster boils as well as steaming clams.

This cooker is completely portable with all parts easily assembled and disassembled for compact transportation and storage, yet it weighs only 40 lbs.

When the control valve is open, a full 100,000 BTUs of powerful heat prepares cooking oil in 3 minutes for frying. Adjust the heat with a touch of the control valve.

Operating Instructions

Place grill on level ground. Insert tapered end of tubing into the hole in the base of the grill. (CAUTION: Make sure the cooker is level and the burner is facing up.)

Attach grill connector to propane cylinder.

Completely open propane valve.

Slightly open control valve at grill connector and light cooker at top of tube immediately (CAUTION: **DO NOT stand directly over cooker when lighting burner**).

Adjust control valve for desired flame height.

When finished cooking, always close both grill connector valve and propane cylinder valve completely.

The **GrillWizard** works with any size of propane tank cylinder and all will give off the same amount of heat. A 20 pound cylinder will provide approximately 6 hours of cooking time if valves are completely opened.

The intense heat produced by the **GrillWizard** allows you to fast fry all foods. The cooking oils of conventional fryers drop in temperature as food is added, but the **GrillWizard** maintains its temperature with just a quick touch of the control valve.

The **GrillWizard** has been designed for easy care. However, keep all dirt and foreign objects out of connectors, hose, valves, and openings. Failure to do so could cause obstruction of gas and greatly diminish the effectiveness of the **GrillWizard.**

CAUTION: If you suspect leaks **DO NOT** light unit before checking.

For outdoor use only.

After washing pan with soap and water, dry thoroughly and coat the entire pan with cooking oil on paper towel to prevent rusting.

FIGURE 5-15 Document for Exercise 3

FTC Consumer Alert

Federal Trade Commission ■ **Bureau of Consumer Protection** ■ **Office of Consumer & Business Education**

Travel Tips: How to Gear Up for a Great Trip

Whether you're off to see the sights, sunbathe on the sand, or ski the slopes, it pays to be an informed travel shopper. To help you avoid vacation frustration, the Federal Trade Commission (FTC), the nation's consumer protection agency, offers these tips.

- **Buy your vacation package from a business you have confidence in.** Ask family and friends to recommend a company with a good track record. Think twice if you can't get a person on the phone to answer your questions. Contact the state Attorney General, consumer protection agency and Better Business Bureau where you live and where the company is based to see if there is a history of complaints on file.
- **Be on the alert for the telltale signs of a travel scam.** Unsolicited mail, email and faxes for deeply discounted travel packages may promise the world, but the fraudsters behind these offers will leave you at the gate.
- **Verify and clarify.** Call to verify your reservations and arrangements. Get the details behind vague promises that you'll be staying at a "five-star" resort or sailing on a "luxury" cruise ship. When you have the names, addresses and telephone numbers of the airlines, car rental companies, and hotels you'll be using, confirm all arrangements for yourself.
- **Get the details of your vacation in writing.** Get a copy of the company's cancellation and refund policies, and ask "What if…?" Consider whether some form of travel cancellation insurance may be appropriate. Make sure the product you're being sold is a licensed insurance policy. The U.S. Travel Insurance Association maintains a list of licensed travel insurance companies.
- **Use a credit card to make your purchase.** If you don't get what you paid for, you may be able to dispute the charges with your credit card company. However, don't give your account number to any business until you've verified that it is reputable.
- **Avoid a travel club flub.** Ask questions before joining a travel club. Sometimes, a "free trial" membership can result in unauthorized charges on your credit card. Find out what you'll get for your money and how you can cancel.
- **Won a "free" vacation?** Not so fast. Scam artists may tell you you've won a "free" vacation, but then claim to need your credit card number for "verification." Tell 'em to take a hike. If the promotion is legit, you never need to pay for a prize.

The FTC works to prevent fraudulent, deceptive and unfair business practices in the marketplace and to provide information to help consumers spot, stop and avoid them. To file a complaint or get free information on consumer issues, visit **ftc.gov** or call toll-free, 1-877-FTC-HELP (1-877-382-4357); TTY: 1-866-653-4261. Watch a video, *How to File a Complaint*, at **ftc.gov/video** to learn more. The FTC enters consumer complaints into the Consumer Sentinel Network, a secure online database and investigative tool used by hundreds of civil and criminal law enforcement agencies in the U.S. and abroad.

May 2011

FIGURE 5-16 Document for Exercise 4

Designing Illustrations

In communicating technical information, you will often need to use illustrations either in addition to words or instead of words to convey your message. How do you determine whether illustrations are really desirable? Ask yourself two questions:

- What do you want the reader to do or think after reading your document?
- How will illustrations help you to achieve your objective?

Quick Tips

Illustrations divide into two categories: tables and figures. Tables display numbers and words in columns and rows. Every other kind of illustration is a figure.

If you want to summarize information to make it easier to remember or retrieve, use a table.

If you want to emphasize information to clarify or reinforce its meaning, use a figure.

CREATING ILLUSTRATIONS

In deciding when and how to use illustrations, remember the following guidelines:

- **Simplify your illustrations.** Keep your illustrations as simple as possible so that your reader has no difficulty understanding your message. Avoid distracting your reader with unnecessary details or decorative flourishes.
- **Use computer applications critically.** Graphics applications and clip art allow you to include a wide variety of illustrations in your document. To make sure your tables and figures are effective, however, you must evaluate the choices available. Graphics applications, for example, might create artistic but misleading graphs, and clip art might exhibit a pictorial style

that isn't quite serious enough or detailed enough to do justice to your subject. It is your job to choose illustrations that display your information clearly and correctly.

- **Consider size and cost.** Calculate the impact of illustrations on the expected length of your document. Illustrations will often increase the size of a document and, if printed, add to the cost of production and distribution.
- **Title your illustrations.** Give each table and figure a title that clearly indicates the message you wish it to convey.
- **Number your illustrations.** If you use several illustrations in your report, number them. Number the tables and figures separately (e.g., Table 1, Table 2, Figure 1, Figure 2).
- **Alert your readers.** Always alert your readers to illustrations by referring to them in the text. Every time you refer to the illustration, use the table or figure number (e.g., see Table 1). Announce the illustration—what it is or shows—then add any verbal explanation your reader will need to fully understand it. Don't lead readers through a complicated explanation and only later refer to the illustration. Point them to the illustration immediately so that they can shift back and forth between the explanation and the illustration as necessary.
- **Position your illustrations strategically.** Place each illustration as close to the passage it explains as possible.
- **Identify your sources.** If you borrow or adapt a table or figure from another source, identify that source (and, if necessary, permission to use it) below the illustration (e.g., SOURCE: *Exposing the Magic of Design: A Practitioner's Guide to the Methods and Theory of Synthesis*, page 99, by Jon Kolko. Copyright 2011 by Oxford University Press. Reprinted by permission.).

Tables.

- Note that the purpose of a table is to summarize information in specific categories to assist the viewer in accessing and retrieving this information.
- Every column in a table should have a heading that identifies the information below it. In a table of numbers, include the unit of measurement, such as "miles per hour." For large numbers, add a designation such as "in thousands" or "in millions" to the column heading (and delete the corresponding zeros from the numeric data). Headings should be brief. If headings need more explanation, include this information in a footnote below the table. Use lowercase letters, numbers, or symbols (e.g., * or +) to indicate footnoted material.
- If possible, box your table to separate it from surrounding paragraphs.
- Keep tables as simple as possible. Include only data relevant to your purpose.
- Consider omitting lines between rows and columns to avoid giving your table a crowded appearance. If possible, use white space to separate rows and columns.

Figures 6-1 through 6-3 show three ways of presenting tabular data.

Table 1.
Population by Sex and Selected Age Groups: 2000 and 2010
(For information on confidentiality protection, nonsampling error, and definitions, see *www.census.gov/prod/cen2010/doc/sf1.pdf*)

Sex and selected age groups	2000		2010		Change, 2000 to 2010	
	Number	Percent	Number	Percent	Number	Percent
Total population	281,421,906	100.0	308,745,538	100.0	27,323,632	9.7
SEX						
Male................	138,053,563	49.1	151,781,326	49.2	13,727,763	9.9
Female...............	143,368,343	50.9	156,964,212	50.8	13,595,869	9.5
SELECTED AGE GROUPS						
Under 18 years	72,293,812	25.7	74,181,467	24.0	1,887,655	2.6
Under 5 years	19,175,798	6.8	20,201,362	6.5	1,025,564	5.3
5 to 17 years	53,118,014	18.9	53,980,105	17.5	862,091	1.6
18 to 44 years	112,183,705	39.9	112,806,642	36.5	622,937	0.6
18 to 24 years	27,143,454	9.6	30,672,088	9.9	3,528,634	13.0
25 to 44 years	85,040,251	30.2	82,134,554	26.6	-2,905,697	-3.4
45 to 64 years	61,952,636	22.0	81,489,445	26.4	19,536,809	31.5
65 years and over	34,991,753	12.4	40,267,984	13.0	5,276,231	15.1
16 years and over	217,149,127	77.2	243,275,505	78.8	26,126,378	12.0
18 years and over	209,128,094	74.3	234,564,071	76.0	25,435,977	12.2
21 years and over	196,899,193	70.0	220,958,853	71.6	24,059,660	12.2
62 years and over	41,256,029	14.7	49,972,181	16.2	8,716,152	21.1

Sources: U.S. Census Bureau, *Census 2000 Summary File 1* and *2010 Census Summary File 1.*

FIGURE 6-1 Table This table is effectively designed using thin lines and generous white space to separate the column headings and the columns from each other, making the entire table look easy to navigate. Note that the row labels are aligned on the left for easy reading while the numerical data in the rows are aligned on the right (or on the decimal point) to allow the easiest possible comparison of information across the rows and columns. The column headings are centered while the subheadings (Number and Percent) are aligned on the right with their corresponding rows of numerical data. Color is used selectively to emphasize the table title, the row of totals, and the two major categories of information in the table. The use of all capital letters for the headings of the two major categories is unnecessary but at least consistent and unlikely to disrupt reading.
Source: U.S. Department of Commerce, Economics and Statistics Administration, U.S. Census Bureau. *Age and Sex Composition: 2010.* U.S. Census Briefs. C2010BR-03. Washington, DC: GPO, 2011. p. 2.

Table 2. Activities of Dolan Springs bus driver, January 27–30, 2009.

Time (PST)	Event	Location	Source
Tuesday, January 27			
3:00 p.m.	Logs on duty, not driving	Mission Hills, CA	Logbook
3:15	Begins driving	Mission Hills	Logbook
3:45	Logs on duty, not driving	Los Angeles, CA	Logbook
4:00	Begins driving	Los Angeles	Logbook
4:30	Logs off duty	San Gabriel, CA	Logbook
Wednesday, January 28			
7:15 a.m.	Logs on duty, not driving	San Gabriel, CA	Logbook
7:30	Begins driving	San Gabriel	Logbook
8:00	Logs on duty, not driving	Los Angeles, CA	Logbook
8:15	Begins driving	Los Angeles	Logbook
10:00	Logs on duty, not driving	Barstow, CA	Logbook
10:15	Logs off duty	Barstow	Logbook
12:45 p.m.	Logs on duty, not driving	Barstow	Logbook
1:00	Begins driving	Barstow	Logbook
3:45	Logs on duty, not driving	Las Vegas, NV	Logbook
4:00	Logs off duty	Las Vegas	Logbook
8:07	Checks into Sahara Hotel	Las Vegas	Hotel records
Thursday, January 29			
9:45 a.m.	Logs on duty, not driving	Las Vegas, NV	Logbook
10:00	Begins driving	Las Vegas	Logbook
10:13	Enters McCarran airport	Las Vegas	RFID[a]/GPS[b]
10:30	Logs on duty, not driving	Las Vegas	Logbook
10:45	Logs off duty	Las Vegas	Logbook
11:31	Leaves McCarran airport	Las Vegas	RFID
12:00 p.m.	Arrives China Buffet restaurant	Las Vegas	GPS
12:49	Departs China Buffet restaurant	Las Vegas	GPS
3:30	Arrives Riviera Hotel	Las Vegas	Video/GPS
4:31	Receives parking warning at Riviera	Las Vegas	Hotel records
6:30	Logs on duty, not driving	Las Vegas	Logbook
6:50	Leaves Riviera Hotel	Las Vegas	Video
7:15	Logs off duty	Las Vegas	Logbook
Friday, January 30			
12:00 a.m.	Goes to bed	Las Vegas, NV	Interview
5:30	On duty, not driving	Las Vegas	Logbook
6:00	Leaves Riviera Hotel	Las Vegas	Video
6:40	Crosses Nevada border	Hoover Dam	Video
6:42	Crosses Arizona border	Hoover Dam	Video
8:00	Arrives at "Sky Station"	Meadview, AZ	Interview
8:15	On duty, not driving	Meadview	Logbook
8:30	Off duty, begins nap	Meadview	Logbook/interview
1:30 p.m.	Nap ends	Meadview	Interview
2:13	Leaves "Sky Station"	Meadview	GPS
2:51	Turns onto US 93 northbound	Dolan Springs, AZ	GPS
3:06	Accident occurs	Dolan Springs	

[a] RFID = radio frequency identification information from McCarran International Airport, Las Vegas.
[b] GPS = global positioning system data from the accident vehicle.

FIGURE 6-2 Table This table is easy to read with effective spacing to separate the columns and rows of information. Major headings are centered and displayed in distinctive white type on black horizontal bars. The subheadings are consistently left-aligned and displayed in bold black type on gray horizontal bars. Two notes are used to clarify important abbreviations. The result is a table that viewers could readily navigate to compare and contrast information or to retrieve specific pieces of evidence. Times in the left column might be easier to read if aligned on the colon.

Source: National Transportation Safety Board. Bus Loss of Control and Rollover, Dolan Springs, Arizona, January 30, 2009. Highway Accident Report NTSB/HAR-10/01 PB2010-916201. Washington, DC: GPO, 2010. p. 12.

Table 4
Pedalcyclists Killed and Injured and Fatality and Injury Rates by Age and Sex, 2009

Age (Years)	Male			Female			Total		
	Killed	Population (thousands)	Fatality Rate*	Killed	Population (thousands)	Fatality Rate*	Killed	Population (thousands)	Fatality Rate*
<5	3	10,887	0.28	0	10,413	0.00	3	21,300	0.14
5-9	12	10,536	1.14	6	10,074	0.60	18	20,610	0.87
10-15	50	12,340	4.05	14	11,767	1.19	64	24,107	2.65
16-20	32	11,166	2.87	5	10,578	0.47	37	21,744	1.70
21-24	23	8,861	2.60	6	8,339	0.72	29	17,200	1.69
25-34	60	21,224	2.83	11	20,343	0.54	71	41,566	1.71
35-44	93	20,857	4.46	12	20,673	0.58	105	41,530	2.53
45-54	124	21,973	5.64	15	22,619	0.66	139	44,592	3.12
55-64	82	16,782	4.89	6	18,005	0.33	88	34,787	2.53
65-74	49	9,593	5.11	4	11,199	0.36	53	20,792	2.55
75-84	18	5,447	3.30	2	7,700	0.26	20	13,148	1.52
85+	3	1,783	1.68	0	3,848	0.00	3	5,631	0.53
Total	**549**	**151,449**	**3.62**	**81**	**155,557**	**0.52**	**630**	**307,007**	**2.05**
Age (Years)	Male			Female			Total		
	Injured	Population (thousands)	Injury Rate*	Injured	Population (thousands)	Injury Rate*	Injured	Population (thousands)	Injury Rate*
<5	**	10,887	**	**	10,413	**	**	21,300	**
5-9	2,000	10,536	172	**	10,074	**	2,000	20,610	107
10-15	6,000	12,340	501	2,000	11,767	135	8,000	24,107	322
16-20	6,000	11,166	510	1,000	10,578	122	7,000	21,744	321
21-24	4,000	8,861	501	2,000	8,339	251	7,000	17,200	380
25-34	8,000	21,224	399	1,000	20,343	68	10,000	41,566	237
35-44	3,000	20,857	152	**	20,673	**	4,000	41,530	86
45-54	6,000	21,973	280	2,000	22,619	81	8,000	44,592	179
55-64	3,000	16,782	187	1,000	18,005	53	4,000	34,787	118
65-74	1,000	9,593	91	**	11,199	**	1,000	20,792	48
75-84	**	5,447	**	**	7,700	**	**	13,148	**
85+	**	1,783	**	**	3,848	**	**	5,631	**
Total	**41,000**	**151,449**	**268**	**10,000**	**155,557**	**65**	**51,000**	**307,007**	**165**

* Rate per million population.
** Less than 500 injured, injury rate not shown.
Source: Fatalities — Fatality Analysis Reporting System, NHTSA.   Injured — General Estimates System, NHTSA.   Population — Bureau of the Census.

FIGURE 6-3 Table This table tries to offer a lot of information in a single location but makes reading and retrieval difficult as a consequence. Notice that bold centered type displayed in horizontal blue bars is used for both first-level and second-level headings. These headings occur both at the top of the table (which is to be expected) but again in the middle of the table (which would be unexpected). Similarly, a row of totals occurs at the bottom of the table (which is to be expected) but also in the middle of the table (which would be unexpected). Unnecessary vertical gridlines and empty cells with double asterisks only exacerbate the visual confusion. At least two separate tables would make for easier reading: one for numbers and one for percents, and/or one for fatalities and one for injuries.
Source: U.S. Department of Transportation, National Highway Traffic Safety Administration. Bicyclists and Other Cyclists. Traffic Safety Facts DOT HS 811 386. Washington, DC: GPO, 2010. p. 3.

Bar and column graphs.

- Note that the purpose of a bar graph is to compare and contrast two or more subjects at the same point in time, whereas the purpose of a column graph is to reveal change in a subject at regular intervals of time.
- Avoid putting excessive information on a bar or column graph and thereby complicating the reader's ability to decipher it. Consider using a separate graph to communicate each point.
- Be sure to label the horizontal or x-axis and the vertical or y-axis—what each measures and the units in which each is calibrated. Readers can't

understand your graph if they don't know what you are measuring or how it is measured.

- For bar graphs, start the x-axis at zero and equally space the intervals on the x-axis to avoid distorting the length of the bars. For column graphs, start the y-axis at zero and equally space the intervals on the y-axis to avoid distorting the height of the columns. On a bar graph, neither axis is a measure of time; on a column graph, the x-axis is ordinarily a measure of time.
- Color can enhance the effect of a graph, but excessive color can reduce comprehension and distort information. Use the same color for all bars or columns that represent the same categories of information. Avoid using color as simple decoration.
- Make the graph accurate. Typical graphics applications allow you to add a range of special effects. However, artistic graphs are not always either effective or accurate. Three-dimensional bars and columns are often deceptive because readers have difficulty visually comparing the relative lengths of the bars and the relative heights of the columns. If you choose three-dimensional bar or column graphs, watch for possible distortion.
- Limit the number of divisions. The more a bar or column is divided, the more difficult it is to understand. Bars or columns with more than four or five divisions are especially challenging for readers and could lead to confusion or misinterpretation.
- For divided bar and column graphs, use color or solid shading to distinguish divisions instead of textured patterns that may create distracting optical illusions.
- Put labels on or near the bars or columns. Keep in mind that explanatory legends (or keys) will slow comprehension because the reader is required to look back and forth between the bars and the legend. Placing labels on bars can be difficult, however, especially if you use colored bars. Even black text will often be difficult to read on any colors but very light ones. In short, use a legend only if you can't use labels. And if you do use a legend, locate it as close to the bars or columns as possible.
- Avoid crowding the bars or columns within a graph. Such visual clutter makes a graph look difficult to interpret. Using three-dimensional bars or columns will also reduce the number that will fit in a given space. Effective and inviting graphs leave generous space between the bars or columns.

See Figures 6-4 through 6-7 for examples of bar and column graphs.

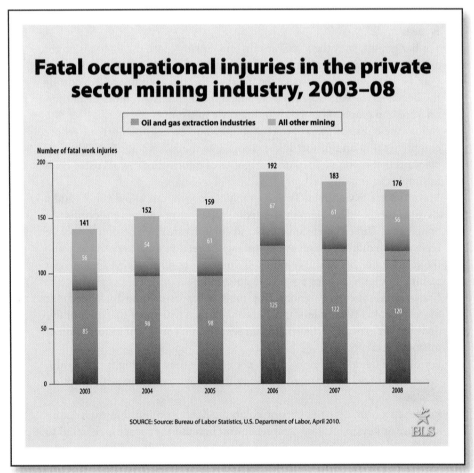

Fatal occupational injuries in the private sector mining industry, 2003–08

■ Oil and gas extraction industries   ■ All other mining

Number of fatal work injuries

200

192
183
176
159
152
141

67
61
56
54
61
56

125
122
120
98
98
85

150

100

50

0

2003   2004   2005   2006   2007   2008

SOURCE: Source: Bureau of Labor Statistics, U.S. Department of Labor, April 2010.

BLS

FIGURE 6-4 Column Graph This divided column graph is clean and concise and makes evident its key point: that is, mining fatalities spiked in 2006 in the oil and gas industry but declined in the following years. The columns are labeled clearly and spaced generously. A white background would allow better contrast, but the colors used for the columns are bright enough to make the beige background a satisfactory design choice. Numerical labeling of each section along with a total for each column makes the horizontal gridlines unnecessary.

Source: U.S. Department of Labor, Bureau of Labor Statistics. Fatal Occupational Injuries and Nonfatal Occupational Injuries and Illnesses, 2008. Report 1028. Washington, DC: GPO, 2011. p. 50.

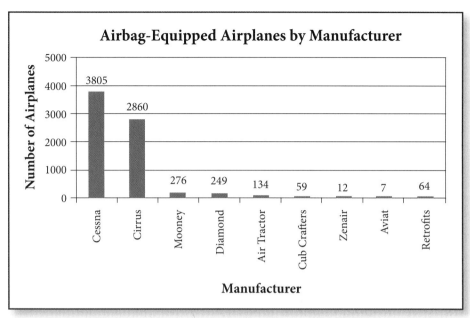

FIGURE 6-5 Column Graph This column graph would be better designed as a bar graph (i.e., with horizontal bars instead of vertical columns). The series of vertical columns aligned on the *x*-axis from left to right might be initially perceived as a chronological progression—the same subject displayed at consecutive points in time. In fact, the figure displays different subjects at the same point in time. Designing the information as a bar graph would avoid any initial misunderstanding and speed the viewer's access to the information. The ordering of the columns from largest to smallest, however, does assist the viewer in making rapid sense of the graphic display. (Notice that the Retrofits category does not refer to a specific manufacturer and might be better reported as a note to the graph, especially given that both the title of the graph and the label for the *x*-axis specify "Manufacturer" as the basis of the display.)

Source: National Transportation Safety Board. Airbag Performance in General Aviation Restraint Systems. Safety Study NTSB/SS-11/01. Washington, DC: GPO, 2011. p. 10.

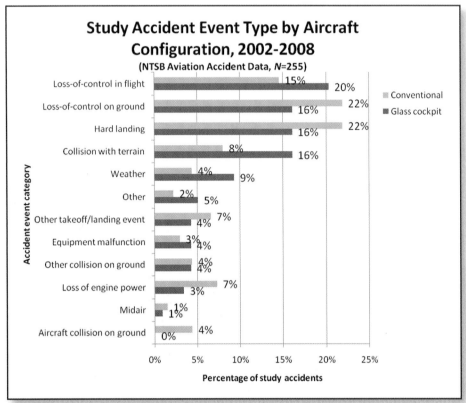

FIGURE 6-6 Bar Graph This bar graph makes a clear and vivid point regarding the frequency of certain types of accidents in aircraft with conventional cockpits versus aircraft with glass cockpits. The two types of aircraft are readily identified by obviously different colors, as explained in a legend conveniently positioned inside the graph. The 12 categories of accident are all crisply labeled for easy reading and understanding. The categories of accidents are positioned on the graph from longest bars at the top to shortest bars at the bottom, according to accidents of aircraft with glass cockpits. It might have made this ordering more readily apparent, however, if the position of the red and blue bars were reversed. The major distraction in the graph is the unusually large size of type used to indicate the quantity of each bar: a smaller size of type is obviously necessary. A better alternative would be to eliminate these numbers altogether and allow the vertical gridlines to do their job. If greater precision is considered vital, it would be wise to specify these numbers to at least one decimal point, instead of rounding, to eliminate the possible confusion created by the different size bars both labeled 1 percent in the Midair category.

Source: National Transportation Safety Board. Introduction of Glass Cockpit Avionics into Light Aircraft. Safety Study NTSB/SS-01/10 PB2010-917001. Washington, DC: GPO, 2011. p. 33.

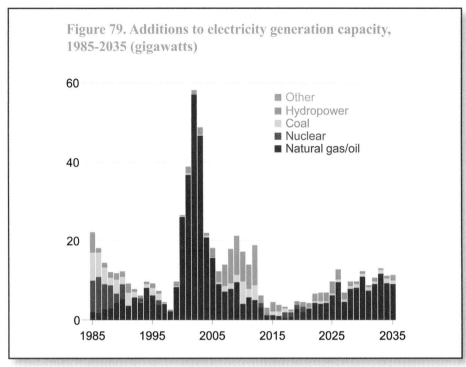

Figure 79. Additions to electricity generation capacity, 1985-2035 (gigawatts)

FIGURE 6-7 **Column Graph** This divided-column graph is difficult to decipher because it displays too many columns and too many divisions of each column in too narrow and short a space. The visual effect makes the data look crowded and cramped instead of readily accessible. Viewers will sometimes find it immensely challenging to determine how many divisions a column really has or which year a specific column is supposed to designate. The graph would be more effective, for example, if only the odd-numbered years were displayed, and if Hydropower was included in the Other category. The alternative, of course, is to allow the entire graph more horizontal and vertical space. The column divisions might also be better labeled with lines pointing to the leftmost column, but at least the explanatory legend is conveniently positioned inside the graph and is easy to interpret.

Source: U.S. Department of Energy, Energy Information Administration. Annual Energy Outlook 2011, with Projections to 2035. DOE/EIA-038. Washington, DC: GPO, 2011. p. 74.

Circle graphs.

- Note that the purpose of a circle graph (also referred to as a pie chart) is to display the number and relative size of the divisions of a subject.
- Restrict the number of segments in a circle graph to seven or eight. A limit exists on the number of segments into which a circle can be divided before comprehension of the relative sizes is jeopardized. If necessary, combine several smaller segments and create a second circle graph to display the composition of that combined segment.

- Watch for possible distortion when you use three-dimensional circle graphs.
- Clearly label all segments. Whether they are placed inside or outside the circle, labels should be horizontal for easier reading. Avoid using explanatory legends (or keys).
- As you segment the graph, begin with the largest section in the upper right-hand quadrant. The remaining segments should be arranged clockwise, in descending order. Color the sections clockwise from darker to lighter so that color reinforces size.

See Figure 6-8 for an example of a circle graph.

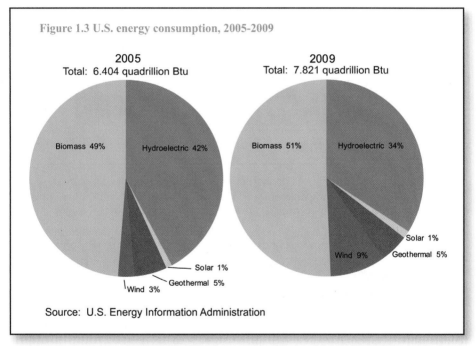

Figure 1.3 U.S. energy consumption, 2005-2009

2005
Total: 6.404 quadrillion Btu

2009
Total: 7.821 quadrillion Btu

Biomass 49%   Hydroelectric 42%

Biomass 51%   Hydroelectric 34%

Solar 1%
Geothermal 5%
Wind 3%

Solar 1%
Wind 9%   Geothermal 5%

Source: U.S. Energy Information Administration

FIGURE 6-8 Circle Graphs This pair of circle graphs uses clear labels for each of its five sections, but these are inconsistently positioned, inside if the label fits inside the section of the circle and outside if it doesn't (with lines from label to corresponding section in 2005 but without lines in 2009). Notice, as a result, that the Wind label is outside in 2005 but inside in 2009. The labels inside the colored sections of the circles are also more difficult to read because of the poor contrast between the black type and dark colors used for the sections. In addition, the sections are arbitrarily ordered and colored. Instead of starting in the upper right quadrant with the biggest piece and progressing clockwise to the smallest piece for easiest reading, the graph fails to puts its information in a logical sequence or use color in a systematic or significant fashion. Here color is only a distracting decoration.

Source: U.S. Energy Information Administration. Trends in Renewable Energy Consumption and Electricity 2009. Washington, DC: GPO, 2011. p. 2.

Line graphs.

- Note that the purpose of a line graph is to show the degree and direction of change relative to two variables.
- Label each axis clearly. Like bar and column graphs, line graphs must have clearly labeled scales to show the variables you are measuring. Ordinarily, the independent variable is placed on the horizontal or x-axis, and the dependent variables are placed on the vertical or y-axis (and, in a three-dimensional graph, on the diagonal or z-axis).
- Choose the scale of each axis to show the appropriate steepness of the slope of the line. Typically, the scales start at zero, with the intervals equally spaced on each axis.
- The major difficulty in designing line graphs lies in choosing the spacing for each axis so that the steepness (slope) of the line accurately measures the actual trend suggested by the data. Typical graphics applications will allow you to adjust the intervals on the x-axis and the y-axis, but your job is to decide whether the slope of the graph accurately depicts your data or gives a distorted impression.
- Avoid using more than three data lines on one graph unless they are separated by visible space. Graphs with lots of overlapping and intersecting data lines are usually difficult for readers to interpret.
- Keep the data lines on your graph distinctive by using either different colors or different styles for each line.
- If possible, label each data line. Avoid explanatory legends (or keys) because these will slow reader comprehension.

See Figures 6-9 and 6-10 for examples of line graphs.

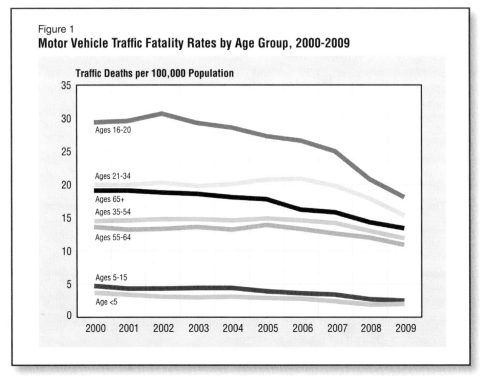

Figure 1

Motor Vehicle Traffic Fatality Rates by Age Group, 2000-2009

Traffic Deaths per 100,000 Population

Ages 16-20
Ages 21-34
Ages 65+
Ages 35-54
Ages 55-64
Ages 5-15
Age <5

FIGURE 6-9 **Line Graph** This line graph uses clear labeling to identify and differentiate its seven data lines. It also uses color, but given that the data lines never intersect, the color does nothing to make reading easier and might only cause confusion as readers try to decide why certain lines are various shades of blue or various shades of gray or why the black line is black. The arbitrary use of color serves only as a decorative distraction to the key point of the graph: that is, traffic fatalities in all age groups dropped from 2000 to 2009 and most precipitously in the 16-20 age group. It is this group that deserves the special visual emphasis of the unique black data line.

Source: U.S. Department of Transportation, National Highway Traffic Safety Administration. Older Population. Traffic Safety Facts DOT HS 811 391. Washington, DC: GPO, 2010. p. 1.

Organization charts.

- Note that the purpose of an organization chart is to map the various divisions and levels of responsibility within an organization.
- Make the chart as simple as the organization itself, with the levels of hierarchy organized highest to lowest and positioned on the chart from top to bottom. The more levels of hierarchy in the organization, the more vertical the chart; the more divisions in the organization, the more horizontal the chart.
- Use the same shape in the same size for all divisions of the organization that are at the same level in the hierarchy.
- Label each division of the organization.
- If space allows, put the labels directly on the division; if not, attach the label to the subject with thin rules (never arrows).

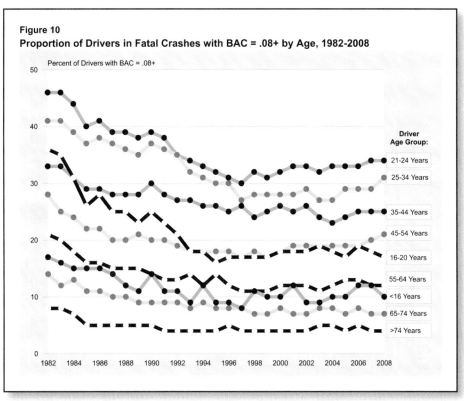

Figure 10
Proportion of Drivers in Fatal Crashes with BAC = .08+ by Age, 1982-2008

FIGURE 6-10 Line Graph This could be the least effective line graph ever designed because it focuses the viewer's attention on all the unnecessary circles instead of the data lines themselves. It even makes it difficult to notice the data lines. The graph does include a label for each line, but the labels are located on the right side of the graph instead of the left side. This unusual position requires readers to read each data line from right to left instead of left to right. The labels might be more effective if positioned closer to the left side of the graph. The graph also uses color to separate the data lines—especially important with intersecting lines—but the use of color here is arbitrary: the key point of the graph is that alcohol-related driver fatalities in all age groups dropped from 1982 to 2008 but most precipitously in the 16-20 age group. Greater emphasis on this point would be achieved if this were the only group displayed with a black data line.
Source: U.S. Department of Transportation, National Highway Traffic Safety Administration. Traffic Safety Facts 2008. DOT HS 811 170. Washington, DC: GPO, 2010. p. 37.

- Position all the labels on the horizontal so that the viewer doesn't have to rotate the page or screen to read the labels.
- Connect each level of the organization to the higher and lower levels with a clear line (never arrows).
- Connect optional, informal, or temporary relationships with a dotted line.

See Figure 6-11 for an example of an organization chart.

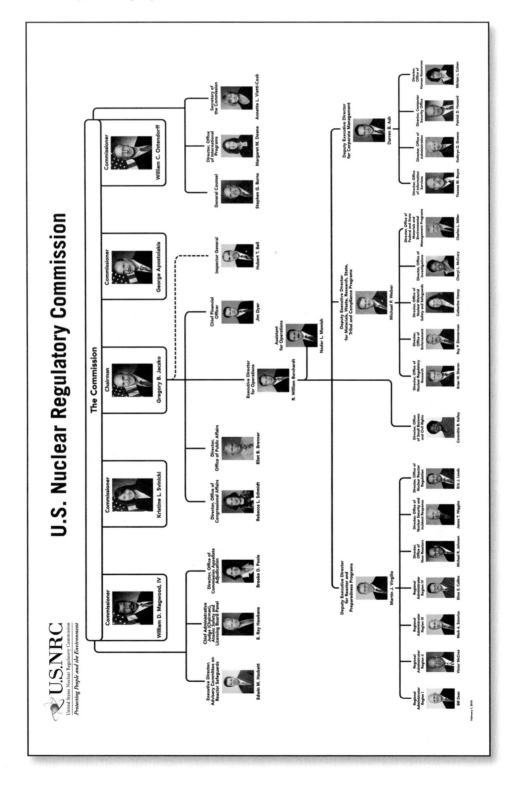

FIGURE 6-11 Organization Chart (see facing page) This organization chart effectively depicts the multiple levels of authority at the U.S. Nuclear Regulatory Commission: for example, Regional Administrators report to a Deputy Executive Director who reports to the Executive Director who reports to the Chair of the Commission. Notice also that certain officials in the organization report to the Chair, while others report to the entire Commission. Photographs of the individuals in each position, diminishing in size according to their level in the hierarchy, bring a sense of humanity to the organization.

Source: U.S. Nuclear Regulatory Commission. NRC Organization Chart. http://www.nrc.gov/about-nrc/organization/nrcorg.pdf.

Flow charts.

- Note that the purpose of a flow chart is to show the sequence of steps in a process or procedure.
- Make the flow chart as simple as the process itself. If a process is simple, design the flow chart so that it progresses in a single direction, usually top to bottom or left to right. Complicated designs that spiral and zigzag imply a more complicated process.
- Use the same shape in the same size for all equivalent steps or phases, but different shapes for steps or phases of a different kind (e.g., circles for the stages in researching a document, squares for the stages of writing, and diamonds for the production stages of printing and binding).
- Label each of the steps or phases.
- If space allows, put the labels directly on the step; if not, attach the label to the step with thin rules (never arrows).
- Position all the labels on the horizontal so that the viewer doesn't have to rotate the page or screen to read the labels.
- Connect each step or phase in the sequence to the next step or phase with a clear directional arrow.
- Connect reversible or interactive steps or phases with double-headed arrows.
- Connect recursive or cyclical steps or phases with circular arrows.
- Connect optional steps or phases with dotted-line arrows.

See Figures 6-12 and 6-13 for examples of flow charts.

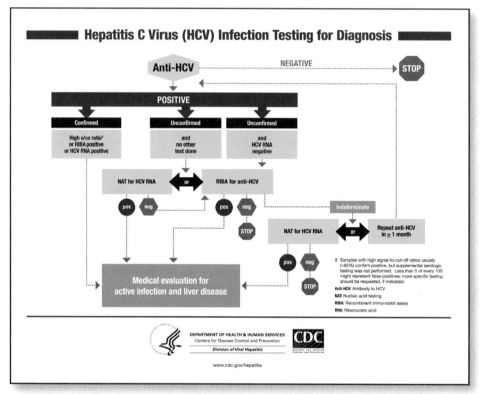

FIGURE 6-12 Flow Chart This flow chart uses a confusing array of shapes and sizes (rectangles, circles, octagons, and hexagons) but at least uses color consistently: for example, orange always indicates a test regardless of shape or size, purple is always a positive test result regardless of shape, and red is always a stop sign regardless of its size. Each stage of the process is also given a legible label. The figure has a fairly straightforward top-to-bottom direction, but the dotted-line arrows might cause confusion by implying that the actions taken after testing are entirely optional.

Source: U.S. Centers for Disease Control and Prevention. Hepatitis C Information for Health Professionals: Laboratory Testing. HCV Infection Testing for Diagnosis Flow Chart, 2008. http://www.cdc.gov/hepatitis/HCV/PDFs/hcv_flow.pdf.

FIGURE 6-13 Flow Chart (see facing page) This flow chart uses simple boxes and arrows in a clear top-to-bottom direction to make a complicated decision process look as easy as possible. Uppercase letters are appropriately used to highlight the critical decisions of YES, NO, STOP, and CONTINUE. The text inside the boxes might be easier to read if it were left-aligned instead of centered.

Source: U.S. Department of Labor, Occupational Safety and Health Administration. Permit-Required Confined Spaces. OSHA 3138-01R. Washington, DC: GPO, 2004. p. 5.

Permit-Required Confined Space Decision Flow Chart

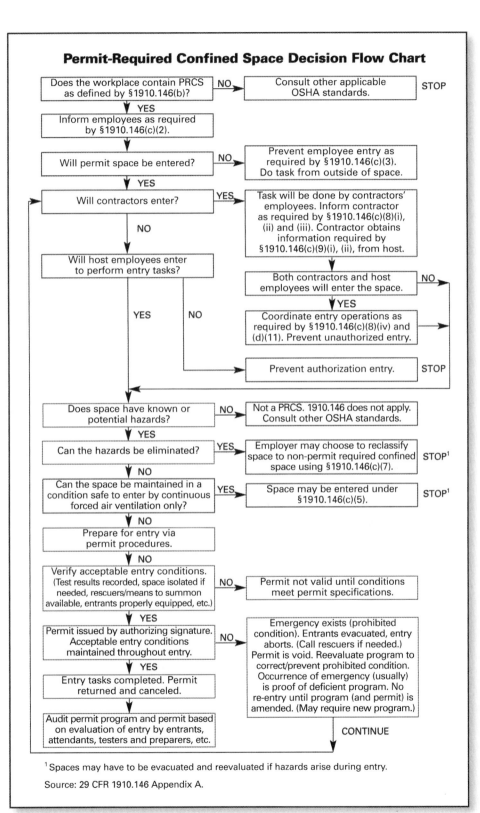

Does the workplace contain PRCS as defined by §1910.146(b)? —**NO**→ Consult other applicable OSHA standards. **STOP**

↓ **YES**

Inform employees as required by §1910.146(c)(2).

↓

Will permit space be entered? —**NO**→ Prevent employee entry as required by §1910.146(c)(3). Do task from outside of space.

↓ **YES**

Will contractors enter? —**YES**→ Task will be done by contractors' employees. Inform contractor as required by §1910.146(c)(8)(i), (ii) and (iii). Contractor obtains information required by §1910.146(c)(9)(i), (ii), from host.

↓ **NO**

↓ Both contractors and host employees will enter the space. —**NO**→

↓ **YES**

Will host employees enter to perform entry tasks? Coordinate entry operations as required by §1910.146(c)(8)(iv) and (d)(11). Prevent unauthorized entry. →

YES / **NO** Prevent authorization entry. **STOP**

↓

Does space have known or potential hazards? —**NO**→ Not a PRCS. 1910.146 does not apply. Consult other OSHA standards.

↓ **YES**

Can the hazards be eliminated? —**YES**→ Employer may choose to reclassify space to non-permit required confined space using §1910.146(c)(7). **STOP[1]**

↓ **NO**

Can the space be maintained in a condition safe to enter by continuous forced air ventilation only? —**YES**→ Space may be entered under §1910.146(c)(5). **STOP[1]**

↓ **NO**

Prepare for entry via permit procedures.

↓ **NO**

Verify acceptable entry conditions. (Test results recorded, space isolated if needed, rescuers/means to summon available, entrants properly equipped, etc.) —**NO**→ Permit not valid until conditions meet permit specifications.

↓ **YES**

Permit issued by authorizing signature. Acceptable entry conditions maintained throughout entry. —**NO**→ Emergency exists (prohibited condition). Entrants evacuated, entry aborts. (Call rescuers if needed.) Permit is void. Reevaluate program to correct/prevent prohibited condition. Occurrence of emergency (usually) is proof of deficient program. No re-entry until program (and permit) is amended. (May require new program.)

↓ **YES**

Entry tasks completed. Permit returned and canceled.

↓

Audit permit program and permit based on evaluation of entry by entrants, attendants, testers and preparers, etc.

CONTINUE

---

[1] Spaces may have to be evacuated and reevaluated if hazards arise during entry.

Source: 29 CFR 1910.146 Appendix A.

Diagrams.

- Note that the purpose of a diagram is to identify the parts of a subject and their spatial or functional relationship.
- Keep the diagram as simple as possible, avoiding unnecessary details or distracting decorations and focusing the viewer's attention on the key features or parts of the subject.
- Label each of the pertinent parts of the subject.
- If space allows, put each label directly on its corresponding part or adjacent to it; if not, connect the label to the part with a thin rule or arrow.
- Position all the labels on the horizontal so that the viewer doesn't have to rotate the page or screen to read the labels.

See Figure 6-14 for an example of a diagram.

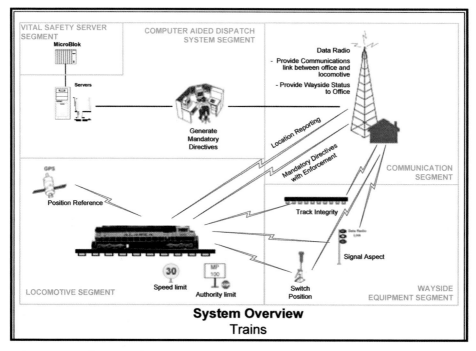

FIGURE 6-14 Diagram This diagram of a collision avoidance system is designed to explain to the public how the safe operation of trains is achieved. Notice the clear labeling and categorization of all key components. The diagram obviously simplifies the relationships among a complicated series of interacting technologies but suits the audience and purpose. The use of color here, however, is usually arbitrary and unnecessary. Viewers might initially perceive the jagged yellow lines as lightning bolts or electricity instead of radio transmissions: double-headed arrows or a note to the figure would avoid this possible confusion.

Source: U.S. Department of Transportation, Federal Railroad Administration. Alaska Railroad Collision Avoidance System (CAS) Project. Research Results RR 09-16. Washington, DC: 2009. p. 2.

Photographs.

- Note that the purpose of a photograph is to show what a subject looks like in realistic detail.
- Keep the photograph as simple as possible, focusing the viewer's attention on the key features or parts of the subject.
- Exercise caution in editing or polishing the photograph. Never insert or delete images. Viewers typically expect a photograph to be a representation of reality, and ethical communicators strive to meet that expectation. Cropping a photograph in order to close in on a subject and eliminate distractions in the background is a standard practice, but never insert or delete objects or change the size or color of objects in a photograph.
- If appropriate or necessary for the viewer's understanding, apply labels for each of the pertinent parts of the subject to direct the viewer's attention.
- If space allows, put each label directly on its corresponding part or adjacent to it; if not, connect the label to the part with a thin rule or arrow.
- Position all the labels on the horizontal so that the viewer doesn't have to rotate the page or screen to read the labels.

See Figures 6-15 and 6-16 for examples of photographs.

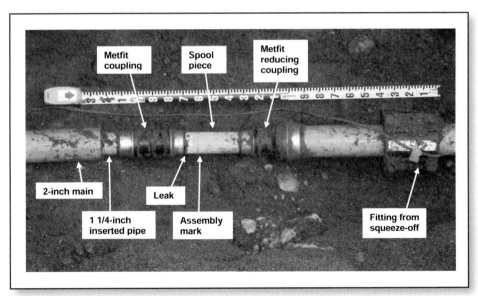

FIGURE 6-15 Photograph This photograph carries clear labels to identify each of the pertinent pieces of pipeline at the site of a fatal accident, with a tape measure inserted to assist with determining relative sizes. The "Leak" label might be better emphasized in all uppercase letters or in a different color as this ought to be the focal point of the photograph that viewers notice immediately.

Source: National Transportation Safety Board. Pipeline Accident Brief: Explosion, Release, and Ignition of Natural Gas, Rancho Cordova, California, December 24, 2008. NTSB/PAB-10/01. Washington, DC: 2010. p. 8.

FIGURE 6-16 Ineffective Photograph This photograph makes viewers look at a lot of distracting detail instead of focusing their attention on essential information. The damaged train is nicely centered in the photograph but on the left and right are transit officials in brightly colored safety vests. Several extraneous items also litter the adjacent platform. The viewer's attention could easily be directed to the specific damage to the train by cropping the photograph and inserting pertinent labels.
Source: National Transportation Safety Board. Collision of Two Municipal Transportation Agency Light Rail Vehicles, San Francisco, California, July 18, 2009. Railroad Accident Brief NTSB/RAB-11/04. Washington, DC: 2011. p. 3.

Animation Clips.

- Note that the purpose of animation is to simulate a process, operation, or incident.
- Keep the animation as simple and straightforward as possible, avoiding unnecessary details or distracting decorations and focusing the viewer's attention on the key actors, equipment, and steps or stages in the process, operation, or incident.
- If appropriate or necessary for the viewer's understanding, insert titles and captions that direct the viewer's attention to pertinent information.

See Figure 6-17 for a screen shot of a sample animation clip.

FIGURE 6-17 Animation This animation video simulates the events leading to the explosion and fire at a chemical facility that killed two operators. The opening 30 seconds are film of the facility's location. This changes to animation of liquids pumping through pipes to a vessel, of operators at computer displays, of the inside of the vessel with liquid boiling and pressure rising, of two operators going to relieve the pressure inside the vessel, and of the explosion and fire itself. The closing 15 seconds are film of the fire and a racing ambulance. The opening and closing sections of film serve to reinforce the reality of the accident, while using animation in the middle section gives viewers a coherent and vivid experience of the accident that is obviously unavailable on film and superior to static images.

Source: U.S. Chemical Safety and Hazard Investigation Board. Animation of Bayer CropScience Pesticide Waste Tank Explosion. Investigation Video. 2011. http://www.csb.gov/videoroom/detail.aspx?VID=48

Film Clips.

- Note that the purpose of a film clip is to depict a process, operation, or incident in realistic detail.
- Keep the film as simple and straightforward as possible, focusing the viewer's attention on the key actors, equipment, and steps or stages in the process, operation, or incident.
- Exercise caution in editing or polishing the film. Viewers typically expect a film clip to be a representation of reality, and ethical communicators strive to meet that expectation. Editing a film for extraneous material is a standard practice, but never change the speed or sequence of the process, operation, or incident (unless the change is altogether obvious) and always make sure that your editing creates no distortions or misrepresentations. In addition,

treat each frame of the film as you would a photograph: never insert or delete objects or actors and never alter the size or color of the items in a frame.

• If appropriate or necessary for the viewer's understanding, insert titles and captions that direct the viewer's attention to pertinent information.

See Figure 6-18 for a screen shot of a sample film clip.

FIGURE 6-18 **Video** This video demonstrates testing of metal dust for combustibility (hypothesized to be the cause of three fires at the same industrial facility in a five-month period). Title cards announce that the video will display the testing in real time and again in slow motion. Using film is essential here to verify the validity of the testing process.

Source: U.S. Chemical Safety and Hazard Investigation Board. U.S. Chemical Safety Board Iron Dust Testing May 26, 2011. Investigation Video. 2011. http://www.csb.gov/videoroom/detail.aspx?vid=52

DESIGNING ILLUSTRATIONS ETHICALLY

Displaying information ethically requires that you make careful choices about the design of your illustrations.

For example, the scale of the x and y axes on a line graph has a significant impact on the data display. In designing a graph, you ordinarily start the x and y axes at 0. Exceptions are possible if beginning at some other point ("suppressing the zero") will not distort information. If several graphs are positioned side by side on a page, thus inviting comparison and contrast of the data, it would be unethical to use differing vertical scales because readers would likely come to incorrect conclusions.

Using distorted graphs, however, isn't the only error that will result in the creation of unethical illustrations. It is unethical to create a drawing that puts features on a product it doesn't really have. It is unethical to design a flowchart that disguises the complexity of a process by making it look relatively simple. It is unethical to stage or doctor a photograph to create a positive or negative impression of your subject that isn't fully justified. It is unethical to edit a film so that a five-minute operation seems to take only four minutes. It is unethical to incorporate illustrations that might be easily misinterpreted (e.g., Figure 6-19).

In addition, if you illustrate information regarding people, you must strive to be sensitive to their humanity. A thoughtless or insensitive illustration could be widely and quickly circulated on the Internet, jeopardizing your organization's reputation for caring about people, especially the people in the communities in which it operates. For example, if you choose a conventional bar graph to depict the human beings killed in mining explosions, you make simple objects of real people with surviving families and friends. In mapping the damage from a tornado, if you ignore the locations of the people who were killed and focus only on demolished buildings, you both diminish the loss of life and give a distorted picture of the disaster. Always consider ways that you might bring a sense of humanity (and thus greater accuracy) to your illustrations. Notice, for example, how the human dimension of a tragic highway accident is made evident in Figure 6-20 by the inclusion of brief demographic details.

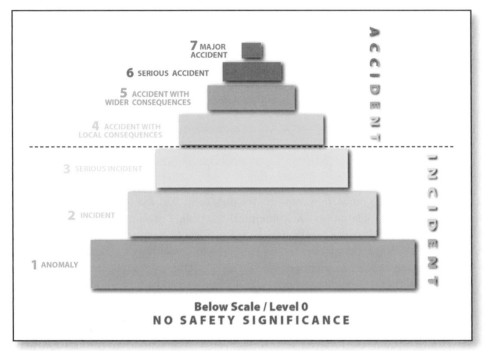

FIGURE 6-19 **Deceptive Illustration** This illustration is designed to depict the scale of severity of nuclear and radiological incidents and accidents, but the shrinking size of the bars implies diminishing severity in spite of the adjacent wording. In addition, viewers might interpret the shrinking size of the bars as indicative of the relative frequency of accidents and incidents: that is, viewers might assume—erroneously— that serious accidents occur more often than major accidents.

Source: International Atomic Energy Agency. The International Nuclear and Radiological Event Scale. 2008. http://www.iaea.org/Publications/Factsheets/English/ines.pdf

Table 2. Passenger vehicle occupant information.

Vehicle	Occupant	Seating Position	Restraint	Injury
2008 Volvo Truck	76-year-old male	Driver	Lap/shoulder (not used)	Serious
2003 Land Rover	49-year-old male	Driver	Lap/shoulder (not used)	Fatal
	51-year-old female	Front right	Lap/shoulder (not used)	Fatal
	12-year-old female	Rear right	Lap/shoulder	Serious
2003 Hyundai Sonata	38-year-old male	Driver	Lap/shoulder	Fatal
	34-year-old female	Front right	Lap/shoulder	Fatal
	06-year-old male	Rear left	Lap/shoulder with booster seat	Fatal
	55-year-old female	Rear right	Lap/shoulder	Fatal
2004 Kia Spectra	52-year-old female	Driver	Lap/shoulder (not used)	Serious
	05-year-old female	Rear left	Lap/shoulder with booster seat	Minor
	06-year-old male	Rear right	Lap/shoulder with booster seat	Minor
2000 Ford Windstar	79-year-old male	Driver	Lap/shoulder	Fatal
	73-year-old female	Front right	Lap/shoulder	Fatal
	71-year-old female	Rear left	Lap/shoulder	Fatal
	52-year-old male	Rear right	Lap/shoulder	Fatal
2004 Ford F350	41-year-old male	Driver	Lap/shoulder	None
	12-year-old female	Front right	Lap/shoulder	None
2008 Chevrolet Tahoe	69-year-old male	Driver	Lap/shoulder	None
	62-year-old female	Front right	Lap/shoulder	Serious
	12-year-old female	Rear left	Lap/shoulder	None
	12-year-old female	Rear right	Lap/shoulder	None

FIGURE 6-20 Table of Injuries and Fatalities Sensitive to Victims This table of information about victims of a highway accident is sensitive to the humanity of the victims. Implicit in the demographic details are the relationships among the passengers in each vehicle. The truly tragic consequences of this accident are obvious and undisguised.

Source: National Transportation Safety Board. Truck-Tractor Semitrailer Rear-End Collision Into Passenger Vehicles on Interstate 44, Near Miami, Oklahoma, June 26, 2009. Highway Accident Report NTSB/HAR-10/02. Washington, DC: 2010. p. 9.

ILLUSTRATION CHECKLIST ✔

Planning

☐ What kinds of illustrations is your audience familiar with?

☐ Do you have information that could be more easily or quickly communicated to your audience visually or in a combination of words and graphics?

☐ Do you have definitions that could be displayed visually in whole or in part?

☐ Do you have any processes or procedures that could be depicted in a flowchart?

☐ Do you have information on trends or relationships that could be displayed in tables and graphs?

☐ Do you have masses of statistics that could be summarized in tables?

☐ Do you need to depict objects? If so, what do you need to display about the objects? Do you need to focus attention on specific aspects of the objects with diagrams? Do you require the realistic detail of photographs?

☐ Do you need to depict incidents or operations? If so, what do you need to display? Do you need to focus attention on specific aspects through animation? Do you require the realistic detail of film?

☐ What are the design conventions of your illustrations?

☐ Are there suitable illustrations you could borrow or adapt? Or will you need to create them yourself?

Revising

☐ Are your illustrations suited to your purpose and audience?

☐ Do your illustrations communicate information ethically?

☐ Are your illustrations effectively located and easy to find?

☐ Are your illustrations numbered and labeled?

☐ Do your verbal and visual elements reinforce each other?

☐ Are your illustrations genuinely informative instead of simply decorative?

☐ When necessary, have you helped your readers to interpret your illustrations with commentary or annotations?

☐ Have you acknowledged the sources for borrowed or adapted tables and figures?

EXERCISES

1. Examine the illustrations used in five journals and magazines in your major field of study. Which types of illustration do you ordinarily find? Which types don't you find? Which occur most often? Which occur least often? What are the

conventions for tables and figures in your field? Summarize your findings in a brief oral presentation with slides that display representative illustrations.

2. Aeschylus Corporation, which designs games for mobile devices, is looking for new employees, especially individuals able to conceive and design state-of-the-art products. It has been a small private corporation for five years and hopes to achieve a major expansion. The president of Aeschylus, Robin Pierce, has asked you to develop recruiting materials for prospective new employees. You've compiled the following information that you believe will be pertinent:

History	Founded in 2007, in Kansas City, Missouri, by Robin Pierce, B.S. in Computer Science, 2004, University of St. Louis; MBA, 2006, Missouri University
Sales	2007: $200,000; 2008: $750,000; 2009: $2 million; 2010: $7 million; 2011: $16 million
Employees	With specialists in design (3), graphics and animation (4), programming (5), video editing (3), production (2), quality assurance (1), documentation (1), sound (1), and music (1)
Products	6 current products, looking to diversify, especially in action–adventure, newest product: Street Maniac (driving game); biggest seller: Trojan War (fantasy role-playing)
Facilities	State-of-the-art equipment, serves both Android and iOS systems
Location	1224 Howard Avenue, Kansas City: new environment friendly building, spacious offices
Salary/benefits	Competitive with industry; excellent medical coverage, 4 weeks vacation each year, 2 weeks paid community-volunteer time each year

Design recruiting materials for Aeschylus Corporation that incorporate as wide a variety of illustrations as possible.

3. In designing your recruiting materials for Aeschylus Corporation, you are surprised by a dilemma. Robin Pierce is willing to hire people with disabilities and would like you to include that information. At this time, Aeschylus has no employees with disabilities, but Jacqueline Brown, a programmer, injured her back in a skiing accident and is temporarily restricted to a wheelchair. Pierce proposes including a photograph of various Aeschylus employees (including Brown in the wheelchair) to indicate to prospective employees that people with disabilities would find a supportive environment at Aeschylus. You mention the idea to staff photographer Kishor Mitra, but he objects, claiming such a picture would be deceptive. As project leader, you have to decide who is right and compose one of two e-mail messages: either to convince Pierce that such a photograph would be unethical or to direct Mitra to take the photograph in spite of his objections. How do you proceed?

4. Examine Figure 6-21. If you were the creator of this document and were given 15 more minutes to make it more effective, what changes would you make?

Workplace shootings

Mass shootings receive a great deal of coverage in the media, as we saw with the Orlando, Fla., office shootings in November 2009 and in the shootings at the manufacturing plant in Albuquerque, N.M., in July 2010. Out of 421 workplace shootings recorded in 2008 (8 percent of total fatal injuries), 99 (24 percent) occurred in retail trade. Workplace shootings in manufacturing were less common, with 17 shootings reported in 2008. Workplace shooting events account for only a small portion of nonfatal workplace injuries.

Over the past 5 years, 2004-08, an average of 564 work-related homicides occurred each year in the United States. In 2008, a total of 526 workplace homicides occurred, or 10 percent of all fatal work injuries. About 4 out of every 5 homicide victims in 2008 were male. The type of assailants in these cases differed for men and women. Robbers and other assailants made up 72 percent of assailants for men, and 51 percent of assailants for women. Relatives and other personal acquaintances accounted for only 4 percent of assailants of homicides for men, but 28 percent for women.[1]

In 2008 there were 30 multiple-fatality workplace homicide incidents, accounting for 67 homicides and 7 suicides. On average, about two people died in each of these incidents.

Shootings accounted for 80 percent of all homicides in 2008 (421 fatal injuries). Co-workers and former co-workers were the assailants in 12 percent of all shootings. Robbers were the assailants in another 40 percent of cases in 2008. Nearly half of these shootings (48 percent) occurred in public buildings, thereby endangering bystanders.

Sales and related occupations accounted for 26 percent of decedents in shootings. Most shootings occurred in the private sector (86 percent) whereas 14 percent of shootings occurred in government. Of the shootings within the private sector, 88 percent occurred within service-providing industries, mostly in trade, transportation, and utilities.

FIGURE 6-21 Document for Exercise 4

Source: U.S. Department of Labor, Bureau of Labor Statistics. Fact Sheet: Workplace Shootings. 2010. http://www.bls.gov/iif/oshwc/cfoi/osar0014.pdf

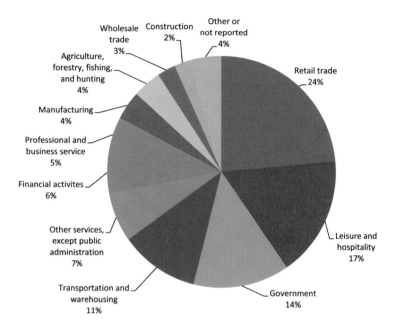

Fatal workplace shootings by industry, 2008

Total fatal injuries = 421

Wholesale trade 3%

Construction 2%

Other or not reported 4%

Agriculture, forestry, fishing, and hunting 4%

Manufacturing 4%

Professional and business service 5%

Financial activites 6%

Other services, except public administration 7%

Transportation and warehousing 11%

Retail trade 24%

Leisure and hospitality 17%

Government 14%

Source: U.S. Bureau of Labor Statistics

[1] For more detailed information on workplace homicides with assailants and circumstance from 1997-2008, see http://www.bls.gov/iif/oshwc/cfoi/work_hom.pdf

Note: Data are revised and final.

Source: Bureau of Labor Statistics (BLS), Census of Fatal Occupational Injuries, July 2010.

FIGURE 6-21 *continued*

PART TWO

Applications

E-mails, Texts, Memos, and Letters

E-mails, text messages, memos, and letters are among the most frequently written business documents. Because people receive so much correspondence, some items may be overlooked or ignored.

Quick Tips

- Prepare readers for the key information in your message by using a clearly worded subject line or opening sentence.
- Put the most important information in the opening paragraph.
- Use formatting techniques to help readers proceed rapidly through your message. The format should help readers recognize the organization and major points of the message.
- Always be concise. Keep sentences and paragraphs short. Readers should not have to read your message more than once to grasp your meaning.
- Try to keep your message to one page or screen.
- If your message is more than one page or screen, use headings to guide your reader through it.

E-MAIL AND TEXT MESSAGES

E-mail and text messages are undoubtedly the most common form of workplace communication. Text messages are by definition brief and thus ideal for urgent notifications and quick acknowledgments—information that can't wait for e-mail. Appropriate e-mail and texting etiquette is continuously evolving, but both kinds of messages must be concise and readable. Keep in mind that typical mobile devices display the list of incoming e-mail messages with the opening five lines of each message and the list of incoming text messages with the opening two lines. You will assist your recipients in navigating their incoming messages if you make sure that your key point is located in the opening lines. Note, for example, the series of emergency messages prepared by the Centers for Disease Control and Prevention (see Figure 7-1). Each is a maximum of 115 characters (including spaces) and puts the essential information right at the beginning.

Memos and Letters

Memos are short, internal communication documents used within organizations. Memos can be posted to a website (including bulletin boards, blogs, and wikis), sent as attachments to e-mail messages, or printed and distributed.

Letters differ from memos in that letters are usually written to individuals outside the writer's organization, but they can be used as official documents within an organization. Like memos, letters can be sent as e-mail attachments. Memos serve as intraorganizational communications only and are not accepted channels for official business with other companies and clients.

Both memos and letters must be worded and formatted for quick skimming and rapid reading. Consider the letters in Figures 7-2 and 7-3. Which would you be more likely to read? Why?

Guidelines for Ensuring Quality

- Watch how you sound when you choose words and put together sentences. Review and proofread messages carefully before you send them. Note especially that any electronic message you send will exist indefinitely and could easily be forwarded to additional readers across the world or obtained by unexpected audiences for years to come.
- Keep the six Cs in mind as you develop e-mails, texts, memos, and letters: be **concise, concrete, complete, correct, courteous,** and **clear**. Be attentive to how what you say can be perceived by your reader. Rephrase anything that you think might be construed in ways you do not intend.
- Be aware of how your message looks. A letter or memo with typographical or formatting errors makes an unfavorable statement about you and your organization. Design e-mail messages with equal care because these may be printed and copies made and distributed.
- Watch for spelling errors as well as errors in sentence structure and word usage. For especially important e-mail messages, consider printing copies before you send them. Editing printed material often reveals errors you may miss as you compose or proofread on your computer screen. Also use the spellcheck tool available on your e-mail application to help you find errors, but keep in mind that spellcheck is no substitute for careful reading.

Text Messages for Mobile Devices

Staying Safe After the Storm

Staying Safe Around Buildings Damaged After a Disaster
Don't enter damaged buildings until inspectors say it's safe. More info from CDC 800-232-4636 http://go.usa.gov/bff.

Leave damaged buildings immediately if you hear unusual noises. More info from CDC 800-232-4636 http://go.usa.gov/bff.

Keeping Children Safe From Drowning in Flooded Areas
Prevent child drownings. Keep kids from playing in or around flood water. More info from CDC 800-232-4636 or http://go.usa.gov/bGa.

Avoiding Carbon Monoxide Poisoning During a Power Outage
Don't use generators/grills in or next to home. Fumes can kill. More info from CDC 800-232-4636 or http://go.usa.gov/bfv.

Don't heat home with gas oven. Keep generators/grills outside. Fumes can kill. More info from CDC 800-232-4636 or http://go.usa.gov/bfv.

Keep generators 25 ft outside door/window. Don't grill inside. Fumes can kill. More info from CDC 800-232-4636 http://go.usa.gov/bfv.

Proper Use of Candles During a Power Outage
If you must use candles, use safe holders far from burnable things. More info from CDC 800-232-4636 or http://go.usa.gov/bfV.

Driving Through Water After a Disaster
Don't drive through floodwater, it can be deeper than you think. More info from CDC 800-232-4636 or http://go.usa.gov/bGc.

Prescription Drugs

Drugs Exposed to Water
Check all drugs. Discard any that may have been contaminated by unsafe water. More info from CDC 800-232-4636 or http://go.usa.gov/jvZ.

You can use lifesaving drugs stored clean and safe if they look normal and dry. Call 1-800-232-4636 http://go.usa.gov/jvZ.

Drug and Supplement Lists
To help care providers, keep a list of drugs and dietary supplements with you. More info from CDC 800-232-4636 or http://go.usa.gov/jvZ.

Lifesaving Drugs
Replace all lifesaving drugs that may have been damaged, as soon as possible. Call 1-800-232-4636 http://go.usa.gov/jvZ.

Cleanup

Preventing Mold After a Disaster
Never mix bleach and ammonia to clean; the fumes can kill. More info from CDC 800-232-4636 or http://go.usa.gov/bws.

See/smell mold? Clean with 1 cup household bleach per 1 gal. water. More info from CDC 800-232-4636 http://go.usa.gov/bfy.

FIGURE 7-1 Text Messages for Public Emergencies

Source: Centers for Disease Control and Prevention. 2011. http://origin.bt.cdc.gov/disasters/psa/textmessages.asp

DEPARTMENT OF HEALTH & HUMAN SERVICES   Public Health Service

_____

                                                          Centers for Disease Control
                                                          and Prevention

                                                          December 16, 2010

Dear Colleague:

We are pleased to announce publication of *Sexually Transmitted Diseases Treatment Guidelines—2010*," in the
Centers for Disease Control and Prevention's (CDC) December 17, 2010 issue of *Morbidity and Mortality Weekly
Report (MMWR) Recommendations and Reports.* These guidelines for the treatment of patients who have sexually
transmitted diseases (STDs) were developed by CDC after consultation with a group of professionals
knowledgeable in the field of STDs who met in Atlanta, Georgia from April 18–30, 2009.

The *Guidelines* are based on newly available evidence and include

- Expanded STD prevention recommendations, including HPV vaccination;
- Revised gonorrhea treatment regimens;
- New treatment regimens for genital warts and bacterial vaginosis;
- The role of *Mycoplasma genitalium* and trichomoniasis in the evaluation of urethritis and cervicitis and
  treatment-related implications; and
- Revised guidance on the diagnostic evaluation and management of syphilis.

Over 19 million cases of STDs occur in the United States each year, with a disproportionate share among young
people and racial and ethnic minority populations. The estimated annual direct medical costs of treating STDs and
their sequelae are $16.4 billion. Left untreated, STDs can cause serious health problems ranging from infertility to
increased risk of HIV infection. The 2010 *Guidelines*, which update the 2006 *Guidelines*, serve as a source of
clinical guidance and advise health care providers on the most effective treatment regimens, screening procedures,
and prevention and vaccination strategies for STDs. CDC revises the *Guidelines* periodically, approximately every
three to four years, using a scientific, evidence-based process that includes CDC and external expert review of
current scientific literature.

To obtain a copy of the *Guidelines*, please go to our website at www.cdc.gov/std/treatment/2010/ or contact CDC-
INFO at 800-CDC-INFO (800-232-4636), 24 hours/day, or e-mail cdcinfo@cdc.gov. You will also be able to order
wall charts and pocket guides on our website or by contacting CDC-INFO. A podcast featuring lead author, Dr.
Kimberly Workowski, will be posted on www.cdc.gov/std/treatment/2010/ on December 20th for viewing. CDC is
also developing iPhone and eBook applications of the *Guidelines*. We encourage you to visit our website for
additional information and updates on all of these products.

Sincerely,

/Charlotte Kent/   /Kevin A. Fenton/
Charlotte Kent, Ph.D.   Kevin A. Fenton, M.D., Ph.D., F.F.P.H.
Director (Acting)   Director
Division of STD Prevention   National Center for HIV/AIDS, Viral Hepatitis,
                                                 STD, and TB Prevention

FIGURE 7-2 Letter

DEPARTMENT OF HEALTH & HUMAN SERVICES   Public Health Service

                                                      Centers for Disease Control
                                                      and Prevention

December 16, 2010

Dear Colleague:

We are pleased to announce publication of **"Sexually Transmitted Diseases Treatment Guidelines—2010,"** in the Centers for Disease Control and Prevention's (CDC) December 17, 2010 issue of *Morbidity and Mortality Weekly Report (MMWR) Recommendations and Reports*.

What's new
The 2010 Guidelines are based on newly available evidence and include
- Expanded STD prevention recommendations, including HPV vaccination
- Revised gonorrhea treatment regimens
- New treatment regimens for genital warts and bacterial vaginosis
- Discussion of Mycoplasma genitalium and trichomoniasis in the evaluation of urethritis and cervicitis and treatment-related implications
- Revised guidance on the diagnostic evaluation and management of syphilis

How to order
To obtain a copy of the 2010 Guidelines, you may
- go to our website at www.cdc.gov/std/treatment/2010/
- call CDC- INFO at 800-CDC-INFO (800-232-4636), 24 hours/day
- e-mail cdcinfo@cdc.gov

How new guidelines are developed
The 2010 Guidelines for the treatment of patients who have sexually transmitted diseases (STDs) were developed by CDC after consultation with professionals knowledgeable in the field of STDs who met in Atlanta, Georgia from April 18 to 30, 2009. CDC revises the Guidelines every three to four years, using a systematic process that includes review by the CDC and external experts of current scientific literature.

What's next
A podcast featuring lead author, Dr. Kimberly Workowski, will be posted on www.cdc.gov/std/treatment/2010/ on December 20. CDC is also developing iPhone and eBook applications of the 2010 Guidelines. We encourage you to visit our website for additional information and updates.

Sincerely,

/Charlotte Kent/   /Kevin A. Fenton/
Charlotte Kent,   Kevin A. Fenton, M.D., Ph.D., F.F.P.H.
Ph.D. Director (Acting)   Director
Division of STD Prevention   National Center for HIV/AIDS, Viral Hepatitis,
                                          STD, and TB Prevention

FIGURE 7-3 Revised Letter

- For text messages on the job, avoid slang and abbreviations unless you know your recipient personally and always keep your messages on point and professional. Always assume your message might be read by your boss.
- For memos, letters, and e-mail messages, use the following structure:

First Paragraph:	States the purpose of the message or the main information the reader needs. If your message delivers unfavorable news, you may want to cushion the reader's disappointment with a gentle and supportive opening.
Middle Paragraphs:	Provide support for or development of the main topic stated in the first paragraph. Limit each paragraph to one idea.
Final Paragraph:	Tells the reader what to do or what position to take. The final paragraph also provides appropriate ending comments.

APPROPRIATE TONE IN E-MAILS, TEXTS, MEMOS, AND LETTERS

Be careful how you sound. What you write always carries with it a sound, an attitude toward the reader and the subject. As they absorb your message, readers often vocalize your sentences and phrases. Anticipate the tone that your reader will attach to what you say. Use a respectful, positive tone and avoid words and phrases that might sound rude, sarcastic, or irritable. Remember: you want to be clear, but you also want to maintain a favorable relationship with your reader.

Avoid phrases that suggest that the reader is careless or unintelligent:

You neglected to . . .
You failed to . . .
I fail to understand how you could . . .

Also avoid phrases that imply that the reader might be lying or exaggerating:

You claim that . . .

Avoid writing what your reader might interpret as excessive flattery. Many people are sensitive to insincerity and suspicious of any attempt to induce them to respond in a certain way:

It is indeed a profound privilege for us to work with you on this project.

We look forward to the opportunity to submit our full proposal. Your firm is known for its commitment to excellence and value, which we are confident we offer.

Attempting to sound objective, however, can often produce impersonal writing:

The changes agreed upon per our conversation are herein included.

Your immediate reply will be greatly appreciated.

Instead, write with a conversational tone that lets your reader know that you are grateful for his or her attention:

> The changes included here were the ones we discussed during our telephone conversations.

> Please let us know your decision as soon as you can.

Many times, in an effort to be clear, writers may sound tactless:

> If your employees had actually read the procedures before trying to install the pump, they would have seen that the installation requires that the sealant be allowed to set for one hour before beginning the second stage of the process. Not following this procedure causes the diagnostic to shut down because the sealant has not dried enough to absorb the test stress. To avoid future installation problems, please see to it that your employees read the procedures and read them thoroughly.

Thinking about the *emotion* that your writing may convey or provoke will help you to present the same idea in a less caustic way:

> Please note in the procedure manual that the second stage of the installation process cannot begin until the sealant has set for one hour. This amount of time is necessary for the sealant to dry enough to absorb the test stress. If the second stage of the installation process is attempted before the sealant has dried, the diagnostic will shut down.

Examine these additional examples and their revisions:

Regrettably, equipment expense reimbursements are not allowed.

Versus

My office can reimburse you for travel related expenses only. Your invoice for equipment may be submitted to the VP of Operations.

We cannot fulfill your request for a list of company positions and annual salaries, as none but company executives are allowed to have access to this information.

Versus

The list of positions and salaries you requested is confidential information limited to use by our company personnel only. For your research, however, we can send you related information on industry-wide trends in similar positions.

GUIDELINES FOR DEALING WITH TONE

As a writer, you cannot anticipate every nuance of meaning that your message will have for your reader. But you can be clear and maintain goodwill with your reader if you keep the following guidelines in mind as you compose any letter, memo, text, or e-mail:

- Allow more time for designing messages that arise from sensitive issues and that may be subject to misreading. Try to avoid sending bad news by text or e-mail.

• Anticipate the effects of messages that will convey negative or unwelcome news. These can be misinterpreted by readers, who can also misjudge your attitude toward them and the information you are transmitting. People often take bad news personally and may be more inclined to take offense or respond with anger.
• Always analyze your reader as carefully as possible, particularly the reader's frame of reference and attitude toward both you and the subject. Always be courteous.
• Read aloud what you have written. When you hear what you have written, you may often detect words and phrases that don't convey the attitude you intend.
• For any especially difficult message, compose the message, save the draft, and then let it cool for a while. Later, read the message aloud to check for clarity and courtesy.

PLANNING AND WRITING CORRESPONDENCE

The following cases (7-1 through 7-5) introduce typical situations on the job in which writers must write a letter, memo, or e-mail message.

Review of Principles

As you plan your e-mails, texts, memos, and letters . . .

10 Questions to Ask Yourself

1. How well do I know the readers?
2. How much do they know about the topic discussed in the message?
3. How will they respond to what I will need to say? In what ways can I use this communication to build rapport for my organization?
4. What exactly am I trying to accomplish with this message?
5. What is their level of knowledge about the subjects discussed?
6. What is their attitude toward me and my organization?
7. What previous business dealings have I/we had with them?
8. How much and what kind of information should I include, based on their profile?
9. How technical can I be in presenting my message?
10. What strategies can I use to make this message easy to read and understand?

Case 7-1: Informational E-mail Message

David McMillan, an administrative assistant to HCI's chief financial officer, must notify 14 division managers of a meeting to deal with looming budget cuts. David decides to attach three documents that those attending will need to have read by the meeting. The e-mail message explains the reason for the meeting, the documents attached, and the proposed agenda. As David explains, everyone should bring the attached documents to the meeting.

This e-mail message exemplifies effective design (Case Document 7-1). Note the clearly phrased subject line, the action-required statement in bold type, and the placement of the main information—the meeting and required attendance—in the opening sentence. The meeting agenda appears as a list, and the managers are told exactly what they must do with the attached materials. The message is concise, and all information is visually accessible.

CASE DOCUMENT 7-1

From: David McMillan [david.mcmillan@hci.com]
Date: February 27, 2012
To: Operations Support Staff
Subject: **Agenda for March 12 Meeting on Proposed Budget Cuts**

Attachments: CFO 1-31.pdf, NSP bid.pdf, OSHA oxygn proc rev.pdf, SHR mntnc cost.pdf

ACTION REQUIRED: Prepare New Cost Figures for Your Projects by March 12

All division managers are required to attend a March 12 meeting to decide how to cut the third and fourth quarter budgets. Please refer to the CFO's memo of January 31 (see attached) for guidelines on cuts.

You will receive a separate e-mail message later today asking you to put this mandatory meeting on your calendar. Please clear your calendar now of any conflicting appointments.

Time and Location: March 12, 8:00-11:00 A.M., Third Floor Conference Room

Please have four copies of your budget prepared with the 15% cut suggested by the CFO's 1/31 memo.

continued

Meeting Agenda
1. Budget presentations and discussion
2. Proposed bid development on the North Shore Power project (see attached)
3. Revision of Procedures to Meet OSHA guidelines on oxygen tanks (see attached)
4. Cost overrun problem with maintenance contractors on the Signal Hill Reclamation project (see attached)

Please review all attached documents and be prepared to discuss viable solutions.

If you have problems or questions, please let me know.

DM

David McMillan
Administrative Assistant
Office of the CFO
HCI, Inc.
889-742-2500

Case 7-2: Instructional Memo

The following memo (Case Document 7-2) announces Quaker Pharmaceutical's new agreement with a local rental car dealership and provides instructions for renting cars for business use. The writer, Maria Ramirez, suggests that readers may want to keep the memo for reference.

CASE DOCUMENT 7-2

MEMORANDUM

TO: Quaker Pharmaceutical sales representatives
FROM: Maria Ramirez
SUBJECT: New Benefits From You-Go Rent-A-Car
DATE: 10/17/11

Quaker Pharmaceutical signed an agreement today with You-Go Rent-A-Car offering a 20% discount for all business-related travel. Please retain this memo for your files.

Business Vehicle Guidelines
- 1 or 2 employees traveling: use compact car; 3 or more employees traveling: use sedan or mini van.
- Luxurious vehicles for transporting clients or potential clients must be approved by your supervisor.
- Please lease the most economical vehicle available.

Regulations
- Employees are expected to follow all traffic laws.
- Employees under 25 cannot drive unless accompanied by fellow employee over 25.
- Vehicle cannot be used to transport persons or property for hire.
- Vehicle cannot be used to tow anything.
- You-Go and **Quaker Pharmaceutical** are not responsible for loss or theft of personal belongings left unattended in the vehicle.

continued

Reservations

To reserve your car for business travel, go online at www.you-go.com or call 1-800-RENTCAR.

- Valid Driver's License needed for reservation
- No deposit required

Online Instructions:

1. Go to http://www.you-go.com
2. Locate login box for Gold Corporate Customers (GCC)
3. Enter Username: QPrental (case sensitive)
4. Enter Password: your last name (all lower case)
5. Follow remaining steps as prompted

*For questions, contact Susan Jones, the Office Services Manager, at 898-757-3478 by call or text.

Case 7-3: Letter Requesting Information

Alicia Forsythe serves as local arrangements chairperson for ASEE's regional meeting. One of her first responsibilities is to locate a hotel in which the regional meeting can be held. She decides to send a letter to seven hotels near the sports arena so that conferees can enjoy sports events during the evenings of the three-day conference. Alicia writes the same letter to all seven hotels requesting information about their facilities.

When Alicia writes to each of the seven hotels, she has a number of questions she needs to be answered: if the hotel can host a convention of 500 people on the dates specified; if the hotel has the number of meeting rooms necessary and the necessary computer and multimedia equipment. Alicia needs each hotel to respond by a specific deadline, and she wants to be sure that every hotel supplies all of the information she requests. With these answers, she can compare costs and services of hotels that are interested in hosting the convention. She uses a **block letter format** with all elements aligned on the left margin. She chooses to conduct this correspondence by formal business letter instead of e-mail in order to make sure she obtains signed paper copies of all promises made by the hotel representatives.

CASE DOCUMENT 7-3

Pittsburg City College
200 Rosser Hall
Department of Civil Engineering
Pittsburg, KS 66760

(date)

(name of convention manager)
(name of hotel)
(mailing address)
(city, state, zip)

Dear (   ):

The South Central Chapter of the American Society of Engineering Education will have its annual meeting in Kansas City, April 22-26, 2013. With the convention 15 months away, the local arrangements committee is seeking a

continued

hotel that will serve as convention headquarters. Our committee would like to consider your hotel as a possible site because of its location and its reputation in handling conventions. By March 1, 2012, I will need answers to the following questions, if you are interested in hosting our convention. I will contact you by telephone no later than March 15, 2012, to arrange an appointment to discuss our needs and your facilities in further detail.

Number of Conferees Expected

Based on registration from past conventions, we expect approximately 500 people to attend. Of that number, approximately 450 will need rooms. Of that number, approximately 250 will require double occupancy rooms.

Conference Accommodations Needed

We need you to provide us answers to the following questions:

1. Can your hotel accommodate 500-600 people, April 22-26, 2013?

2. Since the conference will feature three days of concurrent sessions, do you have available conference rooms in the following configurations:

   - three rooms located in the same general area that will hold 100 people
   - three additional rooms that will hold 50 participants, with six persons per round table.

   We will have three concurrent sessions at each time slot—two in the morning and two in the afternoon.

3. Can your hotel provide the following multimedia equipment for each room?

   - screen
   - projector that can be attached to a variety of mobile devices
   - microphones
   - lectern
   - high-speed Internet connection (please specify wired or wireless)

4. Can the seating arrangements be altered in each room between sessions?

5. Can the hotel provide refreshments during the morning break and afternoon break? Can these refreshments be made available at a location that is convenient to the meeting rooms?

continued

Response Deadline

I will need a written response to each question by <u>March 1, 2012</u>. Also, please include in your reply a price list and menu for refreshments available for conferences.

If you have any questions, please contact me at 797-0244 Monday-Friday. If I am away from my desk, just leave a message on my voice mail and a time when I may return your call.

Sincerely,

Alicia Forsythe

Alicia Forsythe
ASEE Convention Arrangements Chair

Case 7-4: Unfavorable News Letter

Michele Harmon is a highly experienced safety engineer who was interviewed by Fostec Engineering. Ms. Harmon was impressive during the visit to corporate headquarters, but the interview team recommended another finalist for the position. Despite Ms. Harmon's exceptional credentials, the second candidate had qualifications that more clearly matched the company's needs. Ritu Shrivastav, director of personnel, has to write to Ms. Harmon to explain that a job offer will not be forthcoming.

In this situation, Ritu may call Ms. Harmon to give her the disappointing news, but she will also follow the call with a formal letter. Avoid using e-mail or text messages to deliver bad news. Note that the letter gives reasons for Ms. Harmon not being selected, but the news is not explained in a harsh, critical way. It is intended to announce the bad news in as positive and supportive a way as possible. Notice also that Ritu cushions the bad news with a friendly opening and appropriate compliments. Because Ritu was heavily involved with Ms. Harmon during the application and interview process, she addresses her as "Michele." Do not use first names unless you really know the person you are addressing. Ritu uses a **modified block format**, which uses paragraph indentions and shifts the date, closing, and signature line to the right side of the page (Case Document 7-4), because she thinks this format looks a little less stiff and formal.

CASE DOCUMENT 7-4

FOSTEC ENGINEERING, INC. ———————— **ESTABLISHED 1954**
1925 JEROME STREET
BROOKLYN, NY 11205

May 14, 2012

Ms. Michele Harmon
9212 Frost Avenue
Wister, OK 74966

Dear Michele:

All of us here enjoyed the two days you visited with us two weeks ago. Your perception of our clients' needs indicates that you have a firm understanding of the role safety engineering plays in the local contracts we win and manage. While your background would be invaluable to us, we have only

continued

one position available, and we have selected an applicant with international project experience.

As we discussed during your visit, our range of clients has expanded. We now receive RFPs from countries in Europe, South America, and the Pacific Rim. Developing responses to their needs requires us to expand our team, particularly when we can do so with professionals with international experience.

Thank you for considering us. We were genuinely impressed with your professionalism, your analytical skills, and your record as a team player. And I was immensely pleased to have the opportunity to meet you.

Sincerely,

Ritu Shrivastav

Ritu Shrivastav
Manager, Personnel

Case 7-5: Letter of Reply

Rick Evans owns an agricultural equipment business. He has just received an order and a check from Alberto Santoy, who wants to replace an irrigation pump.

Rick needs to write to Mr. Santoy and tell him that the pump he has ordered is being discontinued and replaced by two new pumps, both of which are more expensive but are designed to offer better performance. Rick wants to be sure that Mr. Santoy doesn't think that Rick is simply trying to sell him a more expensive pump when the current model will do the job.

In designing this letter, Rick wants to be sure that he does not suggest to Mr. Santoy that he is the object of a bait and switch. Thus, he opens the letter by telling Mr. Santoy that he has the pump and can ship it immediately (Case Document 7-5). However, he wants Mr. Santoy to know that several improved models are available and that he may wish to choose one of the new models. Rick then presents all the information he believes Mr. Santoy will need to make his decision and then invites Mr. Santoy to contact him. Rick could call Mr. Santoy and talk to him, but in this case a business letter that expresses concern for Mr. Santoy's investment and presents factual information about the alternative pumps will make Mr. Santoy's decision easier. Note that Rick chooses the block letter format: he thinks its formal and straightforward appearance will reinforce his credibility and indicate respect for his customer and their business relationship.

CASE DOCUMENT 7-5

--- Evans Irrigation Manufacturing & Supply Co. ---

19963 Valley Mills Drive
Altair, TX 77412
817 569-3766

(date)

Mr. Alberto Santoy
Route 1, Box 616
Silsbee, TX 77656

Dear Mr. Santoy:

We have received your order and check for $698 as payment for our 15-hp Model XM 21 auxiliary pump. Although we do have several in stock, and we can mail one to you immediately, manufacture of this model has ended. We are

continued

holding your check and order until we hear from you regarding the following alternatives.

Here is the situation. Purchasers of the 15-hp model have indicated that the low output of this pump is generally insufficient to run the new drip irrigation systems currently being manufactured. This particular pump is not designed to handle extensive operation of these larger systems. As a result, we have discontinued the model. We have reduced the price to $548 due to our inability to warranty the motor for more than one year or supply replacement parts for more than two years.

We now manufacture two larger pumps, a 50-hp model and a 75-hp model. The 50-hp model will power a #70 system. The 75-hp model will power a #90 system. Here is a comparison of these three models.

Hypo Motor	Pumps Model	Rating	Warranty	Price
15hp	21	30	1yr = 2 pts	$448
50hp	31	70	full + 5 yr	$1795*
75hp	41	90		$2350*
*Additional warranty available for $125/yr				

While we believe that you will be happier with the reliability and efficiency of either of the larger pumps, if you choose to purchase the 15-hp model, we will ship it immediately and refund the $150 difference in price. I am sending brochures on both new motors. Please look them over and call me at our 800 number, extension 145 if you have any questions. As soon as we hear from you, we will ship you the motor of your choice within two working days.

Sincerely,

Rick Evans

Rick Evans
Owner

CORRESPONDENCE CHECKLIST ✔

Planning

☐ What is your subject and purpose?
☐ What do you want to have happen as a result of your correspondence?
  What will you do to achieve your objective?
☐ Who are your primary readers? Secondary readers? Do your primary
  and secondary readers have different needs? How will you satisfy the
  different needs of all your readers?
☐ Why will your readers read your correspondence?
☐ What is the attitude of your readers toward you? Toward your subject?
  Toward your purpose?
☐ If you are addressing international readers, do you understand their
  cultural practices? What adjustments in your correspondence will their
  cultural practices require?
☐ Will you write an e-mail, text, memo, or letter?
☐ Will you choose a direct or indirect style?

Revision

☐ Are your topic and purpose clearly identified?
☐ Have you satisfied your readers' purpose in reading?
☐ Have you adopted a style suitable to your readers' culture?
☐ Have you avoided jargon and clichés?
☐ Is your message clear, concise, complete, and courteous?

EXERCISES

1. Write a memo to colleagues in your organization in which you solicit their support for the local public library. In your memo, explain the merits of civic engagement for your organization and its history of corporate social responsibility as well as the mission of the library and its contribution to the community.

2. Civil Engineering Associates of Purvis, Ohio, was established in 2007 by Robert B. Davidson and Walter F. Posey, both graduates of the University of Ohio. Business for the company was good, and CEA took on six additional partners between 2007 and 2012: Alvin T. Bennett, Wayne S. Cook, Frank G. Reynolds, John W. Castrop, George P. Ramirez, and Richard M. Burke—all graduates of the University of Ohio.

   For the last five years, the partners of CEA have met every Friday for a working lunch at Coasters, a local restaurant and bar that features attractive young waitresses wearing provocative swimsuits. The customers are almost exclusively men, and the interaction between customers and waitresses is often flirtatious.

This year CEA hired Elizabeth P. Grider, a Missouri University graduate, as a new partner in the firm. She has attended two of the working lunches at Coasters and is uncomfortable in this environment. She does not feel, however, that she can just skip the events, which are the only regular occasions on which all the partners gather. Projects and work assignments are often discussed and decided at these Friday meetings. In addition, the lunches offer the opportunity to establish a comfortable working relationship with the partners. She realizes that "Friday at Coasters" is a long-standing tradition at the firm, and she is reluctant to upset the status quo, but she really wishes they could find a better place to meet.

As Elizabeth P. Grider, write a memo to the senior partner, Robert B. Davidson, explaining your problem and recommending one or more solutions. You would like to speak to Davidson directly, but you think that writing a memo allows you to organize your thoughts. And after the meeting, you could leave the memo with Davidson as a written record of your position.

3. Examine Figure 7-4. If you were the author of this document and were given 15 more minutes to make it better, what changes would you make?

4. A graduate student at a major university posted the following message on his university's e-mail distribution list for graduates of the College of Engineering. His goal was to solicit working engineers to participate in a survey for his dissertation.

Read the original e-mail (Figure 7-5) and then revise it.

Questions to consider: if you were inundated with e-mail messages each day, what would be your initial reaction to this message? What problems in wording and formatting do you notice?

Test the original and your revision on four of your friends. Which version is judged better? Why? E-mail your instructor to report the results of your test. In your message, explain the problems you identified with the original, list the specific changes you made in your revision, and specify which of the changes were considered superior to the original by each of your test participants. Attach a copy of your revision to the e-mail message.

BOARD OF GOVERNORS

OF THE

FEDERAL RESERVE SYSTEM

WASHINGTON, D.C. 20551

DIVISION OF BANKING
SUPERVISION AND REGULATION

SR 11-1

January 25, 2011

TO THE OFFICER IN CHARGE OF SUPERVISION AND APPROPRIATE SUPERVISORY
AND EXAMINATION STAFF AT EACH FEDERAL RESERVE BANK

SUBJECT: Impact of High-Cost Credit Protection Transactions on the Assessment of
Capital Adequacy

This letter provides direction to supervisory and banking organization staff on the
potential impact of high-cost credit protection transactions on their assessment of a banking
organization's overall capital adequacy.

Credit risk mitigation techniques can significantly reduce a banking organization's level
of risk. Depending on the credit quality of the protected assets, among other considerations,
banking organizations may be required to pay high premiums or fees to purchase credit
protection. For specific transactions, it may be appropriate for a banking organization to pay
these costs as part of its overall risk-management strategy.

In some instances, however, the high premiums or fees paid for certain credit protection,
combined with other terms and conditions, call into question the degree of risk transfer of the
transaction and may be inconsistent with safety and soundness. Rather than contributing to a
prudent risk-management strategy, the primary effect of these high-cost credit protection
transactions is to embed a high percentage of expected losses into the premiums and fees paid,
under the premise that the transaction would receive favorable risk-based capital treatment in the
short term and defer recognition of losses over an extended period. Supervisors will scrutinize
such transactions and, based on the factors and analysis described below, may preclude favorable
risk-based capital treatment.

Banking organizations should analyze and document the economic substance of credit
protection transactions that have unusually high-cost or innovative features to assess the degree
of risk transfer and the associated impact on the organization's overall capital adequacy. The
analysis should also specify how the transaction aligns with the banking organization's overall
risk-management strategy. In evaluating the degree of risk transfer of a transaction, banking
organizations should consider and supervisors will assess the following factors, among others, as
applicable:

- A comparison of the present value of premiums relative to expected losses over a variety
of stress scenarios;

Page 1 of 2

FIGURE 7-4 Document for Exercise 3

- The pricing of the transaction relative to market prices;

- The timing of payments under the transaction, including potential timing differences between the banking organization's provisioning or write downs and payments by the counterparty;

- A review of applicable call dates to assess the likely duration of the credit protection relative to the potential timing of future credit losses;

- An analysis of whether certain circumstances could lead to the banking organization's increased reliance on the counterparty at the same time that the counterparty's ability to meet its obligations is weakened;

- An analysis of whether the banking organization can prudently afford the premiums given the banking organization's earnings, capital, and overall financial condition; and

- A review of any internal memos or records outlining the rationale for the transaction and the organization's analysis of the anticipated costs and benefits of the transaction.

Supervisory staff should take high-cost credit protection transactions into account in their assessment of a banking organization's overall capital adequacy. In some cases, supervisory staff may determine that a transaction should be discounted in the assessment of the banking organization's management of its risk profile and capital needs, or that the cost of the transaction should be judged as having a negative impact on the banking organization's earnings and capital. In particular cases, the Board may determine that a transaction should not be recognized as a guarantee for risk-based capital purposes. Misuse of credit protection transactions may negatively impact the organization's supervisory ratings (including management and risk management), its ability to pay dividends and effect equity redemptions and repurchases, and the evaluation of the merits of acquisitions and other applications.

Reserve Banks are asked to distribute this letter to institutions supervised by the Federal Reserve and to supervisory and examination staff. Questions regarding this letter or regarding individual transactions may be directed to Constance Horsley, Senior Supervisory Financial Analyst, at (202) 452-5239, or Chris Powell, Financial Analyst, Capital and Regulatory Policy, at (202) 912-4353.

Patrick M. Parkinson
Director

Page 2 of 2

FIGURE 7-4 *continued*

From: Fred Schotter [fred.schotter@A&M.edu]
Sent: Monday, February 27, 2012 1:15 PM
To: EngrAlumni [engralumni@A&M.edu]

Subject: Please Help with Survey on Psychological Contracts Among Employees

My name is Fred Schotter and I am a Ph.D. student in the Department of Industrial Psychology at your alma mater. I am currently working on my dissertation, which examines the psychological contracts that develop between employees and co-workers in the engineering profession. These "contracts" are the underlying and unspoken relationships that exist in an organization and which greatly influence an employee's desire to go "above and beyond" in terms of demonstrating helping behaviors towards coworkers, supervisors, and, ultimately, even the organization as a whole. I would like to survey a large number of people from the engineering profession. Specifically, I'd like to ask you to consider participating in my study.

An employee satisfaction survey was recently conducted here by the Office of Employee Services in collaboration with the Department of Industrial Psychology to help better understand employee work attitudes and perceptions. That survey included questions about job satisfaction with regard to a wide range of issues about work, life, and the community. The outcomes and trends of those findings will be used to help respond to the needs and interests of university staff and to assure that the university continues to be considered the employer of choice in the region. My survey should not be confused with this on-going collaborative initiative.

If you decide to participate in my study, please know that at least three people will need to participate—an employee, the employee's supervisor, and a co-worker of the employee. All information obtained through this survey will remain confidential and no one outside of my research group will have access to the information provided on the surveys. The survey is voluntary; participants may choose to respond to any or all of the questions. The surveys will require less than 20 minutes per person to complete and may be done online or in hard copy—whichever works better for you. Upon completion of the study later this year I would be more than happy to provide a summary report of the collective results of the entire study to all participating parties.

As you can imagine, it is important for a doctoral student to have access to a broad base for dissertation research. It is sometimes difficult for students to dip into the "real world" without help. I would greatly appreciate it if you would consider participating in this survey and, possibly, asking others within your organization (the more, the better!) to help as well.

If you are willing to participate, please reply to this message. At that time I will work with you on providing a link to the online survey or towards getting you the hard copy of the survey. This survey structure and content have been reviewed and approved by the Institutional Review Board-Human Subjects in Research. Again, please consider that if you choose to participate, I would also need the help of your supervisor and a co-worker to fill out the other appropriate surveys. If you would like to participate and would prefer that I directly e-mail your supervisor and co-worker, I would be more than willing to do so. On the other hand if you are in a supervisory position, I would appreciate it if you could ask two of your employees to participate as well in order to fill the roles of the employee and co-worker. If you have any questions please feel free to e-mail me at any time.

Thank you for your support and for considering this request.

Sincerely,

Fred Schotter

FIGURE 7-5 Document for Exercise 4

Technical Reports

Reports, like correspondence—e-mails, texts, memos, and letters, discussed in the previous chapter—remain the most commonly written workplace documents. Reports serve a variety of functions: they provide information, instructions, analysis, conclusions, and recommendations based on analysis.

Given the quantity of information generated and shared in most work environments, getting your report read has become an increasingly critical consideration. In this chapter, we will explain the basics of designing clear and accessible reports that enhance the likelihood of readers' willingness to find out what you have to say.

Quick Tips

None of your readers will read your entire report, unless it's a single page. Different readers will read different sections of your report according to their needs. Almost all of your readers will read the summary: make sure this section exemplifies clarity and conciseness. The busier your reader, particularly those who receive dozens and hundreds of documents daily, the more important directness, clarity, and conciseness become if you want this reader to read your document.

If a report doesn't have a concise, readable summary, readers will flip to the end to find the conclusions. If they can't find those easily, they likely will not read any portion of the report.

KINDS OF REPORTS

Many routine reports provide information, but others go beyond simple reporting. They categorize and then analyze information or data. From the analysis, the writer may evaluate the information, draw conclusions, and perhaps recommend action based on those conclusions. Analytical reports often defy rigid classification, but for the purpose of learning to write analytical reports, we can generally identify the following types:

- If the analysis focuses on a recommendation, the report may be called a **recommendation report**.
- If the analysis emphasizes evaluation of personnel, data, financial options, or possible solutions to problems or avenues for exploration, the report may be called an **evaluation report**.
- A **feasibility report** analyzes a problem, presents possible solutions to the problem, determines criteria for assessing the solutions, assesses the solutions against the criteria, and then shows the best solution(s) based on the reported analysis of the solutions. The analysis underpins the conclusions and also recommendation is critical. Based on available resources, the writer determines criteria against which possible solutions may be measured and methods of applying criteria and analyzing solutions against criteria selected. Many feasibility reports are long, as they represent the way a problem has been defined, studied, and resolved. Results of feasibility studies can lead to major financial expenditures.
- Many reports both inform and analyze: a **progress report** or a **status report**, which will be discussed in Chapter 9, Proposals and Progress Reports, describes and evaluates the work done on a project, the money expended, and problems encountered.
- A **trip report** documents information gathered on a trip, evaluates this information, and may suggest actions based on findings.
- A **personnel report** describes an employee's performance, analyzes effectiveness, suggests methods of improvement, and estimates the employee's potential for promotion.
- An **economic justification report** explains the cost of a project or action and then argues for the cost effectiveness of the project.

REPORT CATEGORIES—INFORMAL AND FORMAL

Reports can generally be divided into two categories: informal reports, used for daily internal communications in business organizations; and formal reports, generated for readers outside the organization or for major reports developed for internal use. Both kinds of reports share similarities in structure and major components. They differ principally in length and in format.

INFORMAL REPORT HEADING

Internal reports use a memorandum heading that may include many of the following items. Organizations usually have their own specific requirements for internal reports that use a memo heading. Many organizations have a memo template available on the Intranet. Common elements of memo headings usually include the following:

Date:
To:
From:
Subject:
Reference:
Action Required:
Distribution List:

Subject line. The subject line should state clearly—in concise phrasing—the content of the report. The clearer the subject line, the better the odds that your readers will read your report. Your subject line should make your readers want to read your report.

Reference. Many reports respond to previously written reports, to company policies, or to items such as engineering specifications and legal issues. Be sure your readers have what they need and understand how your report links to previous reports and documents.

Action required. If you need your reader(s) to respond to your report by a certain date, then say so here. For example, "Your approval needed by 5/10/2012." (See Case 7-1 on p. 137, which shows a memo with an action-required statement.)

Distribution list. This report segment, which can occur at either the beginning or end of the report, indicates who will receive copies as well as the report's file name for later reference. Be sure to include on this list everyone who should receive a copy. Failing to include all readers can create problems for employees, as omitted readers may think that they are being eliminated from the communication chain.

Parts of an Informal Technical Report

Introduction. Reports should begin with an introduction—a section that introduces readers to the content covered. For routine memo reports, attempt to keep your introduction concise but long enough to ensure that readers understand what they are reading and why they are included on the distribution list. Also remember that reports will be kept in files (virtual and paper) and can be accessed by readers many months and years after you have written the report. The introduction should ensure that all readers understand what follows.

Thus, a memo report introduction should contain the following elements. How much you develop each item will depend on the particular report situation—what you think readers will know.

Subject or report topic.

Report purpose. What do you want your report to accomplish? Often, the report topic and purpose can be combined into one sentence. If possible, begin the report with a sentence or two that states the subject and purpose. For many routine reports, a subject/purpose statement may be all you need.

> As you requested, I have prepared a brief report on the best options in alternative fuels. Current research over the past five years suggests that biofuels, compressed natural gas, and alcohol fuels may present the best alternatives to conventional fossil fuels. This report presents the advantages and disadvantages of each and should offer interesting discussion points for the bi-monthly brown-bag lunch meetings.

Background or rationale. What issues led to the need for this report? Be concise. If you have to have more than a full paragraph, place the background or rationale in a separate paragraph. If your main readers don't need this information, then they can skip this paragraph. Readers on the distribution list or future readers will likely appreciate the information.

> This report recommends that the university begin developing online versions of our high-demand courses, particularly those most requested by students who leave campus for the summer.
>
> The university loses substantial funding when students do not enroll for our summer classes. Many would enroll for online versions of these courses, if we offered them. The loss in revenue has increased over the past three years. Determining the courses we could develop for online/hybrid delivery, the cost required for redesign, and the time required for effective conversion would provide us information on which to make a decision. Discussion of each point follows.

Report development. What topics will you cover? Simply state how you will develop the report, as shown in the previous example and the one below, which indicates three main topics and three main headings. Both examples have the development plan highlighted.

> The effect of organized crime on the U.S. Border States adjoining Mexico has become a major concern. Texas shares the longest border with Mexico via the Rio Grande River, which spans 1,254 miles. Along this area, drug cartels engage in illegal activities that involve a range of crimes, such as racketeering, drug sales, murder, and assassinations. Illegal incursions have been difficult to halt because of the length of the U.S./Mexico border. Mexico's government has been unable to stop the violence and gang wars. Organized crime has continued to thrive in Mexico with sufficient cash flows that allow operations in the United States. This report describes the cartels, describes how they operate, and explains how they adversely affect U.S. foreign policy.

Summary. The report summary determines the success of the report. Many readers who receive copies, simply as information, will read only the introduction and the summary. The summary should tell your readers the essential points and findings in the report. Informal reports may combine the introduction and summary into one paragraph, consisting of the key points and the report purpose.

Discussion. This section develops each point you state you will discuss in the introduction.

Conclusion. The report conclusion ties together what you have presented and states the main ideas you want readers to remember.

Recommendations. If you need to recommend action, then include that here. To improve readability, list and number your recommendations. If you need to discuss them, you can do so following your list.

Attachments. Attachments include any material, provided on hard copy or electronically, needed to support your discussion, conclusions, or recommendations. Attachments may include additional data, calculations, or previously written documents on the same subject.

Case Document 8-1 exemplifies an effective informal report prepared by a student for a study abroad program. Students in the program coming from the United States, Canada, and the United Kingdom developed short reports on a topic of major interest in their state and country to share with other members of the program.

DEVELOPING REPORTS

How reports develop varies, and here we can provide only guidelines and a few examples. In the introduction, you state how you will present your report and the topics that your reader will find. Thus, you can have a main heading for each topic, and readers who have interest in one or two particular issues can go immediately to those issues.

> **Note:** You want to develop a reputation for writing readable, informative, and accurate reports. Don't make readers hunt for information— they won't.

How you arrange the main components should depend on what you believe your readers will want. For example, you may have a

short introduction—subject, purpose, and brief rationale
recommendation
conclusion
discussion

Many reports serve only to inform. Figure 8-1, a report prepared by an engineering company, provides information about radon. The report, requested by the city of Glendale, will be used by employees in the city office to answer questions asked by citizens of the community. The report has no summary, as the report itself summarizes the issue discussed. When you plan to cover several topics, consider listing the topics to alert your readers:

> The Lakefront Advisory Committee has concluded its study of the issues confronting renovation of the property. Our report, which includes citizens' input submitted during the comment period, covers the following main issues:
>
> 1. Financial feasibility of the project
>
> 2. Ability to raise the needed funds
>
> 3. Project maintenance
>
> 4. Shoreline protection
>
> 5. Effect of renovation on changing water levels
>
> 6. Erosion of project materials by water/sand

Bradshaw Engineering
1111 Steering St.
College Station, TX 77840
December 2, 2010

Mr. Henry Rosen
City Attorney
100 City Plaza
Glendale, TX 77844

Subject: Radon Information Report
Dear Mr. Rosen:

     In response to your conversation with Mr. Jerry Bradshaw, I am submitting the report on important radon facts. The purpose of this report is to provide useful information to the City of Glendale staff to be able to answer citizens' questions about radon in their households. The report includes an introduction, a list of answers to frequently asked questions, and a concluding summary of all of the facts presented.

     I will be in Texarkana for a consulting job on pollution, but if any changes need to be made I can work on the edits upon my return.

Sincerely,

Jillian Streigert

Jillian Streifert
Bradshaw Engineer

Enclosed: Radon Information Report
cc: Mr. Jerry Bradshaw

FIGURE 8-1 Informational Report

Radon Causes and Concerns

Introduction

Radon is a radioactive gas which is responsible for the majority of public exposure to radiation. The **EPA (Environmental Protection Agency) estimates that radon causes thousands of cancer deaths in the United States each year**. Radon gas from natural sources can accumulate in buildings, especially in confined areas such as attics and basements. It is also found in some spring waters and hot springs. Radon can be dangerous but severe exposures are preventable with public awareness and home testing. The following information was gathered from epa.gov/radon.

What is Radon?

Radon is a cancer-causing, radioactive gas.
You can't see radon, and you can't smell it or taste it, but it's possibly a problem in your home. Radon is estimated to cause many thousands of deaths each year. That's because when you breathe air containing radon, you can get lung cancer.

Where does Radon come from?

Radon comes from the breakdown of Uranium.
Radon comes from the natural (radioactive) breakdown of uranium in soil, rock, and water and gets into the air you breathe.

Where is Radon found?

Radon is found all over the U.S.
Radon is found at different levels in all areas of the U.S. It can get into any type of building — homes, offices, and schools — and result in a high indoor radon level. But you and your family are most likely to get your greatest exposure at home, where you spend most of your time.

What products is Radon found in?

All natural products contain radioactive elements that can produce radon gas.
Stone, soil, minerals, and sand contain trace amounts of some radioactive elements that can produce measurable amounts of radiation and sometimes radon gas. This includes all concrete products, clay bricks, most non-plastic plates and dishes, coal, natural gas, all glass made using silica (even eye glasses, wine glasses, mirrors, windows, etc.), and granite too. Radon emitted from these sources will generally be insignificant when diluted with the quantity of air in your entire home.

FIGURE 8-1 *continued*

Sources of Radon

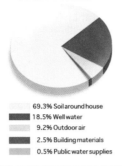

■ 69.3% Soil around house
■ 18.5% Well water
■ 9.2% Outdoor air
■ 2.5% Building materials
■ 0.5% Public water supplies

Source: http://www.radon.com/radon/granite.html

Can I test for Radon?

Yes, testing is inexpensive and easy; it should only take a few minutes of your time.

Testing is the only way to know if you and your family are at risk from radon. The EPA and the Surgeon General recommend testing all homes below the third floor for radon. The EPA also recommends testing in schools. (Refer to Page 4 for How to Test for Radon)

If I have a Radon problem can I fix it?

Yes, Radon reduction systems work and they are not too costly.

Some radon reduction systems can reduce radon levels in your home by up to 99%. Even very high levels can be reduced to acceptable levels.

How does Radon get into my home?

Radon gets in through:
1. Cracks in solid floors
2. Construction joints
3. Cracks in walls
4. Gaps in suspended floors
5. Gaps around service pipes
6. Cavities inside walls
7. The water supply

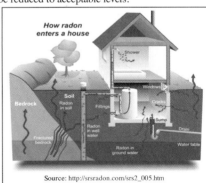

Source: http://srsradon.com/srs2_005.htm

FIGURE 8-1 *continued*

Radon typically moves up through the ground to the air above and into your home through cracks and holes in the foundation. Your home traps radon inside, where it can build up. Any home may have a radon problem. In a small number of homes, the building materials can give off radon, too. However, building materials rarely cause radon problems by themselves.

How to Test Your Home

You can't see radon, but it's not hard to find out if you have a radon problem in your home. The amount of radon in the air is measured in "picocuries per liter of air," or "pCi/L." Many kinds of low-cost "do-it-yourself" radon test kits you can get through the mail and in hardware stores and other retail outlets. You can also hire a qualified tester to do the testing for you. Corrective action should be taken in your home if your radon level is 4 pCi/L, or higher. Radon levels less than 4 pCi/L still pose a risk, but in many cases this level can be reduced.

Two general ways to test for Radon: Short and Long Term

Short-term testing:

Short-term tests remain in your home for two days to 90 days, depending on the device. "Charcoal canisters," "alpha track," "electrets ion chamber," "continuous monitors," and "charcoal liquid scintillation" detectors are most commonly used for short-term testing. Radon levels tend to vary from day to day so if you need results quickly a short-term test followed by a second short-term test may be used to decide whether to take corrective action in your home.

Long-term testing:

Long-term tests remain in your home for more than 90 days. "Alpha track" and "electrets" detectors are commonly used for this type of testing. A long-term test will give you a reading that is more likely to tell you your home's year-round average radon level as opposed to a short-term test which measures the level during a specific time period.

How to Lower the Radon Levels in My Home

Several proven methods to reduce radon in your home exist, but the one primarily used is a vent pipe system and fan. This system pulls radon from beneath the house and vents it to the outside. This system does not require major changes to your home. Sealing foundation cracks and other openings makes this kind of system more effective and cost-efficient. Similar systems can also be installed in houses with crawl spaces. Radon contractors can use other methods that may also work in your home. The right system depends on the design of your home and other factors.

FIGURE 8-1 *continued*

What if I ignore my Radon Problem?

Radon gas decays into radioactive particles that can get trapped in your lungs when you breathe. As they break down further, these particles release small bursts of energy. The particles can damage lung tissue and lead to lung cancer over the course of your lifetime. Not everyone exposed to elevated levels of radon will develop lung cancer. The amount of time between exposure and the onset of the disease may be many years. Smoking combined with radon is an especially serious health risk. Stop smoking and lower your radon level to reduce your lung cancer risk.

Summary

Radon poses a serious health risk at high levels in your home. Your chances of getting lung cancer from radon depend mostly on:

❖ How much radon is in your home
❖ The amount of time you spend in your home
❖ Whether you are a smoker or have ever smoked

Radon is considered a significant contaminant that affects indoor air quality worldwide. It is one of the densest substances that remains a gas under normal conditions and is considered a health hazard due to its radioactivity. Testing is the only way to know your home's radon levels. No immediate symptoms will alert you to the presence of radon. It typically takes years of exposure before any problems surface. Radon exposure is dangerous but it can be prevented with public awareness.

More information about Radon

Radon Hotline:
1-800-SOSRADON (767-7236)
Fax: (785) 532-6952
E-mail: Radon@ksu.edu

EPA:
Website: epa.gov/radon

MedlinePlus: Radon
Website: http://www.nlm.nih.gov/medlineplus/radon.html

FIGURE 8-1 *continued*

Case 8-1

This report was written by a student involved in a study abroad summer program. The professor asked each student to submit a short report that described a major political issue in his or her home country. The audience for these reports were students from other countries in the study abroad program.

CASE DOCUMENT 8-1

TO: James Harold Burton

DATE: December 12, 2010

FROM: Christopher Koehler

SUBJECT: Mexican Drug Cartel Activity in Texas

Introduction

This report surveys the activity of Mexican drug cartels affecting Texas in recent years. The cartels are paramilitary organizations that specialize in illegal drug trafficking. A brief overview of geography and history discussed in this report will help readers understand regional economic and political issues affected by the cartels.

Quick Facts About Texas

- Texas is the second-largest state in the U.S. by both landmass and population (Fig. 1)
  - Landmass approximately the size of France
  - Population approximately half of the United Kingdom
- Texas shares a border with Mexico that is 1,920 km long (see red line in Fig. 1)
  - Border length is approximately 1/6 of United Kingdom coastline

Drug Cartels in Mexico—Brief History

Drug cartels became prominent in Mexico in the 1980's under the leadership of Miguel Ángel Félix Gallardo.[1] Territorial agreements kept competition among rival cartels to a minimum. However, following the arrest of Gallardo in 1989, fragile alliances were broken and cartels began to compete with each other for greater business. Violence escalated while government officials were paid to

continued

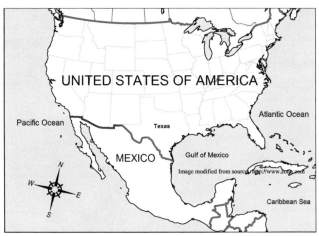

Figure 1. Location and Size of Texas and Mexico
Image modified from source: http://www.zonu.com

be indifferent. By 2006 the cartels had become so powerful that they posed a threat to civil order.

President Felipe Calderon made an open declaration of war on the cartels in 2006 and authorized a rapid escalation of forces. Government-supported troops have numbered approximately 50,000.[2] The maps below reveal current territory estimates (Fig. 2) and drug trafficking routes (Fig. 3) affecting the Texas border. Cooperation with federal and state agencies within Texas is ongoing.

The drug trade today is estimated to account for $991 million per year.[3]

Figure 2. Drug cartel territories
Image modified from source: http://www.economist.com/ blogs/dailychart/2011/01/ drugs_mexico

continued

Figure 3. Drug trafficking routes
Image modified from source: http://www.economist.com/blogs/dailychart/2011/01/drugs_mexico

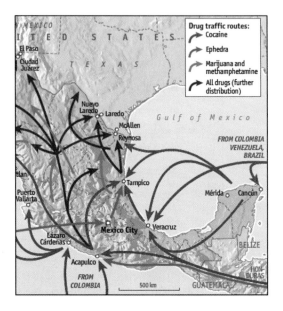

Response by Texas and the United States

Plans to secure the border have been complicated by disagreements between governors of border states and the U.S. government. Texas Governor Perry has asked for a military offensive but has been denied by federal officials.[4] The U.S. government planned to hire defense contractors to build an elaborate border fence but scrapped the project due to costs.[5] Other defensive options include allocating more agents from the U.S. Border Patrol or Texas National Guard. The drug cartels continue to be resilient to these strategies, however: in February 2011 a Texas National Guard member was arrested for cooperation with the cartels.[6]

Mexico continues to insist that the burden is on the United States to diminish the demand for drugs.[7] U.S. President Obama has agreed to put programs in place that encourage drug rehabilitation.[8] In the meantime, the war rages with deaths expected to be in the neighborhood of 10,000-12,000 this year (Fig. 4). Texas border residents are terrified and many are leaving to seek opportunities elsewhere.[9]

continued

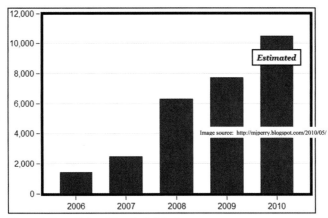

Figure 4. Drug-Related Deaths in Mexico

Sources

[1] New York Times: "In Mexico, Drug Roots Run Deep"
   http://www.nytimes.com/1989/04/16/world/in-mexico-drug-roots-run-deep.html
[2] Los Angeles Times: "Mexico Military Faces Political Risks Over Drug War"
   http://articles.latimes.com/2010/mar/23/world/la-fg-mexico-army23-2010mar23
[3] Viridiana Rios, Harvard University Department of Government: "Evaluating the economic
   impact of drug traffic in Mexico."
   http://www.gov.harvard.edu/people/viridiana-rios-contreras
[4] Governor Rick Perry: "Warning Signs Along Border Must be Heeded by Washington."
   http://governor.state.tx.us/news/press-release/14989/
[5] Arizona Daily Star: "Defense Contractors Botch 'Virtual' Fence on Border"
   http://azstarnet.com/news/opinion/article_c9ed77cc-1ccf-5efd-bd84-dafbb85ca522.html
[6] Brownsville Herald: "Officials Round Up Cartel Suspects in McAllen."
   http://www.brownsvilleherald.com/news/mcallen-123225-officials-round.html
[7] Council on Foreign Relations: Mexico's Drug War
   http://www.cfr.org/mexico/mexicos-drug-war/p13689
[8] Time: "Obama's Other War: Fighting Mexico's Drug Lords"
   http://www.time.com/time/world/article/0,8599,1887535,00.html
[9] Texas Tribune: "Texas Border Residents Seek Better Opportunities"
   http://www.texastribune.org/texas-newspaper/texas-news/texas-border-residents-seek
   -better-opportunities/

ELEMENTS OF FORMAL REPORTS

Long reports should be developed as formal reports. The word "long" generally means 10 pages or more; but as a writer, you have to decide based on the report context. Elements of formal reports should be selected and developed by writers to help readers find their way through the report. The longer the report and the more diverse the readership, the more elements you will need to help readers find what they need. Each element has a different purpose and often targets the needs of different readers. Remember that reports should be developed with the needs of a variety of readers in mind. Reports are not novels: most reports will not be read cover to cover but selectively.

In general, formal reports may include any or all of the following elements. How these elements appear in practice differs widely and depends on the organization preparing the report. We will describe the general characteristics and content of each element and provide several examples.

> Prefatory Elements
> > Letter of Transmittal or Memo of Transmittal
> > Title Page
> > Submission Page
> > Table of Contents
> > List of Illustrations
> > Glossary and List of Symbols
> Abstracts and Summaries
> > Informative Abstract
> > Descriptive Abstract
> > Executive Summary
> Discussion, or Body of the Report
> > Conclusion(s)
> > Recommendation(s)
> > References
> Appendices

Prefatory elements. Readers initially access a report from the prefatory elements. These show readers what your report will discuss and how it will approach the topic. Long, complex reports that will likely be read by many readers require prefatory elements. The letter/memo of transmittal, title page, table of contents, abstract, and/or summary are often your reader's first—and only—experience with the report. Each of these elements should help your readers grasp and accept the rhetorical purpose of the report. Never consider prefatory elements routine "paperwork" needing only perfunctory writing. No matter how well written and researched the report content, the effectiveness of the report begins with the effectiveness of the elements that state the content. Many readers may decide to read the body of the report if they find the prefatory elements compelling.

Letter/memo of transmittal. The letter/memo of transmittal is addressed to the individual who will initially receive the report. This person may not be the primary reader but the individual responsible for routing the report to appropriate readers who will digest and use the content. In consulting reports, the CEO of an organization that has solicited the consulting work is usually the person addressed in the letter of transmittal. Or the transmittal letter can address the person who has authorized and requested the information, analysis, work, or recommendations covered in the report.

Reports prepared for internal distribution will have a memo of transmittal, and reports prepared for external distribution will use a letter of transmittal. Both can be organized the same way.

The letter/memo of transmittal should include the following information at minimum:

- Statement of transmittal—subject and purpose of the report
- Reason for the report

In addition, transmittal documents may include the following items:

- Background material—the larger issue or problem addressed by the report
- Mention of earlier reports (or additional reports that may be needed)
- Information that may be of special interest or significance to the readers
- Specific conclusions/recommendations that might be of special interest to the person to whom the report is addressed
- Financial implications
- Acknowledgments—list of those who provided help in the project

Figure 8-1 includes a transmittal letter. The sample formal report in Appendix C includes a transmittal memo.

Title page. Title pages perform several functions. Basically, they provide critical identifying matter and may contain a number of identifying items to distinguish the report from others on a similar subject or from reports received in response to specific projects. Many organizations have a standard format for title pages. Whatever items you need—or your organization requires you to include—be sure to make the title page attractive. The following information often appears on title pages:

- Name of the company or individual(s) preparing the report
- Name of the company or course for which the report was prepared
- Title and subtitle of the report
- Date of submission
- Code number of the report
- Contract numbers under which the work was performed
- Company or agency logo
- Proprietary and security notices
- Names of contact/responsible individuals
- Descriptive abstract

Submission page. Reports may use a submission page, which includes the list of contributors to the report and/or the names and signatures of the authorizing officer or project leader. Submission pages emphasize the point we make throughout this book: reports require accountability. Signatures on a submission page indicate that the authors stand behind the content. The submission page usually either precedes the title page or follows it. Or the title page and submission page may be combined.

Table of contents. The table of contents (TOC) performs at least three major functions. First, it indicates the page on which each major topic begins and thus serves as a locating device for readers who may be searching for specific information. Second, the TOC forecasts the extent and nature of the topical coverage and suggests the logic of the arrangement and the relationship among the report parts. The TOC contains all major headings used in the report. For that reason, major headings, like the title of the report, should reflect the content of the material that follows. Skimming a table of contents should give readers a clear idea of the topics covered, the content presented under each heading, the amount of coverage devoted to that topic, the development of the report, and the progression of information. (See the table of contents in the report in Appendix C.) While you may wish to use "introduction," "conclusion," and "recommendations," avoid the term "discussion": it tells your reader nothing about how you will present the report content. Third, the TOC should reflect the rhetorical purpose of your report—what you want your readers to know and why your report is important to them.

List of illustrations. If a report contains tables, graphics, drawings, photos—any type of visual—it's customary to use the page heading "Illustrations" or "Exhibits" to list all the visuals. These are usually divided into "tables" and "figures," but specific types may also be listed if you have an array of illustrations: for example, maps, financial statements, photographs, charts, and computer programs.

Glossary and list of symbols. Reports dealing with specialized subject matter often include abbreviations, acronyms, symbols, and terms not known to readers outside a specialized group. Readership should determine if a glossary or list of symbols is needed. Many reports prepared by government agencies for the general public provide glossaries to ensure that any reader can access the report.

Glossaries sometimes appear as prefatory elements, but they can also appear in an appendix at the end of the report. When you first use a symbol or a term that you will include in the glossary, tell your reader where to find the list or the glossary. You may wish to place an asterisk (*) by a word or symbol that will be covered in the glossary. If you have only a few terms that you will need to define, you can define these as footnotes at the bottom of the page and use asterisks (* or **) to alert your readers.

Abstracts and summaries. Abstracts and summaries are the most important prefatory items in a report. The title page, table of contents, abstract, and summary may be the only parts of the report many recipients read. Thus, carefully plan these elements, as each provides a slightly different perspective. While the title page and table of contents outline the report's content and direction, abstracts and summaries provide the essence of the report: topic, purpose, results, conclusions, and recommendations. Each item can stand alone or be designed in conjunction with other prefatory elements, but the wording of the table of contents should echo throughout an abstract or summary. These elements, when well designed, enable readers to quickly find a specific segment in the body of the report.

Often, the abstract follows or appears on the title page. Summaries may also follow the title page. While abstracts and summaries contain similar information, summaries usually provide more extensive information than abstracts and may be written for decision makers whose needs differ from those of readers who want only the essence of a report. (See the table of contents and the summary in Appendix C.)

Abstracts fall into two categories, informative or descriptive. Abstracts, often accompanied by keywords, are prepared for use in online indexes and databases. Keywords allow your report, if it is stored in a database, to be retrieved. Thus, you should think carefully about the keywords that characterize the content of your report. What words will your readers most likely use in a database search? Abstracts with keywords may be separated from the report but linked to the full report. Based on the information in the abstract, readers can decide if they need to move to the full report.

Differences in abstracts have tended to disappear; and some abstracts have the characteristics of both traditional informative and descriptive styles. Organizations and journals usually have specific requirements for abstracts and may require, for example, a short descriptive abstract on the title page and an informative abstract after the table of contents.

Because the quantity of information that bombards readers increases, well-written abstracts have become critical to report access. The abstract should explain the purpose of the report, findings, conclusions, and recommendations—anything of significance. Because many readers now use abstract services, they may read only your abstract, or they may decide to retrieve/order your complete report if the abstract clearly shows the relevance of the content and key points.

A good way to plan an abstract is to create a file that contains the names of its main parts:

Purpose
Methods
Findings or Results
Conclusion(s)
Recommendation(s)

Next, insert information under each heading. When you complete your abstract, you can remove the headings. Be sure to check the length of the abstract; publications rarely want abstracts longer than 100 to 150 words. This method allows you to track length easily. However, some publications want the headings included in the abstract.

Informative abstract. This type of abstract includes the research objectives, research methods used, and findings, including principal results and conclusions.

Recommendations may also be included. Informative abstracts usually range from 50 to 500 words, depending on the length of the report and on the requirements of the disseminating organization and of the abstracting service. Informative abstracts help readers decide if they want or need to access the entire report for more thorough examination. They begin with a statement of the report's purpose, and the remaining sentences give major highlights and conclusions (Figure 8-2).

Descriptive abstract. This type of abstract states what topics the full report contains. Unlike informative abstracts, descriptive abstracts cannot serve as a substitute for the report itself. They begin with the report purpose and then explain content areas or topics covered in the report (Figure 8-3). See also the descriptive abstract on the title page of the sample report in Appendix C.

Executive summaries. Major reports often include executive summaries, which contain all of the items listed at the beginning of this chapter. However, unlike summaries for routine reports, executive summaries provide extensive development of each information segment to allow decision makers the information they need without having to read or search the full report. An example of an

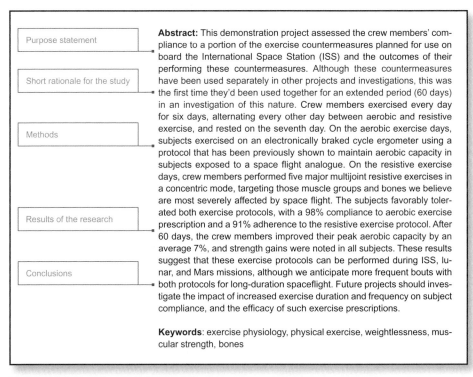

FIGURE 8-2 Informative Abstract

Source: S.M.C. Lee,* M.E. Guilliams,* A.D. Moore, Jr.,* W.J. Williams,* M.C. Greenisen, S.M. Fortney, Exercise Countermeasures Demonstration Project During the Lunar-Mars Life Support Test Project Phase IIA, TM-1998-206537, 1/1/1998, pp. 71, *Krug Life Sciences, Inc. http://ston.jsc.nasa.gov/collections/TRS/_1998-abs.html

1. **Keywords**: motion, motion perception, perception, control, adaptive control

Abstract: The purpose of this report is to identify the essential characteristics of goal-directed whole-body motion. The report is organized into three major sections. Section 2 reviews general themes from ecological psychology and control-systems engineering that are relevant to the perception and control of whole-body motion. These themes provide an organizational framework for analyzing the complex and interrelated phenomena that are the defining characteristics of whole-body motion. Section 3 applies the organizational framework from the first section to the problem of perception and control of aircraft motion. This is a familiar problem in control-systems engineering and ecological psychology. Section 4 examines an essential but generally neglected aspect of vehicular control: coordination of postural control and vehicular control. To facilitate presentation of this new idea, postural control and its coordination with vehicular control are analyzed in terms of conceptual categories that are familiar in the analysis of vehicular control.

FIGURE 8-3 Descriptive Abstract

Source: Gary E. Riccio* and P. Vernon McDonald,** Multimodal Perception and Multicriterion Control of Nested Systems: I. Coordination of Postural Control and Vehicular Control, TP-1998-3703, 1/1/1998, pp. 76, *Nascent Technologies, Ltd. **National Space Biomedical Research Institute. http://ston.jsc.nasa.gov/collections/TRS/_1998-abs.html

executive summary can be seen in the proposal for Project LEAD (Figure 8-4). Even though you know nothing about this project, the executive summary will provide you with extensive information. In many proposals, the summary often determines whether the proposal itself will be read.

Discussion, or body of the report. The main part of the report—the discussion—takes most of the writer's development time. The information to be reported constitutes the discussion. The discussion will explain in detail—information appropriate to the context, the readers, and the purpose of the report—why the report was done, its objectives, methods, findings, results, analysis of results, conclusions emerging from results, and recommendations for dealing with the results. The discussion is the heart of the report: without it, effective summaries and abstracts could not be written. All conclusions and recommendations derive from the discussion. Stated another way, the presentation of information in the discussion allows the report writer to draw conclusions and perhaps recommendations. In short, the discussion must support all conclusions and recommendations.

The discussion can also stand alone. Because the report discussion begins with an introduction, including an explanation of the approach used in developing the report, the discussion is complete in itself. Many discussions end with a factual summary, a concise narrative of the report's main findings.

Ironically, however, the main discussion is the report segment read least. While most readers will look at the summary, abstracts, and table of contents, few will actually delve into the discussion. Nevertheless, the discussion becomes the source, foundation, and documentation for every statement written in the abstract and summary. Your conclusions need to evolve from the discussion. Recommendations

Project LEAD (Leadership Education and Development) for Junior High/Middle Level Preservice and Beginning Teachers

Executive Summary

The College of Education at Texas Tech University proposes to develop a practical project that will address two problems in public education: the teacher shortage caused by beginning teacher attrition and beginning teacher attrition caused by feelings of inadequacy. The present shortage in Texas of 37,000 to 40,000 can be attributed to the attrition of beginning teachers, not the failure of enough new teachers to be certified, according to Ed Fuller, co-director of research at the State (Texas) Board for Educator Certification ("Lawmakers Hear Teacher-Shortage Report," 2002), since it is the certified beginning teachers, 40 to 50 % nationwide, who are the ones who are unwilling to stay in the classroom, this proposed project will seek to address the problem of new teacher attrition and, therefore, the teacher shortage.

The College of Education at Texas Tech University, along with partners from local school districts, proposes to develop a two-part project—LEAD (Leadership Education and Development) for Junior High/ Middle Level Preservice and Beginning Teachers, which will be built around the theme of leadership and which will consist of two distinct but interrelated programs: a preservice and an induction program. The premise is that if beginning teachers are developed as leaders, they will be retained at a higher rate than those young teachers who do not have their courses, their field experience and their first two years of teaching infused with leadership skills. The LEAD group will be better prepared to do well and to be retained because they will begin teaching with training that will give them a sense of control and support as they begin.

LEAD will be developed by a partnership of beginning teachers, selected junior high/middle level principals and their teachers, and faculty and staff of the College of Education at Texas Tech University. This collaboration will

- Define the term *leadership* and determine the leadership outcomes that young teachers need;
- Write the mission and philosophy and the goals and objectives of LEAD;
- Determine the type of students to recruit and how to best recruit them;
- Determine how to best implement and evaluate the determined leadership skills in the preservice courses, including student teaching;
- Develop and implement a Leadership Seminar preservice component;
- Plan and implement a two-year induction program that will continue to emphasize leadership skills and will collaborate with district induction programs;

The project will begin with a selected cohort of 30 junior high/middle level preservice teachers in 2004, and by second and third cohorts of 30 in 2005 and 2006. Group one will participate in two years of induction while group two will have one year, and group three will have none, unless additional funding can be secured. Assessment and evaluation of each aspect of the program will be ongoing, and appropriate annual reports will be made to the funding agency.

Need for LEAD

The College of Education and partners from ISD's in Lubbock County propose to initiate a project to develop teacher leaders. The College of Education is interested in developing this project because of the desire to help address the critical issues of the teacher shortage and the attrition rate of beginning teachers in the public schools. The attrition of certified teachers (40-50%) during the first five years of teaching appears to be a major cause of the teacher shortage across the nation and in Texas (35,000 to 40,000 in Texas alone). Addressing these issues requires a systematic approach that cultivates teacher leaders during their preservice training and supports them during the transition into their teaching careers. Project LEAD (Leadership Education and Development) for Junior High/Middle Level Preservice and Beginning Teachers will consist of two distinct but interrelated programs: a two-year preservice teacher program and an induction program designed to address the critical concerns of teacher shortage and beginning teacher attrition by developing teacher leaders.

FIGURE 8-4 Proposal with Executive Summary

Description of LEAD

Three cohorts of students seeking junior high/middle level certification will be recruited to participate in Project LEAD, based on their perceived level of commitment to the teaching profession at the time of their selection. LEAD will tailor the junior high/middle level certification preservice education courses that these students take to stress leadership skills. Once these students are certified and are beginning teachers in local junior high/middle level classrooms, they will be supported by an induction program, which will help them to implement leadership skills in their classrooms. As a result of stressing leadership in the junior high/middle level preservice courses and in the induction program, LEAD teachers will be better prepared to succeed as educators and to be retained in the profession than will other beginning teachers who do not have this training, for this project will enhance the sense of control and support that are critical to the retention of beginning career teachers.

One important strategy for implementing Project LEAD is for the College of Education to collaborate fully with local ISD's to develop the preservice and induction programs of LEAD. The College of Education faculty and staff will enlist the help of junior high/middle level principals, their teachers, and some of their junior high/middle level beginning teachers who had no special leadership preparation during their preservice courses to advise the faculty and staff on what the preservice and induction components of LEAD should be. For example, they, along with faculty and staff from the COE, will

- Specify what the term *leadership* means for junior high/middle level teachers and schools;
- Determine the leadership outcomes that young teachers need;
- Write the mission and philosophy of LEAD;
- Write the goals and objectives of LEAD;
- Determine the type of students to recruit and how to best recruit them;
- Determine how to best implement and evaluate the determined leadership skills in the preservice courses, including student teaching;
- Develop and implement a Leadership Seminar preservice component;
- Plan and implement a two-year induction program that will continue to emphasize leadership skills and will collaborate with district induction programs;
- Identify Teacher Leaders from the schools who will help with induction;
- Develop and implement an evaluation plan.

Project directors will be especially considerate of the time commitment of ISD participants, being careful not to duplicate programs but to participate in district programming that helps further the goals of both the COE and the district and to provide compensation for students and partners in the ISD's. Mr. Wayne Havens, Interim Superintendent, and Ms. Ann Graves, Assistant Superintendent, of the Lubbock ISD have committed verbally to this project, and we will be receiving a letter of support from them.

The first actual cohort of preservice junior high/middle level teachers will begin in the fall of 2004. This will allow time to develop the partnership with district personnel, to get the items listed above in progress, and to conduct the recruitment of the first cohort. Years 2004-2008 will see three cohorts of 30 each finish their preservice courses and participate in varying times of induction (See Timetable). Assessment and evaluation will be ongoing as will be revisions of the programs given the results of assessment and evaluation.

Timetable

Please see Judy Aycock Simpson for a copy of the timetable.)

Uniqueness of the Project

LEAD will be unique for the following reasons:

- It will be developed as a result of collaboration with Lubbock County ISD's;
- It will target junior high/middle level preservice and beginning teachers;
- It will develop teacher leaders;

FIGURE 8-4 *continued*

• It will enable beginning teachers to be better prepared to succeed because their preservice courses will provide them with the skills to do so;
• It will provide an induction period that will support beginning teachers.

Future Plans

If assessment and evaluation efforts reveal that LEAD results in greater success and retention of beginning teachers, the College of Education will seek funding to implement the full induction program for Cohorts 2 and 3 and to implement a secondary preservice component of LEAD.

Proposed Budget Justification

The budget goal is to provide as much incentive as possible for the partners, the preservice teachers, and the beginning teachers. Because faculty and staff believe so strongly in the value of this project, neither the Principal Investigators, the Project Advisor, nor the faculty and staff of Texas Tech working on the project committee will receive any compensation for services, such as being project director or advisor or the like. A total budget of $33,500.00 is sought for redevelopment of the preservice courses, the development of the induction program, and the coordination and implementation of these programs. This amount equals 16% of the $203,800.00 that is necessary to implement this project. Students, principals, and junior high/middle level teacher leaders and beginning teachers will be the recipients of 81% of the funds sought. The College of Education will commit another $129,237.00 of in-kind contributions to make this project a success.

LEAD Budget

Personnel Preparation Costs

Redevelopment of courses $ 7,500.00
Development of Induction $ 7,500.00
Coordination and Implementation of Seminars $ 3,000.00
Coordination and Implementation of Induction Program $ 3,000.00
Evaluation: $2500 for 1 for 5 yrs. $ 12,500.00
Total Personnel Preparation Costs $ 33,500.00

In-Kind Personnel Support Cost

Graduate Student Worker: 9 months/20 hrs. week/salary, tuition, fringes, $ 81,737.00
Time of 2 Principal Investigators each year: $2500 each for 5 yrs. $ 25,000.00
Time of Project Advisor/Liaison person: $2500 for 5 yrs. $ 12,500.00
Time for COE Committee: $220 each a yr for 5 yrs. $ 10,000.00
Total Personnel Support Costs $ 129,237.00

Partnership Costs

Teacher Leaders from ISD's: $350 each for 190 of 4 yrs. $ 66,500.00
ISD Advisory Groups: $250 for 40 (8 each yr.) for 5 yrs. $ 10,000.00
Parking and Misc. for Teacher Leaders and Advisory Board for 5 yrs. $ 2,000.00
Total Partnership Costs $ 78,500.00

Student and Beginning Teacher Costs

Seminar Materials: Tapes, recorders, white boards, erasers, etc. $ 2,500.00
Seminar Speakers: $100 each for speakers for 14 a year over 4 yrs. $ 19,600.00
Seminar Texts: $100 each for 200 students over 4 yrs. $ 20,000.00

FIGURE 8-4 *continued*

Professional Materials for seminars: $50 each for 200 students over 4 yrs. $ 10,000.00
Leadership Tapes $ 1,200.00
Food for seminars for 4 yrs/200 students $ 4,000.00
Capstone Materials: Texts and Professional Materials for 200 over 4 yrs. $ 8,000.00
Awards Ceremony: Students, partners, etc. for 250 over 2 yrs. At $15 each $ 4,000.00
Stipends for Summer Induction Institute: $350 each for 50 over 2 summers $ 17,500.00
Total Student and Beginning Teacher Costs $ 86,800.00

General Office Supplies

Paper, pens, copying, phones, mailing, brochures, etc. for 8 over 5 yrs $ 5,000.00
Total General Office Supplies $ 5,000.00

Total Money Sought: $ 203,800.00

In-Kind Contribution: $ 129,237.00

FIGURE 8-4 *continued*

need to evolve from the discussion and the conclusions. In a sense, then, the discussion develops as a narrative that comes to a conclusion.

Many readers may need to read parts of the discussion carefully. They will read the introduction, check the table of contents, skip to relevant sections that interest them, and then move to the conclusion or factual summary that pulls together the main results or ideas.

Parts of the discussion. The main body of the report generally begins with an introduction (or introduction + summary) that forecasts what is to follow in the report. It directs the reader's mind to the subject and purpose. It tells the reader how to approach the content by explaining the scope of the report, the plan of development, and any additional information the reader may need. Examine the introduction from a report for the Virginia Department of Transportation (Figure 8-5). Note that it presents the topic, the rationale, and the development plan for the report. Also examine the introduction to the sample report in Appendix C.

Note that the introduction should always include the report subject, purpose, and plan of development. Some reports place the background and the scope in separate sections that follow the introduction, if these two items are extensive. What you include in the introduction depends on readers. If your readers will expect your report, you can write a short introduction. However, if your report will be archived and read later by people who know little about the report context, you will need to provide a longer, more informative introduction. Avoid long introductions: focus on the subject and purpose in terms that explain the relevance of the report to readers. But do anticipate your readers—who will read this report and when—as you plan the introduction. Without a proper introduction, readers will have difficulty following the main discussion.

Collecting and grouping information. As you gather information, try grouping your material and notes into specific categories. Label these categories, and then begin your report. You may want to develop your report according to major sections—introduction, followed by the topics or categories. Open and name the file and begin. For example:

- Introduction: state the purpose of your report—what you expect to accomplish, what you want your reader(s) to know. You can add additional information later. Stating your purpose at the beginning of the draft helps you stay focused.
- Category/topic 1: phrase describing the issue you want to present
- Category/topic 2: etc.
- Category/topic 3: etc.

Next, begin inserting information under each topic or subject category. Focus initially on inserting information that pertains to the topic heading.

This method helps employees who may be trying to work on a report, answer phone calls, answer/send e-mail, and deal with other routine business events

Exiting Conditions Report, U.S. Route 29 Corridor Development Study, Combined Phases II and III From the North Carolina State Line to I-64 in Charlottesville, VA

Chapter 1—Introduction

The objective of the Route 29 Corridor Development Study is to evaluate all modes of transportation within the corridor and to develop both short- and long-term recommendations to preserve and enhance the transportation resources in this important corridor. The importance of U.S. Route 29 was recognized in the Intermodal Surface Transportation and Efficiency Act (ISTEA) passed by the United States Congress in 1991. In ISTEA, Congress designated the 240 miles of Route 29 from Greensboro, North Carolina, to the District of Columbia as a high priority corridor of national significance and directed that comprehensive transportation studies of the corridor be performed. The designation of these high priority corridors was based upon the findings of Congress that:

❑ The construction of the Interstate Highway System connected the major population centers of the nation and greatly enhanced the economic growth in the United States;

❑ Many regions of the nation are not now adequately served by the Interstate System or comparable highways and require further highway development in order to serve the travel and economic development needs of the region; and,

❑ The development of transportation corridors is the most efficient and effective way of integrating regions and improving efficiency and safety of commerce and travel and further promoting economic development.

More recent legislation, the 1998 Transportation Equity Act for the 21st Century (TEA-21), renewed the commitment to completion of important transportation projects by increasing allocations of federal funds to the states. This national legislation affirmed the long-held recognition of Route 29 by the Virginia Department of Transportation (VDOT) as a vitally important principal arterial highway through central Virginia.

For purposes of study, the Route 29 Corridor in Virginia was divided into four sections. The first section, extending from Warrenton to Interstate 66, was studied as part of transportation needs in the I-66 Corridor. The second section extends from Charlottesville to Warrenton, and was studied in the Route 29 Corridor Development Study (Phase I). This Phase I study was completed in the Fall of 1996. The third and fourth sections extend from Lynchburg to Charlottesville and Danville to Lynchburg, respectively. Both of these sections are included in this current study, which is formally entitled the Route 29 Corridor Development Study (Combined Phases II/III).

The background, methodologies and findings of this study are documented in three separate reports. This report, the first of the three, describes the existing transportation system and its operations, as well as current land uses, socioeconomic conditions, and environmental constraints. The second report, *Route 29 Corridor Development Study (Combined Phases II/III) Technical Report,* describes the development of a statement of purpose and need for transportation improvements, the development of transportation demand forecasts, and the development and refinement of various improvement alternatives. The third report, *Route 29 Corridor Development Study (Combined Phases II/III) Recommended Transportation Concept,* describes the final study recommendations for all modes of travel in the corridor.

FIGURE 8-5 Formal Report Introduction

throughout the workday. In short, you can arrange, insert material, save what you have, and add other material as time permits. You may also write notes to yourself or use different colors and fonts for text you may want to move, delete, or revise. See Case 8-2 and the response. How you design your report will depend on (1) the kind of report you are writing, (2) your readers' informational needs, and (3) the purpose of your report.

Strategy for presenting the discussion The discussion should be planned around each topic mentioned in the plan of development. Note that the logic of the discussion should be evident from the headings, as these are repeated in the table of contents.

Each paragraph in the discussion should begin with a topic sentence, followed by supporting sentences, data, and visuals.

Reports with standard arrangement patterns Some kinds of reports have fairly standard arrangement patterns. Many government funding agencies require that all reports submitted follow a specific plan, and content may be inserted into a template and submitted online. Many organizations also have a standard plan for their policies—what sections to include and the order in which they appear. Policy and procedure manuals, detailing the rules that apply to the employees of a business entity, usually follow a standard pattern.

Often, however, as in Case 8-1, you will be writing a report in which you, as the writer, must decide how to present your research or the information you need to convey. Generally, you have two basic choices: topical arrangement and chronological arrangement. In Case 8-1, the writer decides on a topical arrangement that discusses what he believes to be the most pertinent topics his readers should know about drug cartels.

Topical arrangement. In topical arrangement, the order in which you present your ideas should be logical and inclusive. For example, in a report on disease management of citrus fruit, the writer arranges the report by grouping information about specific citrus diseases. He describes, in parallel arrangement, the main diseases:

> Introduction—Description of treatments for citrus diseases
> Disease #1—Melanose
> > Description
> > Factors to be considered before the application of fungicides for
> > melanose control
> > > Table I. Chemical controls for melanose
> Disease #2—Greasy Spot
> > Description
> > Factors to be considered in the management of greasy spot
> > > Table II: Chemical controls for greasy spot
> Disease #3—Foot Rot
> > Description
> > Factors to consider in managing the disease
> > > Table III. Chemical controls for foot rot
> Disease #4—Citrus Nematode
> > Description
> > Sampling instructions to determine presence of citrus nematode
> > > Table IV: Citrus nematode counts considered low, medium, or
> > > high at specific times during the growing season

Conclusion: Factors to consider before applying nematicides
Table V: Chemical controls for nematodes (summary)

Once the citrus researcher has arranged his information, he can begin inserting information beneath each topic heading.

Chronological arrangement. Some topics can be presented by time. You explain or present information sequentially, in the order in which it occurred. The following outline of a literature review, *Cultural Control of the Boll Weevil—A Four Season Approach—Texas Rolling Plains*, illustrates chronological arrangement. This technical report surveys and reviews existing research on how boll weevils can be controlled throughout the agricultural year. Note, too, that the segments use parallel development, and each segment ends with a summary of that segment. This approach allows the reader to choose where to begin and how much to read. For example, the reader may wish to read only the Summary and Introduction and the factual summary for each season:

Summary
Introduction

Spring Cultural Control
    Prepare the land for planting
    Utilize delayed planting
    Use uniform planting
    Summary

Summer Cultural Control
    Shorten the growing season
    Change the microclimate
        Row direction
        Bed shape
        Row spacing
    Summary

Fall Cultural Control
    Utilize harvest-aid chemicals
    Role of planting date
    Terminate irrigations in August
    Summary

Winter Cultural Control
    Eliminate the overwintering habitat
    Modify the overwintering habitat
    Avoid the overwintering habitat
    Summary

Conclusions
Acknowledgments
Supporting Research Studies

Persuasive arrangement and development. Many times reports argue for a specific point or position. When you argue, you need to persuade your readers. Understanding what objections you will need to overcome will be critical to planning your report and the presentation of your arguments. Reports that must produce conclusions and recommendations may require writers to develop a report in which the conclusions and recommendations are not what readers will welcome. Or these reports may be prepared for readers who have no preconceived ideas. In each situation, the report can be designed to anticipate the perspective of readers.

Let's assume, for example, in Case 8-2, that Harper believes the RAMP building should be seriously considered, while Crandall has decided to purchase another site. Crandall told Harper to visit RAMP, but he never expected that RAMP would be another site consideration. To respond to this situation, Harper might begin his report as follows:

> As you requested, I toured the RAMP research facility during my trip to Atlanta October 4-8, 2009. Based on my findings, I believe that you should seriously consider the RAMP facility as the site for our CE operation. RAMP offers us what we need in terms of space and location. Renovation costs can be done in stages to reduce cost, and the facility offers us the space and arrangement we need.

In short, the reader's perspective often determines how persuasive you need to be if you want your ideas considered.

Conclusion(s). Reports end with a statement of the primary issues covered in the discussion. In long reports, a factual summary comes after the discussion and before the conclusions and recommendations. The factual summary does what its name implies: it covers the essential facts but without interpretation. (Interpretation of the factual summary is done in the executive summary.) The longer the discussion, the more useful a factual summary will be to the reader who actually reads the body of the report. The conclusions themselves provide judgments about the subject based on the evidence explained in the discussion.

Recommendations. Recommendations, if required or needed, emerge from conclusions. However, many reports end with only a conclusion. The type of ending depends on the type of report. Recommendations are proposed actions to be taken based on the conclusions.

Appendices. Appendices include documents that support or add to information you include in the discussion. While the appendix may not be read, it serves an important role. An appendix may contain tables of supporting data, statistical studies, spreadsheets, or any material that supports the points or arguments you make in your discussion. If your report recommends an action, having letters or e-mails requesting that action in the appendix provides convincing support for your recommendation.

Case 8-2

Allan Harper was asked to visit a research facility that his firm has discovered is likely going to be for sale soon. Dick Crandall, the VP for operations, asks Allan to provide a brief overview on the usability of the building as a corporate training facility. Allan visits the building, takes notes on major usability features that he knows will interest Dick, and writes a brief report for the VP, known for wanting only important facts and recommendations. Allan begins with a simple report purpose statement, followed by a bulleted list of the facility's features of interest to Dick. Allan uses notes to himself (in color) as he drafts. He concludes with a brief recommendation of what he believes should be done if Dick thinks the building should be purchased. The report responds to the information needs and reading (skimming) style of a specific reader who wants "the facts."

CASE DOCUMENT 8-2

TO: Dick Crandall   DATE: October 9, 2009

FROM: Allan Harper

SUBJECT: Space Assessment of RAMP, 6004 Highway 7

As you requested, I toured the RAMP research facility during my trip to Atlanta October 4–8, 2009. Based on your questions about using the facility for corporate training, I have concluded the following:

Conclusions

- RAMP offers us the space we need and appears to be in excellent condition. Modifications will be necessary, but those required can be done in stages. We can focus on Building 1, then renovate Building 2 and 3 as we want to. The RAMP is composed of two main buildings and one small building (Buildings 1, 2, and 2A on the attached site map).

- Each small office has two internet connections. The main lecture hall has one internet connection and no projection equipment. [Check on price of wireless for the entire building. DC will probably want to know ASAP.]

- The current RAMP buildings are divided into offices for start-up projects. Some of the RAMP income is derived from the space leased by

continued

small start-up companies. Cost: $22/sq. foot. [Is this price low/high?].
[Call Dave Redding about laboratory contracts. Cheryl Kempe has his
phone number.]

- The debt on RAMP is slightly over $12M with approximately $5M
  due in April of 2012. (See p. 4 of the Notes to Consolidated Financial
  Statements.) [Get current balance owed from Fiscal. Perhaps delete for
  now? Call Debbie in Fiscal.]

- For us to use RAMP for training, instead of research, the entire first floor
  of Building 1 would need to be redesigned. We could relocate some of
  the start-up companies to Buildings 2 and 2A, which would preserve the
  income.

- An attached sketch shows how renovation of the first floor of Building 1
  might look. Note:

      Eight office sites for trainers

      Two computer labs

      Five training rooms—two with breakout rooms off the main area.

      One tiered lecture room

Conversion could be made gradually, depending on how many training rooms
are needed ASAP. The attached sketch, included along with the original plan,
shows one redesign plan.

Assessment of the RAMP Building

- The facility seems to be in good repair. Maintenance seems to be
  satisfactory. I found no indication of leaks.

- HVAC system needs to be inspected.

- Wireless capability could be easily installed in the main lecture room.
  ~~The proposed computer laboratories, carved from 12 offices, offer 24
  internet connections.~~

- New projection equipment needs to be purchased. [Cost?]

- Main lecture hall could be converted into a tiered lecture room. The two
  rooms on either side of the lecture hall could be eliminated to further
  expand the main lecture hall. The kitchen would have to be moved or
  eliminated—perhaps moved to Building 2.

continued

- Renovation costs will be high, close to $1M (according to rough estimates by Gavin Newberry—see attached email answer to my query) even if only the first floor of Building 1 is refurbished. Current office furniture is usable, but new furniture, IAV equipment, and computers would need to be purchased for training and meeting rooms. Closets/storage would have to be added to all training rooms. Floor coverings would need to be replaced.

- Location—RAMP is easily accessible from three main arteries.

- Estimated remodeling time: 4 months.

Attachments: 3

LETTER REPORTS

Reports can be prepared as letters. The example report in Figure 8-6, prepared by a graduate of a school district, assesses the quality of the school's programs. The opening paragraph contains qualities of a summary and an introduction. Note the purpose statement and the plan of the report, in addition to the short summary statement. The effective document design allows the report to be read quickly.

EXAMPLE REPORT FOR STUDY

An example report appears in Appendix C. Two additional annotated reports can be found on the book website: **www.oup.com/us/tebeaux.**

WRITING COLLABORATIVELY

In the workplace, you may need to write reports, instructions, and letters on your own and also as part of a team. Collaborative writing occurs in numerous ways that continue to evolve as technology evolves: you may draft a document or part of a document and then submit it, as an e-mail attachment, to several additional employees who will contribute information to your draft. Each writer may suggest changes to others' work by using a comment tool, such as that found in most word

Laura Anne Ranford

September 30, 2008

Mr. David Russell
Project Director for Quality Enhancement
Jasper Independent School District
128 Park Street
Jasper, TX 75951

Dear Mr. Russell:

I appreciate the opportunity to reflect and then assess on my experience in Jasper High School. While much of my academic program was excellent, several areas do need improvement. My report provides an overall assessment, courses needing improvement, courses effective in preparing for college, recommended changes in college-bound curriculum, extracurricular activities assessment, and general recommendations. These recommendations for improving the quality of a Jasper High School experience are as follows:

- Teach challenging and classic literature.
- Require more writing at all levels.
- Offer more opportunities for motivated students to learn, specifically, more AP courses.
- Refocus health course or add a general nutrition course.
- Emphasize depth over breadth of extracurricular involvement; limit: two to three activities.
- Provide more lab time for science courses.

Overall Assessment of My Jasper High School Experience

My Jasper High School experience has proved to be excellent preparation for my college coursework. I took the most challenging courses offered and participated in extracurricular activities that required learning new skills and getting outside my comfort zone. I was fortunate to have instructors that taught students how to learn on their own, think critically, and apply classroom knowledge to everyday situations. However, there were a few courses that have room for improvement.

Courses Needing Improvement

Health

The Health curriculum focused on the topics of sex, drugs, alcohol, smoking, and sexually-transmitted diseases. This approach was ineffective for two reasons. First, long-term consequences, such as lung cancer or liver failure, do not deter teens from smoking and drinking alcohol because they do not plan that far ahead. Second, most teens make lifestyle decisions based on peer pressure, personal values, or rebelling against an authority, not on what they know about personal and public health. I think a health class promoting proper nutrition, regular exercise and a healthy lifestyle would be more effective in helping teenagers make good decisions.

English I & II

Both freshman and sophomore years, English primarily focused on the TAKS test. The novels read for the courses were adaptations of classics or from the *New York Times'* Bestseller list. As a result, no classic

FIGURE 8-6 Letter Report

literature was covered and very little writing instruction was given outside of TAKS writing. Regarding TAKS writing, general characteristics and examples of high-scoring essays were explained. Most writing assignments were given and graded in the TAKS format. Yet, less than 1% of my class grade received a high score on the TAKS writing section sophomore year. Exposure to classic literature and instruction in general composition would improve the quality of underclassman English education.

Courses Effective in Preparing for College

The courses that were most effective in preparing me for college and the key elements each provided are listed below.

Geometry

- Required application of basic concepts. Only general theorems were taught, not specific examples.
- Homework required critical thinking and synthesis of concepts.
- Introduced trigonometry providing a solid foundation for calculus.

AP Chemistry

- Required detailed lab reports demonstrating a grasp of the experiments, chemistry involved, and sources of error.
- Tested over material not covered in class time.
- Expected to synthesize information in problem solving.

Junior English & Dual-Credit English

- Received instruction and constructive feedback on writing.
- Analyzed challenging classic and controversial literature.
- Learned process for writing a research paper.

AP US History

- Expected to prepare for class by reading ahead.
- Taught as a lecture-style course.

AP Calculus

- Created a foundation of theorems, formulas and methods for the Engineering Math courses I have taken at Texas A&M University.

Recommended Changes in College-Bound Curriculum

Offer More Advanced Placement Courses

From my experience, Advanced Placement (AP) courses challenge students to learn on their own, study material before class, come to class prepared to discuss the reading, and express knowledge of subject through writing. The study skills I learned in AP courses have been instrumental to success in college courses. Only Chemistry, US history, and Calculus were offered when I was a student at Jasper High School. For a higher quality college preparatory curriculum, JHS should consider offering additional AP courses such as English, Biology, Spanish, French, and Statistics.

Require Challenging Literature in English I & II

Simply reading well-written literature helps students better understand shorter, less complicated material and literary elements including grammar, sentence structure, punctuation, and style. Exposing students to challenging literature will improve their reading level, writing ability, vocabulary, and standardized test scores.

JHS Evaluation & Recommendations   2

FIGURE 8-6 *continued*

Designate More Lab Time for Science Courses

More lab time should be designated for science courses. Most scientific knowledge was discovered through experimental observation. Additionally, half of the instructional time in college is spent in a lab setting. Spending more time carrying out experiments will better prepare students for college science courses. Increasing class length or having labs before or after school would provide ample time to include more labs in each science curriculum.

Extracurricular Activities: Pros & Cons and Lessons Learned

Extracurricular activities can be beneficial in moderation. However, over-involvement can be detrimental to a student's academic progress and health. Students should pick two or three activities to be involved in each year.

Pros	*Cons*
▪ Working with people teaches teamwork	▪ Easy to join too many
▪ Learning information and skills outside the classroom in realistic situations	▪ Require a lot of after-school hours and weekends
▪ Developing time management strategies	▪ Distract from schoolwork
▪ Competing reveals strengths & weaknesses	▪ Can be a source of stress
▪ Serving the school and community	

Extracurricular activities can provide valuable knowledge and skills that cannot be learned in a classroom. A few of my extracurricular activities and the valuable lessons learned through them are listed below.

Cross-Examination Debate

- ▪ Evaluated the quality of information found in research—whether current and relevant.
- ▪ Developed multiple cases for both sides of a broad topic.
- ▪ Spoke persuasively and answered critical questions with confidence.
- ▪ Asked questions during cross-examination to reveal opponent's weaknesses.
- ▪ Learned to analyze strengths and weaknesses of arguments.
- ▪ Developed note-taking skills.

UIL Academic Competition

- ▪ Emphasized individual learning.
- ▪ Expanded knowledge-base beyond what was required in a given subject.

Sports & One Act Play

- ▪ Learned the importance of preparation and teamwork.
- ▪ Improvement is always possible.
- ▪ Constructive criticism is far more valuable than passive approval or apathy.

Choir

- ▪ Practice and repetition facilitate mastering new ideas and techniques.

Lions' Club

- ▪ Served community through events and fundraising.
- ▪ Organized events in coordination with other clubs.

FIGURE 8-6 *continued*

General Recommendations to Improve the Quality of a Jasper High School Experience

- Teach challenging and classic literature.
- Require more writing at all levels.
- Offer more opportunities for motivated students to learn, specifically, more AP courses.
- Refocus health course or add a general nutrition course.
- Emphasize depth over breadth of extracurricular involvement; limit: two to three activities.
- Provide more lab time for science courses.

   Thank you for the opportunity to participate in this project. I enjoyed reminiscing about my high school experience. Evaluating each course and activity renewed my appreciation for several teachers and mentors who invested in my education and development. They challenged, inspired, and prepared me for what lay ahead.

   If you have any questions regarding my evaluation or my experiences, please contact me at lar@cumberland.com.

Sincerely,

Laura Anne Ranford

Laura Anne Ranford

FIGURE 8-6 *continued*

processing programs. Team members establish a website on the company Intranet and post material that can then be viewed, revised by all team members, and then discussed via the company Intranet.

A team member may establish a blog on the organization's server—never the Internet because of security issues. On the Intranet blog, everyone on the team can contribute information and help "build" the document. The group may then use some type of interactive audio/video tool to discuss the material, particularly if contributors cannot meet face to face.

Team members often cannot collaborate in "real time" because of other work responsibilities. Blogs and other forms of virtual collaboration allow teams to work more flexibly but could also raise questions about information security.

> **Warning:** As we discussed in Chapter 1, the need for security of an organization's intellectual property cannot be underestimated. Hackers can destroy an organization by stealing intellectual property, trade secrets, contracts, and personnel information. The networking software students use in school cannot offer the security needed by business and research organizations.

The secret to effective collaboration is planning:

- Deciding who will do what
- Deciding how to meet the completion time and planning the work schedule for each document segment
- Learning to work together. When people from different countries and cultures collaborate, the need for sensitivity to cultural differences is critical.
- Ensuring one member will assume the task of editing the document to make sure the style shows consistency throughout

The team leader. Collaborative projects must have a team leader. This person may be the project manager or someone appointed. This person will convene meetings, virtual or onsite, and serve as facilitator to keep the project moving. In addition, the team leader

- ensures that all team members know their tasks,
- launches the effort and provides everyone with the document requirements (purpose, audiences, rationale), format, timetable for completion, and methods of communicating about the document (see Figure 8-7),
- monitors development so that the report is completed as required, and
- ensures that the completed document has a single style throughout and contains all information and required segments.

Project Name	
Goals	
Team members	
Responsibilities	
Deliverables	
Timeline	
Meetings	
Initial Outline	

FIGURE 8-7 Collaborative Team Planning Sheets

Requirements of team leaders. Team leaders, in either face-to-face or virtual settings, need to employ a few fundamental strategies:

- Maintain a positive approach
- Be aware of how you sound; be respectful
- Solicit input
- Encourage timely responses from everyone
- Keep records of all communications

After each draft, the team leader should encourage, as time permits, comments by each team member. The comment tool in doc or pdf files allows each team member to recommend changes and assess the effectiveness of the document.

Requirements of team members.

- Keep the schedule as determined by the project leader. If you find you have an issue that threatens your keeping the schedule, notify the team leader immediately.
- Be respectful and accept comments, recommendations, and suggestions from other team members and the project leader. Exhibit a good attitude, even when you feel stressed.
- Do your part of the project. Do not assume that if you get behind another team member can do your work. The quality of the team project stems from the quality of the work performed by the entire team.

REPORT CHECKLIST ✔

Planning

☐ What is the purpose of your report? Have you stated it in one sentence?
☐ What is the scope of your report?
☐ Who are your readers? What are your readers' technical levels?
☐ What will your readers do with the information?
☐ What information will you need to write the report?
☐ How long should the report be?
☐ What format should you use for the report?
☐ What report elements will you need?
☐ What visuals will you need to present information or data?
☐ What elements do you need to include in your introduction?
☐ What arrangement will you use in presenting your report?

Revision

☐ Does your report do the following:
 • Introduce the subject and purpose?
 • Present enough data in words and visuals to justify any conclusions drawn?
 • Discuss and evaluate the data fairly?
 • Summarize the data?
 • Draw logical conclusions from the data?
 • If necessary, present recommendations that are clearly based on the data and the conclusions?
☐ Are your data accurate?
☐ Do your visuals immediately show what they are designed to show?
☐ Is your format suitable for your content, audience, and purpose?
☐ Have you properly documented all information sources?

EXERCISES

1. Visit the website of a major employer in your field. What kinds of reports do you find at this site? What are the elements and characteristics of the reports? How long are the reports? Who are the audiences for the reports? What are the purposes of the reports? Are the reports written by single or multiple authors? What do the reports indicate about this employer? What do the reports indicate about your field? How would you prepare to write a report like one of these?

2. Examine Figure 8-8. If you were the author of this report and were given 15 more minutes to make it better, what changes would you make?

3. Your supervisor asks you to amplify the Figure 8-8 report with detailed explanations and appropriate tables and figures. For this new formal report, identify the major entries you would include in the table of contents and the list of illustrations and compose a 100-word abstract.

4. Figure 8-9 is the Executive Summary from a 124-page accident report of the National Transportation Safety Board. This summary is 322 words. How would you edit it to 300 words? Or 250 words? (The full report is available at http://www.ntsb.gov.)

Agreements Filed with the Federal Trade Commission under the Medicare Prescription Drug, Improvement, and Modernization Act of 2003

Overview of Agreements Filed in FY 2010
A Report by the Bureau of Competition

During the fiscal year 2010 (October 1, 2009 to September 30, 2010), the Federal Trade Commission received 113 final resolutions of patent disputes between a brand and a generic. This preliminary assessment summarizes the types of final settlements received in FY 2010 and describes how the FY 2010 results compare to filings in other recent years.

Overview of Final Settlements

- 31 final settlements contain both compensation to the generic manufacturer and a restriction on the generic manufacturer's ability to market its product.

  o These settlements involve 22 different branded pharmaceutical products with combined annual U.S. sales of approximately $9.3 billion.

- 66 final settlements restrict the generic manufacturer's ability to market its product, but contain no explicit compensation.

  o In 3 of these settlements, the brand and generic companies agreed to provisions that may provide implicit compensation to the generic in order to agree to a restriction on entry. Specifically, these agreements include a declining royalty structure in which the generic's obligation to pay royalties is reduced or eliminated if the brand launches an authorized generic product. Such a provision may achieve the same effect as an explicit agreement by the brand not to compete with an authorized generic and, thus, could be characterized as potentially involving pay-for-delay.

  o 36 of these agreements involve generics not eligible for 180-day first-filer exclusivity that accept restrictions on entry in exchange for the ability to market the relevant product for some period prior to patent expiration. In 32 of these agreements, the settlement occurs with or following the brand's settlement with a first filer.

- 16 final settlements have no restrictions on entry.

FIGURE 8-8 Document for Exercises 2 and 3

Source: Federal Trade Commission. Agreements Filed With the Federal Trade Commission Under the Medicare Prescription Drug, Improvement, and Modernization Act of 2003: Overview of Agreements Filed in Fiscal Year 2010: A Report by the Bureau of Competition. http://www.ftc.gov/os/2011/05/1105mmaagreements.pdf.

Final Settlements Involving First Filers

- 49 settlements involve generics eligible for 180-day first-filer exclusivity.

  o Of these 49 settlements, 26 contain both compensation to the generic manufacturer and a restriction on the generic manufacturer's ability to market its product; and

  o 23 settlements restrict the generic manufacturer's ability to market its product, but contain no explicit compensation.

Comparing FY 2010 to Prior Years

FY 2010 witnessed a significant increase in the number of final settlement agreements filed, as well as the number of settlements potentially involving pay-for-delay. The number of final settlements filed in FY 2010 is almost double the amount received in any previous year. Similarly, the number of potential pay-for-delay settlements and the number of potential pay-for-delay settlements involving first filers substantially increased over any previous year.

	FY2004	FY2005	FY2006	FY2007	FY2008	FY2009	FY2010
Final Settlements	14	11	28	33	66	68	113
Potential Pay-for-Delay	0	3	14	14	16	19	31
Potential Pay-for-Delay Involving First Filers	0	2	9	11	13	15	26

FIGURE 8-8 *continued*

On Wednesday, July 2, 2008, about 1215 eastern daylight time, the 187-foot-long passenger and car ferry MN *Block Island* collided with the 140-foot-long U.S. Coast Guard cutter *Morro Bay* in reduced visibility on Block Island Sound, about 4 nautical miles south of Point Judith, Rhode Island. The ferry, carrying 294 passengers, eight crewmembers, two concession stand employees, and one off-duty employee, had departed Point Judith about 25 minutes earlier and was traveling south, headed for Old Harbor on the eastern side of Block Island, Rhode Island. The cutter, carrying 21 personnel, had departed Naval Station Newport, Rhode Island, about 1015 and was traveling west, headed for Coast Guard Station New London, Connecticut. As the vessels approached the accident site, the visibility decreased due to fog. At the time of the collision, the crew on the *Morro Bay* estimated the visibility at about 500 yards.

As a result of the accident, the *Block Island* ferry sustained about $45,000 in damage and the *Morro Bay* about $15,000. Two ferry passengers were treated for minor injuries and released that same day.

Safety issues identified in this investigation include failure to follow "rules of the road" in reduced visibility, ineffective use of the radars on board both vessels, and lack of safety management systems and voyage data recorders on U.S. passenger ferries.

The National Transportation Safety Board (NTSB) determines that the probable cause of the collision between the ferry *Block Island* and the Coast Guard cutter *Morro Bay* was the failure of the bridge watch officers on both vessels to monitor their radars, sufficiently assess traffic, and compensate for limited visibility. Contributing to the accident was the failure of the bridge watch officers on both vessels to maintain a proper lookout and to sound appropriate fog signals.

As a result of its investigation, the NTSB makes new recommendations to the Coast Guard and to Interstate Navigation Co., and reiterates an existing recommendation to the Coast Guard.

FIGURE 8-9 Document for Exercise 4

Source: National Transportation Safety Board. Collision Between U.S. Passenger Ferry M/V Block Island and U.S. Coast Guard Cutter Morro Bay Block Island Sound, Rhode Island July 2, 2008. Marine Accident Report NTSB/MAR-11/01 PB2011-916401. Washington, DC: GPO, 2010. p. vii.

Proposals and Progress Reports

Proposals and progress reports, two common types of workplace documents, can be written collaboratively or individually depending on the size of the projects. Many projects, such as those funded by the National Science Foundation or the National Institutes of Health, begin with proposals and require regular progress reports during the course of the project once it is funded. This chapter explains development strategies for both types of documents. However, any work done by an employee may require a status (progress) report submitted to one's supervisor to explain what has been accomplished. A project may begin with a verbal agreement between supervisor and employee, but the employee may be required to submit a progress report either as an e-mail message or as a short memo report. Progress or status reports serve as a major source of documentation to show that employees have performed their work.

To help you understand how to design and write proposals and progress reports, we first discuss the development of proposals and use a student's research project proposal as an example. We also provide additional annotated examples of progress reports to illustrate how these occur in work settings.

The proposal, as its name implies, describes proposed work or research, the reasons for the work, the methods proposed to accomplish the work, the estimated time required, and the expected cost.

The progress report, as its name implies, describes and evaluates a project as work occurs. Thus, if an individual or an organization decides to begin a work project or research project, particularly one that requires several months or even several years to complete, the individual or organization will report the progress on that project at intervals agreed upon when the proposal is accepted and the resulting agreement or contract is being negotiated.

Employees may also need to report progress on the full range of projects or problems on which they are working. In situations like these, the employee writes a progress report (or status report, as it may be called) to inform supervisors or other individuals about what has been accomplished in completing a job or solving a problem. The progress or status report thus becomes an official and even a legal record of work performed. Many organizations require employees to prepare annual status reports of their work, their accomplishments, and their objectives for the coming year.

Quick Tips

Keep in mind that proposals and progress reports are persuasive documents. You write to convince your reader of the merit and integrity of your work. In a proposal, you write to persuade your reader that you have a good idea, a good method for implementing the idea, and the experience necessary to manage the implementation—that you can achieve what you propose. In a progress report, you write to persuade the reader either that you are making good progress on your project or that you realize you aren't making good progress but know why and are taking appropriate steps to fix the problem.

PROPOSALS

The starting point of projects is often a proposal. A proposal offers to provide a service or a product to someone in exchange for money. Usually, when the organization—frequently a federal, state, or city government or a business enterprise—decides to have some sort of work or research done, it wants the best job for the best price. To announce its interest, the soliciting organization may advertise the work it wants done and invite interested individuals or organizations to contact the organization. In a university setting, the research and grants office may notify departments that money is available for research projects in a specific area. Faculty members submit project proposals that explain the research they envision; how much time they will need to complete the project; any financial resources required for equipment, salaries, and release time from regular teaching duties; and the goals and benefits of the research to the individual researcher, the university, and perhaps the public.

When an organization disseminates a description of the work it wants done, this document is usually called a request for proposals (RFP) or a statement of work (SOW). The soliciting organization may send selected companies an RFP/SOW that includes complete specifications of the work desired.

Alternatively, the soliciting organization may first describe the needed work in general terms and invite interested firms to submit their qualifications (Figure 9-1). This type of request is usually called a request for qualifications (RFQ). The organization may also place a notice of intent in newspapers,

-NOTICE OF INTENT-Texas Department of Transportation Notice of Intent—
Contract Number 17-8RFP1001. The Bryan District of the Texas Department of
Transportation (TxDOT) intends to enter into two (2) contracts with prime providers pursuant to Texas Government Code, Chapter 2254, Subchapter A, and 43
TAC §§9.30-9.43, to provide the following services. The work to be performed shall
consist of right of way surveys, aerial photography and digital terrain models for
advance planning and PS&E. Work shall include, but is not limited to: on ground
surveys, parcel plats, legal descriptions, right of way maps, establishment of horizontal and vertical control for aerial mapping, etc. for various construction projects
within the Bryan District. A letter of interest notifying TxDOT of the provider's
interest will be accepted by fax at (979)778-9702, or by hand delivery to TxDOT,
Bryan District, 1300 North Texas Avenue, Attention: Mr. Chad Bohne, P.E.; or by
mail addressed to 1300 North Texas Avenue, Bryan, Texas 77803. **Deadline: Letters
of interest will be received until 5:00 p.m. on Wednesday, September 3, 2012.**
For more information regarding this notice of intent, please visit the TxDOT Internet Home Page located at www.dot.state.tx.us/business/professionalservices.htm or
contact Cecelia McCord at (979) 778-9765. 8-10-08

FIGURE 9-1 Example RFQ from a Newspaper

professional journals, or newsletters. The U.S. government posts its RFQs
online at http://www.grants.gov/. The responding organizations explain their
past accomplishments, giving the names of companies for which they performed work, describing the work they did, and giving references who can
substantiate the organizations' claims. Based on the responses it receives, the
soliciting organization will send full descriptions of the work (RFPs/SOWs)
to the groups it believes have submitted the best qualifications. The responses
submitted to an RFQ or a notice of intent may be called letters of interest or
intent (LOIs).

In short, each aspect of the solicitation process, from the RFQ to the RFP/SOW,
has an appropriate use, but one or more of them is necessary to initiate action on
a project.

Example RFP. The vice president for research at a large university has located
funding opportunities for collaborative research grants. These will be available to
faculty across various disciplines. He issues an RFP via e-mail to the university's
research faculty (see Figure 9-2).

The context of proposal development. Because proposals are time-
consuming to write—most require substantial research and analysis on the part of
the proposing organization—individuals and organizations wishing to respond to
an RFP study it carefully. They do not want to submit a proposal that is unlikely

January 5, 2009

MEMORANDUM

TO: Distribution A

FROM: Dr. Rolfe D. Auston
           Vice President for Research

**SUBJECT: 2009 ABC University-Conacyt: Collaborative Research Grant
           Program**

The Office of the Vice President for Research is pleased to issue a request for proposals for the ABCU-Conacyt: Collaborative Research Grant Program. This program
annually awards one-year grants of up to $24,000 to faculty members to advance
inter-institutional cooperation in science, technology, and scholarly activities that
have a direct application in industry or government through the complementary
efforts of scientists and scholars from ABCU and Mexican institutions.

Two main objectives of the Collaborative Research Grant Program are to provide
seed funding to 1) support the completion of a 12-month inter-institutional project,
and 2) support the development and submission of proposals for external funding
of research from competitive granting agencies both domestic and international
(e.g., NSF, NIH, DOE, World Bank, NATO, UNESCO, etc.) and industry.

ABCU and Conacyt have agreed on several research priority areas as noted in the
request for proposals. The research proposed must be linked to the private sector
and have direct application to solving an industrial or governmental problem. All
proposals must include research that directly improves security for the citizens of
the region or explores issues relating to security challenges facing both countries.

A principal investigator (PI) is required from both Texas ABCU and a Mexican
institution. The PI from ABCU must be a tenured or tenure-track faculty member.
The PI from Mexico must be a scientist or scholar from any Mexican institution
of higher education and research that is registered with Conacyt. Other investigators may include faculty from branch campuses or Mexican faculty, postdoctoral
students, graduate students, or research staff. A letter of intent must be received
by 5:00 p.m. on Friday, March 5, 2009, to be eligible to submit a full proposal. Full
proposals must be submitted, routed electronically for appropriate signatures, and
received by 5:00 p.m. on Friday, April 30, 2009. The request for applications is
available on the Web at http://conacyt.abcu.edu.

Additional information may be obtained by contacting Ms. Catharine J. Restivo
(916-555-555; cjr@abcu.edu).

FIGURE 9-2 E-mail RFP

to be accepted. Thus, the proposer—whether a university professor seeking research funds or a highway construction firm seeking to win a contract from a county to upgrade its rural roads—will approach the decision to prepare a proposal carefully.

The individual or the company must first decide whether to respond to the proposal. Can we do the work requested? Can we show that we can do this work, based on what we have already done? Can we do it within the time limit given in the RFP? Businesses responding to RFPs must address economic issues. How much will our proposed approach cost? How much money can we make? Who else will be submitting proposals? What price will competitors likely quote for the same work? Can we compete? What other projects do we have under way? Could problems arise that would make us unable to complete the job on time and at the price we quote? Do we have personnel qualified to work on this project?

The e-mail RFP in Figure 9-2 would elicit other questions. Is my field applicable to the research opportunity described here? Can I develop a collaborative proposal by the deadline? What types of national security topics would be most likely to attract funding? The university research office often has a person who helps answer these questions.

Many business entities requesting proposals will hold a bidders' conference at which companies interested in submitting a proposal can ask questions about the project or seek clarification of the needs described in the RFP. Most RFPs require that proposals be submitted by a deadline and contain specific information. Proposals that miss the deadline or do not contain the information requested are ordinarily omitted from consideration. Therefore, once an organization decides to submit a proposal, staff members carefully study the RFP and identify the information requirements. Each information requirement is given to an individual or a group who will be responsible for furnishing necessary material and data.

Some proposals, such as university research proposals, may be written by one or two persons. In complex proposals, however, different sections may be written by individuals in different areas of the organization. An editor or proposal writer will then compile the final document. This writer/editor may be assisted by readers who help check the developing proposal to be sure that all requested information is included and that the information is correct. Many proposals have to conform to strict length requirements. Proposals that do not conform will be eliminated from consideration.

Once the proposal has been written and submitted, it becomes a legally binding document. The proposing company or individual is legally committed to do what is described in the proposal, at the cost, and within the time limit stated. For that reason, the proposing organization carefully checks all information for accuracy.

When a large number of bidders submit proposals in response to an RFP, the soliciting organization may select several finalists and allow each finalist to give an oral version of the proposal. During oral presentations, the soliciting group asks questions. Representatives of the proposing groups have one more opportunity to argue for the value of what they propose, the merits of their organization, and the justification for the cost attached to the proposed work.

Students may be required to submit proposals for semester research projects or for other university programs, such as research opportunities with faculty. These proposals (two appear in this chapter) provide you with good practice in developing proposals you may write in your career: for example, government grants to fund your research, approvals to launch a work-related project, and actual bid proposals to help your business organization win work projects. Explaining to a potential employer during an interview that you have studied and written at least one proposal and a progress report can help you win a job offer.

Effective argument in proposal development. All writing is persuasive: it must convince the reader(s) that the writer has credibility and that the writer's ideas have merit. However, the success of a proposal rests totally on the effectiveness of the argument—how convincingly the writer argues for a plan, an idea, a product, or a service to be rendered and how well the writer convinces the reader that the proposing organization offers the best qualifications to do the work or research needed. In planning the proposal, the proposer must harmonize the soliciting company's needs with the proposer's capabilities. The writer must be acutely sensitive to what readers will be looking for but not propose action outside the capability of the proposing individual or organization. The proposing individual or organization has an ethical responsibility to explain accurately and specifically what work can be done and not done so that no possibility exists of deceiving readers by making promises that cannot be fulfilled.

The following questions can help you analyze the effectiveness of the argument, from the solicitor's perspective, whether in a written or an oral proposal:

- What does the soliciting organization really want?
- What is the problem that needs to be solved?
- What approaches to the solution will be viewed most favorably?
- What approaches will be viewed unfavorably?
- What objections will our plan elicit?
- Can we accomplish the goals we propose?

To answer these questions, the proposer may be required to do research on the organization, its problems, its corporate culture, the perspective and attitudes stemming from its corporate culture, and its current financial status, goals, and problems. As the proposal develops, the writer should examine it from the intended reader's perspective.

- What are the weaknesses of the plan, as we—the writers—perceive them?
- How can we counter any weaknesses and the reader's potential objections?

- How can we make our plan appealing?
- How can we show that we understand their needs?
- How can we best present our capability to do this project?
- What are our/my strength(s)?
- From our own knowledge of our organization, what are our weaknesses—in personnel and in overall capability to complete this project as proposed?
- Do we need to modify our proposed plan to avoid misleading readers about our ability to perform certain tasks on time, as proposed, and at cost?
- Can we sell our idea without compromising the accuracy of what we can actually do?

As a proposal writer, you should consider each question and determine what evidence you will need to support the merits of your idea and the arguments needed to refute any objections. Every sentence in your proposal should argue for the merits of your plan and your or your organization's ability to complete it. Although the proposal must be designed as a sales document, you have an ethical obligation to present a plan that meets the soliciting organization's needs and requirements. (In considering the ethical issues that confront proposal writers, you will want to review Chapter 3, Writing Ethically.)

Standard sections of proposals. Proposals generally include three main divisions: a summary, a main body, and attachments. The main body focuses on the three main parts of the proposal: the proposal's objectives (technical proposal), methods for achieving objectives (management proposal), and project cost (cost proposal). Proposals vary, but you will see the following segments embedded in some way:

> Project summary
> Project description (technical proposal)
>> Introduction
>> Rationale and significance
>> Plan of the work
>>> - Scope
>>> - Methods
>>> - Task Breakdown
>>> - Problem Analysis
>> Facilities and equipment
> Personnel (management proposal)
> Budget (cost proposal)
> Conclusion
> Appendices

Major business proposals are submitted in complete report format, which requires a letter of transmittal, a title page, a submission page (perhaps), a table of contents, and a summary—all items discussed in Chapter 8. Shorter proposals may be written in a memo or letter format. Many government proposals must be submitted online only. Whatever the format, the main elements will be required, although how they appear will vary with each proposal. In most RFPs, the soliciting organization explains what should be included in the proposal (either specific information to be included or major elements). Often, RFPs indicate the maximum number of pages allowed in a proposal. Writers should follow these instructions carefully to ensure that the proposal is not rejected during the initial screening process because it fails to follow preparation guidelines stipulated by the RFP.

Summary. The summary is by far the most important section of the proposal. Many proposal consultants believe that a project will be accepted or rejected based solely on the effectiveness of the summary, your readers' first introduction to what you are proposing. The summary should concisely describe the project, particularly how your work meets the requirements of the soliciting organization, your plan for doing the work, and your or your company's main qualifications. The summary should be a concise version of the detailed plan, but it should be written to convince readers that you understand what the soliciting firm needs and wants, that what you are proposing can be done as you describe, and that your approach is solid because you have the required knowledge and expertise. After reading the summary, readers should want to read more of your proposal.

Project description (technical proposal). The technical proposal describes what you or your company proposes to do. The description must be as specific as possible. The technical proposal has a number of elements:

Introduction. The proposal introduction should explain what you are proposing, why you are proposing this idea, and what you plan to accomplish. The introduction contains the same elements as any introduction. In short proposals, the summary and introduction can be combined.

Rationale and significance. Much of your success in convincing readers that you should be granted a contract to do the work you propose will rest on your success in convincing them that you understand the project. In the section on rationale and significance, you need to make clear that you understand readers' needs—as stated in the summary or introduction—and that you have designed your goals by analyzing and defining their needs. Although you will clearly be selling your idea, you should recognize and answer any questions your readers may have as you argue the merits of your project. Convincing your readers that you fully understand what they are looking for is critical in establishing your credibility.

In short,

- You may want to define the problem, to show that you understand it.
- You may want to explain the background of the problem and how it evolved, by providing a historical review of the problem.

- If you are proposing a research project, you may want to explain why your research needs to be done and what results can be expected from your research.
- You may want to describe your solution and the benefits of your proposed solution.

Of greatest importance, however, is the *feasibility* of the work you propose. Is your proposed work doable? Is it suitable, appropriate, economical, and practicable? Have you given your readers an accurate view of what you can and will do?

Plan of the work. The section on the work plan is also critical, particularly to expert readers who will attempt to determine whether you understand the breadth of the work you are proposing. In this section, you will describe how you will go about achieving the goals you have stated. You will specify what you will do in what order, explaining and perhaps justifying your approach as you believe necessary. A realistic approach is crucial in that a knowledgeable reader will sense immediately if your plan omits major steps. A flawed work plan can destroy your credibility as well as the merits of the goals or the solution you are proposing.

Scope. The work plan section may need to describe the scope of the proposed work. What will you do and not do? What topics will your study or your work cover and not cover? What are the limits of what you are proposing? What topics will be outside the scope of your project? As the writer of the proposal, you have both an ethical and a legal obligation to make clear to your readers the limits of your responsibility.

Methods. A work plan may also require a statement of the methods you will use. If you are going to do onsite research, how will you do this research? If you plan to collect data, how will you do so? How will you analyze this data? How will you guarantee the validity of the analysis? If your research includes human subjects, how will you make sure that their participation is voluntary and their privacy is protected? If you are going to conduct surveys or interviews, how will you do so and what questions will you ask? If you plan to do historical research or a literature review of a topic, how will you approach such a review to ensure that your findings are representative of what is currently known about a subject area? What precautions will you take to verify that your research is conducted according to applicable ethical and legal standards? A precise, carefully detailed description of your work methods can add to your credibility as one who is competent to perform the proposed work.

Task breakdown. Almost all proposals require you to divide your work into specific tasks and to state the amount of time allotted to each task. This information may be given in a milestone chart, as illustrated in the methods section of the student research proposal (Case 9-1). The task breakdown indicates how much time you plan to devote to each task. A realistic time schedule also becomes an effective argument. It suggests to readers that you understand how much time your project will take and that you are not promising miracles just to win approval of your proposal or business plan.

If a project must be completed by a deadline, the task breakdown and work schedule should indicate exactly how you plan to fit every job into the allotted time. However, do not make time commitments that will be impossible to meet. Readers who sense that your work plan is artificial will immediately question your credibility. Remember, too, that a proposal is a binding commitment. If you cannot do what you propose, what the soliciting organization requires within the required time, you can destroy your professional credibility and leave yourself open to litigation.

Problem analysis. Few projects can be completed without problems. If you have carefully analyzed the problem or work you intend to do, you should anticipate where difficulties could arise. Problems that may be encountered can often be discussed in the rationale section. However, if you discover major obstacles that you believe will occur during the course of the project, you may wish to isolate and discuss these in a separate section. Many organizations that request work or solicit research proposals are aware of problems that may arise. Reviewers in these organizations look carefully at the problem analysis section, wherever it occurs, to see whether the proposer has anticipated these problems and explained the course of action that will be followed in dealing with them. Anticipating and designing solutions to problems can further build your credibility with readers, who will not be impressed if you fail to diagnose points in your work plan that could be troublesome and even hinder your completion of the project as proposed.

Facilities and equipment. The facilities section of the proposal is important if you need to convince the reader that your company has the equipment, plant, and physical capability to do the proposed work. Facilities descriptions are particularly crucial if hardware is to be built at a plant site owned by your organization. Even in research proposals, your readers may want to know what resources you will use. Sometimes existing facilities are not adequate for a particular job and your company must purchase specific equipment. The facilities section enables you to explain this purchase and how it will be included in the cost proposal.

Researchers may need to travel to visit special libraries or research sites. The amount of money needed for this travel will be part of the cost proposal. Thus, the nature of any extra research support, its importance, and its cost to the project should be explained here.

Personnel (management proposal). Any technical proposal or project is only as good as the management strategy that directs it. The management proposal should explain how you plan to manage the project: who will be in charge and what qualifications that person or team has for this kind of work. Management procedures should harmonize with the methods of pursuing the work described in the technical proposal.

Descriptions of your management philosophy and hierarchy should clearly reflect your company's management philosophy and culture. Readers should see the same kind of management applied to the proposed work as to the company and other projects it manages. Any testimony to or evidence of the effectiveness of the management approach will lend credibility to the technical proposal. Proposal reviewers must be convinced that you and your organization have a sound approach supported by good management of that approach.

In research proposals, the researcher who is soliciting funds will want to explain his or her expertise in the subject area proposed. This explanation may focus on educational background, previous projects successfully undertaken, published research on the topic, and general experience.

Budget (cost proposal). The cost proposal is usually the final item in the body of the proposal, even though cost may ultimately be the most crucial factor in industrial proposals. Cost is usually given last and appears as a budget for the length of the proposal period. The technical and management sections of the proposal, with their descriptions of methods, tasks, facilities, required travel, and personnel, should help justify the cost. They should have already explained the rationale for items that will produce the greatest cost. However, any items not previously discussed in the technical and management sections—such as administrative expenses, additional insurance benefits costs, and unexpected legal costs—should be explained. An itemized budget, often submitted as a separate document, includes items such as the proposing organization's liability for not meeting project deadlines, for cost overruns, and for unforeseen labor strikes and work stoppages. Many budget sections include standard statements such as descriptions of union contracts with labor costs, insurance benefits costs, nonstrike costs, and statements of existing corporate liability for other projects—any existing arrangements that affect the cost of the proposed contract. Clearly, the budget should explain exactly how much the project will cost and how the cost is determined. The extensiveness of the budget depends on the magnitude of the project.

Conclusion. The proposal includes a final section that repeats what the proposal offers the potential client or the soliciting agency, why you or your company should be selected to perform the work, and the benefits that the project, when completed, will yield for the client. The conclusion presents the final restatement of your central argument.

Appendices. As in any report, the appendix section includes materials to support information you give in the main body of the proposal—in the technical, management, or cost proposals. For example, the appendix might include résumés of principal investigators, managers, or researchers. These résumés should highlight their qualifications as they pertain to the specific project.

Case 9-1: Research Proposal

The undergraduate research office at a university solicits proposals from under-graduate students who wish to pursue research with a faculty member. Case Document 9-1 is a research proposal written by an undergraduate chemical engineering major, Evan Cherry. The proposal includes sections required by the solicitation for these undergraduate research proposals. Readers for this proposal will be faculty from science and engineering. For that reason, the proposal is highly technical and is prepared to meet the strict length requirements given in the RFP.

EVAN CHERRY

Proposal for Undergraduate Research Scholars Program: Effects of Simvastatin and Fluvastatin on Endothelial Invasion

Summary

Millions of people take cholesterol lowering medications. This proposal investigates whether the cholesterol medications simvastatin (Zocor®) and fluvastatin (Lescol®) can additionally alter a key step of wound healing. We will specifically determine whether these medications affect angiogenesis, the formation of new blood vessels from pre-existing structures using a model of endothelial cell invasion. We hypothesize that simvastatin and fluvastatin may have additional effects unrelated to reducing cholesterol. The specific aims are:

1. Determine the effects of simvastatin and fluvastatin on endothelial invasion.

2. Determine whether the effects on invasion are a direct result of altered cholesterol levels or due to inhibition of HMG CoA Reductase activity.

3. Determine the signaling mechanisms affected by simvastatin and fluvastatin.

Introduction

I. Atherosclerosis and Statins

Cholesterol regulation has become one of the primary methods for preventing heart disease. HMG-CoA Reductase inhibitors (statins), the first line of treatment for inhibiting cholesterol synthesis, lower blood cholesterol levels

continued

and significantly reduce both atherosclerosis[1] and the instance of heart disease by 60%.[2]

Atherosclerosis is the buildup of fatty plaques along blood vessel lining. Various stress factors oxidize the cholesterol transport molecule Low density Lipoproteins (LDL). Oxidized LDL adheres to the lining of blood vessels and encourages foam cell accumulation and plaque growth, which reduces blood flow and can cause heart attack.[3] Plaque rupture can result in a stroke.

The Agency for Healthcare Research and Quality found that in 2005, 29.7 million people purchased statins for an estimated total of 19.7 billion dollars.[4] Two examples of statins are shown below (Figure 1). Simvastatin is derived from lovastatin, a naturally-occurring compound in the fungus Aspergillus terreus. Fluvastatin, a synthetic statin, has a visibly different structure.

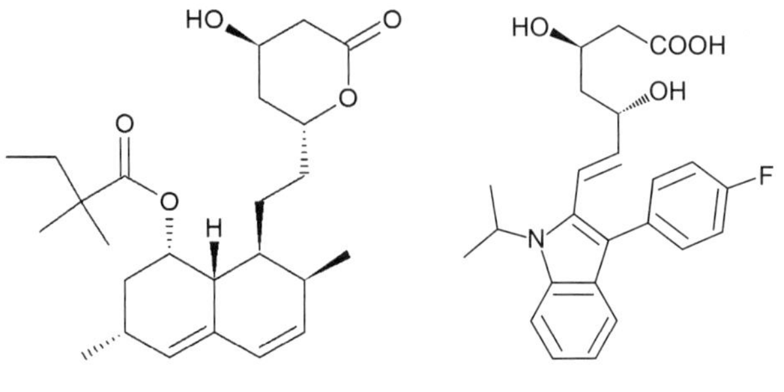

Figure 1: The structures of simvastatin and fluvastatin differ substantially.

II. Angiogenesis

Patients treated with statins exhibit other cardiovascular protective effects, including a lower incidence of cancer.[5] New blood vessel growth, or angiogenesis, is an important part of tumor growth and wound healing. These data have helped form the basis for our hypothesis that statins may affect angiogenesis.

During angiogenesis, endothelial cells lining blood vessels respond to extracellular signals and change into invading structures (Figure 2). The endothelial cells enter the surrounding matrix and form new blood vessel growth. In wound healing, the process relies on platelets, fibroblasts, and neighboring endothelial cells to close the wound. Endothelial cells propagate across the gap until they make contact with other endothelial cells and cease multiplying. The simultaneous combination of lipid inducers and growth factors is required for endothelial invasion.[6]

For our project, we will investigate if statin therapy changes invasion responses in a model reproducing angiogenesis during wound healing.

continued

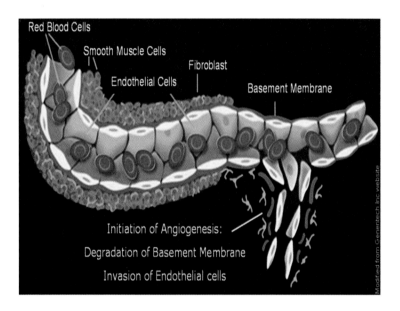

Figure 2. Endothelial invasion begins angiogenesis.

Project Description

We will evaluate the effects of statin therapy on endothelial invasion and whether the effects stem from cholesterol mediation or secondary effects. My project consists of three aims:

1. Determine the effects of statin therapy on endothelial invasion.

We will conduct invasion experiments using statin pre-treated endothelial cells and quantify both the number of cells invading and invasion depth.

2. Determine whether the effects on invasion are a direct result of altered cholesterol levels or HMG CoA Reductase.

We will analyze cholesterol levels in the cells using a commercially available kit and decrease cholesterol levels.

3. Determine how simvastatin and fluvastatin alter signaling.

Preliminary data indicate that several proteins mediate invasion responses. We will analyze levels of activated proteins at various time points of invasion.

Methodology and Timeline

Dr. Bayless' lab implements an artificial angiogenesis model using three-dimensional collagen that mimics the extracellular matrix. We place collagen

continued

solution containing nutritive media and sphingosine-1-phosphate (S1P). S1P is a lipid that signals the endothelial cells to invade the collagen matrix.[7] We add human endothelial cells to the top surface of the collagen. The cells form a single layer and attach to the gel. We then add additional nutritive media and growth factors.

After the cells incubate 18-24 hours, we preserve the cells with formaldehyde before staining with 4′,6-diamidino-2-phenylindole (DAPI), a molecule that causes nuclei to fluoresce under ultraviolet light. This allows us to count the number of invading cells before we stain them with toluidine blue and cut cross-sectional slices. Photographs show invading cells and photography software measures the depth of the invading cells (Figure 3).

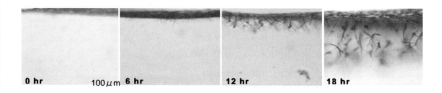

0 hr   100 μm 6 hr   12 hr   18 hr

Figure 3. Endothelial cells invade the 3-dimensional matrix.

To complete *Aim 1* I will place cells pre-treated with simvastatin or fluvastatin in assays as shown in figure 3. The invasion density and depth will be counted. All experiments will be confirmed three times. (n=3)

To complete *Aim 2* we will measure cellular cholesterol levels by using a commercially available kit and measure any differences in cholesterol synthesis between fluvastatin and simvastatin. The cholesterol profile will tell us whether the two compounds comparably inhibit cholesterol.

If we observe any differences in cholesterol levels or invasion, we will assume that these effects are due to decreased HMG CoA Reductase activity. To confirm this we will knockdown HMG CoA Reductase by delivering a small hairpin RNA (shRNA) sequence to the endothelial cells using lentiviruses produced in the Bayless lab. We will check gene knockdown by western blot and analyze the behavior of these cells in our invasion model.

If fluvastatin or simvastatin affect invasion responses, we will assume they are altering signaling events that control invasion. Two of these events are phosphorylation of Akt and p42/44 MAP Kinase (Figure 4). To complete *Aim 3* we will treat cells with simvastatin or fluvastatin and extract proteins over time. For the western blot, we will line up the treated and control extracts on an acrylamide gel and separate them by electrophoresis.

continued

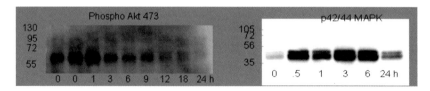

Figure 4. Western blots show Akt and p42/44 levels vary with invasion time.

We will specifically look for differences in activation of Akt and ERK p42/p44. While we do not know all the proteins involved in the invasion response, we do know that these proteins occur early in the process.

The possibility exists that simvastatin and fluvastatin have no effect on these designated proteins; we can then conclude that effects may occur further down the pathway and continue from there.

					Fall 2008						
Week #	1	2	3	4	5	6	7	8	9	10	11	12
Week of	9/21-9/27	9/28-10/4	10/5-10/11	10/12-10/18	10/19-10/25	10/26-11/1	11/2-11/8	11/9-11/15	11/16-11/22	11/23-11/29	11/30-12/6	12/7-12/13
Aim 1	Demonstrating the effects of statins on endothelial invasion											
Aim 2							Measure cholesterol levels					
Report										Compile Data		

					Spring 2009						
Week #	13	14	15	16	17	18	19	20	21	22	23	24
Week of	1/11-1/17	1/18-1/24	1/25-1/31	2/1-2/7	2/8-2/14	2/15-2/21	2/22-2/28	3/1-3/7	3/8-3/14	3/15-3/21	3/22-3/28	3/29-4/4
Aim 3	Transfect cells with HMG-CoA shRNA											
Aim 4						Western blot analysis of pathway proteins					
Report										Draft, review, and finalize thesis		

Table 1. The proposed process spans 24 weeks and finishes early April 2009.

Qualifications

I am a junior chemical engineering major with an interest in medicine and healthcare. I have been employed as a pharmacy clerk and am a phlebotomist. Following graduation, I plan to enter an MD/PhD program. This past summer I worked with Dr. Bayless on the statin project during the Summer Undergraduate Research Program at the Health Science Center and gained experience performing invasion experiments.

I have completed the following elective courses in addition to my major while maintaining a GPA of 3.9.

- Cell & Molecular Biology (BIOL 213)
- Biochemistry (BICH 303)
- Genetics (GENE 301)

continued

References

[1] S. Nissen, S. Nicholls, et al. *Effect of Very High-Intensity Statin Therapy on Regression of Coronary Atherosclerosis,* Journal of the American Medical Association Vol. 295 No. 13 pp. 1556–1565 (2006)

[2] M. Law, N. Wald, A. Rudnicka. *Quantifying effect of statins on low density lipoprotein cholesterol, ischaemic heart disease, and stroke: systematic review and meta-analysis.* The British Medical Journal Vol. 326 (2003)

[3] P. Libby, M. Aikawa, U. Schonbeck. *Cholesterol and atherosclerosis.* Biochimica et Biophysica Vol. 1529 Issues 1–3. pp. 299–309 (2000)

[4] Marie N. Stagnitti, *Statistical Brief #205: Trends in Statins Utilization and Expenditures for the U.S. Civilian Noninstitutionalized Population, 2000 and 2005.* Medical Expenditure Panel Survey (2008)

[5] M. Demierre, P. Higgins, S. Gruber, E. Hawk, S. Lippman. *Statins and Cancer Prevention.* Nature Reviews Cancer 5, pp. 930–942 (2005)

[6] G. Davis, K. Bayless, A. Mavila. *Molecular basis of endothelial cell morphogenesis in three-dimensional extracellular matrices.* The Anatomical Record Vol. 268 Issue 3, pp. 252–275 (2002)

[7] K. Bayless, G. Davis. Sphingosine-1-phosphate markedly induces matrix metalloproteinase and integrin-dependent human endothelial cell invasion and lumen formation in three-dimensional collagen and fibrin matrices. Biochemical and Biophysical Research Communications. Vol. 312 Issue 4 pp. 903–913 (2003)

Case 9-2: **Project Proposal**

The preveterinary honor society at ABC University has invited students to propose and then write, if the proposal is accepted, a discussion of issues important to future veterinarians. Sarah Irving proposes a report that discusses the increasing role of animal rehabilitation in veterinary practice. This proposal includes a summary, a list of topics, methods to be used in developing the topic, a tentative report outline, and an initial list of sources. Since it deals with a non-technical topic, the level of language needs no technical detail. The audience for the report will be other preveterinary students and perhaps faculty who work with the preveterinary society.

CASE DOCUMENT 9-2

MEMORANDUM

TO: Dr. Elizabeth Tebeaux   **DATE:**   February 22, 2010

FROM: Sarah Irving

SUBJECT: Proposal for research paper: Is animal rehabilitation the future
             of veterinary medicine?

Subject and Purpose of the Proposal:

Animal rehabilitation is not currently accepted as a veterinary specialty, and is not widely developed. The growing willingness of owners to pay for rehabilitation treatments is creating a demand for more research into this field and a way to explain animal rehabilitation to the public. A more widespread knowledge of the benefits of this care would encourage more veterinarians to practice or write referrals for animal rehabilitation.

My objective is to create a report that will explain to veterinarians, preveterinary students, and the public where the field of animal rehabilitation is now and how animal rehabilitation will affect the future of veterinary medicine.

Rationale for the Topic and Approach—Its Importance as an Issue

Veterinary patient care is moving toward the level of in-depth planning and quality of care required for human medical care. Owners expect their pets to receive the same level of care they would receive. Options such as physical therapy, prosthetics, and pain management treatments such as acupuncture and medication are often used in treating humans. Though these techniques

continued

are being adapted for animal patients the practice of animal rehabilitation is not widely developed or recommended by veterinarians.

In the last decade many advances in procedures have been made that make animal rehabilitation a feasible part of veterinary medicine. Few veterinarians practice rehabilitation because of the lack of research into rehabilitation methods, results of rehabilitation, and patient benefits.

Growing public awareness of animal rehabilitation is leading to increased demand. The newness of the field leaves few resources for veterinarians, pre-veterinary students, and the public to learn about this growing field. I will research what advances have been made in the field of animal rehabilitation and how animal rehabilitation affects patient care.

I will use articles from peer reviewed journals and answers written by specialists involved in the field to gather data about animal rehabilitation. To get firsthand knowledge from specialists in the animal rehabilitation field I will email surveys to the specialists. To gather articles I will use databases and Google Scholar.

My report will address the issues of:

- What animal rehabilitation is
- Unresolved issues in the field of animal rehabilitation
- Where the field of animal rehabilitation is headed
- Why veterinarians and future veterinarians should practice animal rehabilitation
- How animal rehabilitation relates to the future of veterinary medicine

Methods I Will Use to Research the Report:

To guaranty the validity of my data I will use articles from peer reviewed journals and answers written by specialists involved in the field. These specialists will include veterinary rehabilitation practitioners and researchers in the animal rehabilitation field. To gather articles for my project I will use databases owned by Texas A&M libraries and Google Scholar. These databases include:

- Academic Search Complete
- OmniFile Full Text Mega
- Medline (OVID)

To get firsthand knowledge from specialists in the animal rehabilitation field I will email surveys to the specialists. I have collected names of veterinarians who have written articles about veterinary rehabilitation. I will email them a short three- to five-question survey about their experiences in animal rehabilitation. **Proposed questions include:**

continued

To veterinarians:

- What kinds of treatment do you offer?
- What would you like to tell veterinary students considering rehabilitation practices?
- What would you say the public perception of animal rehabilitation is?
- What is your most common procedure?
- What is the perception of other veterinarians about animal rehabilitation?

To other rehabilitation specialists:

- What would you say the public perception of animal rehabilitation is?
- What is the perception of other veterinarians about animal rehabilitation?
- What would you like to tell veterinary students considering rehabilitation practices?

I will have these emails checked for readability by Dr. Tebeaux before I send them. I will make the emails as easy to answer as possible to get the most responses. I will request that all email replies be sent within two weeks of receiving the email survey so I may use the information in my report.

To make sure my data is the most current data available I will continue researching for the next four weeks. This will give me time to find all sources created up to a month before my report is due.

Work Schedule:

To complete my report on time using the most data available I will follow the schedule below.

Week 1 February 21-27	Draft emails to animal rehabilitation specialists, search for more sources, read sources, and gather names and email addresses of specialists
Week 2 February 28-March 6	Have emails checked for readability, send emails, read sources
Week 3 March 7-13	Continue searching for and reading sources
Week 4 March 14-20	Email replies due by this week, start reading replies, continue searching for and reading sources
Week 5 March 21-27	Turn notes on sources and surveys into rough draft
Week 6 March 28-April 3	Edit rough draft, print, read aloud, edit again
Week 7 April 4-10	Have others edit rough draft
Week 8 April 11-14	Final editing
April 15	Turn in project

continued

Tentative Outline of the Report:

   I. Letter of Transmittal

  II. Title page

 III. Definition of animal rehabilitation

      a. History of animal rehabilitation

      b. Types of animal rehabilitation

          i. Physical therapy

        ii. Hydrotherapy

      iii. Prosthetics

      c. The developing demand for animal rehabilitation

 IV. Unresolved issues in the field of animal rehabilitation

      a. The animal pain management debate

      b. Who is qualified to practice animal rehabilitation

          i. The American Veterinary Medical Association position

        ii. The American Physical Therapy Association position

      c. What certification programs exist?

          i. Canine Rehabilitation Institute

        ii. University of Tennessee College of Veterinary Medicine Certificate Program in Canine Rehabilitation

      iii. Canine and Equine Physiotherapy Training (CEPT) in England

      d. Organizations formed to promote animal rehabilitation

          i. Institute of Registered Veterinary and Animal Physio-therapists (IRVAP)

      e. State government actions to date

      f. Owner involvement in the rehabilitation process

  V. What is the future of animal rehabilitation?

      a. Recent developments in the field

      b. Establishment of a specialty

      c. Animal plastic surgery

      d. Greater public awareness

 VI. Why practice animal rehabilitation?

      a. Good for business, good veterinary practice, good for the clinic's reputation

      b. Advice for pre-veterinary students considering a future as a animal rehabilitation practitioner

 VII. Is animal rehabilitation the future of the veterinary medicine?

VIII. Bibliography

continued

Initial List of Resources

Brockett, John E. "Why Give Pain Medication—Patient Care, Image Or Profit?" *DVM: The Newsmagazine of Veterinary Medicine* 39.2 (2008): 41–. Print.

Downing, Robin. "Putting the New Pain Management Guidelines into Practice." *Veterinary Medicine* 102.11 (2007): 704–5. Print.

Foley, Denise. "Life with a Disabled Pet." *Prevention* 58.2 (2006): 198–201. Print.

Nolen, R. S. "Pet Rehab Becoming Mainstream Practice." *Journal of the American Veterinary Medical Association* 235.7 (2009): 798–9. Print.

Payne, Richard M. "Canine and Equine Physiotherapy." *Veterinary Record: Journal of the British Veterinary Association* 165.4 (2009): 122–. Print.

Sayre, Carolyn, and Robert Horn. "Fake Fins, Plastic Paws." *Time* 170.10 (2007): 49–51. Print.

Skernitvitz, Stephanie. "Rehab Gives Animals Swifter Road to Recovery, DVM Says." *DVM: The Newsmagazine of Veterinary Medicine* 39.10 (2008): 1s–12s. Print.

Smith, Sarah D. "Petting with a Purpose." *Natural Health* 36.3 (2006): 99–100. Print.

Stein, Robert M., and Stephanie Ortel. "Postsurgical Pain Management: Take a Pre-Emptive Approach." *DVM: The Newsmagazine of Veterinary Medicine* 39.7 (2008): 44–6. Print.

Van Dyke, Janet B. "Canine Rehabilitation: An Inside Look at a Fast-Growing Market Segment." *DVM: The Newsmagazine of Veterinary Medicine* 40.7 (2009): 14S–5S. Print.

Verdon, Daniel R. "An Animal Planet." *DVM: The Newsmagazine of Veterinary Medicine* 36.7 (2005): 24–8. Print.

Progress Reports

When a soliciting organization requests a proposal, it often states that a specific number of progress reports will be required, particularly if the project covers a long time period. As their name suggests, progress reports, sometimes known as status reports, tell readers how work is progressing on a project. Their immediate purpose is to inform the authorizing person of the activities completed on a project, but their long-range purpose should show the proposing organization's or the individual's competence in pursuing a task and completing it.

Status reports may also be prepared in paper format and submitted to supervisors. These progress reports help you or your work group provide evidence or documentation of your activities. They generally have three goals:

- To explain to the reader what has been accomplished and by whom, the status of the work performed, and problems that may have arisen that need attention
- To explain to your client how time and money have been spent, what work remains to be done, and how any problems encountered are being handled
- To enable the organization or individual doing the work to assess the work and plan future work

Structure of progress reports. Any work project, such as transportation or construction projects, requires regular progress reports. While these differ, they incorporate the same basic segments: goal of the project, work accomplished (for a given period), work remaining/planned (for the next period), problems encountered, and financial expenditures.

Structure by work performed. This is the standard structure for progress reports.

Beginning
- Introduction/project description
- Summary

Middle
- Work completed   or
  Task 1
  Task 2, etc.
- Work remaining
  Task 3
  Task 4
- Cost

- Task 1
  Work completed
  Work remaining
- Task 2
  Work completed
  Work remaining
- Cost

End
- Overall appraisal of progress to date
- Conclusion and recommendations

In this general plan, you emphasize what has been done and what remains to be done and supply enough of an introduction to be sure that the reader knows what project is being discussed.

For progress reports that cover more than one period, the basic design can be expanded as follows:

Beginning
- Introduction
- Project description
- Summary of work to date
- Summary of work in this period

Middle
- Work accomplished by tasks (this period)
- Work remaining on specific tasks
- Work planned for the next reporting period
- Work planned for periods thereafter
- Cost to date
- Cost in this period

End
- Overall appraisal of work to date
- Conclusions and recommendations concerning problems

Structure by chronological order. If your project or research is broken into time periods, your progress report can be structured to emphasize the periods.

Beginning
- Introduction/project description
- Summary of work completed

Middle
- Work completed
  Period 1 (beginning and ending dates)
    Description
    Cost
  Period 2 (beginning and ending dates)
    Description
    Cost
- Work remaining
  Period 3 (or remaining periods)
    Description of work to be done
    Expected cost

End
- Evaluation of work in this period
- Conclusions and recommendations

Structure by main project goals. Many research projects are pursued by grouping specific tasks into major groups. Then the writer describes progress according to work done in each major group and perhaps the amount of time spent on that group of tasks. Alternatively, a researcher may decide to present a project by re-search goals—what will be accomplished during the project. Thus, progress re-ports will explain activities performed to achieve those goals. In the middle of the plans below, the left-hand column is organized by work completed and remaining, and the right-hand column by goals.

Beginning
- Introduction/project description
- Summary of progress to date

Middle
• Work completed	or	• Goal 1
Goal 1		Work completed
Goal 2		Work remaining
Goal 3, etc.		Cost
• Work remaining		• Goal 2
Goal 1		Work completed
Goal 2		Work remaining
Goal 3, etc.		Cost
• Cost		

End
- Evaluation of work to date
- Conclusions and recommendations

Case 9-3

Recipients of research funds from the preveterinary honor society are expected to submit a progress report. Sarah submits her report several weeks before the research reports will be completed and submitted. Note the detail of her progress, which suggests that her work follows the proposed research methods she included in her proposal.

CASE DOCUMENT 9-3

TO: Dr. Elizabeth Tebeaux   **DATE:**   4/6/10

FROM: Sarah Irving

SUBJECT: Progress on Semester Project

Summary

- Animal rehabilitation is a developing field many veterinarians do not utilize and many pet owners do not know is available. My objective is to create a report that will explain to veterinarians, pre-veterinary students, and veterinary students where the field of animal rehabilitation is now and how animal rehabilitation will affect the future of veterinary medicine.
  - I have narrowed the focus of my report to be a report for students interested in veterinary medicine, veterinary students, and veterinarians. My original audience also included pet owners. I believe these changes will enhance the readability and clarity of my report by preventing the report from being cluttered with information the primary readers would not find useful. I will format the report for pet owners to be able to find information that interests them, while focusing on the audience most in need of this information.

- **My report will address the following issues:**

  - Definition and description of animal rehabilitation
  - Unresolved issues in the field of animal rehabilitation
  - Future of animal rehabilitation
  - Rationale for including animal rehabilitation in veterinary practice

continued

- I have read and taken notes on eleven articles that have information that I can use for my paper. I have four more articles with good information to re-read and take notes on. I have also emailed a survey to fifty veterinarians, veterinary technicians, and physical therapists that practice animal rehabilitation. I have received thirteen responses to my survey. I must read the responses and make a citation for each response. I also must send individual thank you notes to the respondents. The sources I have used and am planning to use are listed below.

- I have made good progress on drafting my report. The articles and surveys left to read will fill the gaps in information in my rough draft. I have also reorganized my report outline. The changes to the outline will enhance the logical flow of the report by grouping similar information. The updated outline can be found on page 4 of this progress report.

Research Consulted:

Articles:

1. **Why Give Pain Medication—Patient Care, Image Or Profit?**
   a. **Citation:** Brockett, John E. "Why Give Pain Medication—Patient Care, Image Or Profit?" DVM: The Newsmagazine of Veterinary Medicine 39.2 (2008): 41–. Print.
2. **Putting the New Pain Management Guidelines into Practice**
   a. **Citation:** Downing, Robin. "Putting the New Pain Management Guidelines into Practice." *Veterinary Medicine* 102.11 (2007): 704–5. Print.
3. **Life with a Disabled Pet**
   a. **Citation:** Foley, Denise. "Life with a Disabled Pet." *Prevention* 58.2 (2006): 198–201. Print.
4. **Underwater Treadmill Therapy in Veterinary Practice**
   a. **Citation:** Jurek, Christine, and Laurie McCauley. "Underwater Treadmill Therapy in Veterinary Practice." *Veterinary Medicine* 104.4 (2009): 182–90. Print.
5. **Pet Rehab Becoming Mainstream Practice**
   a. **Citation:** Nolen, R. S. "Pet Rehab Becoming Mainstream Practice." *Journal of the American Veterinary Medical Association* 235.7 (2009): 798–9. Print.
6. **Canine and Equine Physical Therapy**
   a. **Citation:** Payne, Richard M. "Canine and Equine Physiotherapy." *Veterinary Record: Journal of the British Veterinary Association* 165.4 (2009): 122–. Print.

continued

7. **Rehab Gives Animals Swifter Road to Recovery, DVM Says**
   a. **Citation:** Skernitvitz, Stephanie. "Rehab Gives Animals Swifter Road to Recovery, DVM Says." *DVM: The Newsmagazine of Veterinary Medicine* 39.10 (2008): 1s–12s. Print.

8. **Petting with a Purpose**
   a. **Citation:** Smith, Sarah D. "Petting with a Purpose." *Natural Health* 36.3 (2006): 99–100. Print.

9. **Postsurgical Pain Management: Take a Pre-Emptive Approach**
   a. **Citation:** Stein, Robert M., and Stephanie Ortel. "Postsurgical Pain Management: Take a Pre-Emptive Approach." *DVM: The Newsmagazine of Veterinary Medicine* 39.7 (2008): 44–6. Print.

10. **Canine Rehabilitation: An Inside Look at a Fast-Growing Market Segment**
    a. **Citation:** van Dyke, Janet B. "Canine Rehabilitation: An Inside Look at a Fast-Growing Market Segment." *DVM: The Newsmagazine of Veterinary Medicine* 40.7 (2009): 14S–5S. Print.

11. **An Animal Planet**
    a. **Citation:** Verdon, Daniel R. "An Animal Planet." *DVM: The Newsmagazine of Veterinary Medicine* 36.7 (2005): 24–8. Print.

Survey

- I emailed fifty surveys to veterinarians, veterinary technicians, and physical therapists. The email addresses were found on the University of Tennessee Certificate in Canine Rehabilitation website using the find a practitioner option. As this is one of the two certificate programs in the United States, I felt it would provide a good example of the opinions of certified animal rehabilitation practitioners on the field of animal rehabilitation. I received thirteen responses. Five responses were from veterinarians, seven were from veterinary technicians, and one was from a physical therapist.
  - The surveys I sent to veterinarians contained the following questions:
    1. How would you describe the public perception of animal rehabilitation?
    2. What is the perception of other veterinarians you know about animal rehabilitation?
    3. What kinds of treatment do you offer?
    4. What is your most common procedure?
    5. What would you like to tell veterinary students considering rehabilitation practices?

continued

○ I modified the first and second questions for the surveys I sent to veterinary technicians and physical therapists:

    1. What is the public's perception of animal rehabilitation?

    2. What is the perception of veterinarians about animal rehabilitation?

Work Remaining

Articles to Read:

1. Fake Fins, Plastic Paws
    a. Citation: Sayre, Carolyn, and Robert Horn. "Fake Fins, Plastic Paws." Time 170.10 (2007): 49–51. Print.

2. Changing Times
    a. Citation: Shearer, Tami. "Changing Times." *DVM: The Newsmagazine of Veterinary Medicine* 39.3 (2008): 34–. Print.

3. State Board Lacks Consistency on Standard of Practice
    a. Citation: Marshak, Doug. "State Board Lacks Consistency on Standard of Practice." *DVM: The Newsmagazine of Veterinary Medicine* 38.11 (2007): 38–40. Print.

4. The Price of Pain
    a. Citation: Fiala, Jennifer. "The Price of Pain." *DVM: The Newsmagazine of Veterinary Medicine* 38.10 (2007): 30–2. Print.

Survey

- The thirteen survey responses must also be read, and I must make the citations for the surveys. I also must draft individual thank you notes to each respondent, as some respondents asked questions at the end of their survey responses. These thank you notes will be sent the week of April 5, 2010.

Changes to the Initial Proposal

- I have narrowed the focus of my report to be a report for students interested in veterinary medicine, veterinary students, and veterinarians. My original audience also included pet owners. This change reflects the fact that many sections of my report would not interest most pet owners. Though I have narrowed my audience, it is possible that pet owners could also be a part of my audience, and the report will be formatted for pet owners to be able to find useful information.

continued

- I have added a section defining animal rehabilitation at the beginning of the report, and sections that are required in the major report template. I have also reorganized the report by moving sub-sections into the section called "What is animal rehabilitation." These sections include owner involvement in the rehabilitation process, what certification programs exist, and organizations formed to promote animal rehabilitation. These sub-sections were moved from the unresolved issues in animal rehabilitation section after reading sources that suggested the debate on these issues has been largely completed.

- To describe the field of animal rehabilitation more accurately I have changed the section on prosthetics to a section on assistive devices. This change reflects the realization that most veterinarians consider rehabilitation to be work done postsurgically, and with minimum invasiveness. I believe these changes will enhance the readability and clarity of my report.

Updated Outline:

Letter of Transmittal
Title page with descriptive abstract
Table of Contents
Summary
Introduction
What is animal rehabilitation
    a. Definition of animal rehabilitation
    b. History of animal rehabilitation
    c. Types of animal rehabilitation
        i. Physical therapy
        ii. Hydrotherapy
            1. Benefits of hydrotherapy
            2. What to consider before choosing hydrotherapy
        iii. Assistive devices
    d. The developing demand for animal rehabilitation
    e. Owner involvement in the rehabilitation process
    f. What certification programs exist?
        i. Canine Rehabilitation Institute
        ii. University of Tennessee College of Veterinary Medicine Certificate Program in Canine Rehabilitation
    g. Organizations formed to promote animal rehabilitation
        i. Institute of Registered Veterinary and Animal Physiotherapists (IRVAP)

continued

Unresolved issues in the field of animal rehabilitation
    h. The animal pain management debate
    i. Who is qualified to practice animal rehabilitation
        i. The American Veterinary Medical Association position
        ii. The American Physical Therapy Association position
        iii. State government actions to date
Where animal rehabilitation is headed
    j. Recent developments in the field
    k. Establishment of a specialty
    l. Animal plastic surgery
    m. Greater public awareness
Why practice animal rehabilitation
    n. Good for business, good veterinary practice, good for the clinic's reputation
    o. Advice for pre-veterinary students considering a future as an animal rehabilitation practitioner
Conclusions: Is animal rehabilitation the future of the veterinary medicine?
Bibliography
Appendix A: Proposal
Appendix B: Progress Report

Working Bibliography

Brockett, John E. "Why Give Pain Medication—Patient Care, Image Or Profit?" *DVM: The Newsmagazine of Veterinary Medicine* 39.2 (2008): 41–. Print.

Downing, Robin. "Putting the New Pain Management Guidelines into Practice." *Veterinary Medicine* 102.11 (2007): 704–5. Print.

Fiala, Jennifer. "The Price of Pain." *DVM: The Newsmagazine of Veterinary Medicine* 38.10 (2007): 30–2. Print.

Foley, Denise. "Life with a Disabled Pet." *Prevention* 58.2 (2006): 198–201. Print.

Jurek, Christine, and Laurie McCauley. "Underwater Treadmill Therapy in Veterinary Practice." *Veterinary Medicine* 104.4 (2009): 182–90. Print.

Marshak, Doug. "State Board Lacks Consistency on Standard of Practice." *DVM: The Newsmagazine of Veterinary Medicine* 38.11 (2007): 38–40. Print.

Nolen, R. S. "Pet Rehab Becoming Mainstream Practice." *Journal of the American Veterinary Medical Association* 235.7 (2009): 798–9. Print.

Payne, Richard M. "Canine and Equine Physiotherapy." *Veterinary Record: Journal of the British Veterinary Association* 165.4 (2009): 122–. Print.

continued

Sayre, Carolyn, and Robert Horn. "Fake Fins, Plastic Paws." *Time* 170.10 (2007): 49–51. Print.

Shearer, Tami. "Changing Times." *DVM: The Newsmagazine of Veterinary Medicine* 39.3 (2008): 34–. Print.

Skernitvitz, Stephanie. "Rehab Gives Animals Swifter Road to Recovery, DVM Says." *DVM: The Newsmagazine of Veterinary Medicine* 39.10 (2008): 1s–12s. Print.

Smith, Sarah D. "Petting with a Purpose." *Natural Health* 36.3 (2006): 99-100. Print.

Stein, Robert M., and Stephanie Ortel. "Postsurgical Pain Management: Take a Pre-Emptive Approach." *DVM: The Newsmagazine of Veterinary Medicine* 39.7 (2008): 44–6. Print.

van Dyke, Janet B. "Canine Rehabilitation: An Inside Look at a Fast-Growing Market Segment." *DVM: The Newsmagazine of Veterinary Medicine* 40.7 (2009): 14S–5S. Print.

Verdon, Daniel R. "An Animal Planet." *DVM: The Newsmagazine of Veterinary Medicine* 36.7 (2005): 24–8. Print.

Case 9-4

In business, progress reports are standard. COSMIX (Colorado State Metro Interstate Expansion) posts its reports on road projects on the Internet so that the public can track progress through text and pictures. This transportation progress report provides a list of tasks completed by month throughout a three-year period. This type of online progress report provides transparency and allows the public to see how COSMIX spends highway expansion dollars.

CASE DOCUMENT 9-4

HOME   PROJECT MAPS   CAMERAS   7 DAY OUTLOOK   CONTACT US   NEWS ROOM

◗ **COSMIX**™

PROGRESS

Home   **COSMIX Progress Report and timeline**

Segment
Details
Bijou
Fillmore
Nevada
Rockrimmon
Woodmen -
Academy

Project Maps
Photos

	Jun 2005	Sept 2005	Dec 2005	Mar 2006	Jun 2006	Sept 2006	Dec 2006	Mar 2007	Jun 2007	Sept 2007	Dec 2007
Bijou Interchange											
Filmore Street to Garden of the Gods Road											
Nevada/Rockrimmon Interchange											
Woodmen Road to North Academy boulevard											

October 2007
October marked a significant milestone on the COSMIX project, when the Bijou bridge reopened to traffic. In addition, COSMIX crews began the final piece of work in the North Nevada/Rockrimmon segment when the Rockrimmon/Mark Dabling intersection was closed for reconstruction. Other progress on the project included:

- Continued placement of architectural railings on the Bijou bridge
- Landscaping and streetscape was completed on and near the Bijou bridge
- Completed asphalt paving between South Nevada/Tejon and Cimarron Street
- Utilities and drainage on the Spruce St. cul de sac was completed
- Northbound bridge structure over Colorado Ave. was completed

continued

September 2007
This month, crews worked around the clock to prepare for the opening of the Bijou bridge on October 1. Progress became visible to the traveling public throughout the corridor when three lanes of I-25 became available between North Academy Boulevard and Bijou Street. In addition, crews made progress on the following:

- Completed landscaping behind the Pulpit Rock noise wall.
- Opened three lanes north and southbound between Bijou and Uintah Streets, allowing three lanes throughout the project between North Academy Boulevard and Bijou Street.
- Continued placing decorative railing and light fixtures on the Bijou bridge.
- Continued construction on the landscaping on the northwest corner of Bijou Street and the I-25 interchange, and underneath the Bijou bridge over Monument Creek.
- Continued construction on the I-25 bridges over Colorado Avenue.
- Reopened the Pikes Peak Greenway Trail under the Bijou bridge.
- Prepared for opening of the Bijou bridge.
- Completed paving one-half mile south of North Academy Boulevard, and between the Martin Luther King bypass and Circle Drive.

August 2007
Good weather in August allowed the COSMIX Crews to make quite a bit of progress. Some of the significant COSMIX work in August included:

- Poured concrete on the new I-25 southbound bridge over Colorado Avenue
- Replaced road panels and bridge expansion joints on I-25 southbound between Fontanero and Uintah streets
- Eliminated "the dip" on northbound I-25 at Nevada Avenue with a process known as "mud-jacking"
- Opened the Nevada/Corporate Drive intersection
- Began placing decorative railing on the Bijou bridge
- Installed light fixtures on the Bijou bridge
- Began construction on the aesthetic upgrades on the northwest corner of Bijou Street and the I-25 interchange
- Began landscaping underneath the Bijou bridge over Monument Creek

July 2007
The month of July began with a COSMIX gift to Colorado Springs. Before the July 4th holiday, construction crews opened up the new third lane on north and southbound I-25 between Woodmen Road and Garden of the Gods Road, giving the traveling public three lanes all the way from North Academy Boulevard to Fillmore Street.

continued

In addition, crews also worked on the following:

- Switched traffic onto the new northbound I-25 bridge over Colorado Avenue and began construction of the new southbound I-25 bridge over Colorado Avenue, including caisson drilling and retaining wall construction.
- Continued work on the Corporate Centre Drive/Nevada Avenue connection.
- Completed the new North Nevada Avenue alignment.
- Finished placing panels and staining noise walls at Uintah Street and Pulpit Rock.
- Completed final striping between Woodmen Road and North Academy Boulevard.
- Continued construction to repair concrete panels and bridge joints between Fontanero and Uintah Streets.
- Continued work on the Bijou bridge including:
- Completed paving of the northbound on- and off-ramps
- Completed placement of the bridge deck over Monument Creek and the Union Pacific Railroad
- Completed 75 percent of the sidewalk and median concrete work
- Completed the concrete staining of the abutments and pier columns
- Began architectural stone veneer installation and painting of the decorative railings

June 2007
June 30 marked the two-year anniversary for construction on the COSMIX project. With two years of construction behind us and only six months left on the project, crews made some very visible progress in June, to include:

- Completed concrete staining on most of the North Nevada/ Rockrimmon interchange.
- Completed the Pulpit Rock noise wall.
- Opened the third lane southbound between Nevada Avenue and Fillmore Street.
- Poured the concrete median and sidewalks for the Bijou bridge over I-25.
- Poured two of the four deck sections of the Bijou bridge over Monument Creek and the Union Pacific Railroad.
- Re-opened the southbound I-25 off-ramp at Bijou Street.
- Paved the northbound on- and off-ramps for the Bijou interchange.
- Completed the reinstallation and rehabilitation of the Works Progress Administration (WPA) wall along Monument Creek near Downtown.
- Shifted traffic onto the new portions of the I-25 bridges over Colorado Avenue and the Midland Trail.
- Completed roadway work on the west side of the Bijou bridge.

continued

May 2007

Several major milestones were completed in May, most notably, both north and southbound I-25 were taken off the frontage roads and put back onto the elevated interstate lanes in the Nevada/Rockrimmon area. It took just less than a year to complete the 2.5 miles of new interstate lanes, eight new bridges, and 1.8 miles of retaining walls associated with the interstate in this area. Some of the significant COSMIX work in May included:

- Shifted southbound onto the new interstate in the Nevada/Rockrimmon area on May 4.
- With the southbound traffic shift, the outdated left-hand interstate exit to North Nevada Avenue was permanently eliminated and replaced with a right-hand exit.
- Demolished the old northbound I-25 bridge over the former southbound exit to North Nevada Avenue.
- Shifted northbound I-25 traffic onto the new northbound interstate in the Nevada/Rockrimmon area on May 24.
- Poured the remaining two bridge monuments on the east side of the Bijou bridge.
- Paved northbound I-25 over the Monument Creek and the Works Progress Administration (WPA) Wall.
- Reconstructed and reopened the entry to the parking lot of the Bijou Street Denny's in less than two weeks.
- Began placing noise wall panels for the Pulpit Rock neighborhood sound barrier.

April 2007

Throughout April crews worked to complete the southbound mainline in the North Nevada/Rockrimmon segment in anticipation of shifting traffic off the frontage road and onto the new interstate lanes in early May. Other significant COSMIX work in April included:

- Poured the last of twelve bridge decks in the North Nevada/ Rockrimmon segment on April 6.
- Placed the remaining Bijou bridge girders over Monument Creek and the Union Pacific Railroad.
- Poured two of the four Bijou bridge monuments.
- Poured the northbound I-25 bridge deck over Colorado Avenue.
- Closed Bijou Street from I-25 to Spruce Street to begin raising the grade for the Bijou bridge.
- Began the rehabilitation of the northbound Midland Bridge deck.
- Demolished the remainder of the old northbound I-25 bridge over Monument Creek in the North Nevada/Rockrimmon segment.

continued

- Completed pouring the southbound mainline between the bridges in the North Nevada/Rockrimmon segment.

March 2007

Progress has begun to visibly accelerate in the Colorado Avenue to Bijou Street segment with dramatic changes to the corridor's appearance. Some of the significant COSMIX work in March included:

- Placed the girders for the Bijou Street bridge over I-25 and poured the bridge deck.
- Constructed the north and southbound I-25 lanes under the Bijou Street bridge.
- Shifted northbound I-25 traffic under the new Bijou Street bridge.
- Began the demolition of the south half of the Cimarron Street bridge over Conejos Street and the UPRR.
- Finished pouring piers for the Bijou bridge over Monument Creek and the UPRR.
- Placed girders for the northbound I-25 bridge over Colorado Avenue.
- Placed caissons and columns for the Pulpit Rock noise wall
- Poured the northbound bridge deck over Monument Creek in the Nevada / Rockrimmon area.

COSMIX construction crews reached 40 percent completion on the Bijou Street Interchange last week, when traffic on north and southbound Interstate 25 was shifted onto the new concrete lanes under the Bijou Street bridge. The shift marked the second major milestone in the Bijou segment. The first milestone was accomplished earlier in March, when crews set girders for the Bijou Street bridge over I-25.

February 2007

Construction crews received a reprieve from the unusual amounts of snow in January and February as temperatures began to warm up. Although the snow and cold temperatures returned mid-February, workers made significant progress in the Colorado Avenue to Bijou Street segment and the Nevada/Rockrimmon segment. Some of the significant COSMIX work in February included:

- Shifted northbound I-25 traffic over the Midland bridge to the west to allow for the northbound deck rehabilitation.
- Began placing the northbound retaining wall between Colorado Avenue and Bijou Street.
- Continued with the demolition of the Bijou bridge over Monument Creek and the Union Pacific Rail Road.
- Poured the center piers and placed the abutment panels for the Bijou bridge over I-25.

continued

- Opened the southbound I-25 off-ramp to Garden of the Gods road in its final configuration.
- Re-striped north and southbound I-25 from North Nevada Avenue to Woodmen Road to accommodate the opening of the southbound auxiliary lane from Woodmen Road to Corporate Centre Drive.
- Opened the southbound off-ramp to Corporate Centre Drive.
- Poured the I-25 bridge decks over the Rockrimmon Boulevard extension.
- Poured the southbound I-25 bridge deck over Monument Creek in the Nevada/Rockrimmon area.
- Refreshed the striping throughout the corridor several times after the last few winter storms began to deteriorate the pavement markings.

January 2007
January marked the start of construction on the Bijou bridge. Despite the snow and cold temperatures, crews moved ahead on the demolition of the bridge over I-25 and over Monument Creek and the Union Pacific Rail Road.

Highlighted below are some of the other areas where crews made progress:

- Continued work on the north and southbound I-25 bridges over Monument Creek, Nevada Avenue, Rockrimmon Boulevard, Mark Dabling Boulevard and the Union Pacific Rail Road.
- Continued construction on northbound I-25 over Colorado Avenue.
- Completed rehabilitation work on the southbound bridge over the Midland Trail.
- Completed demolition of the Bijou bridge over I-25.
- Began demolition of the Bijou bridge over Monument Creek and the Union Pacific Rail Road (40 percent complete).
- Continued work on the caissons for the Monument Valley Park Noise Walls.
- Began placing precast columns for the Monument Valley Park Noise Walls.

<u>COSMIX Progress for 2006</u>

<u>COSMIX Progress for 2005</u>

Click on button below
for previous I-25 Web site.

<u>Statewide Weather and Travel Information</u>

Contact Webmaster
Last Modified: Mon, Jan, 07, 2008

STYLE AND TONE OF PROPOSALS AND PROGRESS REPORTS

The proposal and its related report documents serve as sales documents, but writers have an ethical commitment to present information about a project in a clear and accurate manner. Proposals, once accepted, become legally binding documents. Because contracts emerge from proposals, organizations must be prepared to stand behind their proposals. Thus, the style should be authoritative, vigorous, and positive, suggesting the competence of the proposer. Generalizations must be bolstered by detailed factual accomplishments. Problems should be discussed honestly, but positive solutions to problems should be stressed. Neither the proposal nor the progress report should resort to vague, obfuscatory language.

CHECKLIST FOR DEVELOPING PROPOSALS AND PROGRESS REPORTS

Proposals

Planning

☐ Have you made a list of all requirements given in the RFP?

☐ Who are your readers? Do they have technical competence in the field of the proposal? Is it a mixed audience, some technically educated, some not? To whom could the proposal be distributed?

☐ What problem is the proposed work designed to remedy? What is the immediate background and history of the problem? Why does the problem need to be solved?

☐ What is your proposed solution to the problem? What benefits will come from the solution? Is the solution feasible (both practical and applicable)?

☐ How will you carry out the work proposed? Scope? Methods to be used? Task breakdown? Time and work schedule?

☐ Do you want to make statements concerning the likelihood of success or failure and the products of the project? Who else has tried this solution? What was their success?

☐ What facilities and equipment will you need to carry out the project?

☐ Who will do the work? What are their qualifications for doing the work? Can you obtain references for past work accomplished?

☐ How much will the work cost (e.g., materials, labor, test equipment, travel, administrative expenses, and fees)? Who will pay for what? What will be the return on the investment?

continued

CHECKLIST FOR DEVELOPING PROPOSALS AND PROGRESS REPORTS ✔ *continued*

☐ Will you need to include an appendix? Consider including biographical sketches, descriptions of earlier projects, and employment practices.

☐ Will the proposal be better presented in a report format or in a letter or memo format?

Revising

☐ Does your proposal have a well-planned design and layout? Does its appearance suggest the high quality of the work you propose to do? Do your readings both promote and inform?

☐ Does the project summary succinctly state the objectives and plan of the proposed work? Does it show how the proposed work is relevant to the readers' interest?

☐ Does the introduction make the subject and the purpose of the work clear? Does it briefly point out the importance of the proposed work?

☐ Have you defined the problem thoroughly?

☐ Is your solution well described? Have you made its benefits and feasibility clear?

☐ Will your readers be able to follow your plan of work easily? Have you protected yourself by making clear what you will do and what you will not do? Have you been careful not to promise more results than you can deliver?

☐ Have you carefully considered all the facilities and equipment you will need?

☐ Have you presented the qualifications of project personnel in an attractive but honest way? Have you asked permission from everyone you plan to use as a reference?

☐ Is your budget realistic? Will it be easy for the readers to follow and understand?

☐ Do all the items in the appendix lend credibility to the proposal?

☐ Have you included a few sentences that urge the readers to accept the proposal?

☐ Have you satisfied the needs of your readers? Will they be able to comprehend your proposal? Do they have all the information they need to make a decision?

Progress Reports

Planning

☐ Do you have a clear description of your project available, perhaps in your proposal?

CHECKLIST FOR DEVELOPING PROPOSALS AND PROGRESS REPORTS *continued*

- ☐ Do you have all the project tasks clearly defined? Do all the tasks run in sequence, or do some run concurrently? In general, are the tasks going well or badly?
- ☐ What items need to be highlighted in your summary and appraisal?
- ☐ Are there any problems to be discussed?
- ☐ Can you suggest solutions for the problems?
- ☐ Is your work ahead of schedule, right on schedule, or behind schedule?
- ☐ Are costs running as expected?
- ☐ Do you have some unexpected good news you can report?

Revising

- ☐ Does your report have an attractive appearance?
- ☐ Does the plan you have chosen show off your progress to its best advantage?
- ☐ Is your tone authoritative, with an accent on the positive?
- ☐ Have you supported your generalizations with facts?
- ☐ Does your approach seem fresh or tired?
- ☐ Do you have a good balance between work accomplished and work to be done?
- ☐ Can your summary and appraisal stand alone? Would they satisfy an executive reader?

EXERCISES

1. Working individually or collaboratively, write a proposal to a charitable trust or private foundation for funds in support of a local nonprofit organization. Interview a representative from the nonprofit to assist you in identifying appropriate trusts or foundations to apply to as well as the specific projects to which the nonprofit would apply the funds.

2. Write a progress report that details your research and writing efforts on the funding proposal for the nonprofit organization. List the activities you have completed, the activities in progress, and the activities remaining as well as mistakes made, problems encountered, and solutions discovered and implemented.

3. Examine the following proposal (Figure 9-3). If you were the author of this proposal and were given 15 more minutes to make it more persuasive, what changes would you make?

To: Shirley Wallace, President
From: Rick Dominguez, Chief Ethics Officer
Subject: CRO membership
Date: February 12, 2012

Shirley:

I am writing to propose that Artifice Incorporated join CROA (Corporate Responsibility Officer Association), the world's leading organization for issues related to social responsibility, sustainability, ethical operations, and philanthropy.

Artifice would benefit from membership in multiple ways, including industry recognition that we are committed to corporate social responsibility, listing in the CROA membership directory, eligibility for association awards, free registration for the annual CRO Summit, participation in the setting of standards and practices, and access to information resources such as CRO Magazine and CRO.com as well as newsletters, webinars, executive briefings, and peer networks.

As a corporation with revenues of $9 million, Artifice qualifies for the lowest level of annual membership dues: $1495. I know this is a lot of money for us, but I am confident that if we seize this opportunity we could raise the corporate profile and boost the visibility of the literacy project you initiated. I think we could also discover a lot of ways through CROA to manage the several new community efforts you are considering with greater impact and efficiency.

More information about CROA is available at www.croassociation.org. If you have questions, I am available at your convenience.

Rick

FIGURE 9-3 Document for Exercise 3

10

Instructions, Procedures, and Policies

INSTRUCTIONS VERSUS PROCEDURES

Procedures provide general guidelines for performing a task, while instructions provide specific, detailed steps. Procedures—or general guidelines—will be appropriate for some situations, while instructions may be necessary for readers who need detailed directions to perform a job task or process.

Instructions and procedures can appear in several formats: in letters and memoranda (see Chapter 7 for an example instructional memo), in reports, in technical papers or notes, in stand-alone documents to accompany mechanisms or processes, or in complete manuals. Complex procedures and instructions usually appear as manuals, which use many of the report elements exemplified in the formal report in Appendix C. E-mail is not a suitable method of sending instructions/procedures, unless you send these as an e-mail attachment (in a standard rtf, doc, docx, or pdf file) that can be printed or read on the receiver's computer screen. Differences in e-mail applications can produce awkwardly formatted, unreadable text.

CRITICAL ROLE OF INSTRUCTIONS AND PROCEDURES IN THE WORKPLACE

Instructions and procedures often carry heavy legal liability. Because instructions are written for those who need them, most new products and processes have instructions attached. Instructions may also appear on a website, but many of these do not exhibit the qualities of good instructions. When a product fails because instructions lack clarity, completeness, and/or adequate warnings, the manufacturing company can be held responsible for costs incurred from buyers who, in good faith, attempted to follow the instructions. Even worse, when a customer or an employee dies or suffers major injuries because instructions did not provide complete, readable information and safety warnings, the company can be liable for the injuries or death. Companies that sell products that have hard-to-follow instructions on products that must be installed or assembled by the purchasers can lose money on the product when purchasers return the product. Conversely, well-written instructions can improve the image of a company that manufactures products. Many companies will provide onsite, face-to-face instructions for individuals who will have to operate equipment after it is installed. Face-to-face instructions plus written instructions can help purchasers feel confident in the company that sells the equipment. In short, well-designed, clear, complete, accurate instructions can become good sales documents while preventing lawsuits if equipment or products are misused because users did not/could not follow the instructions.

Quick Tips

Many people resist reading instructions. They try to figure out for themselves how to operate a product or perform a task and will turn to the instructions only if all their efforts fail. When they do read the instructions, they want to understand everything immediately without having to read anything twice. A simple design, plain wording, and clear illustrations will be critical to encouraging readers to pay attention to your instructions or procedures:

1. Use concise headings and subheadings to describe and highlight each section.
2. Leave plenty of white space around headings.
3. Use numbers for every step in a chronological process; use bullets for lists of conditions, materials, and equipment.
4. Use white space to make items in lists easy to find and read.
5. Highlight safety information and warnings. Distinguish between danger, warning, and caution.
6. Keep illustrations as simple as possible.
7. Locate illustrations at the point where the reader needs them. Don't expect readers to locate an illustration that is several pages away from the instruction to which it pertains.
8. Label every illustration, and at the appropriate point in the related text, write "See Figure X."
9. Do not begin an instruction at the bottom of one page and complete it at the top of the next page. Insert a "page break" and move the entire instruction to the next page.

Planning Instructions and Procedures

Instructions and procedures should enable those who need them to perform the tasks covered. Successful instructions and procedures can be easily read, easily understood, and correctly followed by the intended users with minimal difficulty. Understanding your target readers and, in some cases, the context in which the documents will be used is paramount. If readers are confused or misled by statements, they can hold the company liable for injury or financial damage suffered because of poorly written instructions or procedures. Instructions, particularly those that involve processes that could be hazardous, should explain the knowledge level required of the target audience.

Who are the readers? What do your readers know about the subject? These questions will determine how much information you provide and the type of language you use. The audience for instructions should be specified, especially if readers not conforming to that audience should not attempt to follow the instructions. For general instructions, remember that many people resist reading instructions. They tend to avoid reading them, if possible, and attempt to perform the task without them. When they do read the instructions, they want to understand them imme diately without having to rercad them. Design features (layout), format, choice of language, and use of visuals can be critical to encouraging readers to focus on the instructions or procedures.

What is your purpose? Successful instructions/procedures require that both you and your readers know your purpose. What should your readers know and be able to do after they read these instructions/procedures? Any information that isn't applicable should be omitted.

What is the context in which the instructions/procedures will be used? Knowing how documents will be read can help you design effective documents. Readers may be focusing on them while they are sitting at their desks. They may need to read the entire document before trying to perform the task, or they may perform the task as they go.

Do your readers need to read the instructions/procedures before they begin? Your telling them how to read the instructions may be necessary. For example, you can include detailed instructions for first-time readers, and then have a summary of steps for readers to use once they are familiar with the longer instructions. Context-sensitive instructions can be found in numerous settings:

- Some sailboards have instructions for how to right the sailboard—if it turns over in the water—on the bottom of the boat where riders can see the instructions if the boat turns over.
- "Quick Start" instructions for many hand-held devices can be found inside the top or lid of the device.

- Some products, such as bookcases, computers, and lamps, for example, come with instructions composed only of pictures to show the steps in assembling the product. However, if the product will be sold in other countries, "picture-only" instructions should be tested for interpretation.
- Instructions used in machine shops and on manufacturing floors are often printed in large type on eye-saver yellow or green paper and laminated to resist grease. These instructions may be in metal loose-leaf notebooks so strong that pages cannot be torn out. Or they may appear on computer screens projected along the assembly line. Again, readability, completeness, and accuracy of these screens can be critical to error avoidance and safety of employees.
- Basic operation instructions and troubleshooting information for large clocks can be found inside the clock mechanism access compartment. These are designed to accompany the booklet that contains detailed instructions.

Will the instructions be available online or in paper? If instructions will be available online, focus on readability of the material. Avoid "text heavy" and lengthy instructions. Partition your instructions into distinct sections hyperlinked in a logical way. Or, you may want to tell your readers immediately that they should print a copy of the instructions if they are too long and complex for online reading.

Planning is particularly critical for writing instructions or procedures. Remembering or even using the document analysis checklist at the end of this chapter will help you determine whether you need instructions or procedures, the delivery medium (online or paper), the content you will include, and any design strategies that could help you produce an effective document. Effective instructions require sensitive attention to readers' information needs, their current knowledge of the topic, and what you want them to know as a result of reading the instructions.

STRUCTURE AND ORGANIZATION

First, analyze the audience, purpose, and context; then, begin to structure your procedures/instructions. Examine the following general guide for what elements to include, but remember that what you decide to include will depend on your topic, your audience, your purpose, and the reader's context. Comprehensive instruction/procedure manuals will usually contain most of these elements, while shorter instructions/procedures may require fewer. To illustrate instructions, we will focus on three examples.

Introduction.   The introduction should familiarize readers with the task to be performed: specifically, what the instructions will allow readers to do and what skill level the person should have to perform the task successfully.

Theory governing the procedure or instruction.   For some types of procedures, readers will perform tasks better if they have a general overview of the process. Knowledge of the process may help them understand when they have made an error and how to avoid errors. If you are going to give instructions for operating a mechanism, some explanation of the value and purpose of the mechanism can prepare readers for the process.

Warnings, cautions, hazards, and notes regarding safety or quality. Given the wide variety of technologically complicated and potentially dangerous products available today, you really cannot "overwarn" readers. And a failure to warn could have costly legal implications for your organization. Any level of hazard needs to be described—what will happen and why—if a particular action is performed. Identify the hazard, followed by the reason or the result, and be sure that all warnings, cautions, and notes are clearly visible. Warnings may also be repeated if they are associated with a particular step or direction. Warnings given at the beginning alert readers to possible problems they may encounter. Be sure that warnings stand out so that readers' eyes are drawn to them. The American National Standards Institute (www.ansi.org) articulates standards for hazard statements. A review of research on hazard messages is available from the U.S. Occupational Safety and Health Administration (www.osha.gov).

Conditions under which the task should be performed. Some instructions, particularly laboratory instructions, may require you to describe the physical conditions required to perform a task: room size, temperature, time required for the entire process and for individual steps, specific safety processes. If time is a constraint, readers need to know how much time will be needed before they begin the task.

Name of each step. For each step, give the following: purpose of the step; warnings, cautions, and notes; any conditions necessary for performing the step; time required to perform the step; and the list of materials needed for the step.

- Place instructions in chronological order.
- Number each step.
- Limit each instruction to one action.
- After you have written the instruction, state in a separate sentence the reason for the instruction, but only if you believe that the reader may not follow the instruction without an explanation. Include warnings whenever necessary. And be sure to explain all warnings if you believe that people will not understand the reason for the warning.

Case 10-1: **Process Instructions**

Stefi Lee, a graduate student who supervises a biochemistry lab, decides that the laboratory instructions for recrystallization are too confusing and decides to revise these before assigning the lab. The original instructions appear in Case Document 10-1a. She will expect students to read the original instructions but also to have the revision available when they actually begin the experiment. Her first step in revising is to do a pre-writing analysis:

Pre-writing Analysis for Revising Recrystallization Instructions

1. Who is/are your reader(s)?
My readers are students new to Organic Chemistry lab. Those enrolled in this course will be required to recrystallize and perform certain tasks in lab they have never done before.

2. What is your reader profile? Background, attitude toward following instructions?
These students have not been previously exposed to Organic Chemistry Lab experiments. They know only basic knowledge from General Chemistry Lab, which does not teach the techniques and methods required in Organic Chemistry Lab. They will have no idea what equipment they will be using nor what each piece of equipment will look like. The only equipment they will have a general idea of are beaker, Erlenmeyer flask, and spatula. They will be totally reliant on the instructions through the entire experiment and won't be able to perform the experiment by memory until they repeat it with the instructions several times. The students want the instructions to be simple and easy to learn, so they understand the general purpose and procedures of the experiment.

3. How much do your readers know about the subject?
The readers don't know anything about this subject because lab experiments in Organic Chemistry Lab are much more advanced and different from General Chemistry Lab.

4. Will you have to define any terms that your readers may not understand?
Yes, some equipment and chemical terms will need to be defined.

5. What do you want your readers to be able to do after reading the instructions or procedures?
I want my readers to fully understand the experiment and be able to learn the steps by memory after following the procedures a few times. After learning to perform the experiment correctly, my readers should know the purpose and intent of the experiment.

6. What is the situation that led to the need for these instructions?

In my first semester of Organic Chemistry lab, I was very confused in lab. The lab manual did not provide very clear instructions on how to set up the equipment. Thus, I performed the experiment very inefficiently and didn't obtain the correct results in the end. The instructions were condensed in long paragraphs, and oftentimes I would lose my place in the procedures. After I finished the experiment, I had no idea what I had done and the purpose of the lab.

7. How will your readers use these instructions? Will they need to read every time, or will they be used only for reference?

My readers will follow these instructions carefully the first few times. They will need to use them several more times until they are able to commit every step of the experiment to memory. Thereafter, they will be able to perform the experiment themselves.

8. What kinds of pictorials will you use?

Graphics of the equipment used and results of the experiment will be provided.

9. What kinds of formatting and page design strategies will you use to make the instructions easy to read?

I will bold headings, provide bullet points, use white space to make the steps easy to see and follow, and underline important steps.

10. What content segments will you include?

I will include descriptive segments for equipments used, personal safety wear for self-protection, experiment procedures, and clean-up procedures.

CASE DOCUMENT 10-1A

Recrystallization

Purpose: To demonstrate the use of recrystallization to purify an impure sample of a solid compound.

Reading: *Techniques:* Recrystallization
Techniques: Melting Points

INTRODUCTION

Organic chemistry tends to be an almost endless adventure into isolation, identification, and/or synthesis of new compounds. Unfortunately, organic compounds have a unique sense of humor and reactions tend never to go to completion. Even if all the starting material has been used, it is a very good bet that more than one product has been formed. Recrystallization is one of four major techniques used to separate and purify organic compounds. Unlike the other techniques, recrystallization requires that the material to be purified be solid.

EXPERIMENTAL PROCEDURE

As soon as you arrive in the laboratory, begin heating 75 mL of water in a 250-mL beaker.

Dissolving the Compound. Weigh approximately 1.5 g of the impure acetanilide into a 125-mL Erlenmeyer flask. Break up the larger lumps with a stirring rod and add a boiling chip to the flask. Add about 25 mL of hot water to the flask containing the impure acetanilide. Heat this mixture on the steam bath. Swirl the flask occasionally (using crucible tongs) to aid in dissolving the solid and to prevent bumping. When recrystallizing an impure solid, it is desirable to use the minimum amount of hot solvent to dissolve the solid (30 mL of hot water are required to dissolve 1.5 g of pure acetanilide). Add small portions of hot water, 1 to 2 mL, until all the acetanilide dissolves. Be careful not to add too much hot water. The impure acetanilide contains water insoluble impurities. If no more material dissolves after you add more hot water, the material left is the insoluble impurity. If the acetanilide forms an oil rather than dissolving, more hot water should be added to dissolve the oil. Be careful not to add too much water.

Filtering Insoluble Impurities. While you are dissolving the acetanilide in hot water, set up a filter flask and a Büchner funnel for a hot vacuum filtration. (The steps required are outlined in *Techniques: Recrystallization*) Then conduct a hot vacuum filtration to remove insoluble impurities.

continued

Recrystallizing the Acetanilide. After completion of the hot vacuum filtration, allow the hot solution to cool slowly. If the solution is cooled too rapidly, small impure crystals form. Notice if an oil forms as the solution cools. If oil droplets are observed, heat the solution until the oil dissolves, add about 5 mL of water, and allow the solution to again cool slowly. After crystallization seems complete (the flask will have cooled to the point that you can comfortably hold it), place the solution in an ice-water bath for about ten minutes to increase the recovery of acetanilide.

Isolating and Drying the Pure Acetanilide. Vacuum filter the ice-cold solution to collect the crystals of acetanilide. Be sure the Büchner funnel is clean if it was used in the hot filtration. Wash the crystals with about 5 mL of ice cold water. The crystals in the funnel will still be quite wet. They should be dried thoroughly before weighing or taking a melting point. Some water may be removed by pressing on the crystals with a spatula while air is being drawn through the funnel by the aspirator. After the crystals have been dried, remove the filter paper and crystals from the Büchner funnel. Place another piece of filter paper on top of the crystals and wrap well in a piece of 15-cm filter paper. Tape with a piece of colored tape as a label. Label the sample with your name, section and course number, and experiment number. Store the sample in your section's storage drawer until the next laboratory period.

The sample of pure acetanilide will be thoroughly dry by the next laboratory period. Weigh the recovered acetanilide and determine its melting point. Compare this weight to the amount of impure acetanilide and determine the percent recovery. Compare the melting point range to the melting point of pure acetanilide reported in the literature.

CLEAN-UP PROCEDURES

The filtrate in the filter flask at the end of the experiment should be poured into the appropriately labeled waste container in the hood. Dispose of the used filter paper in the waste container labeled for this purpose in the hood. Rinse the used equipment with acetone, collect and dispose of the first rinse in the container labeled for this purpose in the hood.

Second Week Lab Period Clean-up Procedures. After you have weighed and determined the melting point of your acetanilide sample, dispose of the acetanilide in the container marked "waste acetanilide." You will also put the filter paper used to store the crystals in this same container. The used melting point capillary tubes should be disposed of in the box designated for broken glass.

SAFETY

Acetanilide is an irritant, avoid getting this on your hands. Wash your hands immediately following contact. You will be using *HOT* water. Use clamps to secure your filter flask to avoid tipping and unnecessary exposure to hot liquids or the acetanilide. Clamps may also be necessary to prevent your flask from tipping over while it is being chilled in the ice-water bath.

Following her analysis of the original lab instructions, Stefi revises the original instructions (see Case Document 10-1b).

CASE DOCUMENT 10-1B

Recrystallization

Step-by-step instructions for carefully and correctly performing Recrystallization.

Recrystallization is a technique used to separate and purify organic[1] compounds from liquid to solid matter.

Before starting this experiment, think safety! These chemicals could be hazardous to your skin and eyes.

For Safety:
- Keep your safety goggles on *at all times*.
- Tie back long hair.
- Wear closed-toe shoes.
- Wear gloves if needed.
- Do not consume any food, drinks, or chemicals during lab.
- Do not wear loose clothing.

Equipment Required:
Check off items ☑ as you collect these before you begin.

☐ 250-mL Beaker
☐ 125-mL Erlenmeyer Flask
☐ Stirring Rod
☐ Boiling Chip
☐ Steam Bath
☐ Clamp
☐ Rubber FilterVac

☐ Crucible Tongs
☐ Filter Flask
☐ Buchner Funnel
☐ Black Tube
☐ Filter Paper
☐ Watch Glass

Chemicals used:

☐ Water
☐ Acetanilide[2]

---

[1] Organic—relating to chemical compounds containing carbon, especially hydrocarbons.
[2] Acetanilide—a white, crystalline, odorless, organic powder, C_8H_9NO, produced by the action of glacial acetic acid on aniline, used chiefly in organic synthesis and formerly in the treatment of fever and headache.

continued

Conducting the Experiment

This experiment requires five steps:

1. Dissolving the compound,
2. Using the balance,
3. Setting up the hot vacuum filtration apparatus,
4. Recrystallizing the acetanilide, and,
5. Cleaning up following the procedure

1. Dissolving the compound

1. Using a graduated cylinder, measure 75 mL of water and add it to a 250 mL beaker.
2. Set the beaker on the cylindrical steam bath on your laboratory desk and turn the **red** knob at the side of your desk to begin heating.
3. While your water is heating, use the balance to weigh approximately 1.5 g of impure acetanilide (Impure acetanilide can be found in a bottle at the front counter). Use a watch glass to accurately weigh the impure acetanilide.

2. Using the balance

1. Obtain a watch glass from your instructor and set it on the balance. Figure 1 is an example of a watch glass.
2. Tare[3] the balance by pushing the "tare" button so that the watch glass has a mass of 0.0 grams.

Figure 1-Watch Glass

3. Then using a spatula, carefully add impure acetanilide onto the watch glass until the balance reads approximately 1.5 grams. Then add the impure acetanilide to the 125-mL Erlenmeyer flask.
4. Break up the clumps of acetanilide with a stirring rod and add a black boiling chip (found at the front counter) to the flask.
5. Add approximately 25 mL of the heated water from the beaker into the flask containing the impure acetanilide.
6. Using crucible[4] tongs, swirl the flask occasionally to prevent clumping. Crucible tongs will protect you from burning your hands. Never pick up hot objects with your hands.

---

[3] Tare—to obtain the weight of a container or wrapper that is deducted from the gross weight to obtain net weight.

[4] Crucible—metal or refractory material employed for heating substances to high temperatures.

continued

7. If all the acetanilide has not dissolved by this step, add 1-2 mL portions of hot water until it dissolves.

8. While the acetanilide is dissolving, set up the hot vacuum filtration apparatus.

3. Setting up the hot vacuum filtration apparatus

Figure 2-Buchner funnel

1. Obtain a Buchner funnel and a filter flask from your instructor. Figure 2 is an example of how your funnel may look, and Figure 3 is an example of a filter flask.

2. Obtain a clamp from your lab drawer and securely clamp the filter flask to the metal frame connected to your desk.

3. Obtain a rubber FilterVac from your lab drawer and place it on top of your Filter flask. Figure 4 is an example of what your FilterVac may look like. Then place the Buchner funnel on top of the FilterVac.

4. Obtain a black long tube from your lower lab drawer. Attach one side of the heavy-walled tube to the side-arm of your flask and the other side to the water aspirator. Figure 5 is a representation of how your entire set-up should look.

Figure 3-Filter flask

5. Obtain a small filter paper and neatly fit it into the Buchner funnel so that it covers all the holes at the bottom of the funnel. Wet the filter paper with 1-2 drops of distilled water. Then turn the water aspirator (green knob) on full blast by turning it all the way to the left. The suction pressure from the water aspirator should suck the filter paper to the bottom of the funnel.

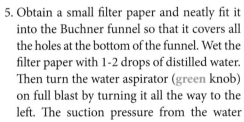

Figure 4-FilterVac

6. At this time, slowly cool the hot solution in the flask by turning down the red knob every few minutes.

7. If oil droplets form, turn up the red knob and heat the solution until the oil dissolves. Then, add about 5 mL of water and allow the solution to cool again slowly. If oil droplets appear again, repeat this step.

Figure 5-Hot Vacuum Filtration Set-up

continued

8. When white clumps begin forming in the flask (sign of crystallization), the solution is ready to be filtered through the Buchner funnel.

4. Recrystallizing the acetanilide

1. With the water aspirator on full blast, vacuum filter the solution by slowing pouring the contents of the flask into the Buchner funnel.

2. Once all your contents are poured, rinse the flask with hot water and pour it into the funnel again. This filtration should produce white crystals that look similar to baby powder.

3. Pour 5 mL of ice cold water into the funnel to wash the crystals formed.

4. Use a spatula to remove the boiling chip and press on the crystals to remove water.

Note: Do NOT turn off the water aspirator until you are ready to clean up!!!

5. After the crystals have dried, carefully dump and wrap the crystals in a 15-cm filter paper. Tape and label the filter paper with your name and section number. Store it in your lab section drawer for next week. By this time, the crystals will be fully dry.

5. Cleaning up following the procedure

1. Do not turn off the water aspirator until the black tube is disconnected from the sidearm of the flask. If water is turned off before the tube is disconnected, water may back up into the freshly cleaned solution and you will have to start over.

2. Pour the filtrate[5] in the filter flask into the waste bottle in the hood at the end of the experiment.

3. Dispose of the small filter paper that was used to filter the solution into the waste container.

4. Carefully take apart the vacuum filtration set-up and wash the equipment thoroughly with acetone in the sink. Return all equipment used to your instructor.

---

[5] Filtrate—liquid that has been passed through a filter.

Case 10-2: Job Instructions

These procedures were written by an employee who had just completed several years as a Runner/Floater at an animal hospital. Before she left, she decided to write a set of instructions for the next person who would take her place. Job procedures have become increasingly important in many organizations. These help the organization in writing job descriptions, training new employees, and evaluating employee performance.

CASE DOCUMENT 10-2

How to Be a Runner at Kingsland Animal Clinic

Congratulations! You have the job! You will now need to learn how to perform your job. These instructions will tell you what you will need to do here at the clinic. Keep these instructions close by until you know all the tasks you will need to perform.

Your First Day

You will be training most of your first day. Read these instructions before you arrive, then observe, listen, and practice. Make notes on the instructions to help you remember what to do.

As you learn the job, you will see other ways that you can help. Always ask questions. The better all employees work as a team, the better service and care the clinic can provide. Every person employed at the clinic has an important job. The Runner's tasks, as you will see, prevent gaps in service and care and improve efficiency.

What the Runner/Floater Does

As the runner/floater, you will experience all aspects of a working veterinary clinic: reception, technical, kennel cleaning, pharmacy, and any other job that the clinic does. If someone needs your help, respond to them immediately. The RF position exists to make everyone's job easier and more efficient.

IMPORTANT: Realize that other employees do not always know when they need help, or they do not want to bother you by asking for it. Learn to know when someone needs you. Take initiative. If someone is having trouble, offer to help. Communicate openly with the receptionists, technicians, and vets to find where you are needed at any given time. Don't be afraid to ask questions about where and how you can help.

continued

CAUTION: Since you will work with animals, remember that sick animals are often frightened. Remain alert and aware of your surroundings. Treat all animals with caution. Just because an owner tells you that her Chihuahua is a "sweetie" doesn't means that it won't try to bite you when you take its temperature.

Your Responsibilities—Discussed in These Instructions

- Knowing the Phone Room
- Helping the Receptionists
- Helping the Technicians
- Completing End of Day Duties
- Working on Other Tasks When You Have Time

The Phone Room

If you are assigned to the phone room, when one of the receptionists is at lunch, or if no one is in the phone room, **answer the phone**. A receptionist will teach you to work the phone.

- Greet callers with "This is [insert your name] at Kingsland Animal Clinic. How can I help you?"
- Always have a note pad ready to write down owner name, animal names, or any other important information.

Most common calls you will receive:

1. **Make an Appointment.** Use the Cornerstone program on the computer in the phone room to make an appointment. A receptionist will show you how to work Cornerstone. Practice using the program so that you don't make mistakes.
2. **Make a Boarding Reservation.** The boarding book should always remain in the phone room, on one of the desks. Write the owner's last name under the requested dates **in pencil**. If the reservation changes, you can easily erase.
3. **Ask about the Status of a Pet.** If the owner dropped off a pet for any reason, the owner may call to find out how the animal is doing. Put the owner on hold; run to the back; and ask the techs: "Does anyone know if [pet name] is ready to go" or "[pet name]'s owner wants to know how he/she is doing. Does anyone know?" When you find out, run to the phone and relay the information.
4. **Ask about Prices.** The price book, like the boarding book, is located in the phone room. This book lists prices for common procedures, surgeries, details, etc. You may put the client on hold for a moment as you find the information.

continued

5. **Ask a Pet Health Question.** Transfer the caller to the phone in the tech station. Put the caller on hold and first make sure a tech can take the call, then transfer the caller. If no tech is free, get the caller's information and tell them a tech will call shortly. Pull the file, and put it in the Drop Off Box with a note attached. Describe question clearly.

6. **Refill Medication.** Simply transfer the caller to the pharmacy station. Check first to make sure someone is available in pharmacy.

7. **Other.** Many calls do not fit into these categories. If you do not know the answer, put the caller on hold and find someone who does know the answer. Any employee will be glad to answer your questions.

NOTE: Make sure to "roll the phones over" when the clinic closes so that no more calls come in.

Helping the Receptionists

The receptionists should never leave the front desk vacant. Your job: make sure they do not leave unless someone else takes their places. You must constantly run between the reception area and the back of the clinic to relay information from the receptionists to the vets and to retrieve animals. This requirement describes the "runner" part of your job. You will keep the receptionists from leaving by doing the following tasks for them:

- When a client drops off a pet, take the pet into the back.

  1. Make a cage card for the animal. Include name, date, and reason for the visit.
  2. Write the animal's name on one of our temporary collars.
  3. Put these in your pocket.
  4. Walk to the front and gently take the animal from the owner. Leave the dog's collar with the owner. CAUTION: Be gentle in dealing with an unknown animal.
  5. Take dogs to the kennel in the back. Take cats to the cat room. Take exotics to the exotics room.
  6. Put the temporary collar on the animal, and tape the cage card on the cage.
  7. Take the animal's folder, which the receptionist will have given you, and place it in the Drop Off box.

- When a pet is ready to go home, you will bring it up to its owner.

  1. Ask the receptionist which animal needs to go home.
  2. Ask the owner for leash and collar or carrier.

continued

3. Find the pet.

4. Take it to its owner.

- When a client arrives for an appointment, the receptionist will prepare the file and hand it to you. Take it to the back and place it in the appropriate appointment slot. Tell the techs that Dr. [vet's name]'s appointment has arrived, or that a walk-in has arrived.

- If a receptionist needs to leave the front for some reason, ask if you can help so that he/she doesn't have to leave. You can help when bathroom breaks are needed.

Helping the Technicians

If the phone room is quiet and the receptionists seem to have things under control, you can head to the treatment area. Here you will find the techs, who can almost always use a hand. How you can help:

1. Restraining an animal. Usually two people are needed to deal with an animal. If you see a tech trying to take an animal's temperature or trim nails with no help, offer to hold the animal. Special ways are needed to restrain the animal for a blood draw: the tech will be glad to show you.

2. Taking Temperatures. You can help hold the animal, particularly the head if the animal decides to bite.

3. Trimming Nails. If you do not know how to trim nails by looking for "the quick," ask a tech to teach you.

4. Weighing an animal.

5. Drawing Blood. If you do not know how and would like to learn, the techs will teach you. This process requires two people.

6. Fecal Tests. A tech will teach you how to attain a fecal sample and set up the fecal test.

7. Giving vaccines. Once you learn how to use needles, the techs and vets will let you draw and administer some vaccines, such as Bordetella and leptospirosis vaccines. You can also learn to give Adequan shots.

8. Pharmacy Work. Once you have worked at the clinic for several months, you will be allowed to fill prescriptions. The tech will print a label, which will tell you how many and what kinds of pills to place in the pill bottles. Apply the label to the bottle and initial it.

9. Anything else the tech asks you to do. NOTE: you will not be asked/ allowed to perform any task for which you have not been trained. Take every opportunity to learn.

continued

End of the Day Duties

End of day clean-up duties depend on how busy the clinic has been that day. Whenever business begins to slow down toward closing time, you can begin working on the following tasks:

- **Take out the trash.** Try to get someone to help you carry the bag to the dumpster.

  1. Every trash can in the clinic must be emptied at the end of EVERY DAY.
  2. Retrieve one large black trash bag from under the sink in the cat room.
  3. Begin dumping the contents of every small trash can into the large bag. You do not need to change the trash bags in the smaller trash cans unless they are particularly dirty.
  4. Make sure you get every trash can—the ICU, employee lounge, and every treatment room. The cans in the cat room and the kennel will be cleaned by the kennel kids.
  5. Take the now full trash bag out to the dumpster.
  6. Replace any of the small bags that you had to throw away.

- **Vacuum**

  1. The vacuum is located in the freezer room, located off the exotics room.
  2. Insert one end of the vacuum into the various outlets in the way.
  3. Begin vacuuming the entire clinic (aside from the cat room and kennel).

Other Tasks to Complete When You Have Time

When you have time, such as a lull in activity or no appointments scheduled, other tasks must be completed.

1. Filing. The receptionists will show and help you with filing.
2. Restock the boxes of flea/tick/heartworm prevention on display in the reception area. (New boxes are stored in the stockroom. One of the vets must unlock that room for you.)
3. Restock the shelves of shampoos, ear cleaners, collars, ointments, etc. Most of these items are stored in the pharmacy area.
4. Clean the lobby. If at any point during the day the lobby looks dirty, sweep it. The broom is stored in the filing hall.

continued

5. Clean up any messes the techs have made in the back (blood, nail trimmings, animal hair, etc.) by spraying the treatment tables with Trifectant found in spray bottles.

6. Clean thermometers with alcohol swabs from the metal tins on the treatment tables.

7. Rinse the fecal loops and cups in the sink and place them in the Trifectant bath along with the urine collection trays.

8. Clean any dirty cages in ICU, isolation, or the cat room. For each cage,

   ○ Remove the mat from the cage and take it to the nearest bathtub.
   ○ Rinse off the mat and spray it with Trifectant. Leave it while you complete the next tasks.
   ○ Remove the newspaper from the cage and throw it away.
   ○ Spray the cage down with Trifectant.
   ○ Wipe the Trifectant with paper towels.
   ○ Line the cage with fresh newspaper found in every room of the clinic.
   ○ Go back to the mat – rinse it, dry it, and put it back in the cage on top of the newspaper.

9. Make sure all the animals have water, unless they will have surgery that day, and that all cats have litter boxes.

10. Check to see if the kennel kids need help cleaning cages, feeding, or walking dogs in the kennel.

Final Words—If you don't understand, always ask!

Case 10-3: Instructional Letter

Jonathan Varner, president of a professional organization, writes the incoming VP to explain how elections for new officers should be conducted.

The letter can be used as a reference by Dr. Dawson as she plans and executes the elections (see Case Document 10-3).

CASE DOCUMENT 10-3

May 12, 2009

Dr. Gabrielle Dawson
Department of Geography
San Diego State University
San Diego, CA

Dear Gabrielle,

As we discussed at AAGG in April, the VP of AAGG is responsible for conducting elections. From my experience in conducting the last election, I recommend that you begin this process immediately. The more persistent you are, the more efficient the process. Do as much as you can before faculty leave campus for the summer.

Time Table

In general, the election process begins during the late spring early summer. Ballots are developed and mailed by mid-September. Ballots should be returned and tabulated by mid-January and the results reported to the vice president. As vice president, you will inform me and then inform each person whose name appeared on the ballot about the results of the election.

Election Procedures

The following procedures should help you conduct the elections. Ultimately, when the AAGG procedures manual is complete, these will appear in the manual. Until that time, however, each president will be responsible for informing the vice-president of election procedures.

Materials Needed

- Election File—contains ballots of previous elections and names of nominating committees
- AAGG Directory—names, phone numbers, and email addresses of all members

continued

Gabrielle Dawson   -2-   May 20, 2009

- Annual Meeting Agendas—protocols for announcing newly elected officers

Step 1: Creating a Nominating Committee

1. At the annual meeting in April, the president asks the general membership to consider individuals who should be asked to run for the office of Vice-President and Member-At-Large. Members are invited to send the names of individuals to the President.

2. The president also organizes a nominating committee. At AAGG, I asked three individuals—Steve Jones, Pam Souther, and Casey Morgan—to serve as the nominating committee. All agreed to serve. Casey Morgan agreed to chair the committee.

   Note: Former officers of the organization are good choices for the nominating committee. They know what is involved in executing the duties of each office. I attempted to select a nominating committee of individuals from different regions in the US. With that point in mind, you could select four members of the committee, but more than four makes the committee unwieldy.

3. The nominating committee must recommend a minimum of six nominees for three member-at-large positions. Eight nominees will be fine, too. Three Vice-President nominees should be chosen. The chair of the nominating committee should ask each candidate for a one-paragraph (150-word) biographical profile.

Step 2: Selecting Nominees for Offices

1. In selecting candidates, you will want to consider several factors:

   - Interest in AAGG and its Activities. Look for people who have shown interest in the organization: attendance at regional and national meetings, people who engage in conversation on the listserv, people who make solid suggestions.

   - Interest in Geography and/or Geoscience. AAGG needs individuals who are effective spokespersons for both as fields of teaching and research: i.e., individuals who are effective and prolific researchers; people who are in charge of programs; people who are regular presenters at meetings.

   - Record of Dependability. VERY IMPORTANT! Try to determine how reliable an individual is. Stay in touch with the nominating committee.

continued

Gabrielle Dawson   -3-   May 20, 2009

Once you get a list of individuals you are considering, please post the list on the Executive Committee listserv. If any of the potential nominees has a track record of non-performance, this is the time to determine that! Many people are "all talk," but slow on performance.

Note: Choose the VP very carefully. This is the person who will succeed you as president of AAGG. Because the president and vice-president have so much responsibility and because they will need to work as a team, be sure you choose someone with whom you can work and someone who will continue to strengthen the organization. AAGG has very strong individuals in its thirty-year history. Each group of officers must be committed to developing AAGG further.

Step 3: Developing the Ballot

1. Be sure to let Casey Morgan know when you want the final list of names. I would suggest that you ask for the list by the second week in September.

2. Contact each individual whose name was submitted by the nominating committee. Be sure that each person has agreed to be nominated and understands what is involved.

3. Develop the ballot and a letter that will be sent along with the ballot.

4. Send the ballot and the letter to Dan Jameson. He will make copies. Try to get this material sent to Dan no later than the third week in September.

Step 4: Monitoring the Election Process

1. Once he has the materials, Dan will duplicate and mail the ballots to the membership. He knows the procedure: each ballot has a self-addressed, stamped return envelope to ensure better response.

2. Dan will want all ballots returned by early January. He will count the ballots and report the results to you. As soon as you have the results, please call—rather than email—each candidate and report the results.

Step 5: Preparing for the Annual Meeting

1. Plan to introduce each of the officers at the meeting. After my farewell speech, I will hand the reins of the organization to you.

2. To help prepare for the meeting, discuss your agenda as president with the incoming VP. I would also suggest that you plan an informal gathering of all the new officers BEFORE the Executive Committee meeting. At the EC, as you are aware, we always have several hours of business to conduct. Meeting with the incoming officers will give you planning time with them.

continued

Gabrielle Dawson   -4-   May 20, 2009

3. Be prepared to tell the general membership at the annual meeting your goals for the next two years. The newly-elected VP and members-at-large should be allotted time to express their concerns. Usually we allot fifteen minutes for this segment of the annual meeting.

Final Thoughts

The election process has been developed to attempt to involve a variety of individuals in the election process. The nominating committee should seek involvement of members in the organization who want to become more involved in AAGG. In no sense does the election process seek to exclude individuals other than those who are not interested in Geography and/or Geoscience and the development of AAGG as an organization.

As you work with the elections, keep notes on ways that the EC can improve the election process. Then add these to the agenda for the 2010 meeting.

As always, if you have any questions, please call me.

Sincerely,

Jonathan

ONLINE INSTRUCTIONS

Online instructions need to follow the same readability considerations as those used in letters, reports, and stand-alone instructions. Otherwise, the instructions will create confusion for many users.

Case 10-4

A university explained how to download class rosters from the faculty e-mail system and insert these into an Excel spreadsheet (see Case Document 10-4a). Note how the application of principles discussed in this chapter improves the instructions (see Case Document 10-4b). The revision supplanted the original, which diminished the number of calls to the computing help desk from faculty who were confused by the original instructions:

CASE DOCUMENT 10-4A

Original Online Instructions

How exactly do I get my roster from NEO, put it into an Excel spreadsheet and make a comma separated value (csv) file for uploading?

1. Log into your neo account, go to the Class Roster tool and go to the appropriate semester. Click on Download Class Roster and you'll see your class roster as a comma separated value (csv) file. Copy and paste this file into a blank excel spreadsheet and save. There's no way right now to actually download it.

2. To get rid of the quotes, go to Edit, then Replace. You want to find every " and replace it with a blank, so in the Find what box, type ", and put nothing into the Replace with box. Click on Replace All, and the quotes disappear.

3. Under File, select Save As option, and save the file as Formatted Text (space delimited)(*.prn). Choose OK and Yes to the questions that pop up. Close the file and answer no to the popup box. You don't want to save the changes.

4. Open the .prn file. The Text Import Wizard will pop up. Leave the file type as delimited and click next. Change the delimiter from tab to comma and click next. Holding the ctrl key down, click on the last four columns, and choose Do not import column (skip), then choose Finish.

5. Under File, select the Save As option. Change the file name to something that does not include the .prn, and save the file as CSV (Comma delimited) (.csv). Always answer yes to the question, "Do you want to keep the workbook in this format?" and when you close the file, answer no to "Do you want to save the changes?". Voila! This is the file the administrator needs.

6. To upload your students into your course, you only need the UIN numbers as a csv file. So, just delete the name columns and any rows above your data, and save. Always answer yes to the question, "Do you want to

keep the workbook in this format?" and when you close the file, answer no to "Do you want to save the changes?" Upload your file according to the directions in CPR. [top]

CASE DOCUMENT 10-4B

Revised Online Instructions

How to Download Your Roster

1. Click on **download class roster**. Note that your class roster now appears as a comma separated value (CSV) file.
2. Without closing the roster on Neo, create an Excel spreadsheet.
3. Go back to your roster. Copy the names.
4. Paste the roster into the Excel spreadsheet just as you copied it.

Get rid of the quotes (" ").

1. Go to **Edit** on the toolbar, then to **Replace**.
   You want to find every " " and replace it with a blank.
2. In the **Find what** box, type " " , and put nothing into the **Replace with** box.
3. Click on **Replace All**, and the quotes disappear.

Prepare to Format the Information in the Excel Spreadsheet.

1. Under **File**, select **Save As** option, and save the file as **Formatted Text (space delimited) (*prn)**.
2. Choose **OK** and then **Yes** to the questions that pop up.
3. Close the file and answer **no** to the popup box.
4. Open the **.prn** file. The **Text Import Wizard** will pop up.

Select the Correct Boxes on the Wizard.

1. Leave the file type as **delimited**. Then click **next**.
2. Change the delimiter from **tab** to **comma**. Then click **next**. You will see the opening rows of your roster appear in neat columns.
3. Under **File**, select the **Save As** option.
4. Save the file as an Excel file. Be sure to save with a name descriptive of the contents.

With your file in an Excel spreadsheet, you can now create a grade or attendance sheet.

CHECKLIST FOR DEVELOPING INSTRUCTIONS/PROCEDURES ✔

Because instructions require careful analysis of readers from many perspectives—the context in which the instructions will be read and used—following a checklist can be helpful in ensuring that you have considered critical issues needed for the instructions:

☐ Who are your readers? Describe them in terms of their knowledge of the subject: educational level, technical level, responsibilities in the organization.

☐ What do you want them to be able to do as a result of these instructions/procedures?

☐ What is the situation that has led to the need for these instructions/procedures to be written?

☐ How will these instructions/procedures be used? Will readers need to read all of them before they begin the task? In what context will readers be using these instructions?

☐ What problems could readers encounter in attempting to use these instructions/procedures?

☐ What types of problems in safety and/or quality control do you need to emphasize? What warnings or notes will you need to include?

☐ What topics do you want to be sure to include/exclude?

☐ What format will you use? Online, online to be printed, paper, manual, poster?

☐ Given the context in which the instructions/procedures will be read, what formatting strategies do you need to use to enhance accessibility?

☐ What types of visuals will you need to include?

☐ What is the basic outline of your instructions? Does this outline meet the needs of your readers? Will it achieve your purpose?

EXERCISES

1. You are employed by a small manufacturer of all-organic ready-to-eat break-fast cereals. The company would like to develop its sales overseas, especially in China. Because ready-to-eat cereals would be relatively new to the majority of the population in China, your package will have to include instructions on how to prepare and eat a serving of cereal. Compose step-by-step instructions, including rough illustrations, to fit on the side of the package.

2. Examine the real instructions given in Figure 10-1. If you were the author and were given 15 more minutes to make the instructions more effective, what changes would you make?

3. Working individually or collaboratively, find a set of instructions you have tried to use with limited success: for example, instructions for posting to a blog or wiki, for checking the security settings on your Internet browser, for operating a new mobile device, or for assembling the several components of a home entertainment system. Develop a slide presentation for your class explaining the deficiencies in the original instructions and the revisions you perceive as necessary.

Print this Page
Close this Window

Printer Friendly Version Of:
http://www.cbp.gov/xp/cgov/travel/id_visa/i-94_instructions/filling_out_i94.xml
Printed:
Thu Jul 14 2011 20:58:14 GMT-0500 (CDT)

Filling Out Arrival-Departure Record, CBP Form I-94, for Nonimmigrant Visitors with a Visa for the U.S.
07/02/2010

For nonimmigrant visitors entering the United States with a visa, there is a requirement to fill a CBP Form I-94 (white form). This form has two specific perforated sections to it. The visitor or the carrier representative must complete both sections of CBP Form I-94 upon arrival in the United States. **The bottom section of CBP Form I-94 is a departure record and must be returned to U.S. officials upon exiting the United States.**

The information requested on the CBP Form I-94, Arrival Record, upper portion, includes:

- Family Name
- First Name
- Date of Birth
- Country of Citizenship
- Sex (Male or Female)
- Passport Number
- Airline and Flight Number **(if applicable)**
- Country Where You Live – Lawful Permanent Residence
- City Where You Boarded **(if applicable)**
- City Where Visa was Issued **(if applicable)**
- Date Issued (Day/Mo/Yr) **(if applicable)**
- Address While in the United States (Number and Street)
- City and State

The information requested on the CBP Form I-94, Departure Record, lower portion, includes:

- Family Name
- First Name
- Date of Birth
- Country of Citizenship

After the successful completion of processing the applicant, a CBP officer stamps the applicant's **CBP Form I-94, Arrival and Departure Records, and** the passport. The CBP Declaration, used at air and sea ports of entry, may also be stamped by the CBP officer. The CBP officer retains the arrival portion of the CBP Form I-94 and returns the departure portion of the CBP Form I-94 and passport to the applicant.

The departure portion of CBP Form I-94 and passport is to be in the applicant's possession at all times until the applicant departs the United States. If an applicant boards a commercial conveyance to depart the United States, the transportation carriers are:

1. To remove the departure portion of the CBP Form I-94 from the applicant's passport.
2. Annotate the reverse of the departure portion of the CBP Form I-94 with the facts of the applicant's departure from the United States.
3. Return the departure portion of the CBP Form I-94 to the nearest CBP office.

It is your responsibility to ensure that your I-94/I-94W is turned in to Customs and Border Protection (CBP) at the end of your visit to the United States.

FIGURE 10-1 Document for Exercise 2

- If you are departing by air, please turn the I-94/I-94W into the airline prior to departure.
- If you are departing by sea, please turn the I-94/I-94W into the shipping line prior to departure.
- If you are departing by land and you will not be returning to the United States within 30 days, please turn the 1/94/1/94W into the Canadian authorities when crossing the Canadian border and to a U.S. Official when crossing the Mexican border.

In general, if you have been admitted to the United States under most visa classifications if you take a short trip (30 days or less) to Canada or Mexico, you may retain your I-94/I-94W, so that when you resume your visit to the United States you are readmitted for the balance of the time remaining on your I-94/I-94W.

For those admitted as academic students or exchange visitors (F or J classifications), if you take a short trip (30 days or less) to Canada, Mexico, or the Adjacent Islands, you may retain your I-94 and your SEVIS form I-20 or SEVIS Form DS-2019, so when you resume your visit to the United States you are readmitted for the balance of the time required for you to complete your program.

Both 8 CFR 214.1 and 22 CFR 41.112 contain legal guidance on the procedures for the readmission of a traveler and automatic revalidation of a visa that has expired.

However, because each traveler's individual circumstances may vary (such as your current status in the United States, foreign destination, and the nationality of the traveler); it is recommended that you contact CBP at the port of your departure and prior to your departure if you have any questions regarding these issues.

FIGURE 10-1 *continued*

11

Oral Reports

Your ability to give oral reports can be as critical to your success as your ability to write reports. In today's work environment, knowing how to speak effectively and use presentation slides has become an increasingly valuable asset, whether you work in an academic or a nonacademic environment. In applying for a job or admission to a graduate program, you may need to give an oral presentation on a specific topic or perhaps on a research project you have conducted. As an employee, you may need to prepare a written document of an oral presentation you have given. Or, an employer may ask you to make an oral presentation of a written document. Whatever the venue, you will benefit from knowing and then practicing basic strategies of developing effective oral presentations.

Quick Tips

- In the introduction, interest the audience in the subject, and enumerate the key points you will cover (e.g., "I will cover the following five points.").
- In the discussion section, help your audience pay attention and track where you are in your presentation by numbering each point as you cover it (e.g., "Now let's proceed to my second point.").
- When you reach the conclusion, announce it. You want your audience to pay extra attention. Audiences know that you will now summarize what you've said, and they can catch anything they missed earlier. Once you've said "in conclusion," you have about a minute before you must stop talking. Audiences grow hostile to speakers who promise to stop but then don't. In the remaining minute of your presentation, fix in the audience's mind the one or two ideas you want them to remember or take away from your presentation.
- Keep your presentation as short as possible. Nobody wants to listen to a long presentation.

Understanding the Speaking-Writing Relationship

Effective oral and written presentations share the following requirements:

• Analyze your audience. Know what they will expect.
• Articulate your purpose clearly.
• Develop sufficient and appropriate supporting material.
• Understand the context in which your presentation will be received.
• Organize the material so that your audience can follow your points easily.
• Choose a speaking style—level of language, approach to the subject, and tone—suitable to your role as well as your audience and purpose.
• Select the presentation format—text, text + visuals, text + sound and/ or animations—that will enhance your audience's understanding of your message.

Analyzing the Audience

Analyzing your listening audience follows the same principles discussed in Chapter 2:

• How much does my audience know about the subject?
• How much do they know about me?
• What do they expect from me?
• How interested will they be in what I say?
• What is their attitude toward me?
• What is their attitude toward my subject?
• What is their age group?
• What positions do they occupy in the organization?
• What is their educational background?
• What is their cultural/ethnic background?
• What is their economic background?
• What are their political and religious views?
• What kinds of biases will they likely have toward me and my topic?

To be an effective speaker, you must know your audience, establish an effective relationship between you and them by being sincere and knowledgeable about the subject, and then conform to their expectations about dress, demeanor, choice of language, and attitude toward them and the topic. When you speak to people from other countries, you should plan to research the culture of that country. Be aware that hand gestures you use routinely may have different meanings in other cultures. Also, the clothing you choose to wear should be selected with the culture of the audience in mind: you want your audience to pay attention to what you are saying instead of what you are wearing.

Determining the Goal of Your Presentation

Oral presentations, like written presentations, must be designed for a specific purpose. By knowing what they will hear from the beginning of the presentation, audiences can understand the reason for the content. State your goal in one sentence, as you begin to plan. Announce your purpose early in the presentation to prepare your audience for the main ideas to come.

Remember that oral presentations, like written presentations, can enhance your reputation within an organization. Therefore, consider every speaking opportunity an opportunity to sell not only your ideas but also your competence and your value to the organization.

Choosing and Shaping Content

Preparing the oral presentation often requires careful research:

- Determine what information you will need.
- Choose information that will appeal to your audience—particularly their attitudes and perspectives toward the topic.
- Consider a variety of information types: statistics, testimony, cases, illustrations, history, and particularly narratives that help convey the goal you have for your presentation. Be sure that every item you include pertains to the goal of your presentation.

Analyzing the Context

Analysis of context and analysis of audience are often inseparable:

- What broader concerns underlie the need for the presentation?
- What immediate issues underlie the presentation?
- How does your presentation relate to these issues?
- What will be happening in the organization when you make your presentation?
- How does your presentation fit into the organizational situation?
- If you are one of several speakers, what kinds of presentations will other speakers make?
- In what surroundings will you make the presentation?

Choosing the Organization

Like written communications, oral presentations must reflect your audience's needs and perspective:

- Does your audience have interest in what you will say?
- What main ideas do you want to convey?

- Based on your purpose and the needs and expectations of the audience, in what order should you present these ideas?

Answers to these questions will help you decide how to go about organizing your presentation. Generally, however, like the written presentation, oral presentations have distinct parts—an introduction, a main body, and a conclusion. The introduction should clearly tell the audience what the presentation will cover so that the audience is prepared for what is to come. The body should develop each point stated in the introduction, and the conclusion should reiterate the ideas presented and reinforce the purpose of the presentation.

As you do your research and collect content for your presentation, begin organizing your information. Divide your content into main categories of ideas:

    I. Idea 1
    II. Idea 2
    III. Idea 3, etc.

Once you have the main content "chunks" or divisions, begin to subdivide each main idea. Order the subdivisions so that the information moves in a logical sequence:

    I. Idea 1
        A, B, C . . .
    II. Idea 2
        A, B, C . . .
    III. Idea 3
        A, B, C . . .

Introduction: Be sure that you state your goal near the beginning. Even if you use some type of opening statement to interest your audience, state the goal of your presentation next. Then, state how you will proceed in your presentation: what main issues you will discuss. The main ideas should be announced and enumerated here.

Main Body: Here you must explain each of your key ideas in order. Also try to include at least one example or anecdote for each point to make your ideas more vivid and memorable. If you make your presentation easy for your listeners to follow and understand, the more they (and you) will profit from your presentation.

Conclusion: At a minimum, restate the main issues you want your audience to remember, but be concise. Nothing is worse than a conclusion that drags on and doesn't conclude. Tell your audience exactly what you want them to remember from your presentation. Try to find a concluding narrative or statement that impacts your audience. The conclusion should leave the audience with a positive feeling about you and your ideas.

CHOOSING AN APPROPRIATE SPEAKING STYLE

How do you sound when you speak? You may have effective content and ideas and accurate and supporting statistics. However, how you speak your ideas can "make or break" the effectiveness of what you say. Avoid sounding patronizing, rude, overly solicitous, gushing, or insincere. Use a conversational style: short sentences, concrete language, speech that suggests to your audience that you are really talking with them. Remember that your organizational role and your relationship to your audience will dictate the tone and degree of formality of your presentation. Avoid speaking too rapidly.

- Do they know you?
- Is your rank in the organization above or below them?
- Are you speaking to an audience of individuals from all levels within the organization?
- What demeanor, approach, and level of formality does the organization usually expect from those giving oral presentations?
- Is the audience composed of people who understand American English? How well do they understand American English?

If you are speaking before a group composed largely of people from another country, determine beforehand their fluency in American English. If they are not comfortable with American English, speak more slowly, avoid idiomatic expressions, choose concrete words, and speak in relatively short sentences. Limit each sentence to one idea.

Choosing Visuals to Enhance Your Purpose and Your Meaning

Because we live in a time when communication is visual and verbal, illustrations can make your ideas more persuasive and more professional. Many of the guidelines for using visuals in oral presentations mirror those for written documents: they need to exemplify simplicity and clarity and fit the needs of the audience.

Formal presentations should use PowerPoint or similar presentation software to help listeners follow the ideas. PowerPoint allows you to give your listeners the outline of your presentation and insert pictures, graphs, tables, drawings, photographs, diagrams, and flow charts as well as sound and video. But because these will be seen while the audience is listening to you, be sure that all visuals are as simple and as easy to read as possible. The slide presentation in Figure 11-1 exemplifies effective use of the following guidelines:

- Limit the information on any single slide.
- Use a typeface that can be easily read.
- Use a nondistracting background that does not overpower content. Figure 11-4 shows a simple but effective background.
- Limit the typefaces you use to two per visual.
- Avoid using all caps.
- Use a typeface—size and font—that contrasts distinctly with the background.

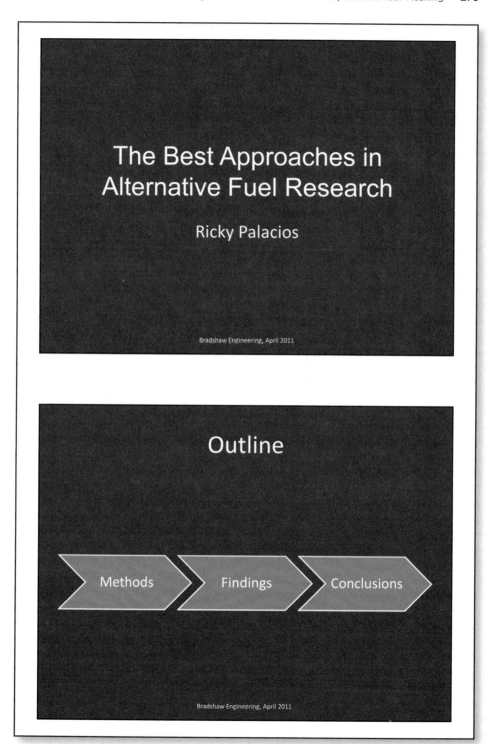

FIGURE 11-1 A PowerPoint Presentation Prepared for a Brown-Bag Luncheon

Methods

- Research using technical databases from Bradshaw Engineering
- Qualitative Analysis
  - Weigh pros and cons
  - Focus on cost and scalability
- Suggest best approach based on results

Bradshaw Engineering, April 2011

Biofuel

Process
- Biomass from corn and algae common
- Microorganisms ferment biomass
- Forms bioalcohols used as fuel

Pros
- Renewable source
- Environmentally friendly
- Used extensively in USA

Cons
- Scaling up difficult
- Food vs. Fuel
- Deforestation for farming

Bradshaw Engineering, April 2011

FIGURE 11-1 *continued*

Alcohol Fuel

Process
- Fossil fuels broken down
- Methanol, ethanol, and butanol produced
- Used in combustion engines

Pros
- Existing infrastructure
- Good fuel efficiency
- Easily transported as a liquid

Cons
- Cost of raw materials
- Causes engine corrosion

Bradshaw Engineering, April 2011

Hydrogen

Process
- Oxygen and hydrogen burn in a fuel cell
- Water is a byproduct
- Cell produces energy

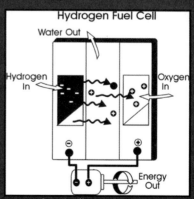

Hydrogen Fuel Cell

Source: http://www.alternative-energy-news.info/images/technical/hydrogen-fuel-cell.jpg

Bradshaw Engineering, April 2011

FIGURE 11-1 *continued*

Hydrogen

Pros
- No CO_2 emissions
- Efficient compared to gasoline

Cons
- Lots of storage space
- Highly explosive
- Manufactured from nonrenewable sources

Bradshaw Engineering, April 2011

Compressed Air

Process
- Electricity compresses air
- Air stored at high pressures in tank
- Gas expands and pushes pistons
- Pistons produce work

Pros
- Less expensive than fossil fuels
- No emission
- Disposing of old engines less hazardous

Cons
- Short driving ranges
- Long charging time
- Heat in the engine

Bradshaw Engineering, April 2011

FIGURE 11-1 *continued*

Alternative Fossil Fuel

Process

- Retrograde condensation extracts gas from ground
- Gas stored at high pressures
- Distributed in cylindrical containers

Pros

- Existing infrastructure
- Burns cleanly
- Less flammable than gasoline

Cons

- Finite source
- Lots of storage space

Bradshaw Engineering, April 2011

Nuclear Power

Process

- Nuclear fission in reactor
- Water turns to steam
- Steam spins turbine
- Turbine produces work
- Water recycled back to reactor

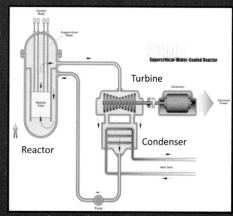

Source: http://www.inl.gov/featurestories/i/scwr.gif

Bradshaw Engineering, April 2011

FIGURE 11-1 *continued*

Nuclear Power

Pros
- Cheap raw materials
- Scaling up economical
- Almost no emissions

Cons
- High capital investment
- Slow approval process
- Emergency health risks

Bradshaw Engineering, April 2011

Conclusions

Biofuels, Alcohol Fuels, Alternative Fossil Fuels
- Low emissions, but
- Finite resources do not last forever

Compressed Air
- Not enough power to scale up

Hydrogen
- Energy efficient, but
- Hydrogen manufactured from nonrenewables

Bradshaw Engineering, April 2011

FIGURE 11-1 *continued*

Final Suggestion

Nuclear Power is the best approach

- High energy output with low long-term cost
- Technology increasing raw material pool
- Scalable and already provides 15% of world energy
- Environmentally friendly

Bradshaw Engineering, April 2011

Notes

1. United Nations Environment Programme. Energy Branch. *Towards sustainable production and use of resources: Assessing Biofuels*. 2009,16.

2. Clean Fuels Development Coalition. *The Ethanol Fact Book*. 2007, 47.

3. Ulf Bossel. "Does a Hydrogen Economy Make Sense?" *Proceedings of the IEEE*. October 2006, 1836.

4. " Study Indicates Air Hybrid Could Improve Fuel Economy 64 Percent in City Driving Conditions; Findings Presented During SAE 2003 World Congress." *SAE International*. http://www.sae.org/news/releases/airhybrid.htm (accessed March 25, 2011).

5. "Natural Gas Vehicle Safety." *International Association for Natural Gas Vehicles*. http://www.iangv.org/natural-gas-vehicles/safety.html (accessed March 25, 2011).

6. Dr. Andrew Martin. "The Benefits of Nuclear Power." *University of Melbourne Writing Center*. http://nuclearinfo.net/Nuclearpower/TheBenefitsOfNuclearPower (accessed March 25, 2011).

Bradshaw Engineering, April 2011

FIGURE 11-1 *continued*

Other problems that can surface with slide presentations:

- Avoid "busy" or complicated visuals as in Figures 11-2.
- Avoid making your audience study your slides. Figure 11-3, for example, will require your audience to study the map. If they have to focus to decipher your slides, they will not listen to you. Bar graphs, circle graphs, simple diagrams, and pictures exemplify standard types of visuals. Whatever visual you decide to use, limit content to the concept, data, or point you are trying to make. Figure 11-8 shows a good example of a line graph.
- Do not read your slides to your audience. Let them read each slide as you make it available, then begin to comment.
- Be sure that what the visual says is immediately evident, a requirement that Figures 11-2 and 11-3 fail to meet.

Avoid using too many slides. Listeners will grow restless if you talk too long and inundate them with too many slides. The engineer who prepared Figure 11-1 was asked to explain, in a 12-minute presentation, the most promising alternative fuels to the members of his company composed of engineers and technologists from a variety of engineering areas.

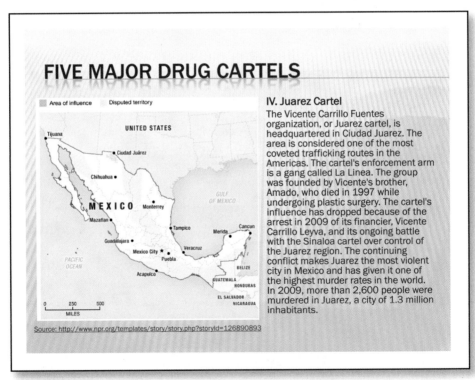

FIGURE 11-2 This slide, from a presentation describing the problems that drug cartels create for Texas, includes too much descriptive text to explain the map.

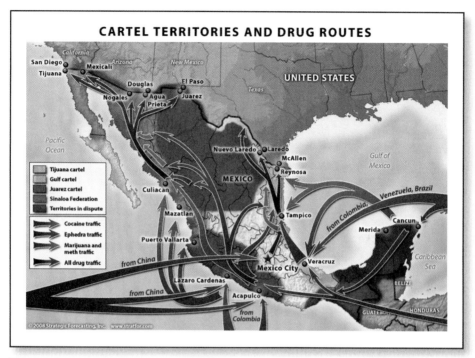

FIGURE 11-3 Contains a map selected from an online source. The quantity of information included could be daunting in a slide but helpful in a report, in which readers have time to study the information.

As shown in the next single-slide examples, PowerPoint allows you almost unrestricted use of color and background, but too much color or an ornate slide background can distract your audience. If you need to prepare slides or transparencies for video conferencing, use the plain background and a typeface color that contrasts with the background to enhance readability. The organization for which you work may have a template for their employees to use for all company presentations.

Figure 11-4 exemplifies effective use of a background that does not distract but supports the content of the slides.

Figure 11-5 exemplifies a three-dimensional pie chart, created with Excel and transported into PowerPoint. Viewers have to connect the legend with the segments and read the percentages on each segment. This chart could become more readable if each segment were labeled along with the percentages. See Figure 11-6. As shown in Figure 11-7, the boxed labels improve readability.

FIGURE 11-4 This slide exemplifies effective use of a background that does not distract but supports the content of the slide. The sound of the pistol firing occurs when this page appears.

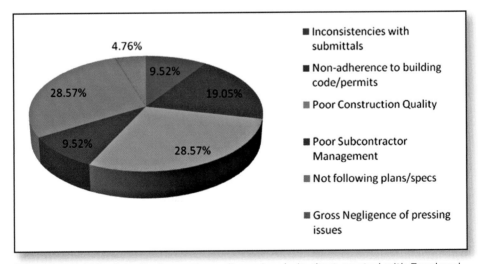

FIGURE 11-5 This slide displays a three-dimensional pie chart created with Excel and transported into PowerPoint. Use of a legend creates difficulties for listeners.

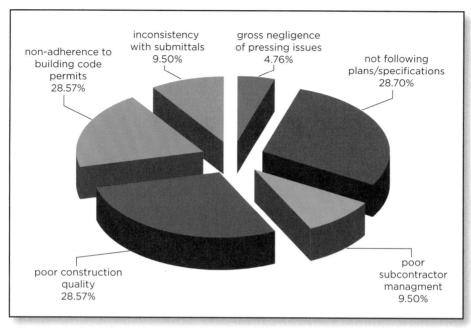

FIGURE 11-6 Figure 11-5 reconfigured to place segment labels outside the graph. The exploded view helps readers see the segment sizes.

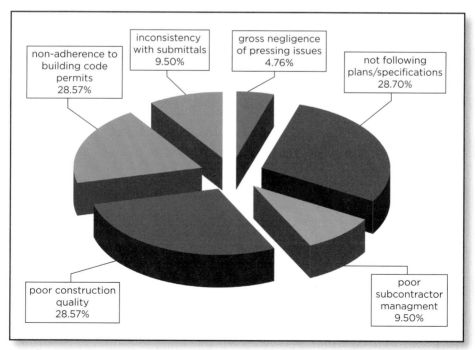

FIGURE 11-7 Use of Boxed Labels

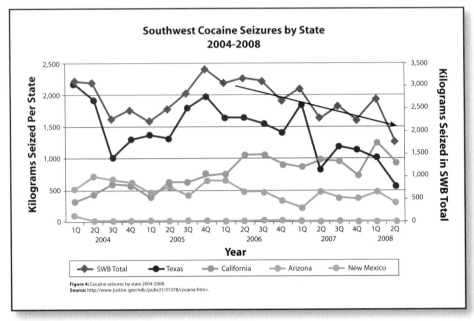

Figure 4: Cocaine seizures by state 2004-2008.
Source: http://www.justice.gov/ndic/pubs31/31378/cocaine.htm>.

FIGURE 11-8 Effective Slide with a Line Graph

PLANNING YOUR PRESENTATION—QUESTIONS YOU NEED TO ASK

Analyze each point listed above by answering the following questions, just as you did in planning your written communication.

Audience.

- Who is my audience?
- What do I know about my audience—background, knowledge, position in the organization, attitudes toward me and my subject?

Purpose.

- What is my purpose in giving this oral presentation?
- Is there (should there be) a long-range purpose?
- What is the situation that led to this presentation?
- Given my audience's background and attitudes, do I need to reshape my purpose to make my presentation more acceptable to my audience?

Context.

- Where will I be speaking?
- What events will be transpiring in the organization (theirs or mine) that may affect how my audience perceives what I say?

Content.

- What ideas do I want to include and not include?
- Based on the audience and the context, what difficulties do I need to anticipate in choosing content?
- Can any ideas be misconstrued and prove harmful to me or my organization?

Graphics.

- What kinds of visuals will I need to enhance the ideas I will present?
- Where should I use these visuals in my presentation?

Style.

- What kind of tone do I want to use in addressing my audience?
- What kind of image—of myself and my organization—do I want to project?
- What level of language do I need to use, based on my audience's background and knowledge of my subject?
- What approach will my audience expect from me?
- How formal should I be?

Speaking to Multicultural Audiences

As organizations become more international, you may find that you need to give presentations to groups in other countries. Because you will want any audience to respond positively to your presentation, you will need to do research to understand how people from other cultures will likely interpret what you say, how you say it, how you dress, and how you act in your dealings with them. The visuals you use may also have to be changed, as symbols in one culture may have an entirely different meaning in another culture.

In your library and online, you will find a list of resources and books that can help you understand the perspectives of international audiences. As you consider your audience and the content you want to present to this audience, remember that your understanding of the cultural profile of your listeners is perhaps as important as your correctly discerning their knowledge of your topic and their interest level.

Designing Each Segment

The oral presentation has to have thoughtful structure for one main reason: once you have said something, the audience cannot "rehear" what you said. In reading, when you do not understand a sentence or paragraph, you can stop and reread the passage as many times as necessary. To help your audience follow what you say, you must design your presentation with your audience's listening limitations in mind.

Audiences generally do not enjoy long presentations. Listening is difficult, and audiences will tire even when a presentation is utterly fascinating. For that reason, look for ways to keep your message as concise as possible. Don't omit information your audience needs, but look for ways to eliminate nonessential material. Again, without carefully analyzing your audience—their attitude toward the subject, their background knowledge of the topic, their perspective toward you—you cannot decide either content or arrangement of content.

Choose an interesting title. Grab your audience's attention by developing a title that, at the very least, reflects the content of your presentation but does so in an interesting way. The title of an oral presentation should prepare your audience for the content you will present.

Develop your presentation around three main divisions. Helping your audience follow your message requires that you build into your structure a certain amount of redundancy. That means that you reiterate main points. In the introduction, you "tell them what you are going to tell them"; in the main body, you "tell them"; and in the conclusion, you "tell them what you told them." This kind of deliberate repetition helps your audience follow and remember the main points you are making. (Again, readers can "reread" text, but listeners cannot "rehear" oral remarks.) To design your presentation with planned repetition, you must clearly know your purpose and what you want your audience to know.

Plan the introduction carefully. During the introduction you focus your audience's attention on your theme and the way you plan to present the theme. Unless the introduction is effective and interests the audience, you will have difficulty keeping your audience's attention. The effective introduction thus tells your audience how to listen, what to expect, and the path you will follow in presenting your message. You may also wish to introduce your topic with an attention-getting device: a startling fact, a relevant anecdote, a rhetorical question, or a statement designed to arouse your audience's interest. Again, the device you choose will depend on the audience, the occasion, and the purpose of the presentation.

Or, if your audience is unreceptive or unfamiliar with the subject, you may want to include background material to help them grasp and process your main points:

1. Acknowledge that you perceive the problem that your audience has with you or your topic.
2. Establish a common ground with the audience—your points of agreement.
3. Attempt to refute (if you can do so efficiently) erroneous assumptions that you believe the audience may have about you or the subject.
4. Ask the audience to allow you the opportunity to present your information as objectively as possible.

Design the body. In the introduction you state the main issues or topics you plan to present. Thus, in designing the body of the presentation, you develop what you want to say about each of these main points or ideas. You may want to present your ideas in a chronological sequence, a logical sequence, or a simple topical sequence. This method will help your audience follow your ideas if you are giving an informative speech, an analytical speech, or a persuasive speech. The important point, however, is that you need to demarcate and announce each point in the body as you come to it so that your audience knows when you have completed one point and begun another.

Design the conclusion. The conclusion reinforces the main ideas you wish your audience to retain. How you design the conclusion will depend on your initial purpose. A strong conclusion is nearly as important as a strong introduction, as both the beginning and the end will be the parts most likely remembered.

CHOOSING AN EFFECTIVE DELIVERY STYLE

Avoid speaking in a "written" style. Use phrases, and use a variety of sentence lengths. Avoid excessively long, complex sentences, as listeners may have difficulty following your ideas. In general, keep your sentences short. If you concentrate on getting your point across by having a conversation with the audience, you will likely use a natural, conversational style. Many suggestions for clarity in writing also apply to clarity in speaking:

- Avoid long, cumbersome sentences. Long sentences can be as hard to hear as they are to read.
- Avoid abstract, polysyllabic words. Instead, use concrete language that your audience can visualize.
- Avoid jargon, unless you are sure that your audience will be readily familiar with all specialized terms.
- Use short, active voice sentences.

TECHNIQUES TO ENHANCE AUDIENCE COMPREHENSION

Because your audience cannot "rehear" ideas, once you have stated them, look for ways to help your audience easily follow your ideas:

1. Be sure you clearly demarcate the beginning and end of each point and segment of your presentation:

   - Announce each main topic as you come to it so that your audience knows when you have completed one topic and are beginning the next one.
   - Allow a slight pause to occur after you have completed your introduction, and then announce your first topic.

- After completing your final topic in the main body of your presentation, allow a slight pause before you begin your conclusion.

2. Speak slowly, vigorously, and enthusiastically. Be sure you pronounce your words carefully, particularly if you are addressing a large group or a multicultural group.

3. Use gestures to accentuate points. Move your body deliberately to aid you in announcing major transition points. In short, avoid standing transfixed before your audience.

4. Maintain eye contact with your audience. Doing so helps you keep your listeners involved in what you are saying. If you look at the ceiling, the floor, or the corners of the room, your audience may sense a lack of self-confidence. Lack of eye contact also tends to lessen your credibility. In contrast, consistent eye contact enhances the importance of the message. By looking at your audience, you can often sense their reaction to what you are saying and make adjustments in your presentation if necessary.

5. Do not memorize your presentation. You don't want it to sound like something you are reciting to your listeners. You want it to seem like your turn in a conversation you are having with your listeners.

6. Do not read your slides to your audience. Allow them to see the information on your slide before you begin discussing the material or points on each slide.

7. Rehearse your presentation until you feel comfortable. Try walking around, speaking each segment, and then speaking aloud the entire presentation. Rephrase ideas that are difficult for you to say—these will likely be hard for your audience to follow. Be sure to time your presentation so that it does not exceed the time limit. Keep your presentation as short as possible.

8. If possible, record your speech. Listen to what you have said as objectively as possible. As you listen, consider the main issues of audience, purpose, organization, context, content, and style.

9. Listen for tone, attitude, and clarity. Is the tone you project appropriate for your audience and your purpose? Is each sentence easy to understand? Are you speaking too rapidly? Are the major divisions in your presentation easy to hear? Are any sentences difficult to understand?

10. Try not to provide the audience handout material before you begin. To do so encourages your audience to read rather than listen. If you must provide written material, be sure the material is coordinated with your presentation so that you keep your audience's attention on what you are saying as you are saying it.

11. When you use slides, tell the audience what they will see, show them the slide, give them time to digest what they are seeing, and then comment on the slide. Do not begin talking about another topic while a slide depicting a past topic is still showing. Remember: people cannot see and listen at the same time. Avoid using too many slides.

12. When you are planning your presentation, determine how you will handle questions. Prepare for questions your audience may ask and decide how you will answer each one. Again, unless you have analyzed your audience and the reason for your presentation, you will not be able to anticipate questions that will likely arise.

13. Keep the question and answer time moving briskly. Answer each question as concisely as possible, and then move to the next question. If you are faced with a difficult question, reword the question or break the question into several parts. Then answer each part. Be sure to restate questions if listeners in the back of the room are unable to hear questions asked by those near the front.

DESIGNING AND PRESENTING THE WRITTEN PAPER

Papers presented at professional meetings are frequently read from written manuscripts if the material to be delivered is complex. These papers may then be published in the official proceedings of the professional society.

However, presentations may need to be read for other reasons:

1. A presentation that discusses company policy, a sensitive issue, or a topic that must be approved by someone in the organization before the presentation. In situations like these, the presentation is carefully written and read from the approved, written manuscript to ensure accuracy.

2. A presentation that will be circulated or filed as documentation. In a situation like this one, a spokesperson may read a carefully prepared statement, particularly if a possibility exists that material may be misconstrued by those in the audience.

3. Inexperienced speakers who must deal with a difficult problem may be more comfortable reading from a prepared manuscript. With the manuscript in front of you on the lectern, you don't have to worry about losing your train of thought or forgetting important details.

Written presentations can be effective if the speaker plans and writes the presentation carefully and then utilizes a number of delivery techniques to enhance the effectiveness of the oral reading.

Structuring the written speech. The structure of the written speech is the same as the extemporaneous speech. The speech has three main parts: the introduction, the main body, and the conclusion. Each section should be structured like the extemporaneous speech. However, you will need to write each section completely. If you know that the speech will be published, you may wish to write it like an article for publication or a report and use headings and subheadings to reveal the content and organization of the speech.

Writing the speech. After you have designed the content of your paper and made final revisions in your ideas, you will need to give close attention to your sentences and paragraphs, since you will be reading these directly from the page.

1. Be sure that each section is clearly demarcated from other sections. This means that each section should have an overview that clearly announces that the section is beginning. Each paragraph should also begin with a topic sentence that summarizes the content of the paragraph. In short, in writing a speech to be read, you are making a concerted effort to accentuate every device for revealing organization, since your audience cannot stop and re-hear what you have just said.

2. Limit each section and each paragraph within sections to one idea. Watch length so that your audience will not lose track of the main idea you are presenting.

3. Avoid excessive detail.

4. Use enumeration to help your audience follow your main points and to know when one point has ended and the next point is beginning.

5. Avoid long sentences. Long sentences are as difficult (or more difficult) to hear and follow as they are to read.

6. Prune every sentence to make it as clear and concise as possible.

7. Use active voice whenever possible so that your sentences will preserve the natural quality of spoken language.

8. Type your presentation in a large type—12 point type or larger. Triple space and leave wide margins on each side of the page.

9. With a marker, draw a "break" line after the introduction, between each main point in the body, and before the conclusion.

10. Underline or highlight important phrases or sentences throughout the presentation.

11. Consider using visuals, even though these may not be published separately.

Again, choose visuals that will clarify any difficult or important points.

Practicing the presentation.

1. Read each sentence aloud. Rewrite sentences that are difficult for you to say.

2. As you practice reading the presentation, try to look directly at your audience and speak important phrases or sentences to the audience.

3. Use overviews and topic sentences to announce each major topic as you come to it. To further alert your audience to the beginning of a new point, pause briefly; look at your audience; then read your overview statement or topic sentence. If possible, try to speak these to your audience instead of reading them.

4. As you practice reading your presentation, continue to listen for any sentences or words that are difficult to articulate. Recast sentences and paragraphs that do not sound organized, logical, and clear. If possible, replace difficult words with others that are easier to speak.

5. As you read, speak slowly and enunciate clearly and distinctly.
6. Once you can read each sentence with ease and without haste, time your presentation to be sure that it does not exceed a time limit if you have been given one.
7. Read your speech into a recorder. Allow some time between recording and listening so that you can gain some objectivity. As you listen, check for sentences that are hard to follow. Listen for breaks between major sections and major points.

CHECKLIST FOR PREPARING ORAL REPORTS ✔

continued

Audience

☐ Who is your audience?
☐ What do you know about your audience—background, knowledge, position in the organization, attitudes toward you and your subject?
☐ What is the relationship between you and your audience?
☐ What is the attitude of your audience toward you and your presentation likely to be?
☐ Is your audience from a culture markedly different from yours? What adjustments to your presentation will any such differences require?

Purpose

☐ What is your purpose in giving this oral presentation?
☐ Is there (should there be) a long-range purpose?
☐ What is the situation that led to this presentation?
☐ Given your audience's background and attitudes, do you need to adjust your purpose to make your presentation more suitable for your audience?

Context

☐ Where and when will you be speaking?
☐ What events will be transpiring in the organization (theirs or yours) that may affect how your audience perceives what you say?
☐ What equipment, applications, and materials are available to you?
  - Slideware?
  - Audio?
  - Video?
  - Internet connection?
  - Chalkboard?
  - Flipchart and easel?
  - Handouts?

continued

CHECKLIST FOR PREPARING ORAL REPORTS ✔ *continued*

Content

☐ What ideas do you want to include and exclude?
☐ Based on the audience and the context, what difficulties do you need to anticipate in choosing content?
☐ Can any ideas be misconstrued and prove harmful to you or your organization?
☐ Do you have a good opening that will interest your audience and create a friendly atmosphere?
☐ Have you limited your major points to fit within your allotted time?
☐ Does your talk contain sufficient examples, analogies, narratives, and data to support your generalizations? Have you repeated key points?
☐ Can you relate your subject matter to some vital interest of your audience?

Graphics

☐ What kinds of visuals will you need to clarify or reinforce the ideas you will discuss?
☐ Where should you use these in your presentation?
☐ Are these visuals immediately readable and understandable?
☐ Do they successfully focus the listeners' attention and augment and clarify your message?
☐ Do they meet the four criteria that govern good graphics?
　• Visibility
　• Clarity
　• Simplicity
　• Controllability

Style

☐ What kind of tone do you want to use in addressing your audience?
☐ What kind of image—of yourself and your organization—do you want to project?
☐ What level of language do you need to use, based on your audience's background and knowledge of your subject?
☐ What approach will your audience expect from you?
☐ How formal should you be?
☐ Which delivery technique will be more appropriate? Extemporaneous? Manuscript?
☐ If you are speaking extemporaneously, have you prepared a speech outline to guide you?

continued

**CHECKLIST FOR
PREPARING ORAL REPORTS** ✔ *continued*

☐ If you will be reading from a manuscript, have you introduced a conversational tone into your talk? Is your typed manuscript easy to read from?

☐ Do you have a good ending ready, perhaps a summary of key points or an anecdote that supports your purpose? If you began with a story, do you want to go back to it now?

☐ Have you rehearsed your talk several times?

Questions and Answers

☐ What questions might the audience ask? Are you prepared to answer these questions?

☐ How will you keep your answers concise and direct?

☐ Do you have a specific time limit for questions? How will you keep track of your time?

EXERCISES

1. Choose one of the chapters in this book and adapt the material as a series of slides to accompany your 15-minute oral presentation on the subject of technical communication for professionals in your field.

2. If you were adapting the document in Figure 11-9 as a slide presentation for new taxi drivers, which pieces of information would you consider especially important to display? How would you display this information to make it easy for your audience to read and remember?

3. Prepare a five-minute/seven-slide presentation explaining to new majors in your field the job opportunities available to graduates of the program.

4. Prepare a slide presentation of your major semester project, including a copy of your slides to distribute to your audience as a pdf file for their mobile devices.

5. Examine the following real slide presentation in Figure 11-10. If you were the author and were given 15 more minutes to make the slide presentation more effective, what changes would you make? For more information on FDA Advisory Committees, visit http://www.fda.gov/AdvisoryCommittees.

OSHA® FactSheet

Preventing Violence against Taxi and For-Hire Drivers

Taxi drivers are over 20 times more likely to be murdered on the job than other workers. By recognizing the hazards that lead to violent incidents and using proven prevention and control measures, employers and drivers can create safer working conditions.

For-hire and taxi driver homicides

The Bureau of Labor Statistics' (BLS) data indicates that annual homicide rates for taxi drivers (and chauffeurs) from 1998 to 2007 ranged from 9 per 100,000 workers, to 19. During that period the rate for all workers was at or below 0.5 per 100,000 workers. In other words, taxi drivers' homicide rates were between 21 and 33 times higher than the national average for all workers.

Workers' Homicide Rates 1998 - 2007

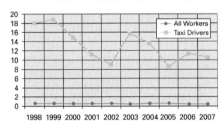

	1998	1999	2000	2001	2002	2003	2004	2005	2006	2007
	49	51	42	34	30	45	38	25	32	35

Number of Taxi Driver Homicides

Risks that may lead to violence

Taxi drivers face many of the same risk factors as other workers in potentially violent occupations. These include working:
- With cash (making them targets for robbery);
- Alone and in isolated areas;
- At night and in poorly lit settings;
- In high-crime areas;
- With people under the influence of alcohol.

Reducing the Risks

Reducing risks requires employers and/or taxi drivers to assess their potential hazards and consider physical and procedural methods for reducing them. Generally, physical or "engineering" controls should be considered first since they create physical barriers between drivers and the hazards. Procedural methods require changes in behavior, such as not accepting cash, to reduce risks.

Physical Controls
Potential physical controls include:
- Barriers – such as bullet-resistant glass – between drivers and passengers prevent robberies, injuries and death.
- Security cameras record activities within the vehicle, discouraging violent behavior, and aiding in identifying passengers, if an assault does occur.
- Silent alarms (such as an external light) and/or radio communication allow drivers to safely request help.
- Vehicle tracking devices, such as global positioning satellite (GPS) systems, allow drivers in distress to be located.
- Improved lighting inside the taxi allows the driver to be aware of passenger behavior.

Procedural Controls
Procedural controls include:
- Establishing police protocols – including authorizing police stops.
- Promoting the use of credit card payments to limit the amount of cash in the taxi and thereby discourage robberies.
- Providing safety training to teach drivers, dispatchers and company owners about protective measures.

Employer Responsibilities

OSHA citations can only be issued for violations of standards, regulations, and the General Duty Clause. Section 5(a)(1) of the OSH Act, the "General Duty Clause," provides that "Each em-

FIGURE 11-9 Document for Exercise 2

ployer shall furnish to each of his employees employment and a place of employment which are free from recognized hazards that are causing or likely to cause death or serious physical harm to his employees" [29 U.S.C. 654(a)(1)].

Employers are required by law to communicate to workers their rights under the OSH Act. Posters containing these and other rights are available free of charge from OSHA's area offices or can be downloaded from OSHA's website— www.osha.gov.

Taxi companies that only use the services of drivers who are independent contractors are not subject to OSH Act coverage. It should be noted however, that the suggested safety measures listed here are likely to help reduce the risks for independent contractors to the same extent as employees.

Worker Rights

Section 11(c)(1) of the OSH Act provides: "No person shall discharge or in any manner discriminate against any employee because such employee has filed any complaint or instituted or caused to be instituted any proceeding under or related to this Act or has testified or is about to testify in any such proceedings or because of the exercise by such employee on behalf of himself or others of any right afforded by this Act" [29 U.S.C. 660(c)].

Conclusion

Employers are responsible for taking measures to protect the health and safety of their workers. In addition, it is the duty of taxi drivers to follow proper safety procedures. OSHA has recommended these safety controls to help reduce work-related violence. Employers, dispatchers and drivers can use a combination of the suggested controls, which apply to their individual work situations.

This fact sheet is not a standard or regulation, and it creates no new legal obligations. It contains recommendations as well as descriptions of mandatory safety and health standards. The recommendations are advisory in nature, informational in content, and are intended to assist employers in providing a safe and healthful workplace. The Occupational Safety and Health Act requires employers to comply with safety and health standards and regulations promulgated by OSHA or by a state with an OSHA-approved state plan. In addition, the Act's General Duty Clause, Section 5(a)(1), requires employers to provide their employees with a workplace free from recognized hazards likely to cause death or serious physical harm. This information will be made available to sensory impaired individuals upon request. The voice phone is (202) 693-1999; teletypewriter (TTY) number: (877) 889-5627.

For more complete information:

OSHA® Occupational Safety and Health Administration

U.S. Department of Labor

DEP 4/2010

FIGURE 11-9 *continued*

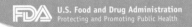

Menthol Report Subcommittee:
The Logistics of
Writing the Report

Karen M. Templeton-Somers, Ph.D.
Center for Tobacco Products, FDA

FIGURE 11-10 Document for Exercise 5

Menthol Report Subcommittee

- Established for the purpose of developing a report on the issue of the impact of the use of menthol in cigarettes on the public health, including such use among children, African-Americans, Hispanics, and other racial and ethnic minorities.

- All voting TPSAC Members, and the non-voting Industry Representatives, were invited to participate

FIGURE 11-10 *continued*

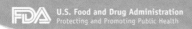

Meetings

At least two subcommittee meetings, held in open session

September 27, 2010

    - organizational; to discuss the timelines and structure of the required report

February, 2011

    - compilation of the chapters, discussion, deliberation, and final edits to the full report before referral to TPSAC

FIGURE 11-10 *continued*

Writing Process

- FDA will not write any portion of the report
- Workgroups of 2-3 SGE members of the Subcommittee will collaborate to write drafts of the chapters of the report

FIGURE 11-10 *continued*

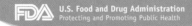

Writing Process

- Workgroups
  - Will deal with trade secret and confidential commercial information.
    - will not work in open session
    - will not include non-SGE participants

FIGURE 11-10 *continued*

Writing Process

- Consultants
  - As necessary, SGE consultants will work with workgroups to provide necessary expertise.
  - Workgroups will not consult with anyone else in the creation of the report

FIGURE 11-10 *continued*

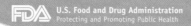

Writing Process

- Science Writer
  - Will provide technical writing assistance to committee
  - Will not deliberate on science or contribute to the scientific analysis

FIGURE 11-10 *continued*

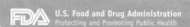

Ground Rules and Logistics

- Conflict of interest screening must be kept current throughout the writing process.
- The drafts-in-progress are to be kept confidential and cannot be shared with anyone other than the chair, the DFO, and the science writer.
- The DFO (or designee) will participate in any workgroup meetings or telecons, and will be the channel for exchanging drafts.

FIGURE 11-10 *continued*

Ground Rules and Logistics

Scientific Information

- Report will be based upon background materials, public submissions, presentations, and the deliberations and discussions occurring at TPSAC meetings
- In drafting the report, members will bring their expertise to bear in analyzing and synthesizing the science presented to TPSAC

FIGURE 11-10 *continued*

Ground Rules and Logistics

New Scientific Information

- If a member plans to rely upon scientific studies or information not presented to TPSAC, the member should provide the information to the DFO
- FDA will review the new information and present it, as appropriate, at a TPSAC meeting for discussion
- Once the information has been presented to TPSAC it may be relied upon in the report.

FIGURE 11-10 *continued*

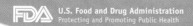

Participation of the Industry Representatives

- Because workgroups will review trade secret and confidential commercial information, the Industry Representatives will not participate in the workgroups.

FIGURE 11-10 *continued*

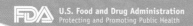

Participation of the Industry Representatives

- Included in the Menthol Report Subcommittee – participation in the discussions at both the first and last meeting, and at the TPSAC review of the Report.
- CTP would like to ask the Industry Representatives to collaborate on a document that would serve as the industry perspective.

FIGURE 11-10 *continued*

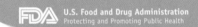

Support from CTP

- CTP will continue to obtain previously requested information to support the writing of the report.
- The DFO will track the progress of the drafts, and keep copies of intermediary versions.
- CTP will provide other administrative support, as necessary.

FIGURE 11-10 *continued*

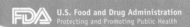

Questions?

FIGURE 11-10 *continued*

Résumés and Job Applications

Quick Tips

Finding a job is itself a job. Sites such as CareerBuilder (www.careerbuilder .com) or Monster (www.monster.com) offer important resources to support your search, but you can't be timid or passive. You have to search actively and assertively for opportunities.

You will likely experience both excitement and disappointment in your search. It will be exciting to imagine yourself working for different companies and living your life in different cities. It will also be disappointing if you don't immediately get your dream job. The search process is often a roller coaster of emotions—highs and lows.

Keep in mind that a variety of factors entirely aside from your credentials are involved in every hiring decision. If you aren't offered a job for which you applied, don't take it personally and don't be discouraged. The key to finding a satisfying job is perseverance.

THE CORRESPONDENCE OF THE JOB SEARCH

A persuasive letter of application, sometimes called a *cover letter*, and a clear and organized résumé won't guarantee that you get a job, but ineffective ones will usually guarantee that you don't. Also essential is to make sure that nothing in your online profiles or postings at social networking sites such as Facebook, LinkedIn, or Twitter would raise questions in a potential employer's mind about your suitability for a job. Verify especially that details mentioned in your letter of application or

303

listed on your résumé are identical to the information in your profiles (e.g., names of previous employers, dates of previous employment). Keep in mind that potential employers will almost certainly check your online profiles and postings because it is quick and easy to do so: how you characterize yourself here won't necessarily win you a job but could stop you from getting a job or from keeping a job.

Letter of application. Plan the mechanics of your letter of application carefully. Use a standard typeface. Don't use italics or bold. Make sure your letter is mechanically perfect and free of grammatical errors. Be brief, but not telegraphic. Keep the letter to a single page unless you have extensive pertinent experience to emphasize and explain.

More and more organizations direct job candidates to apply online for positions. If this is the case, you will go online to the organization's job site, enter your name and contact information, identify which job you are applying for, and upload your letter and résumé in the specified format. If no format is specified, submit your materials in one of the widely used formats (e.g., as a doc file, docx file, pdf file, or rtf file) so that it might be easily accessed by the recipient. Make the file read-only so that nothing will be later inserted or deleted.

If you are applying for jobs in the traditional manner, however, make sure to buy high-quality white bond paper and envelopes. This is no time to skimp. Don't send a letter or résumé that has been duplicated. Each copy of your letter must be individually addressed, printed, and signed. Accompany each letter with your résumé.

Pay attention to the style of the letter and the résumé that accompanies it. The tone you want in your letter is one of self-confidence. You must avoid both arrogance and timidity. You must sound interested and eager, but not obsequious or desperate. Don't give the impression that you must have the job, but, on the other hand, don't seem indifferent about getting it.

When describing your accomplishments in the letter and résumé, use action verbs. They make your writing concise and specific, and they make you seem dynamic and energetic. For example, instead of reporting that you worked as a sales clerk, explain that you maintained inventories, promoted merchandise, prepared displays, implemented new procedures, and supervised and trained new clerks. Here's a sampling of such action verbs:

administer	edit	oversee
analyze	evaluate	plan
conduct	exhibit	produce
create	expand	reduce costs
cut	improve	reorganize
design	manage	support
develop	operate	promote
direct	organize	write

You cannot avoid the use of *I* in a letter of application, but take the you-attitude as much as you can. Emphasize what you can do for the prospective employer—how your getting this job will benefit the company. The letter of application is not the place to be worried about salary and benefits. Above all, be mature and dignified. Avoid tricky and flashy approaches. Write a well-organized, informative letter that highlights the skills you have that the company desires in its employees.

The beginning. Start by explaining that you are applying for a job and by identifying the specific job for which you are applying. Don't be strident or inventive here. A beginning such as "WANTED: An alert, aggressive employer who will recognize an alert, aggressive young programmer" will usually direct your letter to the reject pile. If you can do so legitimately, a bit of name dropping is a good beginning. Use this beginning only if you have permission and if the name you drop will mean something to the prospective employer. If you qualify on both counts, begin with an opening sentence such as this:

> Dear Mr. Dominguez:
>
> Professor Theresa Ricco of Nebraska State University's Department of Biochemistry has suggested that I apply for a research position in the virology division of your company. In June I will receive my Bachelor of Science degree in Biochemistry from NSU. I have also worked as a research assistant in Dr. Ricco's lab for two years.

Remember that you are trying to arouse immediate interest about yourself in the potential employer.

Sometimes the best approach is a simple statement about the job you seek, accompanied by a description of something in your experience that fits you for the job, as in this example:

> Your opening for a researcher in the virology division has come to my attention. In June of this year, I will graduate from Nebraska State University with a Bachelor of Science degree in Biochemistry. I have also worked part-time for two years in a cell and molecular research laboratory at NSU. I believe that both my education and my work experience qualify me for this position.

Be specific about the job you want. Quite often, if the job you want is not open, the employer may offer you an alternative one. But employers are not impressed with general statements such as, "I'm willing and able to work at any job you may have open in research, production, or sales." Instead of indicating flexibility, such a claim usually implies that your skills and interests are unfocused—that you would be adequate at several things but truly exceptional at nothing.

In addition, make it clear in this opening that you know something about the company—its history, its achievements, its special projects, its reputation in the industry—anything that will demonstrate that you did your research and picked this company to apply to because something about it was impressive, something about it made you think you could make a key contribution to its success.

The body. In the body of your letter you highlight selected items from your education and experience that show your qualifications for the job you seek. Remember always that you are trying to show the employer how well you will fit into the job and the organization.

For this section, you need to know what things employers value the most. In evaluating recent college graduates, employers look closely at the major, academic performance; work experience; awards and honors; and extracurricular activities. They also consider recommendations, standardized test scores, military experience, and community service.

Try to include information that employers typically consider important, but emphasize those areas in which you are especially noteworthy. For example, if your grades are good, mention them prominently: otherwise, maintain a discreet silence about your academic record. Speak to the employer's interests, and at the same time highlight your own accomplishments. Show how it would be to the employer's advantage to hire you. The following paragraph, an excellent example of the you-attitude in action, does all these things:

> The advertisement for this position indicated that extensive interaction with international colleagues, especially from South America, would be expected. I would like to note that I studied Spanish and Portuguese in college and have a high fluency in both languages. I also visited Argentina and Brazil two years ago for a six-week intensive summer session. I am familiar with the major cities as well as the history and key traditions. I would thus be a confident and articulate representative of the company.

Be specific about your accomplishments: otherwise, it will sound like bragging. It is much better to write, "I was president of my senior class" instead of "I am a natural leader." "I was president" is a piece of evidence; "I am a natural leader" is a conclusion. Your aim is to give employers the evidence that will lead them to the right conclusions about you.

One tip about job experience: the best experience relates to the job you seek, but mention any job experience, even if it does not relate to the job you seek. Employers believe that a student who has worked is more apt to be mature than one who has not. If you have worked at a job, you are more likely to have effective work habits and a real work ethic. If you have worked at a job, it indicates that another employer once judged you worthy of hiring.

Don't forget hobbies that relate to the job. You're trying to establish that you are interested in, as well as qualified for, the job.

Don't mention salary unless you're answering an advertisement that specifically asks you to discuss your expectations. Keep the you-attitude. Don't worry about insurance benefits, vacations, and holidays at this point in the process. Keep the prospective employer's interests in the foreground. Your self-interest is taken for granted. If you are offered the job, that's the time to inquire about such details if they are not readily provided to you.

If you are already working, you will emphasize your work experience more than your college experience. Identify your responsibilities and achievements on the job. Do not complain about your present employer. Such complaints will lead the prospective employer to mistrust you.

In the last paragraph of the body, refer the employer to your enclosed résumé. Mention your willingness to supply additional information such as references, letters of recommendation, writing samples, or college transcripts.

The ending. The goal of the letter of application is to get you an interview with the prospective employer. In your final paragraph, you request this interview. Your request should be neither apologetic nor aggressive. Simply indicate that you are available for an interview at the employer's convenience, and give any special instructions needed for reaching you. If the prospective employer is in a distant city, indicate (if possible) a convenient time and location that you might meet with a representative of the company, such as the upcoming convention of a professional association. If the employer is really interested, you may be invited to visit the company as its expense.

The complete letter. Figure 12-1 shows a complete letter of application. The beginning of the letter shows that the writer has been interested enough in the

---

Letter of application

300 East 5th Street
Long Beach, CA 90802
January 23, 2012

Mr. Richard Hernandez
Office of Information Technology
Price Insurance Corporation
2163 Artesia Drive
St. Louis, MO 63136

Dear. Mr. Hernandez:

Identifies specific job and demonstrates knowledge of company	I am writing to apply for the position of computer security analyst listed in the March issue of *IT Professionals*. Price Insurance has a growing reputation for innovative security solutions, and I believe my education and experience would contribute to your efforts.
Highlights education	I am graduating in May of this year from the University of California at Long Beach with a bachelor's degree in Computer Science. I have completed courses in software verification and validation, fault-tolerant computer systems, web-based software systems, analysis of algorithms, communication networks, database management systems, and human-computer interaction.
Highlights work experience	In addition, I have a year of experience as a programmer and database manager at a local Internet service provider. I know how to take a project from application of principles through risk analysis, resource management, and adaptation of improvement techniques, to delivery and billing. I have also worked in computer support, developing both my technical skills and my ability to interact courteously and effectively with customers.
Refers to résumé	You will find more detailed information about my education and work experience in the résumé enclosed with this letter. I could also supply descriptions of the courses I have taken, copies of the projects completed in those courses, and a complete list of my job duties at each place of employment.
Requests interview	In April, I will attend the regional meeting of the Society for IT Professionals in St. Louis. Would it be possible for me to visit with a representative of Price Insurance at that time?

Sincerely yours,

Gillian Woods

Gillian Woods

Enclosure

FIGURE 12-1 Complete Letter of Application

company to investigate it. The desired job is specifically mentioned. The middle portion highlights the writer's course work and work experience that relate directly to the job she is seeking. The ending makes an interview convenient for the employer to arrange.

Keep in mind that a personnel officer skims your letter and résumé in about 30 seconds. If you have not grabbed his or her interest in that time, you are probably finished with that organization.

The résumé. A résumé provides your prospective employer with a convenient summary of your education and experience. As in the letter of application, good grammar, correct spelling, neatness, and brevity—ideally, only one page—are of major importance in your résumé.

The two most widely used résumés are chronological and functional résumés. Each has advantages and disadvantages.

Chronological résumés. The advantages of a chronological résumé (Figure 12-2) are that it's traditional and acceptable. If your education and experience show a steady progression toward the career you seek, the chronological résumé portrays that progression well. Its major disadvantage is that your special capabilities or accomplishments may sometimes get lost in the chronological detail. Also, if you have holes in your employment or educational history, they show up clearly.

Put your address at the top. Include your e-mail address and your telephone number (including the area code). If you have a fax number, include it.

For most students, educational information should be placed before work experience. People with extensive work experience, however, may choose to put it before their educational information.

List the colleges or universities you have attended in reverse chronological order—in other words, list the school you attended most recently first; the one before, second; and so on. Do not list your high school. Give your major and date, or expected date, of graduation. Do not list courses, but list anything that is out of the ordinary, such as honors, special projects, and emphases in addition to the major. Extracurricular activities also go here if they are pertinent to the job you seek.

As you did with your educational experience, put your work experience in reverse chronological order. To save space and to avoid the repetition of *I* throughout the résumé, use phrases rather than complete sentences. The style of the sample résumés makes this technique clear. As in the letter of application, emphasize the experiences that show you in the best light for the job you seek. Use nouns and active verbs in your descriptions. Do not neglect less important jobs of the sort you may have had in high school, but use even more of a summary approach for them. You would probably put college internships and work–study programs here, though you might choose to put them under education. If you have military experience, put it here. Give the highest rank you held, list service schools you attended, and describe your duties. Make a special effort to show how your military experience relates to the civilian work you seek.

Lawrence Hendrich
lhend@tamu.edu

Local Address   307 B Spruce College Station, TX 77840 (713) 806 - 1603
Permanent Address 22922 Governorshire Katy, TX, 77450 (281) 395 - 0096

EDUCATION   **Texas A&M University, College Station TX**
Bachelor of Science Degree
Double Major: Biomedical Science and Entomology
Graduated: December 2011
GPR: 3.3/4.0

EXPERIENCE   **Texas A&M University, College Station TX**
The History of Medicine Study Abroad, Germany, Summer 2010
- Shadowed and Observed a triple bypass surgery, North Rhine Westfalia Heart and Diabetes Center
- Visited German veterinary cloning facilities in Bayer Healthcare Target Research Facilities, Chemical Research Facilities, and fermentation facilities
- Participated in research on "Nazi Medicine"

St. Joseph's Hospital, Bryan TX
Day Surgery Tower Volunteer, August 2009 – present
- Assisted patients and their families while at the hospital.
- Aided doctors, nurses, and staff in various duties.

International Student Volunteers (ISV) Conservation Project
- Traveled to Australia to work with a team on trail building in national forests, planting over 1,000 trees, sages, and grasses, and removing invasive species from devastated swamp lands.

ACTIVITIES   **Sigma Nu National Fraternity**
- Executive Council
  - Candidate Marshall – Fall 2011
  - Lieutenant Commander (Vice President) Spring 2010 – Spring 2011
  - Sentinel and Risk Reduction Fall 2009 – Spring 2010
- Head of Philanthropy Committee 2010-2011, Recruitment Committee, Academic Chair – Spring 2010, Social Chair – Fall 2008, House Manager – Spring 2008, Candidate Class Social Chair – Fall 2007

Biomedical Science Association (BSA) Fall 2007 – present
Texas A&M Pre-Med Society Fall 2009

AWARDS   **Sigma Nu Fraternity**
- Commander's Award 2010 – Spring 2011
- Man of the Year Fall 2010 – Spring 2011
- Scholar of the Year Fall 2009 – Spring 2010
- Big Brother of the Year Fall 2009 – Spring 2010

Study Abroad Fellowship & International Education Scholarship
National Scholar's Honor Society – inducted Fall 2010

FIGURE 12-2 Chronological Résumé

You may wish to provide personal information. Personal information can be a subtle way to point out your desirable qualities. Recent travels indicate a broadening of knowledge and probably a willingness to travel. Hobbies listed may relate to the work sought. Participation in sports, drama, or community activities indicates that you enjoy working with people. Cultural activities indicate you are not a person of narrow interests. If you are proficient in a language aside from English, mention this: more and more organizations are looking for employees with the potential to support international business activity.

If you choose to indicate that you are married or have a family, you might also emphasize that you are willing to relocate. Don't discuss your health unless it is to describe it as excellent.

You have a choice with references. You can list several references with addresses and phone numbers or simply put in a line that says "References available upon request." Both methods have an advantage and a disadvantage. If you provide references, a potential employer can contact them immediately, but you use up precious space that might be better used for more information about yourself. Conversely, if you don't provide the reference information, you save the space but put an additional step between potential employers and information they may want. It's a judgment call, but your first goal is to interest the potential employer in you. If that happens, then it will not be difficult to provide the reference information at a later time. If, however, one of your references is a prestigious individual in the discipline or industry, be sure to list your references on the résumé.

In any case, do have at least three references available. Choose from among your college teachers and past employers—people who know you well and will say positive things about you. Get their permission, of course. Also, it's a smart idea to send them a copy of your résumé. If you can't call on them personally, send them a letter that requests permission to use them as a reference, reminds them of their association with you, and sets a time for their reply:

Dear Ms. Zamora:

In May of this year, I'll graduate from Watertown Polytechnic Institute with a B.S. in metallurgical engineering. I'm getting ready to look for a full-time job. If you believe that you know enough about my abilities to give me a good recommendation, I would like your permission to use you as a reference.

As a reminder, during the summers of 2009 and 2010, I worked as a laboratory technician in your testing facility at Watertown. They were highly instructive summers for me and reinforced my college studies.

I want to start sending my résumé out to some potential employers by March 1 and would be grateful for your reply by that time. I've enclosed a copy of my résumé so that you can see in detail what I've been doing.

Thanks for all your help in the past.

Best regards,

At the bottom of the traditional paper résumé, place a dateline—the month and year in which you completed the résumé. Place the date in the heading of scannable and e-mail résumés.

Functional résumés. A main advantage of the functional résumé (Figure 12-3 and Figure 12-4) is that it allows you to highlight the experiences that show you to your best advantage. Extracurricular experiences show up particularly well in a functional résumé. The major disadvantage of this format is the difficulty, for the first-time reader, of discerning a steady progression of work and education.

The address portion of the functional résumé is the same as that of the chronological. After the address, you may include a job objective line if you like. A job objective entry specifies the kind of work you want to do and sometimes the industry or service area in which you want to do it, like this:

Work in computer security.

or like this:

Work in computer security for a medical insurance corporation.

Place the job objective entry immediately after the address and align it with the rest of the entries (as shown in Figure 12-3).

For education, simply give the school from which you received your degree, your major, and your date of graduation. The body of the résumé is essentially a classification. You sort your experiences—educational, business, extracurricular—into categories that reveal capabilities related to the jobs you seek. Remember that in addition to professional skills, employers want good communication skills and good interpersonal skills. Possible categories are *technical, professional, team building, communication, research, sales, production, administration,* and *consulting.*

The best way to prepare a functional résumé is to brainstorm it. Begin by listing some categories that you think might display your experiences well. Brainstorm further by listing your experiences in those categories. When you have good listings, select the categories and experiences that show you in the best light. Remember, you don't have to display everything you've ever done, just those things that might strike a potential employer as valuable. Finish off the functional résumé with a brief reverse chronological work history and a date line, as in the chronological résumé.

For example, Lawrence's chronological résumé (Figure 12-2) is impressive, but he realized it would not help him in applying for a research assistant position in entomology that had been advertised on campus. He developed a functional résumé (Figure 12-3) and submitted it to the entomology professor who needed the research assistant. The functional résumé emphasized what Lawrence knew about entomology and research, which was exactly what the professor wanted, and Lawrence got the job. He finished that research position but needed a new job for the summer. Lawrence revised his résumé again (Figure 12-4), adding what he had learned from the first research position, and submitted it for the second position.

Lawrence Hendrich
lhend@tamu.edu

Local Address   **Permanent Address**
22922 Governorshire   307 B Spruce
College Station, TX 77840   Katy, TX, 77450
(713) 806 - 1603   (281) 395 - 0096

EDUCATION   **Texas A&M University, College Station TX**
Bachelor of Science Degree
Double Major: Biomedical Science and Entomology
Graduated: December 2011,   GPR: 3.3/4.0

LABORATORY QUALIFICATIONS

Collegiate Science Coursework

- General Chemistry w/ lab I & II
- General Biology w/ lab I & II
- Physics w/ lab I & II
- Organic Chemistry w/ lab I & II
- Biochemistry
- Microbiology w/ lab
- Basic knowledge of diseases

Collegiate Entomology

- Identifying Species of Insects
- Collection of Insects
- Forensic Entomology
- Medical Entomology w/ lab
- Veterinary Entomology w/ lab
- General Entomology w/ lab
- Insect Morphology w/ lab

Other Skills

- Microsoft Office – Word, Excel, PowerPoint, and Access

EXPERIENCE

The History of Medicine Study Abroad, Germany, Summer 2010

- Shadowed and Observed a triple bypass surgery, North Rhine Westfalia Heart and Diabetes Center

FIGURE 12-3 Functional Résumé

Lawrence Hendrich --2

- Visited German veterinary cloning facilities in Bayer Healthcare Target Research Facilities, Chemical Research Facilities, and fermentation facilities

- Participated in research on "Nazi Medicine"

St. Joseph's Hospital, Bryan TX

Day Surgery Tower Volunteer, August 2009 – present

- Assisted patients and their families while at the hospital.
- Aided doctors, nurses, and staff in various duties.

International Student Volunteers (ISV) Conservation Project

- Traveled to Australia to work with a team on trail building in national forests, planting over 1,000 trees, sages, and grasses, and removing invasive species from devastated swamp lands.

ACTIVITIES   Sigma Nu National Fraternity
                      Coastal Conservation Association
                      Biomedical Science Association (BSA) Fall 2007 – present
                      Texas A&M Pre-Med Society Fall 2009

AWARDS

Sigma Nu Fraternity

- Commander's Award, Fall 2010 – Spring 2011. The chapter president recognizes one exceptional individual within the chapter.

- Man of the Year, Fall 2010 – Spring 2011. The Fraternity recognizes the individual who has demonstrated excellence in the area of leadership.

- Scholar of the Year, Fall 2009 – Spring 2010. The Fraternity recognizes the individual who has demonstrated excellence in the area of scholarship.

- Big Brother of the Year, Fall 2009 – Spring 2010. The Fraternity recognizes an exceptional Big Brother in the chapter.

Study Abroad Fellowship and International Education Scholarship

National Scholar's Honor Society – inducted Fall 2010

References Furnished Upon Request

FIGURE 12-3 *continued*

Lawrence Hendrich
lhend@tamu.edu

Local Address	**Permanent Address**
22922 Governorshire	307 B Spruce
College Station, TX 77840	Katy, TX, 77450
(713) 806 - 1603	(281) 395 - 0096

EDUCATION   **Texas A&M University, College Station TX**
Bachelor of Science Degree
Double Major: Biomedical Science and Entomology
Graduated: December 2008, GPR: 3.3/4.0

LABORATORY EXPERIENCE & QUALIFICATIONS

Texas A&M University, Department of Entomology – Dr. Michel Slotman

- Polymerase Chain Reaction
- Gel Electrophoresis
- Ligation & Cloning
- DNA Extraction
- Basic Lab skills and safety

Collegiate Science Coursework

- General Chemistry w/ lab I & II
- General Biology w/ lab I & II
- Physics w/ lab I & II
- Organic Chemistry w/ lab I & II
- Biochemistry
- Microbiology w/ lab
- Basic knowledge of diseases

Collegiate Entomology

- Identifying Species of Insects
- Collection of Insects
- Forensic Entomology
- Medical Entomology w/ lab
- Veterinary Entomology w/ lab
- General Entomology w/ lab
- Insect Morphology w/ lab

Other Skills

- Microsoft Office – Word, Excel, PowerPoint, and Access

EXPERIENCE

The History of Medicine Study Abroad, Germany, Summer 2010

- Shadowed and Observed a triple bypass surgery, North Rhine Westfalia Heart and Diabetes Center

FIGURE 12-4 Functional Résumé

Lawrence Hendrich --2

- Visited German veterinary cloning facilities in Bayer Healthcare Target Research Facilities, Chemical Research Facilities, and fermentation facilities

- Participated in research on "Nazi Medicine"

St. Joseph's Hospital, Bryan TX

Day Surgery Tower Volunteer, August 2009 – present

- Assisted patients and their families while at the hospital.

- Aided doctors, nurses, and staff in various duties.

International Student Volunteers (ISV) Conservation Project

- Traveled to Australia to work with a team on trail building in national forests, planting over 1,000 trees, sages, and grasses, and removing invasive species from devastated swamp lands.

ACTIVITIES   Sigma Nu National Fraternity
                     Coastal Conservation Association
                     Biomedical Science Association (BSA) Fall 2007 – present
                     Texas A&M Pre-Med Society Fall 2009

AWARDS

Sigma Nu Fraternity

- Commander's Award, Fall 2010 – Spring 2011. The chapter president recognizes one exceptional individual within the chapter.

- Man of the Year, Fall 2010 – Spring 2011. The Fraternity recognizes the individual who has demonstrated excellence in the area of leadership.

- Scholar of the Year, Fall 2009 – Spring 2010. The Fraternity recognizes the individual who has demonstrated excellence in the area of academics.

- Big Brother of the Year, Fall 2009 – Spring 2010. The Fraternity recognizes an exceptional Big Brother in the chapter.

Study Abroad Fellowship and International Education Scholarship

National Scholar's Honor Society – inducted Fall 2010

References Furnished Upon Request

FIGURE 12-4 *continued*

This new job would require him to work with two professors—one in crop sciences and one in entomology. Both were impressed and Lawrence was again hired.

Ordinarily, you will prepare your résumé as a traditional formatted document, but you might instead be asked to fill in fields at a job site online that will automatically generate your résumé according to a standardized template.

Traditional formatted résumés. As Figures 12-2, 12-3, and 12-4 illustrate, in a traditional résumé you use variations in type and spacing to emphasize and organize information. Make the résumé look easy to read—leave generous margins and white space. Use distinctive headings and subheadings. The use of a two-column spread is common, as is the use of boldface in headings. You might use a 12-point type like Arial for headings and a 10-point type like Times for the text. Be sparing, however, with the typographical variation: you want to organize the page of information visually without pulling the reader's attention away from your abilities.

If you are printing your résumé, use a high-quality bond paper in white or off-white. Your letter and résumé should be on matching paper. If you are attaching the résumé as an electronic file to an e-mail message or uploading it to a job site, again make sure you submit it as a read-only file in a widely used format (e.g., doc, docx, pdf, or rtf) for easy access by the recipient.

Who is the recipient for your letters and résumés? When answering an advertisement, you should follow whatever instructions are given there. You might be directed, for example, to a company-wide job site to submit your application electronically. Otherwise, direct the materials, if at all possible, to the person in the organization who directly supervises the position for which you are applying. This person often has the power to hire for the position. Your research into the company may turn up the name you need. If not, don't be afraid of calling the company switchboard and asking directly for a name and title. If need be, write to human resources directors. Whatever you do, write to a specific individual by name.

Sometimes, of course, you may gain an interview without having submitted a letter of application—for example, when recruiters come to your campus. Bring a résumé with you and give it to the interviewer at the start of the interview. The résumé gives the interviewer a starting point for questions and often helps to focus the interview on your qualifications for the job.

Online-generated résumés. A lot of companies allow you to submit résumés as documents generated electronically by filling in the fields on a series of pages at the site. The fields solicit the details of your address, credentials, and objectives and allow you to identify the job or jobs for which you are applying. This information is automatically compiled in a standardized format for access by hiring managers. Because you can't organize the information yourself to emphasize your knowledge and experience, using keywords to highlight your suitability for the job will be critical.

Follow-up letters. Write *follow-up letters* (1) if after two weeks you have received no answer to your letter of application; (2) after an interview; (3) if a company fails to offer you a job; and (4) to accept or refuse a job.

No answer. If a company doesn't acknowledge receipt of your original letter of application within two weeks, write again with a gracious inquiry such as the following:

Dear Mr. Petrosian:

On 12 April I applied for a position with your company. I have not heard from you, so perhaps my original letter and résumé have been misplaced. I enclose copies of them.

If you have already reached a decision regarding my application or if there has been a delay in filling the position, please let me know at your earliest opportunity.

I look forward to hearing from you.

Sincerely yours,

After an interview. Within a day's time, follow up your interview with a letter. Such a letter draws favorable attention to yourself as a person who understands business courtesy and good communication practice. Express your appreciation for the interview. Emphasize any of your qualifications that seemed to be especially important to the interviewer. Express your willingness to live with any special conditions of employment, such as relocation. Make clear that you want the job and feel qualified to do it. If you include a specific question in your letter, it may hasten a reply. Your letter might look like this one:

Dear Ms. Kuriyama:

Thank you for speaking with me last Tuesday about the computer security position you have open.

Working in computer security relates well to my experience and interests. The job you have available is one I am qualified to do. I am working this semester on a research report that examines the legal and ethical issues regarding electronic retrieval of patient records in public hospitals. May I send you a copy next week when it is completed?

I understand that the position would include working alternating weekends. This requirement presents no difficulty for me.

I look forward to hearing from you soon.

Sincerely yours,

After being refused a job. When a company refuses you a job, good tactics dictate that you acknowledge the refusal. Express thanks for the time spent with you and state your regret that no opening exists at the present time. If you like, express the hope of being considered in the future. You never know; a new job might come available at a later time. In any case, you want to maintain a good reputation with this employer and its representatives. These are people working in the same industry as you: you may encounter them at professional conferences or meetings of the local chapter of your professional association. They may later come to work at your same company as your colleague, your supervisor, or your subordinate. The few minutes you devote now to a courteous reply will create a lasting impression on them of your extraordinary professionalism.

Accepting or refusing a job. Writing an acceptance letter presents few problems. Be brief. Thank the employer for the job offer, and accept the job. Determine the day and time you will report for work, and express pleasure at the prospect of joining the organization and working with your new colleagues. A good letter of acceptance might read as follows:

> Dear Mr. Gafaiti:
>
> Thank you for offering me a job as research assistant with your firm. I happily accept. I will report to work on 1 July as you have requested.
>
> I look forward to working with Price Industries and particularly to the opportunity of doing research with Dr. Ertas.
>
> Sincerely yours,

Writing a letter of refusal can be difficult. Be as gracious as possible. Be brief, but not so brief as to suggest rudeness or indifference. Make it clear that you appreciate the offer. If you can, give a reason for your refusal. The employer who has spent time and money in interviewing you and corresponding with you deserves these courtesies. And, of course, your own self-interest is involved. In the future you may wish to work for this organization even though you must decline the opportunity at this time. A good letter of refusal might look like this one:

> Dear Ms. White:
>
> I enjoyed my visit to the research department of your company. I would very much have liked to work with the people I met there. I thank you for offering me the opportunity to do so.
>
> After much serious thought, I have decided that the research opportunities offered to me in another job are closer to the interests I developed at Nebraska State University. Therefore, I have accepted that job and regret that I cannot accept yours.
>
> I appreciate the great courtesy and thoughtfulness that you and your associates extended to me during the application and interview process. The individual you do hire will be blessed with exceptional colleagues.
>
> Sincerely yours,

INTERVIEWING

The immediate goal of all your preparation and letter and résumé writing is an interview with a potential employer.

The interview. If you have prepared properly, you should show up at the interview knowing almost everything about the organization, including its basic history, chief locations, key products and services, financial situation, and mission.

You should have the following with you: your résumé; a portfolio of your work, if appropriate; pen and notebook; a list of your references; and your business card.

The interviewer will probably start with a bit of social conversation to put you at ease before proceeding to questions aimed at assessing your skills and interests and how you might be of value to the organization. You might anticipate questions such as the following:

- What can you tell me about yourself?
- What are your strengths and weaknesses?
- What do you want to be doing five years from now?
- Why would you want to work for us?
- Why should we hire you?
- What accomplishment are you most proud of?
- What is the biggest problem you've encountered and how did you solve it?

To the question, "What can you tell me about yourself?" the interviewer really doesn't expect an extended life history. This question provides you the opportunity to talk about your work and educational experiences and your skills. Try to relate your skills and experience to the needs of the organization. Don't overlook the people and communication skills essential to nearly every professional job.

In your answer to this and other questions, be specific in your examples. If you say something like "I have good managerial skills," immediately back it up with an occasion or experience that supports your statement. Focus on offering the specific evidence that will lead the interviewer to the right conclusions about you. Such specifics are more memorable than unsupported claims and will help you stick in the interviewer's mind.

In answering questions about your strengths and weaknesses, be honest, but don't betray weaknesses that could eliminate you from consideration. Admit to weaknesses that would have no impact on the specific job for which you are interviewing: for example, if the job has no managerial duties, it would be okay to acknowledge that your managerial skills are undeveloped.

To the question, "What do you want to be doing five years from now?" a good answer would identify a job with greater responsibilities at the same company.

The question, "Why do you want to work for us?" allows you to display what you have learned about the organization. In answering this question, you should again show that what you have to offer fits with what the company needs.

In the final portion of the interview you will typically be given a chance to ask some questions of your own. It's a good time to get more details about the job or the working environment. Ask about the organization's goals. "What is the company most proud of?" is a good question. Or "What are you looking for in the candidate for this position?" "What will you want him or her to accomplish in the first year on the job?" Don't ask naive questions—questions you ought to know the answers to already from your research—like the size of the company or the number of employees. Don't ask questions just to ask questions. The interview is a good time for you to find out if you really want to work for this organization. Not every organization is going to be a good fit for what you have to offer and what you want to do. Avoid questions about salary and benefits unless the interviewer has raised this subject.

If you really want to go to work for the organization, make that clear before the interview ends. But don't allow your willingness to appear as desperation. Companies don't hire desperate people. At some point in the interview, be sure to get the interviewer's name (spelled correctly), title, address, phone number, e-mail address, and fax number. You'll need them for later correspondence. When the interviewer thanks you for coming, thank him or her for seeing you and leave. Don't drag the interview out when it's clearly over or linger at the door.

If you are invited for a site visit as a finalist for the position, you will find yourself informally interviewed by a variety of potential colleagues and supervisors during lunches or dinners, while waiting for elevators, while walking from office to office, or while driving to and from the airport. For this series of informal interviews or conversations, prepare one-minute answers to each of the formal interview questions: that is, abbreviate your usual three-minute or five-minute answer in a cogent emphasis on your key selling point. If time allows, you could always elaborate, but if the conversation is interrupted or the subject abruptly changes, you will at least have made your point and proven yourself articulate.

Negotiation. Interviewers rarely raise the subject of salary and benefits until they either see you as a good prospect or are sure they want to hire you. If they offer you the job, the negotiation is sometimes done in a separate interview. For example, your future boss may offer you the job and then send you to negotiate with the human resources staff.

Sometimes, the negotiator may offer you a salary. At other times, you may be asked to name a salary. Now is the time to put to good use the information you may have received through your networking activities. Or check the online job finding services or specialized services such as Salary.com (www.salary.com) for their estimates of earnings for different positions in different industries.

Your research in these sources will give you not a specific salary but a salary range. If asked to name a salary, do not ask for the bottom of the range. Ask for as near the top as you believe is reasonable given your education and experience. The negotiator will respect you the more for knowing what you are worth. However, balance the compensation package—vacations, pension plans, health care, educational opportunities, and so forth—against the salary. Some compensation packages are worth a good deal of money and may allow you to accept a lower salary.

The location of the job is also a critical factor to consider. Online services such as Salary.com (www.salary.com) offer cost-of-living calculators that determine the comparative worth of salaries by location. For example, $50,000 in New York City could be the equivalent of $35,000 in Chicago, $26,000 in Houston, or $43,000 in Los Angeles.

Before and after the interview.   If you have not participated in job interviews before, you would be wise to practice with several friends. Using the information that we have given you and that you have gathered for yourself, practice several interviews, with two of you as interviewer and interviewee and the remainder as observers. Ask the observers to look for strengths and weaknesses in your answers, diction, grammar, and body language and to give you a candid appraisal. Practice until you feel comfortable with the process.

After you finish each interview, write down your impressions as soon as possible. How did your clothes compare to the interviewer's? Were there unexpected questions? How good were your answers? What did you learn about the organization? What did you learn about a specific job or jobs? Did anything make you uncomfortable about the organization? Do you think you would fit in there? By the next day, get a thank-you note (letter, e-mail, or fax) off to the interviewer.

JOB SEARCH CHECKLIST

The Letter and Résumé

Planning

☐ Your letter of application:
- What position are you applying for?
- How did you learn about this position?
- Why are you qualified for this position?
- What interests you about this company?
- What will you do for the organization?
- How will the employer reach you?

☐ Your résumé:
- Do you have all the necessary details about your education and experience (e.g., dates, job descriptions, schools, majors, degrees, extracurricular activities)?
- Which résumé format will suit your experience and abilities, chronological or functional?
- Do you have permission to use the names of at least three people as references?

Revising

☐ Your letter of application:
- Do you seem self-confident but not arrogant or boastful?
- Does your letter show how you could be valuable to the employer?
- Does your letter reflect interest in a specific job?
- Have you emphasized the education and experience that suit you for this job?
- Have you made it clear you would like to be interviewed? Have you made it easy for the employer to arrange the interview?

continued

JOB SEARCH CHECKLIST ✔ *continued*

- Is your letter completely free of grammatical and spelling errors? Is it designed for easy reading and skimming?

☐ Your résumé:
- Have you picked the résumé type that suits your experiences and qualifications?
- Have you listed your education and job experience in reverse chronological order?
- Have you used active verbs and appropriate keywords to describe your education and experience?
- Is your résumé completely free of grammatical and spelling errors? Is it designed for easy reading and skimming?

The Interview

Planning

☐ Have you completed your research about the organization? Are you familiar with its history, goals, products, locations, and reputation in the industry and region?
☐ Have you practiced your answers to likely questions?
☐ Do you have good questions to ask the interviewer?

Reviewing

☐ Did you answer all the questions effectively? Which questions could you have answered better?
☐ Were you asked questions that you didn't expect?
☐ How did the interviewer answer your questions? Did he or she seem to think you asked good questions?
☐ Do you think you will be offered the job? Why or why not?
☐ Do you think you are a good fit for this organization? Why or why not?

EXERCISES

1. Investigate a potential employer of majors in your field. Locate information available from the employer's website as well as online job-finding services. Are all the profiles of this employer basically similar? Do you notice important differences? Locate additional information available in newspapers, magazines, and government documents about this employer. What is the public perception

of this employer? What is its reputation in the industry? Interview employees or managers for their perspectives on the advantages and disadvantages of working for this employer. Compile the findings of your research in a slide presentation for majors in your field.

2. Given the findings of your investigation of a major employer in your field, list the characteristics of this employer's ideal job candidate. What would be the ideal job candidate's education and experience? What would be his or her special skills, dispositions, and achievements? How are you similar to this ideal job candidate? How do you differ?

3. Given the findings of your investigation of a major employer in your field and your inventory of the ideal job candidate, tailor your typical letter of job application and résumé to the needs and interests of this employer. What changes will you make in your usual version of each document? How will these changes increase the likelihood of your being interviewed for a job?

4. If a friend of yours were applying for a position as a technical writer at Google, which of the following two résumés (see Figures 12-5 and 12-6) would you advise she include with the letter of application? If you were given 15 more minutes to make this résumé more effective, what changes would you make? How would your advice differ if your friend were applying for a job at IBM?

Ty Williams
1221 Cooper Avenue
Dallas, TX 75123
214-555-4433
ty.williams@texas.edu

Employment Objective

Position as a Technical Communicator, with opportunities to utilize my experience and skills in technical editing and document design

Education
Texas University
Dallas, TX

B.A., Technical Communication, May 2012
GPA: 3.5.
GPA in Major: 3.75

Employment Experience

Crisp Communications
Dallas, TX
2011-2012

- Compose, edit, and design a variety of documents for clients of this consulting firm, including brochures, newsletters, reports and manuals.
- Supervise small projects.
- Coordinate project staff and schedule.
- Maintain billing records.

Mercury Computers
Dallas, TX
2010-2011

- Provided customer support for hardware and software products.
- Researched customer problems, identified appropriate solutions, and replied to customers.
- Served average of 50 customers daily.

Special Skills

- Proficient in all Adobe applications
- Read/write/speak Spanish

Scholastic Honors

- Sigma Pi Delta Honor Society, 2012
- R.T. Brookings Scholarship Recipient, 2011
- Dean's Academic Honor Roll, 2010-2012

Professional Memberships

IEEE Professional Communication Society
Society for Technical Communication (STC)

References

Available upon request from the Career Planning and Placement Center, Texas University, Smith Hall, Room 225, Dallas, TX 75124-1005.

February 2012

FIGURE 12-5 Document for Exercise 4

Ty Williams
1221 Cooper Avenue
Dallas, TX 75123
214-555-4433
ty.williams@texas.edu

Employment Objective	Position as a Technical Communicator specializing in technical editing and document design
Education	Texas University Dallas, TX B.A., Technical Communication, May 2012
Communication Skills	<ul><li>Compose, edit, and design a variety of documents, including brochures, newsletters, reports and manuals.</li><li>Create projects using all Adobe applications</li><li>Provide customer support for hardware and software products</li><li>Research customer problems, identify appropriate solutions, and reply to customers by telephone or e-mail message.</li><li>Read/write/speak Spanish</li><li>Graduating with Honors: GPA: 3.5; GPA in Major: 3.75</li></ul>
Project Management	<ul><li>Supervise small document design projects from initial meeting with client through publication and delivery</li><li>Coordinate project staff and schedule.</li><li>Maintain billing records.</li></ul>
Professional Involvement	<ul><li>Sigma Pi Delta Honor Society</li><li>Association for Computing Machinery (ACM)</li><li>IEEE Professional Communication Society</li><li>Society for Technical Communication (STC)</li></ul>
Work Experience	<ul><li>Crisp Communications Dallas, TX, 2011-2012, document design</li><li>Mercury Computers, Dallas, TX, 2010-2011, customer support</li></ul>
References	Available upon request from the Career Planning and Placement Center, Texas University, Smith Hall, Room 225, Dallas, TX 75124-1005.

February 2012

FIGURE 12-6 Document for Exercise 4

Appendix A

Brief Guide to Grammar, Punctuation, and Usage

ab ◆ ABBREVIATIONS

Every field uses standard and specialized terms that may be abbreviated for convenience and conciseness.

First, decide whether your audience is familiar enough with the unabbreviated term to allow you to use it without defining it. Second, decide whether your audience is familiar enough with the abbreviation for you to use it without spelling it out.

If you decide that an abbreviation is appropriate and must be explained, place the abbreviation in parentheses following your first use of the unabbreviated term. Thereafter, use the abbreviation by itself. If necessary, after the parentheses, provide a definition of the term. Make the definition as detailed as necessary for your purpose and audience:

> Fluid catalytic cracking (FCC) changes crude oil to gasoline by breaking the long-chain molecules that are characteristic of hydrocarbon liquids. The process involves exposing the oil to a special chemical agent under high temperature and pressure. FCC is the key conversion process at oil refineries.

Use Latin abbreviations like *i.e.* (that is) and *e.g.* (for example) in parenthetical explanations, or in tables and figures if space is limited.

Avoid starting sentences with abbreviations: spell out the abbreviation or revise the sentence to shift the abbreviation to a later position in the sentence.

Check the appropriate style guide or publication manual in your field for specific guidelines on abbreviations.

apos ◆ APOSTROPHES

Use apostrophes to indicate the possessive case of nouns (e.g., singular: manager's; plural: managers') and the missing letters in contractions (could've: could have).

With coordinated nouns, use apostrophes to make all possessive in order to indicate individual ownership. To indicate joint ownership, make only the final noun possessive.

- Maria's and David's reports are late. (i.e., The reports written by Maria and the reports written by David are late.)

• Maria and David's reports are late. (i.e., The reports written together by Maria and David are late.)

Also use apostrophes to indicate the possessive case of indefinite pronouns ending in –one or –body as well as *either, neither, another,* or *other*:

- Everyone's paycheck is incorrect because of a computer error.
- The change must have raised somebody's profits this quarter.
- I asked both managers and either's approval is enough to proceed.
- I asked both managers but neither's approval was forthcoming.
- We preferred each other's answer.
- She preferred another's answer.

acro ◆ ACRONYMS

Acronyms are names for objects or entities formed from a combination of the initial letters of the words in a title or phrase. Unlike abbreviations (e.g., UN for United Nations), acronyms are pronounced as words (e.g., UNICEF for United Nations International Children's Emergency Fund).

First, decide whether your audience is familiar enough with the acronym to allow you to use it without showing the phrase from which it is derived. Second, decide whether the phrase from which it is derived is itself a sufficient definition or explanation of the acronym.

If you decide that an acronym is appropriate, place the phrase from which it is derived in parentheses following your first use of the acronym. If necessary, supply additional explanation immediately following. Thereafter, use the acronym by itself:

The mysterious illness was identified as SARS (Severe Acute Respiratory Syndrome), a disease similar to pneumonia but viral in nature and thus impervious to antibiotics. SARS killed 299 people in Hong Kong in a 2003 epidemic.

brackets ◆ BRACKETS

Use brackets inside quotations or parentheses to insert a clarifying note or comment:

- "This is the highest level of membership in the organization [8.1% of 375,000] and indicates exceptional professional achievement."
- If you would like more information about this policy, please call my office (M-F 8-5 [EDT], 866-555-7243).

cap ◆ CAPITALIZATION

Capitalize months but not seasons. (e.g., January was unusually mild this winter.)

Capitalize geographic areas but not directions. (e.g., The stores were all originally in the Southeast, but soon spread not so much north as west.)

Capitalize titles preceding names but not following or in isolation:

- The invitation is from President Juanita Solis Ybarra.
- Juanita Solis Ybarra, president of the company, arrived earlier this morning.
- The president of the company is Juanita Solis Ybarra.

colon   ◆   COLON

Use a colon to introduce quotations, lists, or supporting statements:

- Dr. Smith's testimony was unequivocal: "This test has no predictive value and should not be promoted as though it does."
- The company has five locations: Cairo, Hong Kong, Los Angeles, Paris, and Rio de Janeiro.
- The book explains the maieutic method: that is, the practice of teaching by asking questions that stimulate thinking and elicit new ideas.

Never use a colon immediately following a verb or a preposition:

WRONG: The five stores are located in: Cairo, Hong Kong, Los Angeles, Paris, and Rio de Janeiro.
WRONG: The locations of the five stores are: Cairo, Hong Kong, Los Angeles, Paris, and Rio de Janeiro.
RIGHT: The stores are in five locations: Cairo, Hong Kong, Los Angeles, Paris, and Rio de Janeiro.
RIGHT: The stores are located in the following cities: Cairo, Hong Kong, Los Angeles, Paris, and Rio de Janeiro.

Use a colon to separate two independent clauses if the second clause explains or amplifies the first:

- Analytical skills are necessary but insufficient: we must also develop the ability to synthesize information.
- The new facility uses icons to identify its various services: for example, a picture of a glowing question mark identifies the information booth.

Use a colon following the salutation of a business letter.

Dear Mr. Ramirez:

c   ◆   COMMA

Use a comma before a coordinating conjunction (*and, but, or, nor, for, yet*) that joins two independent clauses:

- The engineers arrived at their recommendation almost immediately, and the supervisor supported their judgment.
- The engineers arrived at their recommendation almost immediately, but the supervisor questioned their judgment.

Use a comma after an introductory word, phrase, or clause:

- Unfortunately, the company must declare bankruptcy.
- In appreciation of their efforts on the project, the president awarded each of the scientists a $500 bonus.
- After you have completed the usability testing, the engineers will modify their design of the product.

Use commas to separate nonrestrictive modifiers from the remainder of the sentence.

RESTRICTIVE: Cotton farming that is conducted without artificial irrigation lowers the cost of production but raises the risk of a poor crop.
NONRESTRICTIVE: Cotton farming, which typically involves the use of defoliants as well as herbicides and pesticides, has high costs for the environment.

A restrictive modifier is necessary to the meaning of the sentence. The writer has thus restricted the subject of cotton farming to that which is conducted without artificial irrigation. The writer here is making a single claim: cotton farming without artificial irrigation has lower costs but higher risks.

A nonrestrictive modifier supplies additional information about the subject without restricting it. The writer here is making two claims: cotton farming usually has high costs for the environment, and cotton farming usually involves defoliants, pesticides, and herbicides.

Use commas to separate items in a series of words, phrases, or clauses.

- This unit of the facility produces ethylene oxide, ethylene dichloride, and polyethylene.
- Ethylene contributes to the ripening of fruit, the opening of flowers, and the shedding of leaves.
- Florists complain about the impact of ethylene exposure on the life of their flowers, grocers worry about high-ethylene products like bananas, and shippers focus their efforts on good temperature controls to minimize the chemical's release.

Use commas to separate dates, geographical locations, and titles:

- On Wednesday, June 18, 2011, the case was closed.
- The marble sculpture was shipped from Palermo, Sicily, by boat to Galveston, Texas, and transported from there by truck to Albuquerque, New Mexico.
- The new members of the citizen review board are Gillian Kelly, Ph.D., and Xiling Li, J.D.

dm   ◆   DANGLING MODIFIER

A dangling modifier occurs whenever a modifying word or phrase is used without a suitable noun for it to modify:

WRONG: Assuming the contamination was widespread, the eggs were discarded.

RIGHT: Assuming the contamination was widespread, the manager discarded the eggs.

dash ◆ DASH

The dash serves the same function as parentheses (i.e., separating a tangential or explanatory comment from the remainder of the sentence), but the dash does so with greater emphasis—like a shout instead of a whisper.

ell ◆ ELLIPSIS

Use three spaced periods to indicate that words have been omitted from a quotation. If the quotation is at the end of a sentence, use four periods (i.e., three spaced periods for the ellipsis and a period for the sentence).

- "In a work context, these readers . . . will feel no commitment to read what you write unless your messages are useful to them as they do their own work."
- "In a work context, these readers, all of whom come from a variety of educational and cultural backgrounds, will feel no commitment to read what you write unless your messages are useful to them. . . ."

If the quotation is obviously incomplete, skip the ellipsis.

According to the investigator, their actions were "deliberate and malicious."

exc ◆ EXCLAMATION POINT

Avoid using exclamation points in the writing of reports, letters, memos, and e-mail messages so that you never come across as easily excited or agitated. If writing instructions, use exclamation points as necessary with cautions and warnings.

frag ◆ FRAGMENT

A sentence fragment is a phrase or a clause punctuated as though it were a complete sentence. This error is usually fixed by connecting the fragment to the preceding sentence.

WRONG: The findings were exactly as expected. Although we were hoping for better news.

RIGHT: The findings were exactly as expected, although we were hoping for better news.

WRONG: The report came straight from the investigating committee. Which included two forensic scientists and the city's medical examiner.

RIGHT: The report came straight from the investigating committee, which included two forensic scientists and the city's medical examiner.
WRONG: The city council voted to change the policy. Surprising all of us at the meeting.
RIGHT: The city council voted to change the policy, surprising all of us at the meeting.

hyphen ◆ HYPHEN

Use a hyphen with the following suffixes and prefixes:

- -elect: president-elect
- -in-law: brother-in-law
- all-: all-around team player
- ex-: ex-employee
- quasi-: quasi-empirical study
- self-: self-starter

Also use hyphens with prefixes preceding capitalized words (e.g., pre-Olympics competition), prefixes preceding numbers (e.g., post-9/11 security), and prefixes preceding acronyms and abbreviations (e.g., anti-HIV medication).

In addition, use a hyphen between words joined together to modify a word:

- It was a labor-intensive process.
- The waiting room has black-and-white-striped chairs.
- She makes six-, eight-, and twelve-string guitars.
- Nicholas is a well-connected manager for this project.

ital ◆ ITALICIZATION

Italicize titles of books, journals, magazines, plays, films, radio and television programs, sculptures and paintings, ships, aircraft, and spacecraft.

Italicize words that are considered foreign to the English language.

Italicize Latin words for genus and species. (e.g., The zoological designation for the American toad is *Bufo americanus*.)

Italicize words, letters, and numbers identified as words, letters, and numbers.

The words *compose* and *comprise* have opposite meanings.
His middle initial is *A*.
She said it scored a *5* on the grading scale.

Italicize letters used as statistical symbols:

- *M* (i.e., mean)
- *N* (i.e., number in the population studied)

- *p* (i.e., probability)
- *SD* (i.e., standard deviation)

mm ◆ MISPLACED MODIFIER

A misplaced modifier is a word, phrase, or clause put in the wrong position in the sentence and thus modifying a word the writer never intended to be modified.

WRONG: This machine was repaired almost for $100.
RIGHT: This machine was repaired for almost $100. (*or* This machine was almost repaired for $100.)
WRONG: He was trying to find a job for two years.
RIGHT: He was trying for two years to find a job. (*or* He was trying to find a two-year job.)
WRONG: The computer was available at a new store that he tried a week ago.
RIGHT: The computer that he tried a week ago was available at a new store. (*or* The computer was available at a new store that he visited a week ago.)

np/ag ◆ NOUN-PRONOUN AGREEMENT

In all formal communication, collective nouns such as *each, everyone, either, neither, anybody, somebody, everybody,* and *no one* use singular pronouns and singular verbs:

FORMAL: Each has his or her machine.
FORMAL: Everybody was given his or her ticket.

For informal communications, the plural pronoun is widely used:

INFORMAL: Each has their own machine.
INFORMAL: Everybody was given their ticket.

A better solution is to revise the wording:

- All have their machines.
- Each has a machine.
- All were given their tickets.
- Everybody was given a ticket.

The same issue arises with nouns used in a generic sense, such as the word *employee* in the following:

FORMAL: The employee must complete his or her training within one week of being hired.
INFORMAL: The employee must complete their training within one week of being hired.

Again, a better solution is to revise the wording:

- All employees must complete their training within one week of being hired.
- The employee must complete the training within one week of being hired.

With collective nouns such as *team, group, class,* or *committee,* use the singular pronouns *it/its* if you are referring to the unit and the plural pronouns *they/their/them* if you are referring to the constituents.

- The usability team will conduct its tests according to the schedule that it posted on its website.
- The usability team will pick up their passports before they leave on this trip.

num ◆ NUMBERS

Ordinarily, use words for numbers from zero to nine and numerals for numbers 10 and higher.

In a series of numbers, if any one of the numbers is 10 or higher, use all numerals:

- The experiment involved eight vehicles and four drivers.
- The experiment involved 8 vehicles, 4 drivers, and 16 passengers.

Never start a sentence with a numeral: either use words for the number or revise the sentence to shift the number from the opening position.

- Twenty-five people were involved in the experiment.
- The experiment involved 25 people.

With two adjacent numbers, use words for one and numerals for the other in order to avoid confusion.

- He ordered twelve 100-item boxes.
- The list includes 15 ten-digit numbers.

Always use numerals for dates, addresses, exact time, exact sums of money, measurements, and cross-references.

- 1 February 2012 or February 1, 2012
- 4307 55th Street
- 2:00 P.M. (but two o'clock)
- $7,988.97 (but about eight thousand dollars)
- 17 km
- 35 g
- see page 86
- see Table 4

paral   ◆   PARALLELISM

Use the same grammatical structure for items in a series:

> WRONG: This job candidate is proficient at writing proposals, publication management, usability tests, and designing websites.
> RIGHT: This job candidate is proficient at writing proposals, managing publications, running usability tests, and designing websites.
> RIGHT: This job candidate is proficient at proposal writing, publication management, usability testing, and website design.

paren   ◆   PARENTHESES

Use parentheses to separate a tangential or explanatory comment.

Never put any mark of punctuation before an opening parenthesis, but put any required marks of punctuation inside the parentheses and after the closing parenthesis:

- Use parentheses to separate a tangential or explanatory comment (including definitions, clarifications, examples, quotations, or statistics) from the remainder of a sentence.
- Latin words are used to designate genus and species in zoological classification (e.g., *Bufo americanus* for the American toad). (Note that these scientific names are always displayed in italics.)

pron   ◆   PRONOUN

Use the subjective case of a pronoun (*I*, *he*, *she*, *we*, *they*) if it serves as the subject of a clause:

- She and I will work on this project.
- He visited the manufacturing facility yesterday, even though she and I made the same trip a week ago.

Use the objective case of a pronoun (*me*, *him*, *her*, *us*, *them*) if it is the object of a verb or the object of a preposition:

- The manager congratulated them and us for fixing the problem.
- The investigating committee interviewed him and her at the same time.
- The manager distributed copies of the report to them and me.
- This project will be difficult for him and me to complete on time.

quot   ◆   QUOTATION MARKS

Use quotation marks for brief quotations:

- As Clarence Weisman has noted, "The intelligent solution would be to limit the population of this species."

- According to Gloria Moore, "Almost 250 billion pounds of nurdles are manufactured annually. This growing continent of plastic pellets is a looming disaster for the world's environment, especially its oceans."

For quotations of four or more lines, skip the quotation marks and indent and single space the quotation.

Use quotation marks around titles of articles from journals and magazines:

- The article "Polymers are Eternal" was originally published by Marco Quesada in 1986.
- Andrea Kolosov's "The Geologic Heritage in Dispute" claims that investment in crop diversity is dwindling.

Always put commas and periods inside the quotation marks:

- According to Andrea Kolosov's "The Geologic Heritage in Dispute," investment in crop diversity is dwindling.
- Marco Quesada is the author of "Polymers are Eternal."

Put all other marks of punctuation outside the quotation marks unless they are part of the quotation.

- In 1986, Marco Quesada published his article "Polymers are Eternal": it was greeted with derision by the plastics industry.
- Andrea Kolosov's "The Geologic Heritage in Dispute" asked the question, "What are the avoidable contributors to this growing environmental crisis?"

run-on ◆ RUN-ON SENTENCE

A run-on sentence is two independent clauses joined with only a comma or with no punctuation at all.

Two independent clauses may be punctuated as two separate sentences (each with a period) or may be joined with a semicolon, a colon, or a comma and a conjunction (*and, but, for, nor,* or *yet*):

WRONG: A corporate code of conduct has legal and ethical implications, it must address multiple audiences both inside and outside the organization.
RIGHT: A corporate code of conduct has legal and ethical implications. It must address multiple audiences both inside and outside the organization.
RIGHT: A corporate code of conduct has legal and ethical implications; as a consequence, it must address multiple audiences both inside and outside the organization.
RIGHT: A corporate code of conduct has legal and ethical implications, and thus it must address multiple audiences both inside and outside the organization.

A run-on sentence may also be repaired by changing one or the other of the independent clauses to a dependent clause or phrase:

> RIGHT: Because a corporate code of conduct has legal and ethical implications, it must address multiple audiences both inside and outside the organization.
> RIGHT: A corporate code of conduct has legal and ethical implications, making it necessary to address multiple audiences both inside and outside the organization.

semi ◆ SEMICOLON

Use a semicolon to join related independent clauses. (e.g., The mysterious illness shared symptoms of pneumonia; however, unlike typical pneumonia, this illness was viral and unresponsive to antibiotics.)

Use a semicolon to separate items in a series if the items are internally punctuated with commas. (e.g., The equipment order included security cameras for all exits; fire extinguishers, smoke detectors, and carbon monoxide detectors for both floors; projectors, computers, and screens for all twelve classrooms; and computers and telephones for thirty-five offices.)

av/ag ◆ SUBJECT-VERB AGREEMENT

Note that the words *each*, *either*, and *neither* take a singular verb regardless of intervening words:

- Each is qualified.
- Each of the job candidates for the two supervisor positions is qualified.
- Either is qualified.
- Either of the job candidates that we interviewed yesterday is qualified.
- Neither is qualified.
- Neither of the job candidates who interviewed yesterday with us is qualified.

In a coordinated subject joined by *or* or *nor*, make the verb agree with the closer noun or pronoun:

- The original letter or my copies are available for examination.
- My copies or the original letter is available for examination.
- Neither the original letter nor my copies are available for examination.
- Neither my copies nor the original letter is available for examination.

In a coordinated subject joined by *and*, the verb is always plural:

- The original letter and my copies are available for examination.
- My copies and the original letter are available for examination.

With collective nouns such as *team*, *group*, *class*, and *committee*, use a singular verb if you are referring to the unit and a plural verb if you are referring to the constituents.

The usability team is in the conference room.
The usability team are in line for big raises this year.

WW ♦ WRONG WORD

The following words are often confused and misused. Here are examples of correct usage:

We **accept** your explanation.
The portfolio included everything **except** his résumé.

The price of gasoline **affected** [influenced] the company's profits.
The product failure **effected** [caused] the company's bankruptcy.

The reports were **already** written.
We were **all ready** to write the reports.

The supervisors were **all together** [united] in their opposition to the proposal.
The supervisors were **altogether** [completely] opposed to the proposal.

We don't purchase office supplies from that company **anymore**.
We don't need **any more** office supplies.

We talked **awhile** but came to no agreement.
We talked for **a while** but came to no agreement.

The designers think that **canvas** will be a durable material for this product.
The managers will **canvass** their employees for opinions about the new policy.

He failed to **cite** sources in his report.
The **site** of the accident was inaccessible to emergency vehicles.

The illustrations **complemented** the step-by-step instructions.
The supervisor **complimented** the writers on their efforts.

Six employees and one supervisor **compose** the grievance committee.
The grievance committee **comprises** six employees and one supervisor.

The boiler is **continually** [repeatedly] overheating.
The technicians worked **continuously** [without interruption] all afternoon to fix the boiler.

The **council** [committee] of advisors was in agreement.
The president was grateful for their **counsel** [advice].

She was always **discreet** [prudent] in discussing confidential issues.
Each item on the agenda is **discrete** [separate].

She is considered a truly **eminent** authority on homolytic fission.
The arrival of the safety investigators is **imminent**.

Their **everyday** routine includes a period of stretching exercises.
She bicycles to the office **every day**.

He realized the refinery was five miles **farther** [distance].
The committee decided to investigate **further** [degree].

We tallied **fewer** [number] accidents this month.
We noticed **less** attention [amount] to safety.

The company is moving **forward** with new technologies.
This report will include a **foreword** of two pages.

The report **implied** [suggested] that the engineer was incompetent.
The manager **inferred** [concluded] that closer supervision of the project was necessary.

It's [it is] no longer under warranty.
Its warranty has expired.

He ordered testing for **lead** contamination.
The manager **led** the team through a difficult project.

We rejected the **principal** recommendation of the report.
The **principal** of the mortgage is slowly shrinking.
We rejected the recommendation on **principle**.

This **quotation** will reinforce the urgency of the report's recommendations.
We will probably **quote** the president in this report.

The judge talked **respectfully** to the members of the jury.
The offices in Portland and Salem were closed on July 1 and July 15, **respectively**.

She bought **stationary** bicycles for the exercise room.
She bought white paper for the company's **stationery**.

I know that **they're** flying to the district office later today.
She was aware of **their** departure.
He was also going **there** in the morning.

The **weather** this year has been unusual.
The profits for the industry hinge on **whether** the price of gasoline rises.

Whose division reported the highest sales?
Who's joining the company?

I appreciate that **you're** working on the report.
I am grateful for **your** work on the report.

Appendix B

Using Sources of Information

Effective technical communication is built on a foundation of clear, credible, pertinent, and sufficient information. The effective communicator, as a consequence, must develop the six skills of information literacy:

1. Locate sufficient sources of information: Given your audience and purpose, you will have to decide on the nature and scope of potential information sources: interviews, surveys, books, articles, blogs, websites, videos, and government documents.

2. Examine sources for pertinent information: With the possible sources of information compiled, you must review each for information related to your subject. This effort includes the ability to skim a table of contents and a list of illustrations, search for keywords, and navigate a subject index.

3. Evaluate sources for credibility: You must judge the accuracy of the information in your sources. Ordinarily, the more reliable the source or the more sources offering the same information, the more likely it is you have information that deserves to be trusted. No source is infallible, but credible sources typically identify their sources of information, have a track record of offering valid and reliable information, or publish their information only after rigorous review by editors and subject specialists.

4. Summarize information in sources clearly and correctly: You will have to make sure that your abridged version of the information in a source is neither misleading nor mystifying. If you are unsure of the right wording, consider integrating quotations judiciously.

5. Synthesize information across sources. Your job isn't only to list the information in each of your sources but to piece together the information from all of your sources so that it creates a coherent picture of your subject. This effort includes explaining the relationships among the pieces of pertinent information that you have located (e.g., causal, chronological, comparative) and making sure that your assertions are supported by evidence and clarified by examples.

6. Cite sources of information appropriately. According to your audience and purpose as well as the practices of your organization, choose a formal or informal method of identifying your information sources. In the majority of documents that you write (e-mail messages, blog postings, letters, and memos), informal citation will be satisfactory (e.g., "According to the book *Risk and Safety Analysis*, . . ." or "The video at www.worldnews.com/video/031711/nuclearsafety.html makes clear that . . ."). In proposals and reports

using multiple sources of information, especially if circulated outside your organization, a formal system of documentation will be necessary to assist readers in weighing the merits of your research and keeping track of your sources: that is, in addition to specifying which sources supplied which information, a formal system makes evident the number of sources you used, the variety of your sources, and the frequency with which you relied on each source.

Applications such as EndNote (www.endnote.com) or Zotero (www.zotero.org) will assist you with managing, citing, and annotating your sources, but your conscientious efforts are critical to developing the skills of information literacy. No application is a substitute for your cautious judgment about information that is clear, credible, pertinent, and sufficient.

THE MLA SYSTEM

In the MLA (Modern Language Association) system of documentation, cite sources parenthetically by author's last name (or by authoring organization or by title if no author is identified). If you cite a specific passage or quote from a source, include specific pages:

> Publishing the instructions in a picture-intensive but unconventional medium (e.g., playing cards, wall calendars) could offer "unexpected solutions to such problems as delivering information to remote populations or communicating with inattentive or resistant audiences" (Malone 59).

In a list titled Works Cited, detail your sources in alphabetical order by the author's last name (or by authoring organization or by title if no author is identified). If several of your sources are by the same author, list the items in alphabetical order by title and substitute three hyphens for the author's name on the second and subsequent entries.

If you used a paper copy of the source, close the entry with the word *Print*. If you accessed the source through the Internet, close the entry with the word *Web* and specify the date of access (include the URL, in angled brackets, only if it is important to finding the source). If neither Print nor Web, specify other media as appropriate (e.g., E-mail, Television, Radio, Performance, DVD).

Book:
Sethi, Priti. *Setting International Standards: Guidelines for Multinational Corporations.* 2nd ed. New York: Dolphin, 2012. Print.

Collection:
Van Pelt, Carolyn, ed. *Visual Communication in a Digital World.* Boston: Beacon Hill, 2005. Print.

Essay or article in a book:
Handa, William, and Alice Felmier. "Computer-Mediated Classrooms: Bridging Academic and Industry Environments." *Collaborative Writing: Investigations in Theory and Practice.* Ed. Mary M. Karis and William M. Lay. Chicago: Radius, 1991. 170–205. Print.

Article in a professional journal:
Malone, Edward A. "The Use of Playing Cards to Communicate Technical and Scientific Information." *Technical Communication* 55.1 (2008): 49–60. Print.
Northcut, Kathryn M. "Insights from Illustrators: The Rhetorical Invention of Paleontology Representations." *Technical Communication Quarterly* 20.3 (2011): 303–326. Web. 30 July 2011.

Article in a monthly publication:
Raffael, Pauline. "Living with Gorillas." *Natural Life,* Oct. 2009: 48–59. Print.

Article in a daily newspaper:
"Bike-Friendly Culture Inspires Business Community" *The Long Beach Times* 14 Jan. 2011. Web. 3 Sept. 2011.

Government publication:
United States. Dept. of Transportation. National Highway Traffic Safety Administration. *An Analysis of the Significant Decline in Motor Vehicle Traffic Accidents in 2008.* DOT HS 811 346. Washington: GPO, 2010. Web. 18 Nov. 2011.

Article in an online news source:
Ramirez, Juanita. "Bird Flu Strikes Nicaragua." *INN.org.* International News Network. 17 Dec. 2011. Web. 19 Dec. 2011.

Page of a website:
"History of WHO." World Health Organization. 2011. Web. 12 May 2011.

Online multimedia source:
Ramirez, Juanita. "What is Bird Flu?" Video. *INN.com.* International News Network. 17 Dec. 2011. Web. 19 Dec. 2011.

Posting to an e-mail distribution list:
Cooper, Geoffrey. "A Virtual Ethics Frontier." Message to ATTW Distribution List. 9 Oct. 2011. E-mail. <http://lyris.attw.org/read/messages?id10091124>

Posting to a blog or bulletin board:
Brookie, Drew. "Rural Veterans and the Tyranny of Distance." *The White House Blog.* 3 Aug. 2011. Web. 7 Aug. 2011.

THE CHICAGO SYSTEM

The Chicago (*Chicago Manual of Style*) notes system of documentation includes a numerical list of citations (i.e., Notes) in the order cited as well as a list of sources (i.e., Bibliography) in alphabetical order by author's last name (or by authoring organization or by title if no author is identified). For online sources, include the Digital Object Identifier (DOI), a unique alphanumeric designator of the source's fixed location on the Internet. If no DOI is available, include the URL.

For each source cited, insert a superscript number in the text corresponding to the appropriate source in the numerical list:

> Publishing the instructions in a picture-intensive but unconventional medium (e.g., playing cards, wall calendars) could offer "unexpected solutions to such problems as delivering information to remote populations or communicating with inattentive or resistant audiences."[2]

Notes:

1. Priti Sethi, *Setting International Standards: Guidelines for Multinational Corporations,* 2nd ed. (New York: Dolphin, 2012), 117.
2. Edward A. Malone, "The Use of Playing Cards to Communicate Technical and Scientific Information." *Technical Communication* 55 (2008), 59.
3. Sethi, *Setting International Standards,* 89.
4. Malone, "The Use of Playing Cards," 53.

Following are a variety of sources as each would be displayed in numerical Notes and in the alphabetical Bibliography:

Book:

1. Priti Sethi, *Setting International Standards: Guidelines for Multinational Corporations,* 2nd ed. (New York: Dolphin, 2012), 117.

Sethi, Priti. *Setting International Standards: Guidelines for Multinational Corporations.* 2nd ed. New York: Dolphin, 2012.

Collection:

2. Carolyn Van Pelt, ed., *Visual Communication in a Digital World* (Boston: Beacon Hill, 2005), iii–iv.

Van Pelt, Carolyn, ed. *Visual Communication in a Digital World.* Boston: Beacon Hill, 2005.

Essay or article in a book:

3. William Handa and Alice Felmier, "Computer-Mediated Classrooms: Bridging Academic and Industry Environments," in *Collaborative Writing: Investigations in Theory and Practice,* ed. Mary M. Karis and William M. Lay (Chicago: Radius, 1991), 181.

Handa, William, and Alice Felmier. "Computer-Mediated Classrooms: Bridging Academic and Industry Environments." In *Collaborative Writing: Investigations in Theory and Practice,* edited by Mary M. Karis and William M. Lay, 170–205. Chicago: Radius, 1991.

Article in a professional journal:

4. Edward A. Malone, "The Use of Playing Cards to Communicate Technical and Scientific Information," *Technical Communication* 55, no. 1 (2008): 59.

Malone, Edward A. "The Use of Playing Cards to Communicate Technical and Scientific Information." *Technical Communication* 55, no. 1 (2008): 49–60.

5. Kathryn M. Northcut, "Insights from Illustrators: The Rhetorical Invention of Paleontology Representations," *Technical Communication Quarterly* 20, no. 3 (2011): 303–326, accessed August 1, 2011, doi:10.1080/10572252.2011.578236.

Northcut, Kathryn M. "Insights from Illustrators: The Rhetorical Invention of Paleontology Representations." *Technical Communication Quarterly* 20, no. 3 (2011): 303–326. Accessed August 1, 2011. doi:10.1080/10572252.2011.578236.

Article in a monthly publication:

6. Pauline Raffael, "Living with Gorillas," *Natural Life,* October 2009, 51.

Raffael, Pauline. "Living with Gorillas." *Natural Life,* October 2009, 48–59.

Article in a daily newspaper, anonymous:

7. "Bike-Friendly Culture Inspires Business Community," *The Long Beach Times,* January 14, 2011, http://www.lbtimes/com/011411/bike.html.

"Bike-Friendly Culture Inspires Business Community." *The Long Beach Times,* January 14, 2011. http://www.lbtimes/com/011411/bike.html.

Government publication:

8. U.S. Department of Transportation, National Highway Traffic Safety Administration, *An Analysis of the Significant Decline in Motor Vehicle Traffic Accidents in 2008*, DOT HS 811 346 (Washington, DC: U.S. Government Printing Office, 2010), 12, http://www-nrd .nhtsa.dot.gov/Pubs/811346.pdf.

U.S. Department of Transportation, National Highway Traffic Safety Administration. *An Analysis of the Significant Decline in Motor Vehicle Traffic Accidents in 2008.* DOT HS 811 346. Washington, DC: U.S. Government Printing Office, 2010. http://www-nrd.nhtsa .dot.gov/Pubs/811346.pdf.

Article in an online news source:

9. Juanita Ramirez, "Bird Flu Strikes Nicaragua," *INN.com*, December 17, 2011, http://www .inn.com/2011/HEALTH/conditions/12/17/hm.flu/index.html.

Ramirez, Juanita. "Bird Flu Strikes Nicaragua," *INN.com*, December 17, 2011. http://www .inn.com/2011/HEALTH/conditions/12/17/hm.flu/index.html.

Page of a website:
10. World Health Organization, "History of WHO," accessed April 7, 2010, http://www
.who.int/about/history/en/index.html.

World Health Organization. "History of WHO." Accessed April 7, 2010. http://www.who
.int/about/history/en/index.html.

Online multimedia source:
11. Juanita Ramirez, "What is Bird Flu?" Video, *INN.com*, December 17, 2011, http://www
.inn.com/2011/HEALTH/conditions/12/17/hm.flu/index.html#innSTCVideo.

Ramirez, Juanita. "What is Bird Flu?" Video. *INN.com*. December 17, 2011. http://www
.inn.com/2011/HEALTH/conditions/12/17/hm.flu/index.html#innSTCVideo.

Posting to e-mail distribution list:
12. Geoffrey Cooper, "A Virtual Ethics Frontier," ATTW E-mail Distribution List, online
posting, October 9, 2011, http://lyris.tu.edu/read/messages?id5406780.

Cooper, Geoffrey. "A Virtual Ethics Frontier." ATTW E-mail Distribution List, online posting, October 9, 2011. http://lyris.tu.edu/read/messages?id5406780.

Posting to a blog or bulletin board:
13. *The White House Blog*, "Rural Veterans and the Tyranny of Distance," blog entry by Drew
Brookie, August 3, 2011, http://www.whitehouse.gov/blog/2011/08/03/rural-veterans-and-
tyranny-distance.

White House Blog, The. "Rural Veterans and the Tyranny of Distance." Blog entry by Drew
Brookie, August 3, 2011, http://www.whitehouse.gov/blog/2011/08/03/rural-veterans-and-
tyranny-distance.

THE APA SYSTEM

The APA (American Psychological Association) system of documentation cites
sources parenthetically using the author's last name (or authoring organization or
title if no author is identified) and the year of publication, separated by a comma.
If emphasizing or quoting a specific passage, also cite specific pages using the abbreviation *p.* or *pp.* as necessary:

> Publishing the instructions in a picture-intensive but unconventional medium (e.g.,
> playing cards, wall calendars) could offer "unexpected solutions to such problems as
> delivering information to remote populations or communicating with inattentive or
> resistant audiences" (Malone, 2008, p. 59).

In a list titled "References" and organized alphabetically by author's last name (or
by authoring organization or by title if no author is identified), detail your sources.
If available, include the Digital Object Identifier (DOI), a unique alphanumeric

designator of the source's fixed location on the Internet. If the source was accessed online but has no DOI, include the URL. If the online source is subject to change (e.g., wiki, website), include the date of retrieval.

Book:
Sethi, P. (2012). *Setting international standards: Guidelines for multinational corporations* (2nd ed.). New York: Dolphin.

Collection:
Van Pelt, C. (Ed.). (2005). *Visual communication in a digital world.* Boston: Beacon Hill.

Essay or article in a book:
Handa, W., & Felmier, A. (1991). Computer-mediated classrooms: Bridging academic and industry environments. In M. M. Karis & W. M. Lay (Eds.), *Collaborative writing: Investigations in theory and practice* (pp. 170–205). Chicago: Radius.

Article in a professional journal:
Malone, E. A. (2008). The use of playing cards to communicate technical and scientific information. *Technical Communication, 55,* 49–60. doi:10.4321/TC012345678

Northcut, K. M. (2011). Insights from illustrators: The rhetorical invention of paleontology representations. *Technical Communication Quarterly, 20,* 303–326. doi:10.1080/10572252.2011.578236

Article in a monthly publication:
Raffael, P. (2009, October). Living with gorillas. *Natural Life, 38,* 48–59.

Article in a daily newspaper, anonymous:
Bike-friendly culture inspires business community (2011, January 14). *The Long Beach Times.* Retrieved from http://www.lbtimes/com/011411/bike.html

Government publication:
U.S. Department of Transportation, National Highway Traffic Safety Administration. (2010). *An analysis of the significant decline in motor vehicle traffic accidents in 2008* (DOT HS 811 346). Washington, DC: GPO. Retrieved from http://www-nrd.nhtsa.dot.gov/Pubs/811346.pdf

Article in an online news source:
Ramirez, J. (2011, December 17). "Bird flu strikes Nicaragua." *INN.com.* Retrieved from http://www.inn.com/2011/HEALTH/conditions/12/17/hm.flu/index.html

Page of a website:
History of WHO. (2010). *World Health Organization.* Retrieved April 7, 2010,
  from http://www.who.int/about/history/en/index.html

Online multimedia source:
Ramirez, J. (2011, December 17). *What is bird flu?* [Video]. *INN.com.* Retrieved from
  http://www.inn.com/2011/HEALTH/conditions/12/17/hm.flu/index.html
  #innSTCVideo

Posting to e-mail distribution list:
Cooper, G. (2011, October 9). A virtual ethics frontier. Message posted to ATTW
  electronic mailing list, archived at http://lyris.ttu.edu/read/messages?id5406780

Posting to a blog or bulletin board:
Brookie, Drew. (2011, August 3). Rural veterans and the tyranny of distance
  [Blog post]. Retrieved from http://www.whitehouse.gov/blog/2011/08/03/rural
  -veterans-and-tyranny-distance

Appendix C

Report for Study

The following report was prepared by a preveterinary student. The preveterinary honor society at ABC University invited students to propose and then write, if the proposal were accepted, a discussion of issues important to future veterinarians. The proposal for this report appears in Chapter 9.

Sarah's report illustrates effective organization and development of the idea she proposed. Note the integration of her letter of transmittal, summary, table of contents, and discussion. Note also that she uses a casual, conversational style to present her findings and useful visuals to illustrate animal rehabilitation methods and devices.

MEMORANDUM

| TO: | Dr. Elizabeth Tebeaux | **DATE:** | 4/15/10 |
| FROM: | Sarah Irving | | |

SUBJECT: **Transmittal of the final report on the field of animal rehabilitation**

A copy of my report on the field of animal rehabilitation is attached. The purpose of this report is to allow veterinarians, veterinary students, and others interested in the field of animal rehabilitation to understand the current state of the field.

Animal rehabilitation allows animals to have a higher quality of life. Animal rehabilitation includes pain medications and physical rehabilitation. Since a veterinary license is not required to practice animal rehabilitation, and pain medications can only be prescribed by a veterinarian, pain medications are not described in this report. Common types of physical rehabilitation are briefly described to provide an overview of methods animal rehabilitation practitioners could use to help animals.

The field of animal rehabilitation is rapidly expanding. Pet owners are using the Internet to learn about alternative treatments for their pets. Pet owners see rehabilitation as a cheaper and safer option than surgery.

Veterinarians see rehabilitation as a way to gain revenue and expand their practices. This report describes the current state of the field, the issues remaining to be solved, and where the field is headed. The report then has a section of advice from current rehabilitation practitioners for those considering opening a rehabilitation practice. This report concludes by stating that animal rehabilitation is changing the future of veterinary medicine.

I would like to acknowledge the help I received from veterinarians, veterinary technicians, and physical therapists who responded to my survey. These include Dr. Davidson, Dr. Sanchez, Dr. Horn, Dr. Downing, Dr. Jess, Robert J. Porter III, Kimberley Knap, Margaret Waluk, Kristen Hagler, Margaret Rudoy-Resnik, Roxanne Mazurkiewicz, Debora Carroll, and Sandra Hudson.

Animal Rehabilitation

An Expanding Field

Sarah Irving

English 301
4/15/2010

Abstract

This report has been prepared to help those interested in animal rehabilitation gain a basic view of this emerging field. This report describes animal rehabilitation and the current state of the field. This report also contains a list of consulted sources and the initial progress report and proposal for the project.

Table of Contents

Summary

Purpose of the report

This report serves as a guide to help veterinarians, veterinary students, and those interested in the field of animal rehabilitation understand the current state of the field of animal rehabilitation.

Research methods used

To gather information about the field of animal rehabilitation I searched online journal articles, veterinary publications, and interest group websites. I also surveyed certified rehabilitation practitioners. These practitioners included veterinarians, veterinary technicians, and physical therapists.

Understanding animal rehabilitation

Animal rehabilitation is working to reduce animal pain while speeding the healing process. Animal rehabilitation includes physical rehabilitation and pain medication. The field was originally developed for injured race horses. The idea of rehabilitation then spread to helping sporting dogs. In the last decade rehabilitation has begun to be seen as a viable mainstream practice of veterinary medicine.

The field of animal rehabilitation includes pain medication and physical rehabilitation. Since pain medications may only be prescribed by a licensed veterinarian, and a veterinary license is not required to practice animal rehabilitation, pain medications are not described in this report. Common types of physical rehabilitation, including physical therapy, underwater treadmill therapy, and assistive devices, are briefly described to provide an overview of what an animal rehabilitation practitioner could use to help an animal.

Current status of the field

As many baby boomers receive physical therapy for injuries their appreciation for animal rehabilitation services for their pets is increasing and the field of animal rehabilitation is growing. Veterinarians are also seeing the benefits of rehabilitation as patients recover faster and rehabilitation revenue helps veterinary clinics expand.

Animal rehabilitation requires a large amount of effort from the pet owners. Many animals must attend rehabilitation sessions two or three times a week. Physical therapy is then needed to continue the rehabilitation process and the animal's improvement. This means that owners are involved in exercises specifically designed for each patient at home.

Signs of the growth of the field are seen in the institutions promoting continuing education for professionals. Two animal rehabilitation certification programs currently exist in the United States. These are the University of Tennessee College of Veterinary Medicine Certificate in Canine Rehabilitation and the Canine Rehabilitation Institute. Both programs train licensed veterinarians, veterinary technicians, and physical therapists in animal rehabilitation.

The American College of Veterinary Sports Medicine and Rehabilitation and the Institute of Registered Veterinary and Animal Physiotherapists are working for a higher rehabilitation standard in the United States and England. The American College of Veterinary Sports Medicine and Rehabilitation is also working to make rehabilitation a recognized veterinary specialty in the United States.

Unresolved issues in the field of animal rehabilitation

Two large issues remaining in the animal rehabilitation field are the need for pain management and who may receive rehabilitation certification.

The first issue is whether animals need pain management to heal. Some veterinarians do not use pain medications and other rehabilitation methods for their patients. Others say pain treatments are too expensive for rural clients. Another group of veterinarians say pain medication and physical rehabilitation should be required for all surgery patients.

This debate is complicated by the fact that many state veterinary boards have no pain management standards. In the case of Dr. Seemann in Michigan, his license was revoked after he did not give pain medication to a dog following surgery at his rural clinic. Dr. Seemann protested the revoking of his license, and the issue has been brought to the state courts. Michigan is one of many states that had no standards of veterinary pain management at the time. Veterinarians continue to debate the importance of having pain management protocols.

The second unresolved issue in the animal rehabilitation field is defining who is qualified to practice animal rehabilitation. The American Veterinary Medical Association (AVMA) insists that only veterinarians are licensed and trained to treat animal patients. The American Physical Therapy Association (APTA) insists that only a licensed physical therapist can perform rehabilitation, regardless of the species of the patient. The two animal rehabilitation certification programs in the United States currently allow veterinarians, veterinary technicians, and physical therapists to become trained in animal rehabilitation. This issue will ultimately be decided by individual state legislatures.

Future of animal rehabilitation

The American College of Veterinary Sports Medicine and Rehabilitation and the Institute of Registered Veterinary and Animal Physiotherapists are promoting a broader recognition of animal rehabilitation as an integral part of veterinary medicine. As interest in animal rehabilitation increases so does its availability. Veterinarians are referring more clients to rehabilitation clinics or are receiving training to offer rehabilitation themselves. They are viewing it more and more as a legitimate service and less as an unproven alternative treatment.

The Alameda East Veterinary Hospital, featured on the popular Animal Planet show "Emergency Vets," recently opened a rehabilitation clinic. The television coverage of animal rehabilitation will help the availability of animal rehabilitation to become common knowledge. Pet owners are also finding information on animal rehabilitation online.

Why practice animal rehabilitation?

Rehabilitation helps patients heal faster and improves patients' quality of life. Rehabilitation also helps veterinary clinics to earn more revenue and expand their practice. Pet owners view veterinarians who offer rehabilitation as more compassionate, even if they do not choose to use rehabilitation for their pets. Rehabilitation also saves some pets from euthanasia, by giving pet owners a less expensive option than surgery. Practicing rehabilitation or making referrals to rehabilitation clinics is good veterinary practice, good for business, and good for a clinic's reputation.

Is animal rehabilitation the future of veterinary medicine?

Animal rehabilitation is an expanding field in veterinary medicine. It is changing how animal pain is viewed and treated. Many veterinarians are seeing their patients recover faster and have a higher quality of life with rehabilitation. Owners are seeking out rehabilitation for their pets. Even without being officially considered a veterinary specialty, animal rehabilitation is changing the future of veterinary medicine.

Advice for those considering a future as an animal rehabilitation specialist

As an epilogue this report contains a section of advice for those considering practicing animal rehabilitation. The advice was provided by current veterinarians, veterinary technicians, and physical therapists practicing animal rehabilitation.

Animal Rehabilitation
An Expanding Field

Introduction

The field of animal rehabilitation is growing rapidly as word about the effectiveness of rehabilitation for animal patients spreads. Pet owners see rehabilitation as a cheaper and safer option than surgery to help their pets to have a better quality of life. Veterinarians see rehabilitation as a way to expand their practice. This report describes what animal rehabilitation is, where the field is today, what issues remain to be solved, and where animal rehabilitation is headed. This report concludes by stating that animal rehabilitation is changing the future of veterinary medicine. The report then has a section of advice from current rehabilitation practitioners for those considering opening a rehabilitation practice.

This report is intended to help those interested in the field of animal rehabilitation obtain a broad understanding of the field. Those wishing to practice animal rehabilitation must then complete one of the two certification programs in the United States. Currently only licensed veterinarians, veterinary technicians, and physical therapists may earn a certification in animal rehabilitation.

Understanding animal rehabilitation

Definition of animal rehabilitation

Animal rehabilitation is the process of helping an animal to return to full health. Rehabilitation reduces pain, prevents bone and muscle atrophy, and allows the patients to recover faster from an injury. Animal rehabilitation includes pain medication and physical rehabilitation.

History of animal rehabilitation

Animal rehabilitation began in the 1960s with the growth of popularity of horse races. The growth of horse racing led to more injured horses in need of rehabilitation. Animal rehabilitation then spread to the canine sporting industry. By the 1980s canine rehabilitation had grown into a mainstream practice in Europe, but canine rehabilitation was still not widespread in the United States.

American veterinarians were behind European veterinarians in considering physical therapy to be a viable option for animals. It was not until 1996 that the American Veterinary Medical Association added the words "veterinary physical therapy" to its guidelines[1]. Currently seventeen veterinary colleges in the United

States offer canine rehabilitation classes, but only two canine and equine rehabilitation certification programs exist in the United States to date[1].

Animal rehabilitation has developed from an option used only by horse owners and sporting dog enthusiasts to a mainstream treatment over the last decade. This development stems from the fact that "pet owners in general have come to expect their companions will have access to the same medical options they themselves have[2]". Pet owners are realizing that physical therapy can lead to increased mobility, reduced pain, and a higher quality of life for their pets.

Treatment methods are often adapted from techniques used in human rehabilitation for use on animal patients. This may include using rubber exercise balls to re-teach animals balance, treadmills to teach animals to use a healing leg again, and custom made devices to help animals from the smallest kitten to the largest elephant[3].

Though awareness of rehabilitation has increased in the veterinary community, most veterinarians do not suggest rehabilitation to their clients. Veterinary surgeons and specialists most commonly refer cases to rehabilitation clinics[4]. The American College of Veterinary Sports Medicine and Rehabilitation is currently working to have the American Veterinary Medical Association recognize rehabilitation as a veterinary specialty.

Types of animal rehabilitation

Animal rehabilitation is a broad field that includes many different types of treatments. Veterinarians, veterinary technicians, and physical therapists with animal rehabilitation certification were asked to provide information on the types of treatments they offer. These treatments are listed in the blue box to the right. Some of the more commonly practiced types of animal rehabilitation include physical therapy, underwater treadmill therapy, and assistive devices. These techniques are explained below.

Physical therapy

Physical activities, modified for each patient, can be designed to exercise certain muscles or joints. The length of time, pace, and frequency of the exercise must be carefully varied to prevent over-stressing an animal[10]. Rehabilitation practitioners carefully monitor the exercises to ensure the

Rehabilitation Treatments [4][5][6][7][8][9]
- *underwater treadmill*
- *physioball*
- *balance balls*
- *therapeutic ultrasound*
- *cold laser*
- *land treadmill*
- *hot and cold packs*
- *electro-muscular stimulation*
- *home exercises*
- *therapeutic massage*
- *acupuncture*
- *stem cell therapy*
- *custom braces and carts*
- *swimming*

animal is moving the affected section of the body correctly. Therapists also watch for signs of the exercise stressing the patient, and as a result can change the physical therapy plan to a less stressful procedure.

Other types of physical therapies include massage, acupuncture, and balance balls[11]. Pet massage can help with circulation, muscle tone, breathing, flexibility, and digestion. It may also help with emotional health and immune response[12]. Balance balls can help an animal learn to stand correctly. Acupuncture can relieve tension in muscles.

Figure 1: Dog using a balance ball
Source: http://www.handicappedpets
.com/www/index.php/pet-care
-articles/pet-health-treatments/
29-physical-therapy-for-pet-paralysis
.html

Underwater treadmill therapy

Underwater treadmills allow the patient to have a correct and slower gait which allows for exercises not possible without water supporting the body weight. Walking on an underwater treadmill also helps improve joint flexibility. Underwater treadmill exercises are most useful to patients who have recently had joint surgery or who are overweight[13]. Underwater treadmills work by providing an environment where the water supports the weight of the patient's body. This relieves the stress on the patient's joints. The resistance caused by walking in water makes the patient slow their gait and the warm water relaxes their muscles[14].

1. Benefits of underwater treadmill therapy[13]

- Faster recovery after injury or surgery
- Increased muscle strength
- Improved joint flexibility
- Weight loss

2. What to consider before choosing underwater treadmill therapy

- Patients with upper respiratory diseases have difficulty breathing in water
- Newly sutured areas, large wounds, incontinent patients, and patients with diarrhea should not use hydrotherapy

Figure 2: Golden retriever walking on an underwater treadmill
Source: http://aquadogrehab.com/

page 3

Passive range-of-motion exercises or standing exercises may be used in water by rehabilitation practitioners before the treadmill is used. These exercises involve the rehabilitation practitioner physically moving the animal's limbs in the desired motion. This helps patients who are in too much pain to start exercising on the treadmill and patients who are not used to being in water.

Assistive devices

Assistive devices for animals include carts, slings, braces, and prosthetics. Dogs and cats that lose control of their back limbs can be strapped into small carts[15]. These carts resemble tiny wheelchairs specially modified for their patient and must be custom ordered[16]. Assistive devices for animals, often crafted out of ordinary materials, must be developed for the many unique types of patients treated by veterinarians. Examples of prosthetics that have been invented include prosthetic paws, an elephant leg, fins, and artificial beaks[16].

Figure 3: Dog using a cart to walk
Source: http://www.handicappedpets.com/ www/index.php/pet-videos/209-denali-dog -on-wheels.html

There has been an increase in interest in assistive devices for animals in recent years. Owners see their animals as a part of their families. They are more willing to put in the effort to live with a disabled pet than in the past. Equipment such as pet wheelchairs, diapers, slings, braces, protective booties, and ramps allow animals to lead good lives if their owners are willing to put in the effort[17]. Most assistive devices are custom made, and can be expensive. The amount of effort required from the owner to care for the animal must be considered along with the cost when making decisions about assistive devices.

"The public seems to be intrigued by animal rehab. Most of my clients have had some sort of injury and have benefited from rehab, so have an understanding and appreciation for rehab for their animals." **Sandra Hudson, veterinary technician** [4]

Prosthetic limbs can be attached using a cuff on the prosthetic limb, or can be inserted into the bone. In the later case a porous metal is attached to the bone, and the muscle and ligament tissues grow into the metal. This provides a seal that prevents infection. Implanted prosthetics are still being developed, and are not yet widely used[16].

page 4

Current Status of the Field

The developing demand for animal rehabilitation

Pet owner interest in animal rehabilitation is growing. Pet owners, many of whom are baby boomers, often have had rehabilitation after a surgery or know others who speak highly of rehabilitation. They understand the benefits of rehabilitation for people and expect the availability of rehabilitation for their pets. They see the importance of rehabilitation for their animals after an injury or surgery.

Other pet owners see rehabilitation as an alternative to euthanasia for an aging pet[7]. They see rehabilitation, such as underwater treadmill therapy for arthritic dogs, as a way to help their pet maintain a high quality of life. Animal rehabilitation is less expensive than surgery, and can possibly help animals who are at high risk of complications from surgery heal with less risk.

Veterinary interest in the field is also growing. As more clients ask for rehabilitation services, more veterinarians are seeing rehabilitation as a way to expand their practice. They are willing to invest the time and money into the training and equipment of a rehabilitation practice, or they are willing to refer clients to a rehabilitation practitioner.

Owner involvement in the rehabilitation process

Home exercises are often an important component of a rehabilitation program. These exercises are specially designed and are taught to the owner by the rehabilitation practitioner. Owners must be willing to invest their time between rehabilitation sessions for the continued improvement of their pet. A physical rehabilitation practitioner can teach an owner passive range of motion, massage, and joint compression techniques to relieve pain[18]. Passive range-of-motion techniques can be used to maintain flexibility. Massage and joint compression help relax tensed muscles.

"It can be stressful at times, but I think that more and more vets are becoming aware of the importance of incorporating rehab and alternative services into their practices, because that is what the client wants now, and they are willing to pay for it."
Margaret Rudoy-Resnik

Owners should ask themselves how their animal will move around with the disability. Many animals adapt easily to using a pet wheelchair or other assistive device. Owners should also consider if they are willing to put the personal effort into caring for a disabled pet. The extra work required can include time, money, and emotional investment[17].

What certification programs exist

The following certification programs are the only animal rehabilitation programs recognized by veterinary interest groups in the United States for giving good rehabilitation training. Classes from these programs are recognized as continuing education classes for licensed veterinarians, veterinary technicians, and physical therapists.

Canine Rehabilitation Institute

The Canine Rehabilitation Institute offers courses in clinics in Maryland and Florida, and at Colorado State University's College of Veterinary Medicine. The courses are offered to veterinarians, veterinary technicians, physical therapists, and physical therapy assistants. The Institute also offers continuing education courses for certified rehabilitation practitioners. Students practice on live dogs of varying backgrounds, ages, and needs. The certificates from the Canine Rehabilitation Institute are approved by the American Association of Veterinary State Boards[19].

University of Tennessee College of Veterinary Medicine Certificate Program in Canine Rehabilitation

The University of Tennessee College of Veterinary Medicine trains veterinarians, veterinary technicians, physical therapists, and physical therapy assistants in canine and equine rehabilitation. The program was founded by a physical therapist and Dr. Darryl Millis, professor of orthopedic surgery at the University of Tennessee College of Veterinary Medicine[2]. The program operates in the veterinary college.

Organizations formed to promote animal rehabilitation

Institute of Registered Veterinary and Animal Physiotherapists (IRVAP)

The Institute of Registered Veterinary and Animal Physiotherapists, based out of England, is a society of veterinary therapists and surgeons formed to create high standards for animal physiotherapy practices[20]. The institute strives to be a resource to current and future animal physiotherapists. The institute is currently developing a certification program called Canine and Equine Physiotherapy Training. The first classes were launched in the fall of 2009.

American College of Veterinary Sports Medicine and Rehabilitation (ACVSMR)

The American College of Veterinary Sports Medicine and Rehabilitation (ACVSMR) was founded by Dr. Sheila Lyons[21]. It has been proposed to the American Veterinary Medical Association as a new specialty in veterinary medicine. The American Veterinary Medical Association will be voting on the pro-

page 6

posed specialty at the end of April 2010. The proposed American College of Veterinary Sports Medicine and Rehabilitation specialty will focus on rehabilitation of all species. If the specialty passes it will create a specialization process with internships and residencies as well as new opportunities in continuing education for veterinarians.

Dr. Lyons is also the founder of Homecoming Farm Inc[22]. Homecoming Farm is a nonprofit organization founded to promote the establishment of the ACVSMR as a veterinary specialty. Homecoming Farm conducts research and education on equine rehabilitation.

Unresolved issues in the field of animal rehabilitation

The animal pain management debate

Recent studies show that pain causes decreased sleep, fatigue, delayed healing, decreased energy, and suffering[23]. Animal behaviorists suggest that animals are less likely to show signs of pain in the veterinary office because they do not associate the office with safety. Animals are more likely to demonstrate signs of pain at home with their owners present. An article in DVM magazine recommends providing owners with a set of "pain-assessment guidelines to engage them in the pain-management processes[18]". These guidelines should explain to the owners how to decide if higher doses of pain medication or the use of an additional medication is needed.

> *Ways veterinarians ensure good treatment of pain*
> - *Create a pain scoring system for staff to use*
> - *Apply pain management protocols for every surgical patient*
> - *Assess and record observations of pain during all examinations*
> - *Reassess patients with chronic pain often*

Older veterinarians do not always use pain management in their practices. The recent case of Dr. Carl Seemann in Minnesota has brought the controversy surrounding pain management procedures to the attention of the veterinary community. Dr. Seemann's license was suspended after he did not give a dog pain medication following a surgery[24]. Dr. Seemann is 84 years old, and has been practicing in rural Minnesota for many years. He argued that most of his clients did not wish to pay for the medication, so he did not offer it.

Veterinarians writing to the veterinary professional magazines, such as DVM magazine, have been debating whether his license should have been revoked, since Minnesota, and most other states, have no clear guidelines for veterinary pain management[25]. Pain management is a recent addition to the curriculum of veterinary teaching hospitals, and is not consistently practiced in veterinary clinics. The case continues to be fought in the Minnesota legal system, while the debate continues in the veterinary community on the ability of state boards to create standards of veterinary pain management[26].

Those against mandating pain management as a part of veterinary medicine say that states that enforce regulations for pain management should clearly define and point out the protocols. This would prevent lawsuits caused by animals dying from adverse reactions to the pain medication. Some surgeons say that pain management should be optional. They believe pet owners should decide if they want the veterinarian to give pain medication to their animal.

There is also a disagreement between those who believe animal patients experience the same level of postsurgical pain as human patients. Some veterinarians believe that the pain medication given to animals post-surgically only gains more profit and makes the veterinarian look more caring[27]. Others believe the practice of post-surgical pain management is beneficial to the animals and prevents long term pain[18].

Pain management is good business, since the pain medication brings in good revenue. It is also a good practice, since the patients will heal faster. Pain medication allows the veterinarian to show compassion for the patient, which helps to build a bond with the clients. When clients see a veterinarian doing more for their animal than other veterinarians do, they value the clinic more, which leads to an increased number of visits and client recommendations[23].

Who qualifies to practice animal rehabilitation

The American Veterinary Medical Association and the American Physical Therapy Association disagree over who is qualified to practice animal rehabilitation. This debate will ultimately be decided by state legislatures. Those interested in practicing animal rehabilitation should check the laws of their state to see if licensing requirements exist.

The position of the American Veterinary Medical Association (AVMA)
The AVMA believes that only a licensed veterinarian or a physical therapist trained in non-human anatomy and physiology should practice physical therapy on animals. They believe only a veterinarian or a veterinary technician understands an animal's anatomy well enough to develop effective treatments for animal patients.

The position of the American Physical Therapy Association (APTA)
According to the Animal Physical Therapy Special Interest Group (SIG) Strategic Plan, "The mission of the Animal Physical Therapy SIG of APTA's Ortho-

pedic Section is to define, advance, and promote the role of the physical therapy profession in the field of animal rehabilitation through education, collaboration, communication, advocacy, and ethical practice[28]". This plan includes the goals of developing educational guidelines for physical therapists interested in rehabilitation, tracking government decisions on animal rehabilitation regulations, and promoting animal rehabilitation as a practice for physical therapists. They argue that all patients receiving physical therapy should be treated by a licensed physical therapist regardless of the species.

State government actions to date

The ultimate decision on who can practice physical therapy on animals rests with the state legislatures. The legality of who may practice animal rehabilitation is not defined in most states. The American Veterinary Medical Association and the American Physical Therapy Association are currently lobbying legislatures to resolve the issue.

Nevada allows physical therapists to complete a certification process to practice animal rehabilitation with a referral from a veterinarian[1]. Colorado passed a bill in 2007 allowing physical therapists to work with animals. The law defined the training, practical experience, and joint work between the veterinarian and physical therapist required to practice animal rehabilitation[1]. As the field of animal rehabilitation grows, more state legislatures will define who may practice animal rehabilitation and what state governing board will watch over animal rehabilitation practitioners.

The future of animal rehabilitation

Greater public awareness

Alameda East, the veterinary clinic featured on Animal Planet's TV show "Emergency Vets," recently opened a 12,000 foot rehabilitation clinic[29]. Showing animal physical therapy on television will lead to more requests from pet owners for their animals to receive physical therapy. Pet owners are also using the Internet to find alternative treatments for their pets. This will help advance the development of animal rehabilitation as a specialty by showing that demand exists for animal rehabilitation.

Recent developments in the field

As public awareness of the availability of animal rehabilitation grows, the amount of certification programs and the variety of rehabilitation services are also growing. The Institute of Registered Veterinary and Animal Physiotherapists recently created a program called Canine and Equine Physiotherapy Training

(CEPT) based out of Nottingham University's School of Veterinary Medicine and Science in England. The first class was held in October of 2009[30]. The Institute and the two established certification programs in the United States are continuing to develop classes as new types of rehabilitation services are developed.

Why practice animal rehabilitation

Good for business and good veterinary practice

Practicing animal rehabilitation or referring to rehabilitation clinics is good for business and good veterinary practice. Rehabilitation is a new source of revenue and jobs for veterinary clinics. Clients who are not willing to risk their animal developing complications from surgery have the option of rehabilitation improving an animal's quality of life. Rehabilitation also saves some pets from euthanasia by giving pet owners a less expensive option than surgery.

Animal rehabilitation is also good veterinary practice since it helps patients heal faster and improves patients' quality of life. Rehabilitated patients live longer with less pain than those not rehabilitated after an injury or surgery. Pet owners view veterinarians who offer rehabilitation as more compassionate, even if they do not choose to use rehabilitation for their pets. Clients appreciate when veterinarians care about their pets, which improves the clinic's reputation.

Animal rehabilitation: the future of veterinary medicine?

Animal rehabilitation is an expanding field in veterinary medicine. It is changing how animal pain is viewed and treated. Many veterinarians are seeing their patients recover faster and have a higher quality of life with rehabilitation. Owners are seeking out rehabilitation for their pets. Even without being officially considered a veterinary specialty, animal rehabilitation is changing the future of veterinary medicine.

Advice for those considering a future as an animal rehabilitation practitioner

Veterinarians, veterinary technicians, and physical therapists were asked to provide advice on becoming an animal rehabilitation practitioner.

1. Margaret Waluk, a physical therapist, suggested that if you are in private practice and wish to make animal rehabilitation available to your clients, make sure that practitioners have the proper education and credentials before referring to them[31].

page 10

2. "They could start with simple equipment and increase to a full rehab facility. I would recommend attending one of the animal rehabilitation schools to be trained and to have resources of faculty and other rehabilitation practitioners." Sandra Hudson, Veterinary Technician[4].

3. "Depending on your practice area, it may or may not be a profitable venture." Roxanne Mazurkiewicz, Veterinary Technician[5].

4. "Research the web as much as you can. Try and stay with as much scientific backed material as possible and after you do all of that contact me or someone else that has been in the field for a long time with more specific questions." Robert J. Porter III, Veterinary Technician[10].

5. Rehabilitation practices "are typically an asset as long as the staff have been properly trained. Rehab is a great adjunctive therapy for many common conditions." Kimberly E. Knap, Assistant Director of Teaching Services at the University of Illinois Veterinary Teaching Hospital[6].

6. "Having an understanding of how the body works as a whole, not just broken down into systems as you have studied in school will help you treat patients more effectively. The combination of traditional medicine, complementary/alternative medicine, and animal sports medicine and rehabilitation really helps to provide the best patient care. The field of veterinary pain management is also growing, something which veterinary rehabilitation takes into consideration when treating patients." Kristen Hagler, Veterinary Technician[7].

7. "Rehabilitation is an ancillary part of the overall treatment for various orthopedic and neurologic cases. Often for the best results both surgery and rehab are required. Rehab is here to stay so don't hold off rehab as an option for your cases. Owners are finding out and seeking it out. They become very unhappy with their veterinarian or practice if they were not informed of the option even if your facility is unable to provide this valuable service. Rehab is not a panacea for all situations but when used early has great benefits to the overall outcome of cases. Don't wait until it is too late to start rehab." Dr. Joel Jess, DVM[32].

8. "It's very important to learn as over time it will become the standard of care especially post surgical orthopedic cases. Specialization will be for non-surgical cases, neurological diseases, etc. Most likely an orthopedic surgeon will have some level of training in the practice to do therapy in the office." Dr. Jeffrey Horn, DVM[33].

9. "Clients get turned off from 'conventional' treatments, and really appreciate a vet that can think outside the box. You don't have to know a lot, but at least know whom you can refer to, even that impresses." Margaret Rudoy-Resnik, Veterinary Technician[35].

10. My advice: "participate in a clinical experience—either at their vet school or another school—for a few weeks. If they want to focus on rehabilitation, then

they should inquire about the ACVSMR (or consider a dual degree in physical therapy). If they are graduating this spring, they should definitely look into one of the CE courses, and also inquire about the ACVSMR within the next year. If they're currently looking for a job, the practices with the most opportunity for being involved with rehabilitation are stand-alone rehabilitation businesses (there are a few—not many). For most veterinarians doing rehabilitation, they are either in a veterinary specialty practice with surgeons, or work closely with a surgical specialty practice who will refer rehabilitation cases to them. Lastly, some degree of rehabilitation can be incorporated into most any general private practice. There is generally more opportunity for rehabilitation in practices that perform orthopedic and neurologic surgery. Regardless of the practice, the key is for the veterinarian to be well educated in the specialty." Dr. Jacqueline Davidson, DVM, Clinical professor at Texas A&M College of Veterinary Medicine and Biomedical Science[34].

References

1. van Dyke JB. Canine rehabilitation: An inside look at a fast-growing market segment. DVM: The Newsmagazine of Veterinary Medicine 2009 07;40(7): 14S-5S.
2. Nolen RS. Pet rehab becoming mainstream practice. J Am Vet Med Assoc 2009 10;235(7):798-9.
3. Thai Elephant Motala prosthetic, prosthesis, artificial leg, landmine, Asia, repaired Damage Updates 2009 Pictures Operation prosthetic leg 1999 to 2009 Thailand Hospital Landmine Soraida Salwala Friends of the Asian Elephant FAE [Internet] [cited 2010 3/19/2010]. Available from: http://animom.tripod.com/motala.html.
4. Hudson S. Survey of rehabilitation specialists.
5. Mazurkiewicz R. Survey of rehabilitation specialists.
6. Knapp K. Survey of rehabilitation specialists.
7. Hagler K. Survey of rehabilitation specialists.
8. Sanchez DM. Survey of rehabilitation specialists.
9. Downing DR. Survey of rehabilitation specialists.
10. Porter RJI. Survey of rehabilitation specialists.
11. Physical therapy for pet paralysis [Internet] [cited 2010 4/13/2010]. Available from: http://www.handicappedpets.com/www/index.php/pet-care-articles/pet-health-treatments/29-physical-therapy-for-pet-paralysis.html.
12. Smith SD. Petting with a purpose. Natural Health 2006 03;36(3):99-100.
13. Home—Aqua Dog [Internet] [cited 2010 4/13/2010]. Available from: http://aquadogrehab.com/.

14. Jurek C, McCauley L. Underwater treadmill therapy in veterinary practice. Vet Med 2009 04;104(4):182-90.
15. Walkin Wheels—Dog On Wheels [Internet] [cited 2010 4/13/2010]. Available from: http://www.handicappedpets.com/www/index.php/pet-videos/209-denali-dog-on-wheels.html.
16. Sayre C, Horn R. Fake fins, plastic paws. Time 2007 09/03;170(10):49-51.
17. Foley D. Life with a disabled pet. Prevention 2006 02;58(2):198-201.
18. Stein RM, Ortel S. Postsurgical pain management: Take a pre-emptive approach. DVM: The Newsmagazine of Veterinary Medicine 2008 07;39(7):44-6.
19. Canine Rehabilitation Institute | Welcome [Internet] [cited 2010 4/9/2010]. Available from: http://www.caninerehabilitation.com/.
20. IRVAP—The Institute of Registered Veterinary and Animal Physiotherapists [Internet] [cited 2010 4/11/2010]. Available from: http://www.irvap.org.uk/index.html.
21. acvsmr.com [Internet] [cited 2010 4/11/2010]. Available from: http://www.acvsmr.com/.
22. Home [Internet] [cited 2010 4/11/2010]. Available from: http://www.homecomingfarm.org/.
23. Downing R. Putting the new pain management guidelines into practice. Vet Med 2007 11;102(11):704-5.
24. Fiala J. The price of pain. DVM: The Newsmagazine of Veterinary Medicine 2007 10;38(10):30-2.
25. Shearer T. Changing times. DVM: The Newsmagazine of Veterinary Medicine 2008 03;39(3):34-.
26. Marshak D. State board lacks consistency on standard of practice. DVM: The Newsmagazine of Veterinary Medicine 2007 11;38(11):38-40.
27. Brockett JE. Why give pain medication—patient care, image or profit? DVM: The Newsmagazine of Veterinary Medicine 2008 02;39(2):41-.
28. Orthopaedic Section—American Physical Therapy Association [Internet] [cited 2010 4/11/2010]. Available from: http://www.orthopt.org/sig_apt.php.
29. Verdon DR. An animal planet. DVM: The Newsmagazine of Veterinary Medicine 2005 07;36(7):24-8.
30. Payne RM. Canine and equine physiotherapy. Veterinary Record: Journal of the British Veterinary Association 2009 07/25;165(4):122-.
31. Waluk MM. Survey of rehabilitation specialists.
32. Jess DJ. Survey of rehabilitation specialists.
33. Horn DJ. Survey of rehabilitation specialists.
34. Davidson DJ. Survey of rehabilitation specialists.
35. Rudoy-Resnik M. Survey of rehabilitation specialists.

Index